Wittgenstein and Heidegger

Ludwig Wittgenstein and Martin Heidegger are arguably the two most influential philosophers of the twentieth century. Their work not only reshaped the philosophical landscape but also left its mark on other disciplines, including political science, theology, anthropology, ecology, mathematics, cultural studies, literary theory, and architecture.

Both sought to challenge the assumptions governing the traditions they inherited, to question the very terms in which philosophy's problems had been posed, and to open up new avenues of thought for thinkers of all stripes. And despite considerable differences in style and in the traditions they inherited, the similarities between Wittgenstein and Heidegger are striking.

Comparative work of these thinkers has only increased in recent decades, but no collection has yet explored the various ways in which Wittgenstein and Heidegger can be drawn into conversation. As such, these essays stage genuine dialogues, with aspects of Wittgenstein's elucidations answering or problematizing aspects of Heidegger's, and vice versa. The result is a broad-ranging collection of essays that provides a series of openings and provocations that will serve as a reference point for future work that draws on the writings of these two philosophers.

David Egan finished his Doctor of Philosophy at Oriel College, Oxford, and has since taught at McMaster University and Christ Church, Oxford.

Stephen Reynolds completed his Doctor of Philosophy at Oriel College, Oxford, before teaching at Magdalen and New Colleges. He is currently an Astbury Scholar at Middle Temple, UK.

Aaron James Wendland is a Doctor of Philosophy Candidate at Somerville College, Oxford.

Routledge Studies in Twentieth-Century Philosophy

Wittgenstein and Heidegger

**Edited by David Egan,
Stephen Reynolds, and
Aaron James Wendland**

Routledge
Taylor & Francis Group

NEW YORK AND LONDON

First published 2013
by Routledge
711 Third Avenue, New York, NY 10017

Simultaneously published in the UK
by Routledge
2 Park Square, Milton Park, Abingdon, Oxon OX14 4RN

*Routledge is an imprint of the Taylor & Francis Group,
an informa business*

Library of Congress Cataloging-in-Publication Data

Wittgenstein and Heidegger / Edited by David Egan, Stephen Reynolds,
    and Aaron James Wendland.
        pages cm. — (Routledge studies in twentieth-century philosophy ; 35)
    Includes bibliographical references and index.
    ISBN 978-0-415-50998-5 (hardback : alk. paper) — ISBN 978-0-203-38271-4 (ebook)
1. Wittgenstein, Ludwig, 1889–1951.   2. Heidegger, Martin, 1889–1976.   I. Egan, David.
    B3376.W564W543   2013
    192—dc23
    2013002605

ISBN: 978-0-415-50998-5 (hbk)
ISBN: 978-0-203-38271-4 (ebk)

Typeset in Sabon
by Apex CoVantage, LLC

Printed and bound in the United States of America by Publishers Graphics,
LLC on sustainably sourced paper.

This book is dedicated to:
Kieran and Susanna Egan
Paul and Mary Reynolds
Eugen, Ilse, Eugene, and Debbie Wendland

Contents

x   *Contents*

Acknowledgments

The editors thank the team at Taylor & Francis, especially Felisa Salvago-Keyes, for their patience and support, and for their faith in this project. In addition, our special thanks are due to Stephen Mulhall, who has been a mentor to all three of us, and who has served as a model and a guide in developing our own interests in Wittgenstein and Heidegger.

David Egan thanks the Social Sciences and Humanities Research Council of Canada, the Clarendon Fund, Oriel College, and Oxford's Faculty of Philosophy, all of whom have provided financial support during the process of working on this book, as well as the family and friends who have provided ever-important nonfinancial support. His thanks are also due to Warren Goldfarb and Stanley Cavell, who first gave direction to his passion for philosophy.

Stephen Reynolds is grateful to the Arts and Humanities Research Council, Oriel College, and the University of Oxford's Philosophy Faculty for financial support over the years. He would also like to thank Martin Warner, Michael John Kooy, and Stephen Houlgate for introducing him to philosophy and showing him its value. His greatest thanks, though, go to his wife, Rebecca, for her limitless patience and abiding optimism.

Aaron James Wendland would like to express his gratitude to Somerville College, Oxford, for a generous scholarship that made editing this book possible. He is also indebted to Jeff Noonan and Heather MacIvor for sparking his interest in philosophy, and to Gad Horowitz, Charles Taylor, and John Gray for their guidance and inspiration. Marii Väljataga reminded him that Apollo only gets it half right. Finally, a special thank you is reserved for Eugen and Ilse Wendland as well as Eugene and Debbie Wendland. Aaron's accomplishments are as much theirs as they are his own.

Abbreviations

1   WORKS BY WITTGENSTEIN

AWL	*Wittgenstein's Lectures: Cambridge, 1932–1935: From the Notes of Alice Ambrose and Margaret Macdonald*
BB	*The Blue and Brown Books: Preliminary Studies for the "Philosophical Investigations."*
BTS	*The Big Typscript*
Conv	*Wittgenstein: Conversations 1949–1951*
CV	*Culture and Value*
LC	*Lectures and Conversations on Aesthetics, Psychology and Religious Belief*
LFM	*Lectures on the Foundations of Mathematics: Cambridge, 1939*
LPP	*Wittgenstein's Lectures on Philosophical Psychology: 1946–47*
LWL	*Wittgenstein's Lectures: Cambridge, 1930–32*
LWPPI	*Last Writings on the Philosophy of Psychology*
LWPPII	*Last Writings on the Philosophy of Psychology*
LWVC	*Ludwig Wittgenstein and the Vienna Circle: Conversations Recorded by Friedrich*
NB	*Notebooks, 1914–1916*
OC	*On Certainty*
PG	*Philosophical Grammar*
PhR	*Philosophical Remarks*
PI	*Philosophical Investigations*
PO	*Philosophical Occasions: 1912–1951*
PPF	*Philosophy of Psychology—a Fragment*
RC	*Remarks on Colour*
RFM	*Remarks on the Foundations of Mathematics*
RPPI	*Remarks on the Philosophy of Psychology*
RPPII	*Remarks on the Philosophy of Psychology*
SP	*Wittgenstein: Sources and Perspectives*
TLP	*Tractatus Logico-Philosophicus*
Z	*Zettel*

2   WORKS BY HEIDEGGER

AM	*Aristotle's Metaphysics Q 1–3: On the Essence and Actuality of Force*
Basic	*Basic Concepts*
BaT	*Being and Truth*
BCAP	*Basic Concepts of Aristotelian Philosophy*
BH	*Becoming Heidegger: On the Trail of His Early Occasional Writings*
BP	*The Basic Problems of Phenomenology*
BQ	*Basic Questions of Philosophy: Selected "Problems" of "Logic."*
BT	*Being and Time*
BW	*Basic Writings*
CP	*Contributions to Philosophy (From Enknowing)*
CPC	*Country Path Conversations*
DT	*Discourse on Thinking*
EGT	*Early Greek Thinking: The Dawn of Western Philosophy*
EP	*Einleitung in die Philosophie (GA 27)*
ET	*The Essence of Truth On Plato's Parable of the Cave Allegory and Theaetetus*
FCM	*The Fundamental Concepts of Metaphysics: World, Finitude, Solitude*
FS	*Four Seminars*
GA	*Gesamtausgabe*
HCT	*History of the Concept of Time: Prolegomena*
HH	*Hölderlin's Hymn "The Ister."*
HR	*The Heidegger Reader*
ID	*Identity and Difference*
IM	*An Introduction to Metaphysics*
IPR	*An Introduction to Phenomenological Research*
ITP	*Introduction to Philosophy—Thinking and Poetizing*
KPM	*Kant and the Problem of Metaphysics*
LQT	*Logic: The Question of Truth*
M	*Mindfulness*
MFL	*The Metaphysical Foundations of Logic*
N	*Nietzsche*
OBT	*Off the Beaten Track*
OHF	*Ontology—the Hermeneutics of Facticity*
OWL	*On the Way to Language.*
P	*Parmenides*
PIA	*Phenomenological Interpretations of Aristotle Initiation into Phenomenological Research*
PIE	*Phenomenology of Intuition and Expression*
PIK	*Phenomenological Interpretation of Kant's Critique of Pure Reason*

PLT   *Poetry, Language, Thought*
PM   *Pathmarks*
PR   *The Principle of Reason*
PRL   *The Phenomenology of Religious Life*
PS   *Plato's Sophist*
PT   *The Piety of Thinking*
QT   *The Question Concerning Technology and Other Essays*
SA   *The Self-Assertion of the German University*
STF   *Schelling's Treatise on the Essence of Human Freedom*
Supp   *Supplements: From the Earliest Essays to* Being and Time *and Beyond*
TB   *On Time and Being*
TDP   *Towards the Definition of Philosophy*
WCT   *What Is Called Thinking?*
WIP   *What Is Philosophy?.*
WP   *Why Do I Stay in the Provinces?*
WT   *What Is a Thing?*
Zo   *Zollikon Seminars: Protocols—Conversations—Letters*

3 OTHER WORKS CITED WITH ABBREVIATIONS

AT   *Oeuvres Complètes de René Descartes*
CPR   *Critique of Pure Reason*

Contributors

Lee Braver is Associate Professor of Philosophy at Hiram College. He is the author of *A Thing of This World: A History of Continental Anti-Realism* (Northwestern, 2007), *Heidegger's Later Writings: A Reader's Guide* (Continuum, 2009), and *Groundless Grounds: A Study of Wittgenstein and Heidegger* (MIT, 2012), as well as number of articles and book chapters. He is presently working on two books: *Heidegger: Thinking of Being*, and *Unthinkable*. He is also considered by many to be a Master Griller.

Taylor Carman is professor of philosophy at Barnard College, Columbia University. He is author of *Heidegger's Analytic* (Cambridge, 2003), and *Merleau-Ponty* (Routledge, 2008), which appeared in the Routledge Philosophers Series. He is coeditor of *The Cambridge Companion to Merleau-Ponty* (Cambridge, 2004) and has written articles on various aspects of phenomenology and philosophy of mind.

David R. Cerbone is Professor of Philosophy at West Virginia University. He is the author of *Understanding Phenomenology* (Acumen, 2006) and *Heidegger: A Guide for the Perplexed* (Continuum, 2008), as well as numerous articles on Heidegger, Wittgenstein, and the phenomenological and analytic traditions more generally. He is (with Søren Overgaard and Komarine Romdenh-Romluc) editor of the series *Routledge Research in Phenomenology*.

David Egan has taught at McMaster University and Christ Church, Oxford. His publications include "Pictures in Wittgenstein's Later Philosophy" (*Philosophical Investigations*, 2011) and "*Das Man* and Distantiality in *Being and Time*" (*Inquiry*, 2012).

Simon Glendinning is a Reader in European Philosophy in the European Institute at the London School of Economics and Political Science. He is the author of *On Being with Others: Heidegger—Derrida—Wittgenstein* (Routledge, 1998) and *In the Name of Phenomenology* (Routledge,

2007). A previous essay on Heidegger and Wittgenstein, "The End of Philosophy as Metaphysics," was published in *The Cambridge History of Philosophy 1870–1945*, ed. Thomas Baldwin (Cambridge, 2004). His current work is centred on the Philosophy of Europe.

Charles Guignon is currently Professor of Philosophy at the University of South Florida. He has written extensively on Heidegger, is the author of *On Being Authentic* (Routledge, 2004) and coauthor of a critical study of psychology titled *Re-envisioning Psychology* (Jossey-Bass, 1999), and he has edited or coedited a number of books, including *Richard Rorty* (Cambridge, 2003), *The Good Life* (Hackett, 1999), two works by Dostoevsky—*The Grand Inquisitor* (Hackett, 1993) and *Notes from the Underground* (Hackett, 2009)—and two volumes of readings by and about existentialists.

Denis McManus is Professor of Philosophy at the University of Southampton. He is the author of *The Enchantment of Words: Wittgenstein's Tractatus Logico-Philosophicus* (Oxford, 2006) and *Heidegger and the Measure of Truth* (Oxford, forthcoming). He is the editor of *Wittgenstein and Scepticism* (Routledge, 2004) and *Heidegger, Authenticity and the Self* (Routledge, forthcoming).

Edward Minar is Associate Professor in the Philosophy Department at the University of Arkansas. He works primarily on topics in philosophy of mind, epistemology, history of analytic philosophy, and continental philosophy. Relevant publications include "Heidegger, Wittgenstein and Skepticism" (*Harvard Review of Philosophy*, Spring 2001); "Heidegger's Response to Skepticism in *Being and Time*," (in *Future Pasts: Reflections on the History and Nature of Analytic Philosophy*, ed. Juliet Floyd and Sanford Shieh (Oxford, 2001)); and "Wittgenstein's Response to Skepticism in *On Certainty*," (in *Readings of Wittgenstein's* On Certainty, ed. William Brenner and Danielle Moyal-Sharrock (Palgrave MacMillan, 2005)). He is editor of the journal *Philosophical Topics*.

Stephen Mulhall is Professor of Philosophy at New College, Oxford. He has published extensively on Wittgenstein and Heidegger. His most recent books are *Wittgenstein's Private Language* (Oxford, 2006), *The Conversation of Humanity* (Virginia, 2007), and *The Wounded Animal* (Princeton, 2009). A book of essays, *The Self and Its Shadows*, is due to appear with Oxford University Press in 2013.

Herman Philipse is a distinguished professor of philosophy at the University of Utrecht. He is the author of books such as *Heidegger's Philosophy of Being: A Critical Interpretation* (Princeton, 1998), and *God in the Age of Science? A Critique of Religious Reason* (Oxford, 2012). Philipse has written many philosophical articles in Dutch, both scholarly

and popular, and published papers such as "The Absolute Network Theory of Language" (*Inquiry* 33, 1990), "Transcendental Idealism" (*The
Cambridge Companion to Husserl*, 1995), "Heideggers philosophisch-
religiöse Strategie" (*Zeitschrift für philosophische Forschung* 57, 2003),
and "Overcoming Epistemology" (*The Oxford Handbook of Continental Philosophy*, 2007).

Stephen Reynolds completed his DPhil in philosophy at Oriel College, Oxford, before teaching at Magdalen and New Colleges. He is currently an
Astbury Scholar at Middle Temple.

Anthony Rudd is Visiting Associate Professor of Philosophy at St. Olaf Col-
lege, Minnesota, USA. He is the author of *Expressing the World: Skepti-
cism, Wittgenstein and Heidegger* (Open Court, 2003), as well as *Self,
Value and Narrative: A Kierkegaardian Approach* (Oxford, 2012) and
Kierkegaard and the Limits of the Ethical (Oxford, 1993). Recent papers
include "Narrative, Expression and Mental Substance" (*Inquiry*, 2005),
"Skepticism, Sublimity and Transcendence" (*International Philosophical
Quarterly*, 2008), and "In Defence of Narrative" (*European Journal of
Philosophy*, 2009).

Theodore R. Schatzki is Dean of Faculty and Professor of Philosophy and
Geography in the College of Arts and Sciences at the University of Ken-
tucky. He is the author of *Social Practices: A Wittgensteinian Approach
to Human Activity and the Social* (Cambridge, 1996), *The Site of the
Social: A Philosophical Account of the Constitution of Social Life and
Change* (Pennsylvania State, 2002), *Martin Heidegger: Theorist of Space*
(Steiner, 2007), and *The Timespace of Human Activity: On Performance,
Society, and History as Indeterminate Events* (Lexington, 2010).

Joseph K. Schear is University Lecturer and Tutorial Fellow in Philosophy at
Christ Church, Oxford. He has published a number of essays in phenom-
enology and philosophy of mind, and he has edited the volume *Mind,
Reason, and Being-in-the-World: The McDowell-Dreyfus Debate* (Rout-
ledge 2012). He is currently writing a book, *Horizons of Intentionality:
From Husserl to Heidegger*.

Aaron James Wendland is a doctoral student at Somerville College, Oxford.
His thesis is on Heidegger's appeal to the creative use of language as the
site and source of cultural transformation. An essay entitled "Contra-
dictory Freedoms: Kant on Moral Agency and Political Rights" recently
appeared in *Philosophy Study*, and a paper entitled "The Metaphysics of
Modern Technology" is forthcoming in *The European Legacy*.

1 General Introduction

*David Egan, Stephen Reynolds,
and Aaron James Wendland*

Ludwig Wittgenstein and Martin Heidegger are widely recognized as two of the most influential and important philosophers of the twentieth century. Born into German-speaking families in the same year, each emerged as the star pupil and anointed successor of the leading figure in their respective traditions: Bertrand Russell with Wittgenstein in analytic philosophy and Edmund Husserl with Heidegger in phenomenology. Russell and Husserl expected their protégés to continue the work they had begun, but Wittgenstein's *Tractatus Logico-Philosophicus* and Heidegger's *Being and Time* radically questioned and cast serious doubt on that work. Yet Wittgenstein and Heidegger did not stop there. After turning away from their mentors' teachings, they both went on to revise their own earlier thought. And although the extent of this revision is open to debate in each case, both clearly came to view their later thought as a response to—and criticism of—their more youthful philosophical endeavors.

In addition to these biographical similarities, Wittgenstein and Heidegger share a certain philosophical temperament. First, Wittgenstein's later work accords with Heidegger's anti-foundationalism.[1] In other words, both reject the impulse to find a solid, indubitable foundation upon which to build the human artifice. Second, both opt instead for a holistic and pragmatic approach, seeking understanding through the connections between things and seeing thought as embedded in a broad range of human activities. Finally, each rejects Descartes' mind-body dualism and Plato's attempt to interpret the everyday world in terms of a more essential reality.

Methodologically, Wittgenstein and Heidegger are uncomfortable with the prospect of advancing new philosophical theses and theories, and both occasionally characterize their work as simply offering descriptions or reminders that no one would disagree with. In the face of this apparent humility, they have revolutionized philosophy—not by erecting new edifices, but by calling into question the grounds upon which all philosophical edifices have been established. Lastly, both have been associated with the notion of an "end to philosophy," because they do not so much offer a new way forward (as Russell and Husserl hoped to) but dispute the very idea of progress as a model for philosophy.

Despite the biographical, philosophical, and methodological similarities between Wittgenstein and Heidegger, relatively little comparative work has been done on them. The reason for this oversight is as simple as it is unfortunate: for roughly the last hundred years there has been a divide between "analytic" philosophy, which has dominated Anglophone universities, and "continental" philosophy, which has had a prominent role in French and German thought.[2] Analytic philosophers claim Wittgenstein as one of their own and often dismiss Heidegger as an obscurantist, whereas continental philosophers, although more charitable to Wittgenstein, have never fully embraced his work. In addressing this paucity of comparative work, this volume aims to bridge the analytic-continental divide by placing a key figure from one tradition in contact with a prominent voice from the other. Yet the chapters collected here are not simply concerned with comparing and contrasting Wittgenstein and Heidegger. Rather they stage genuine dialogues, with aspects of Wittgenstein's thought elucidating, answering, or problematizing aspects of Heidegger's, and vice versa. And we hope that such dialogues will give rise to new lines of inquiry—much like the work of Wittgenstein and Heidegger themselves—lines that are neither strictly Heideggerian nor strictly Wittgensteinian, but that shed light on important philosophical issues.

Although we have left it to our contributors to offer a detailed analysis of the relation between Wittgenstein's and Heidegger's writings, this introduction offers a few words about the life and work of our protagonists (sections 1 and 2) as well as the scholarship surrounding their thought as a whole (section 3). Finally, we've provided a brief summary of each chapter in the collection for our readers' convenience (section 4).

1   WITTGENSTEIN: LIFE AND WORKS

Ludwig Wittgenstein was born into an assimilated Jewish-Catholic family in Vienna on April 26, 1889. His father, Karl, was a self-made man and steel magnate, who combined engineering prowess and business acumen to become one of the wealthiest men in Europe. Ludwig was the youngest of nine children, and grew up in an intense and talented family. Of his four brothers, three committed suicide and Ludwig and his surviving brother Paul also entertained thoughts of suicide at points in their lives. The family was exceptionally musical: Ludwig's oldest brother, Rudi, was a prodigiously talented musician, as was Paul, who enjoyed a successful career as a concert pianist despite losing his right arm in the First World War. Ludwig himself was exquisitely sensitive to music, and his notebooks contain many remarks about music. In general, the Wittgensteins were energetic patrons of the arts: Karl was an important supporter of the Secession movement and the Wittgensteins' palatial home hosted concerts by Brahms and Mahler.

Ludwig looked to be the most likely of Karl Wittgenstein's sons to follow his father into industry, and he initially trained as a mechanical and aeronautical engineer. During his studies in Manchester, however, he was drawn to foundational questions in mathematics, and sought the advice of Gottlob Frege in Jena. Frege suggested that Wittgenstein study under Bertrand Russell in Cambridge, and thus he arrived unannounced at Russell's rooms on October 18, 1911, in an encounter that would prove pivotal in both men's lives. Despite some initial reticence, Russell quickly came to regard Wittgenstein as a genius who could carry forward his research in mathematical logic and analytic philosophy. In the following two years of intense collaboration, the roles of teacher and pupil were reversed, and Russell later reflected, "Getting to know Wittgenstein was one of the most exciting intellectual adventures of my life" (Russell 1951, 298).

In 1913, Wittgenstein moved to the village of Skjolden in Norway to work in isolation, and began to develop a conception of logic as of "a *totally* different kind than any other science" (*NB* 120). To Wittgenstein, Russell and Frege's universalist conception of logic, according to which logic consists of "maximally general truths" (Ricketts 1996, 59), seemed insufficiently radical in distinguishing logic from the sciences. Far from expressing maximally general truths, Wittgenstein came to think of logical propositions as not *expressing* anything at all: they are *senseless*—limiting cases of propositions with sense. Logical form is something *shown* in the way that non-logical propositions manage to depict facts about the world.

Wittgenstein's work on logic was interrupted and deepened by the First World War. Although he was excused from the military draft due to a double hernia, Wittgenstein volunteered for service in the Austro-Hungarian army. He constantly sought out dangerous assignments, and was decorated several times for bravery. During his time at the front, Wittgenstein's earlier atheism gave way to a religious mysticism, particularly as expressed in Tolstoy's *The Gospel in Brief*. This mysticism finds expression in the later sections of the *Tractatus Logico-Philosophicus*, which took shape during Wittgenstein's military service. Toward the end of the war, Wittgenstein was captured by the Italian army, and posted to Russell a completed manuscript of the *Tractatus* from a prisoner-of-war camp in Cassino. After some difficulties in finding a publisher, the *Tractatus* was published in German in 1921, and in an English translation by C.K. Ogden and Frank Ramsey in 1922.

The *Tractatus* presents a conception of logic, language, and the world as mirroring one another: language consists of bipolar propositions that depict facts, which may be true or false depending on how the world contingently is, and which can depict the world by sharing a logical form with the facts that they depict, and with the senseless propositions of logic. These latter say nothing, but show the logical structure of the world. On this account, propositions that do not describe the world, but rather try to speak about the world as a whole, or make evaluative statements, are ill-formed and therefore nonsensical. Because the propositions of the *Tractatus* are themselves not descriptive in the required sense, Wittgenstein claims that they are themselves nonsensical, serving instead as a ladder that the reader must "throw away . . . after he has climbed up it" (*TLP* 6.54).[3]

Although Wittgenstein's later philosophy differs from the *Tractatus* in many respects, this early work exhibits a number of methodological features that abide throughout his philosophical career. First, Wittgenstein regards the conceptual puzzlement that gives rise to philosophy as resulting from illegitimate questions rather than from elusive answers. Second, philosophy puts an end to questioning by making the questions disappear or lose their urgency. And third, the way to put an end to questioning is to achieve a clear presentation of the issues about which questions arise. Such a presentation dispels the need for questioning.

Wittgenstein returned to civilian life in 1919 in a state of personal crisis. The war had changed him deeply, and, with the completion of the *Tractatus*, he felt he had given a final and definitive answer to the philosophical problems that troubled him. He had inherited a vast fortune from his father, who had died in 1913, but gave it all away, mostly to his siblings. As Wittgenstein saw it, their own great wealth meant that they could not be further corrupted by money. Instead, Wittgenstein chose a life of austere simplicity, training as a schoolteacher and taking on a number of posts in the mountains of rural Austria. Wittgenstein's aristocratic bearing and exacting standards caused friction with the villagers, and he left his post in Otterthal in 1926 under a cloud after beating a student. Returning to Vienna, Wittgenstein collaborated with his friend Paul Engelmann in designing a spare, modernist house for his sister, Margaret.[4]

In the late 1920s, Wittgenstein gradually returned to philosophy. The *Tractatus* had become a keystone text of the Vienna Circle, and Wittgenstein engaged in a series of discussions with Moritz Schlick, Rudolf Carnap, Friedrich Waismann, and Herbert Feigl. In 1929, he returned to Cambridge, where the *Tractatus* was accepted as his PhD thesis.

With the support of a fellowship at Trinity College, Cambridge, Wittgenstein's later philosophy began to take shape in the 1930s. In particular, the *Tractatus* vision of logic as crystalline, pure, and sublime began to give way to a vision of logic and language as parts of variegated human forms of life, and answerable to no higher authority than the human practices in which they are used. Whereas the earlier philosophy entertained the idea of a general form of propositions, Wittgenstein's later work insists that there are "countless different kinds of use of all the things we call 'signs,' 'words,' 'sentences'" (*PI* §23). As with his earlier work, Wittgenstein struggled to find the appropriate form for expressing his views: he saw himself not as advancing new theories but as resolving conceptual confusion, a method that requires a different form from standard modes of philosophical argumentation. Through meticulous drafting and redrafting of his thoughts, the *Philosophical Investigations* gradually took shape. The main body of the text was completed by 1946, but, in accordance with Wittgenstein's wishes, it was published only posthumously, in 1953. Since that time, a number of other collections of Wittgenstein's notebook material have also been published, such as *On Certainty*, *Remarks on the Foundations of Mathematics*, and *Zettel*.

Wittgenstein had an intense personality, and the number of memoirs about him attests to the strong impression he made on those who knew him. He was a mercilessly demanding friend, but he was even more demanding of himself, especially as regards personal honesty. In the 1930s, he made a series of "confessions" to various friends, aiming to weed out any dishonesty or vanity, and he lived a life of Spartan simplicity. For Wittgenstein, honesty was a matter not simply of truthfulness but also of courage, and he saw genius as "*courage in one's talent*" (*CV* 44). Being true to his talent, for Wittgenstein, was a test of character as much as a test of intellect.

In 1939, Wittgenstein was elected Professor of Philosophy at Cambridge following G. E. Moore's retirement. He also became a naturalized British citizen, which permitted him to travel to Austria—recently united with Nazi Germany in the 1938 *Anschluss*—to negotiate a settlement with the Nazi authorities that would allow his sisters to remain in Vienna unmolested. During the Second World War, Wittgenstein sought work as a medical orderly at Guy's Hospital in London, and also assisted in medical research in Newcastle.

Wittgenstein resigned his professorship in 1947 and spent the remaining years of his life writing and living with friends in the United States, Ireland, and Norway as well as in Great Britain. He succumbed to prostate cancer on April 29, 1951, and is buried in the Parish of the Ascension Burial Ground in Cambridge. On his deathbed, shortly before losing consciousness, he told his doctor's wife: "Tell them I've had a wonderful life" (Monk 1990, 579).

2 HEIDEGGER: LIFE AND WORKS

Martin Heidegger was born into a modest home in Meßkirch, Germany, on September 26, 1889. Heidegger's parents were active parishioners at the Catholic church of St. Martin, and Heidegger's early education prepared him for the priesthood. From 1903 to 1906, he attended a Gymnasium in Constance where he lived in the Jesuit house for theology students, and in 1906 he moved to the Berthold-Gymnasium in Freiburg where he received an education in classics. From 1909 to 1911, Heidegger was a member of the diocesan seminary in Freiburg and a student of theology at Freiburg University. During the course of his doctrinal training, Heidegger was presented with a copy of Franz Brentano's book, *On the Several Senses of Being in Aristotle*. And although this text inspired his lifelong attempt to elucidate the meaning of Being, Heidegger's early interest in Brentano and Aristotle prompted him to leave the seminary in 1912 in order to register in Freiburg's Philosophy Faculty. Under the supervision of Arthur Schneider, Heidegger produced a doctoral dissertation, *The Doctrine of Judgment in Psychologism*, in 1913. And with the oversight of Heinrich Rickert, he completed his *Habilitationsschrift*, *The Categories and the Doctrine of Meaning in Duns Scotus*, in 1915.

Apart from two brief periods of service in the First World War, Heidegger held various teaching and administrative posts at Freiburg between 1916 and 1922. Here Heidegger had the opportunity to lecture on Plato and Aristotle, Medieval Scholasticism, Kant and German Idealism, and the writings of St. Paul, St. Augustine, and Martin Luther. He quickly developed a reputation as an exceptional teacher who, over his career, attracted a group of students as diverse and influential as Hannah Arendt, Hans-Georg Gadamer, Hans Jonas, Emmanuel Levinas, Karl Löwith, Herbert Marcuse, and Leo Strauss. As a lecturer at Freiburg, Heidegger privately studied Kierkegaard and Nietzsche as well as several German poets, including Stefan George, Friedrich Hölderlin, Rainer Maria Rilke, and Georg Trakl. He also began reading Dilthey's *Introduction to the Human Sciences*, which taught him much about the historical nature of human understanding. However, the most decisive influence on Heidegger's intellectual and professional development came when the founder of phenomenology, Edmund Husserl, was appointed to Freiburg's Chair of Philosophy in 1916 and subsequently hired Heidegger as his assistant. Husserl's call to bracket our scientific explanations of the world so that we can describe how phenomena actually appear to us anticipates Heidegger's attempt in *Being and Time* to come to terms with the meaning of Being through an analysis of human beings in their average everydayness. Husserl's concept of evidence prefigures Heidegger's discussion of truth as the unconcealment of beings. And Husserl's stature surely helped the scarcely published Heidegger secure a professorship in Marburg in 1923.

Heidegger's classes at Marburg combined Husserl's analysis of phenomena as they are presented to human consciousness with Aristotle's emphasis on the practical wisdom implicit in every human endeavor. Heidegger also drew on Dilthey and Kant for a series of lectures on "The History of the Concept of Time." And as a result of these collective reflections, the first two divisions of Part I of *Being and Time* appeared in print in the spring of 1927. Heidegger's provisional aim in *Being and Time* is to offer an "interpretation of *time* as the possible horizon for any understanding whatsoever of Being" (*BT* 1/19), and he tentatively argues that the Being of an entity is determined or disclosed through the temporal nature of human activities. Given the intimate link between Being and human activity, *Being and Time* offers a detailed description of the essential aspects of human existence. Heidegger's word for human being is *Dasein*, literally, being-there, and it is meant to capture the fact that the essence of a particular human is determined by the space, place, or world she finds herself in. Of course, as human beings, we are all born into a specific historical situation that presents us with different ways of living our lives. And when we adopt a specific activity that our *past* makes available by choosing to carry that activity into the *future*, entities and aspects of the world show up *as* the entities and aspects that they are in light of that activity. Hence, Heidegger claims that the Being of an entity is determined by the temporal horizon of human activity. Heidegger never completed the full plan for *Being and Time*, consisting of two parts, each with three divisions, but the first two divisions published alone established Heidegger as one of Germany's preeminent thinkers. And on the basis of this text, Heidegger was appointed to the Chair of Philosophy at Freiburg when Husserl retired in 1928.

Although Heidegger's writings on Kant and phenomenology in the late 1920s built on the basic assumptions of *Being and Time*, sometime in 1930 Heidegger's thinking began to turn away from his earlier philosophy and to his later thought of the 1940s and 1950s. Throughout the 1930s, Heidegger lectured extensively on Nietzsche and Hölderlin. The essence of art and truth became increasingly important themes in Heidegger's work, and these motifs featured prominently in Heidegger's public presentation of "The Origin of the Work of Art" in 1935. In this essay, Heidegger says that "art is truth setting itself to work" (*PLT* 38). The truth at work in a work of art is not the accurate *representation* of reality through a piece of art, but rather the initial *presentation* of reality that is achieved in the work. Truth, in other words, happens in artworks when they reveal aspects of reality that were previously concealed. And whereas *Being and Time* identified human activity with world-disclosure, "The Origin of the Work of Art" seems to shift the site of world-disclosure to specific things—namely, artworks. The precise nature of this shift is a matter of much debate, but Heidegger himself characterized it as a change in emphasis from *Dasein* (human being) to *Sein* (Being). And if one thing is clear about the turn in Heidegger's thinking in the 1930s, it is this: in order to adequately articulate the meaning of Being, Heidegger thought it necessary to drop the Kantian transcendental vocabulary of *Being and Time* for a slightly more poetic tone (*BW* 231).

As Heidegger's thought evolved in the early 1930s, Germany was experiencing a radical political transformation. Hitler was appointed Chancellor on January 30, 1933. Heidegger was elected Rector of Freiburg University on April 22, 1933, and on May 1, 1933, he joined the Nazi Party. Heidegger sought to align the university with National Socialism, and in his Rectoral Address he urged his colleagues to advance the spiritual mission of Germany through labor service, armed service, and the service of knowledge (see *SA*). Although a series of conflicts with faculty and party officials forced Heidegger to resign as Rector in April 1934, he remained a member of the Nazi Party until its dissolution at the end of the war.

In 1945, Freiburg's Denazification Committee banned Heidegger from teaching at the university for the next five years. Unable to teach, he gave occasional lectures on the essence of technology to a businessmen's club in Bremen and at the Bavarian Academy of Fine Arts in Munich. These lectures have had a profound influence on deep ecology and the philosophy of technology. In them, Heidegger characterizes the reduction of the world to resources for production and consumption as the crisis of modernity. This reduction counts as a crisis insofar as our failure to treat the world as a sacred place worthy of our respect leads to the violation of nature and thus the destruction of our home. In response to this crisis Heidegger seeks a releasement from our technological way of life such that we no longer see the world as a gigantic resource for our production and consumption. When properly released, Heidegger says we are capable of "letting beings be." Yet the world-disclosure accomplished when released from our technological mode of Being is neither a matter of human activity (as in *Being and Time*) nor is it attained through the creation of an artwork (as in "The Origin of the Work of Art"). Instead, it is achieved through a receptivity to and reverence for what Heidegger now sees as the fourfold division of Being between earth, sky, divinities, and mortals. Characterizing the way in which we overcome the crisis confronting modernity as *receptivity* to the earth, our sky, divinities, and our mortality means that human *activity* cannot counter the danger. And Heidegger followed his own thought to its logical conclusion in an interview with *Der Speigel* when he said: "only a god can save us" (*HR* 313–33).

The University of Freiburg restored Heidegger's right to teach in 1950. In 1951–52 Heidegger delivered his final official lecture course, "What is Called Thinking?" In this lecture, he identifies humans as beings with the ability to think, but then claims that what is "*most thought-provoking is that we are still not thinking*" (WCT 4). Heidegger's point is that thinking is always ahead of us, and this point is consistent with Heidegger's interpretation of the Pre-Socratics in the 1960s as well as the preface he penned for his collected works just before his death in 1976. In this preface, Heidegger claims that his thinking has been constantly "underway in the field paths of the self-transforming asking of the many-sided question of Being," and he concludes by saying that his aim has always been to "awaken a confrontation with the question concerning the topic of thinking" (in Petzet 1993, 224).

3   WITTGENSTEIN AND HEIDEGGER: INFLUENCE AND SCHOLARSHIP

As noted earlier, Wittgenstein and Heidegger are two of the most influential philosophers of the twentieth century, and their impact is evident in the diversity of philosophical movements they inspired. With that said, their importance as philosophers comes despite the fact that—or more likely, because—neither is a philosopher in the ordinary modern mold. Throughout his life, Wittgenstein felt uneasy in university settings, exhibited little interest in the history of philosophy, and occasionally uses the language of pathology in talking about philosophy. Heidegger had a more traditionally academic career, but his later work in particular seeks a way beyond traditional philosophy toward what he calls "thinking," and even in *Being and*

Time, he calls for the "destruction" of the history of ontology (*BT* §6). Because both Wittgenstein and Heidegger struggled to articulate thoughts that constituted something more and something other than responses to the traditional philosophical problems they inherited, their influence spreads well beyond their contributions to particular philosophical problematics. In this section, however, we focus primarily on their impact on philosophy, briefly reviewing the major lines of influence and scholarship of each in turn before considering some points of connection and convergence in that scholarship.

3.1   Wittgenstein

Besides the impact Wittgenstein had on the work of philosophers he knew personally, such as Russell, Moore, and Ramsey, the first major reception of his thought took place in the Vienna Circle from the mid-1920s. Leading figures of the circle, such as Moritz Schlick and Rudolf Carnap, embraced the *Tractatus* as providing a clear demarcation between sense and nonsense that would banish metaphysical speculation and help forge a more scientific philosophy. The ideas of the Vienna Circle reached the English-speaking world via A. J. Ayer in Britain and Ernest Nagel and Charles Morris in America, and by the outset of the Second World War, many of the leading figures of the predominantly Jewish Vienna Circle had moved permanently to America.[5] Although W. V. O. Quine (1951) is generally thought to have radically undermined the central tenets of logical positivism, many of the methods, and some of the results, of this diverse group of Austrian philosophers remain influential in analytic philosophy to this day. Furthermore, the *Tractatus* stands as one of the major works of the early analytic tradition that prompted a "linguistic turn," elevating the analysis of language to a central place in philosophy.

Wittgenstein's later philosophy has had a broader and less definite impact. Much as the *Tractatus* found currency in interwar Vienna, so did the *Investigations* in postwar Oxford. As with the Vienna Circle, it would be a mistake to suggest the postwar Oxford philosophy spoke in a single, united voice, or that Wittgenstein's influence upon this group of philosophers was uniform. Nevertheless, Wittgenstein's influence can be felt in the work of Gilbert Ryle, H. L. A. Hart, and P. F. Strawson, among others. Although less directly impressed with Wittgenstein, J. L. Austin exhibits marked affinities: both he and Wittgenstein exhibit sensitivity to the subtleties of ordinary language and skepticism toward more technical methods in philosophy.

But Wittgenstein's later philosophy is significant not so much for spawning a particular school of thought, as for influencing lines of argument across analytic philosophy—especially in the philosophy of language and the philosophy of mind. In the philosophy of language, Wittgenstein offers a significant challenge to referential and truth-conditional theories of meaning, and his work has inspired a number of attempts at "use" theories of meaning, inferential role semantics, and various forms of contextualism. His rule following considerations has also had significant impact on discussions of the normativity of meaning. In the philosophy of mind, Wittgenstein has inspired anti-Cartesian and anti-dualist arguments, and his discussion of the possibility of a private language has inspired critical appraisals of the idea of phenomenal content and private experience. Wittgenstein's treatment of both language and mind has influenced arguments for externalism about mental content, and against mentalism more generally. Wittgenstein has also had a marked influence on the philosophy of action and epistemology. Wittgenstein's impact can be felt in the work of such mainstream analytic philosophers as Donald Davidson, Daniel Dennett, Michael Dummett, Saul Kripke, John McDowell, Hilary Putnam, and Crispin Wright.

Wittgenstein's centrality to analytic philosophy has declined in recent decades, as his robustly anti-metaphysical stance clashes with the rise of analytic metaphysics, and his methodological pronouncements sound increasingly alien to philosophers who draw their conception of research and progress from the model of the natural sciences. However, as "analytic philosophy" becomes an increasingly broad term, and terms like "post-analytic philosophy" emerge to challenge the governing orthodoxy, Wittgenstein retains a strong presence in contemporary philosophy.[6] Wittgenstein has made less of an impression outside the English-speaking world, but a number of major European philosophers have made fruitful use of his work, including Jürgen Habermas, Karl-Otto Apel, Ernst Tugendhat, and Jacques Bouveresse.[7]

Wittgenstein scholarship has been vigorous in the sixty years since his death, and shows no sign of abating.[8] At present, one can roughly distinguish an "orthodox" interpretation of Wittgenstein from a range of revisionist readings that have blossomed particularly in the last twenty years, notably championed in Crary and Read (2000). Whereas orthodox interpretations find in Wittgenstein a brilliant representative of philosophy in the analytic tradition, revisionist readings question the extent to which Wittgenstein can be assimilated to the standard aims and methods of that tradition. However, this rough distinction must not obscure the diversity of orthodox and revisionist readings, nor mislead the reader into thinking that orthodox or revisionist readings of the early work necessarily complement their counterpart with regard to the later work.[9]

With regard to *Tractatus* scholarship, the main point of contention is how one ought to understand Wittgenstein's claim at *TLP* 6.54 that the reader should recognize the propositions of the *Tractatus* as nonsensical. According to the orthodox interpretation, accepting this claim does not require us to reject the idea that the *Tractatus* advances a picture theory of meaning, a conception of logic as consisting of senseless tautologies, and so on. Rather, it helps us to see that these claims are, strictly speaking, ineffable, and show themselves only in the correct analysis of propositions with a sense. By contrast, the so-called "resolute" reading, primarily associated with Cora Diamond and James Conant, insists on taking Wittgenstein at his word: if the propositions that constitute the body of the *Tractatus* are nonsensical, there is no sense in which we can even meaningfully entertain a picture theory of meaning and the like. Instead, this reading suggests, the *Tractatus* leads us through the imaginative exercise of trying to make sense of its propositions, and recognizing their collapse frees the reader from the temptation to philosophical theorizing.[10]

The "orthodox" interpretation of Wittgenstein's later philosophy—which, to repeat, is completely independent of the orthodox interpretation of the *Tractatus* provided in the previous paragraph—finds its most comprehensive expression in the commentaries of G. P. Baker and P. M. S. Hacker.[11] On this interpretation, Wittgenstein is sharply critical of much traditional philosophy, in particular dismantling metaphysical pictures of language and reality, but he also performs the positive task of mapping segments of the grammar of our language, and providing a surveyable representation of fragments of the conceptual landscape so as to relieve conceptual confusion. Dissension from this interpretation is more varied than the (nevertheless diverse) range of "resolute" readings of the *Tractatus*, but a common thread is a reluctance to attribute any strong positive claims to Wittgenstein. Perhaps the strongest resistance to a "positive" reading of the later Wittgenstein finds expression in the therapeutic reading of Gordon Baker (see Baker 2004), although very different (from each other as well as from Baker) dissensions from the "orthodox" reading find powerful expression in the work of Stanley Cavell, Cora Diamond, and John McDowell.[12]

3.2 Heidegger

Heidegger's influence has touched almost every corner of European philosophy, but is perhaps most notable in France. A list of Heidegger's inheritors reads like a who's who of twentieth-century continental philosophy. Michel Foucault, who makes no overt reference to Heidegger, nevertheless remarks: "For me Heidegger has always been the essential philosopher. . . . My entire philosophical development was determined by my reading of Heidegger" (Foucault 1988, 250). And even Jürgen Habermas, who opposes Heidegger in many respects, acknowledges that "[a]n intensive engagement with the early Heidegger left its marks on my . . . work" (Habermas 1992, 205). Although Heidegger's influence on Anglophone philosophy is less pervasive, his ideas have nevertheless had a considerable impact there.

The first major reception of Heidegger's work came in France via Alexandre Kojève and Kuki Shuzo, and sparked the blossoming of French existentialism, most notably represented by Jean-Paul Sartre. Sartre and his colleagues drew particular inspiration from the themes of anxiety and authenticity in *Being and Time*. Other notable French thinkers who encountered Heidegger's work before the Second World War include Maurice Merleau-Ponty, Emmanuel Levinas, Jacques Lacan, and Georges Bataille.[13] Heidegger's "turn" in the early 1930s distanced him from the existentialism he had inspired, but his post-turn writings influenced a further generation of postwar philosophers in France. The most notable among these was Jacques Derrida, whose deconstruction elaborated on Heidegger's own *Destruktion*, but Heidegger had a profound impact on post-structuralism and postmodern thought in France more generally.

Heidegger also exercised a powerful influence in German philosophy, both through his writings and through his many notable students.[14] Gadamer's development of hermeneutics owes a considerable debt to Heidegger, and adding hermeneutics to existentialism and post-structuralism, Heidegger can be said to have sparked at least three major movements in twentieth-century continental thought, as well as making a decisive contribution to phenomenology. Heidegger also exercised a marked influence on Asian philosophy, particularly in Japan, and he has had a major impact on a number of other disciplines, most notably theology, literary studies, and scholarly work on architecture.

Far more than Wittgenstein, Heidegger seems to inspire extremes of adulation and condemnation. The first generation of Marxist thinkers of the Frankfurt School in interwar Germany reacted strongly against Heidegger, and postwar philosophers associated with the Frankfurt School, most notably Habermas, share this critical orientation. But whereas this criticism takes Heidegger to task for saying the wrong things, criticism from within the analytic tradition frequently dismisses Heidegger as not having said anything at all. The first salvo launched at Heidegger from this quarter came from Rudolf Carnap (1932), who famously argued that a logical analysis of sentences like "The nothing itself nihilates" (*BW* 103) reveals them to be nonsensical. Many analytic philosophers have shared Carnap's assessment that Heidegger's work amounts to little more than pretentious nonsense.

Yet as early as 1928, Heidegger was receiving a sympathetic hearing in Anglophone philosophy. Ryle's review of *Being and Time* is not shy in its criticism, but neither is it niggardly in its praise:

> [Heidegger] shows himself to be a thinker of real importance by the immense subtlety and searchingness of his examination of consciousness, by the boldness and originality of his methods and conclusions, and by the unflagging energy with which he tries to think behind the stock categories of orthodox philosophy and psychology. (Ryle [1928] 2009, 222)

That said, Heidegger's reception in America has been much warmer than in Britain. An early champion was J. Glenn Gray, and other American philosophers of the postwar generation to draw inspiration from Heidegger's work include William Barrett, Marjorie Grene, and William J. Richardson.[15] In the last quarter of the twentieth century, Heidegger's thought became central to a number of prominent philosophers with a hearing in the analytic tradition, most notably Richard Rorty, Charles Taylor, and Hubert Dreyfus,[16] and both Dreyfus and John Haugeland have wielded Heideggerian ideas in engaging with analytic philosophy of mind and cognitive science.[17]

Dreyfus in particular has been an energetic promoter of Heidegger in Anglophone philosophy, and his former students are among the most prominent

Heidegger scholars in America, some of them contributors to this volume. Like Rorty, Dreyfus places particular emphasis on the pragmatic aspects of Heidegger's philosophy, and his efforts to make Heidegger's thought accessible to an analytic audience has been lauded for its clarity and rigor and criticized for creating a "philosophical Frankenstein" derided as "Dreydegger" (Woessner 2011, 208).[18] Other American scholars, such as David Farrell Krell, keep their Heidegger at arm's length from the analytic tradition, aiming at greater fidelity to Heidegger's own idiom (see, e.g., Krell 1992).[19]

3.3 Wittgenstein and Heidegger: Points of Contact

If it is surprising that fairly little scholarship has connected the work of Wittgenstein and Heidegger, it's worth noting first of all that, despite their many similarities, Wittgenstein and Heidegger themselves seemed to have little awareness of, or interest in, one another. Heidegger leaves no recorded mention of Wittgenstein, and from Wittgenstein we have only a single elusive remark, beginning: "To be sure, I can imagine what Heidegger means by being and anxiety" (*LWVC* 68).[20]

Philosophy in Germany was particularly poised to take up connections between Wittgenstein and Heidegger, not just because both of these philosophers wrote in German, but because Germany has remained more hospitable to analytic philosophy than France and to continental philosophy than Britain. Karl-Otto Apel is particularly notable in this regard (see especially Apel 1980 and 1998a), but Habermas and Tugendhat have also both drawn on Wittgenstein in their criticisms of Heidegger. Furthermore, Gadamer, although primarily a disciple of Heidegger's, engages fruitfully with Wittgenstein (see especially Gadamer 1976). In France, Pierre Bourdieu, although working in a tradition more deeply influenced by Heidegger, draws particular inspiration from Wittgenstein as well: "Wittgenstein is probably the philosopher who has helped me most at moments of difficulty" (Bourdieu 1990, 9). And Jean-François Lyotard also makes frequent reference to Wittgenstein (see, for example, Lyotard 1984).

A number of Heidegger's proponents in the orbit of analytic philosophy found in Wittgenstein a more widely accepted figure through whom to bring out Heidegger's relevance. Rorty is a prominent example, highlighting the pragmatic aspect of both philosophers, and drawing them into dialogue to forge new paths in the philosophy of language and philosophy of mind (see especially Rorty 1979 and 1993). Taylor also makes thorough use of both philosophers, elaborating on their anti-representational stance, and insisting on the significance of a background of shared understanding for a proper appreciation of language and other social practices.[21] Dreyfus and a number of his followers draw on Wittgenstein, especially to elaborate the pragmatic aspect of Heidegger's philosophy, and to explore Heidegger's conception of Being-with.[22] And Robert Brandom also draws on both Wittgenstein and Heidegger in his treatments of semantics and intentionality (see Brandom 1994 and 2002).

In the other direction, a number of scholars have found Heidegger a helpful foil in emphasizing Wittgenstein's affinity to themes in continental philosophy. The connection with Heidegger has particular appeal to readers who resist the assimilation by orthodox interpreters of Wittgenstein's thought to standard problems and debates within analytic philosophy. Stanley Cavell is an early pioneer in this area (see especially Cavell 1988a), whose thought has a strong influence on the comparative work of Mulhall (2001a), and to a lesser extent Glendinning (1998). Wittgenstein's waning influence in the mainstream of analytic philosophy has opened space for further explorations in this direction, as has Heidegger's adoption by a number of analytically oriented philosophers.

Finally, the number of book-length studies giving thorough consideration to Wittgenstein and Heidegger together is small but growing, and includes Sefler (1974), Gier (1981), Edwards (1990), Mulhall (1990, 2001a), Standish (1992), Glendinning (1998), Rentsch (2003), Rudd (2003), Camerlingo (2011), Flatscher (2011), and Braver (2012).

4   CHAPTER SUMMARIES

The chapters in this volume cover a wide variety of topics. The collection begins with chapters exploring what might broadly be termed "methodological" issues. In "The Meaning of Being and the Possibility of Discourse," **Stephen Mulhall** contends that Heidegger's conception of fundamental ontology and Wittgenstein's conception of grammatical investigation are more closely akin than is often recognized. Mulhall takes his cue from Rush Rhees's reading of Wittgenstein. Rhees views natural language as a unified whole, with its various "games" interlocking to lend one another intelligibility. He fears that Wittgenstein fails to account for this dialogical unity, but Mulhall contends that his fears are misplaced. As Mulhall sees it, such dialogical unity lies at the heart of Wittgenstein's understanding of grammatical investigation—and it is formally analogous to the unity that underpins Heidegger's understanding of ontology. Mulhall concludes by examining the implications of this parallel for our view of philosophy's nature and its place within our culture.

Simon Glendinning's "Wittgenstein and Heidegger and the 'Face' of Life in Our Time" stages what is arguably a more controversial rapprochement between our two thinkers. He attempts to combat a Wittgensteinian criticism of Heidegger—namely, that Heidegger's use of the term "Being" generates philosophical confusion. In pursuing an interpretation of Heidegger that is consistent with some of Wittgenstein's central concerns—and thus resistant to the foregoing charge—Glendinning asks what might account for not only the diversity but also the unity of Being. The answer, he avers, is *us*—or Dasein itself.

In "The Provocation to Look and See: Appropriation, Recollection, and Formal Indication," **Denis McManus** explores the notion that Heidegger's insights are not capable of being articulated in propositional form. Mc-Manus makes sense of this notion by turning to Heidegger's remarks on "formal indication"—the mysterious methodological motif Heidegger frequently refers to in the early 1920s. McManus's principal proposal is that *Being and Time* as a whole might be seen as formally indicative, which is to say, it prompts us "to look and see," indicating what it is we ought to attend to, rather than handing it to us on a plate. McManus reaches this conclusion through analyzing not only Heidegger's remarks on formal indication but also—crucially—his Wittgensteinian approach to philosophical confusion.

In "The Authenticity of the Ordinary," **David Egan** argues that we can unearth something like a Heideggerian appeal to authenticity in Wittgenstein's appeal to ordinary language. The latter is of course central to Wittgenstein's later philosophy: he reminds us that our words find meaning in the ordinary practices and forms of life in which they are used. But at first sight this emphasis on the ordinary appears to clash with Heidegger's claim that average, everyday understanding is marked by inauthenticity: if Heidegger is right, surely Wittgenstein's emphasis on ordinary language is fundamentally inauthentic. Egan argues that it is not, and that, in fact, Wittgenstein's emphasis on the ungroundedness of our ordinary practices parallels Heidegger's discussion of anxiety and uncanniness.

Charles Guignon's "Wittgenstein, Heidegger, and the Question of Phenomenology" explores the extent to which the philosophical methods of Wittgenstein and Heidegger converge. Having demonstrated that there is no evidence of one actually influencing the other, he goes on to show that both are keenly aware of contextualism, and of the linguistic constitution of our sense of reality. In short, Guignon argues that despite undeniable differences, our protagonists share a deep-lying conception of how philosophy can approach the problems it addresses.

With **Edward Minar**'s "Understanding the Being of the 'We': Wittgenstein, Heidegger, and Idealism," we turn to some of the central concerns of the Western philosophical tradition. Minar's focus is the way in which both thinkers seek to undermine idealism despite appearing to espouse a conception of the world as shaped by our own understanding and activity. As Minar sees it, although both recognize that idealism yields some important insights, they aim to expose the explanatory pretensions that make it appear necessary.

"Heidegger and Wittgenstein on External World Skepticism," by **Herman Philipse**, moves us from idealism to the related topic of external world skepticism. Such skepticism takes various forms in contemporary philosophy, with present-day analytic philosophers advancing numerous solutions. Yet both Heidegger and Wittgenstein contended that the skeptical "problem" does not make sense. We might therefore wonder whether today's mainstream philosophical community has overlooked the lessons of Heidegger and Wittgenstein. Philipse claims that Heidegger's "destruction" of the problem of the external world is inadequate, but that a Wittgensteinian dissolution of it may be more promising.

In "What Science Leaves Unsaid," **Taylor Carman** observes that both Heidegger and Wittgenstein saw philosophy as radically different from science, and that they both saw a deep connection between the factual language of science and schematic pictorial representation. He goes on to note that recent "austere" readings of the *Tractatus* correctly state that Wittgenstein's picture conception of language prohibits its own positive expression as a theory, but he adds that those same readings fail to distinguish illusory riddles from what Wittgenstein called "the unsayable." His contention, ultimately, is that Heidegger's language allowed him to say what Wittgenstein could not: namely, that propositions and facts have the character of a picture.

Lee Braver's "Disintegrating Bugbears: Heidegger and Wittgenstein on Basic Laws of Thought" explores the approaches taken by Wittgenstein and Heidegger to fundamental philosophical principles. Whereas Wittgenstein purports to flout the Law of Non-Contradiction by disarming contradictions, Heidegger purports to flout the Principle of Reason by accepting ungrounded phenomena. Braver argues that in these ways both thinkers encourage us to accept as justificatory unjustifiable—yet contingent and effective—ways of understanding the world. As Braver sees it, this encouragement is ultimately a call to acknowledge human finitude.

Joseph K. Schear's "Understanding as a Finite Ability" takes us to the philosophy of mind. Schear's central claim is that Heidegger and Wittgenstein both characterize human understanding as a finite ability. His chapter surveys the different ways each develops that characterization—first, explaining what it amounts to, and second, using it to shed light on their respective projects. In doing so, Schear demonstrates that Wittgenstein *exhibits* the finitude of understanding by participating in the temptation to be infinite, while Heidegger *explains* it by contrasting it with the infinite intellect.

Theodore R. Schatzki investigates the relevance of Heidegger and Wittgenstein to an area of philosophy that barely existed when they themselves wrote: the philosophy of action. In "Human Activity as Indeterminate Social Event," Schatzki argues that each figure uncovers a profound aspect of human activity and that together these aspects anchor a unified account of that phenomenon. Whereas Heidegger reveals that activity is an indeterminate event, Wittgenstein points toward the social constitution of action. Schatzki explores the complementary nature of these two aspects and identifies the ways in which each thinker's work points to the aspect uncovered by the other.

Our final four chapters explore the connections between our two philosophers in the context of religious and artistic thought. In "Heidegger's Religious Picture," **Stephen Reynolds** argues that Heidegger's understanding of Dasein exemplifies what Wittgenstein termed a "religious picture." Reynolds proceeds in two stages. First, he contends that Heidegger's analysis of the call of conscience articulates a Lutheran conception of human existence. Second, he argues that this conception operates in such a way as to satisfy Wittgenstein's notion of a religious "picture." His central suggestion, then, is that the role played by Heidegger's Lutheran view of humanity corresponds to that which Wittgenstein ascribes to religious beliefs.

Heidegger's express comments on art form the basis of **Aaron James Wendland**'s chapter, "Words as Works of Art." In "The Origin of the Work of Art," Heidegger claims that art is the medium through which our world is presented to us before going on to classify all art as poetic language. Yet in that important essay he fails to explain *how* that presenting is accomplished. Wendland's aim is to establish just that. He does so by looking back to *Being and Time*, forward to Heidegger's later essays on language, and laterally to the writings of Wittgenstein.

In the penultimate chapter of the volume, **Anthony Rudd**'s focus is the fusion of modernism with romanticism. The principal claim of "Wittgenstein and Heidegger as Romantic Modernists" is that both Wittgenstein and Heidegger inherit a romantic vision in which Cartesian dualism is overcome through a "re-enchantment" of the world. Rudd describes how early twentieth-century modernism involved a revival of this romantic outlook, amounting to a romantic modernism, and he contends that Wittgenstein and Heidegger should be seen as its philosophical representatives. He concedes that the romantic vision did have to struggle against countervailing tendencies in both philosophers, but suggests that this conflicted outlook was itself characteristic of the modernist revival of romantic themes.

We remain with modernism for the final chapter in the collection. As the title suggests, **David R. Cerbone**'s contribution, "Dwelling on Rough Ground: Heidegger, Wittgenstein, Architecture," moves us away from stock philosophical concerns to investigate our thinkers' broader cultural context. Cerbone considers Heidegger and Wittgenstein in relation to the modernist architecture that became prominent during their own lives. Using Le Corbusier's image of the House-Machine as the exemplar of modernist architecture, Cerbone looks at how both Heidegger and Wittgenstein can be seen as resisting that image. He argues that the source of their resistance is a shared appreciation of the organic dimensions of language—and that as a result, they can be read as anticipating the "existential" failings that later critics of modernism (such as Charles Jencks and Robert Venturi) would develop.[23]

NOTES

1. A "resolute" reading of the *Tractatus* (see ahead) would also interpret that early work as anti-foundationalist.
2. The distinction between "analytic" and "continental" philosophy is far from straightforward, especially since the application of "analytic philosophy" has expanded well beyond the focused research program launched by Russell and Moore over a century ago to encompass a broad range of only loosely allied methods and projects. The mismatch between the name of a method ("analytic") and a geographical designator ("continental") suggests the distinction may be something of a case of apples and oranges anyway. We will rely on this distinction as a heuristic to sketch out the philosophical terrain, but do not

wish to place much weight upon it. For a concise and persuasive criticism of the distinction, which concludes that it is merely sociological, see William Blattner's reflections at http://www9.georgetown.edu/faculty/blattnew/contanalytic.html.

3. How to interpret this "throwing away the ladder"—whether Wittgenstein believes the propositions of the *Tractatus* gesture at ineffable truths or whether he holds a more "austere" conception of their nonsensicality—is a central point of contention in *Tractatus* scholarship, explored by a number of the authors in the present volume.

4. The connections between Wittgenstein's philosophy and his work as an architect are explored in more detail in David R. Cerbone's contribution to this volume.

5. Ayer (1936) offers the best known advocacy for logical positivism in English. Hanfling (1981) provides a good overview of this movement, and Ayer (1959) provides a helpful anthology.

6. Hacker (1996) provides an excellent history of analytic philosophy, which tracks Wittgenstein's place in the evolution of that tradition.

7. See, for example, Habermas (1988, 1998); Apel (1980); Tugendhat (1986); and Bouveresse (1987, 1995, 2003).

8. Helpful summaries of Wittgenstein scholarship can be found in Kahane, Kanterian, and Kuusela (2007a) and Glock (2007).

9. To give just one example, toward the end of his life, Gordon Baker advanced a revisionist therapeutic reading of Wittgenstein's later philosophy while retaining an orthodox reading of the *Tractatus*.

10. For representative expressions of the orthodox interpretation of the *Tractatus*, see Anscombe (1959); Black (1964); Hacker (1986); and Kenny (2006). For representative expressions of the "resolute" reading, see Diamond (1991c); Goldfarb (1997a); Conant (2002); Conant and Diamond (2004); and McManus (2006). For critical responses to this reading, see Hacker (2000) and Proops (2001).

11. Baker later defected to a therapeutic reading of Wittgenstein, and Hacker completed and more recently revised the commentaries on his own.

12. See, for example, Cavell (1976a, 1979); Diamond (1991) (especially the introduction and first chapter); and McDowell (2000). See also Mulhall (2001a) for a Cavell-inspired reading of Wittgenstein.

13. For more on this aspect of Heidegger's influence, see Kleinberg (2005).

14. For more on this aspect of Heidegger's influence, see Wolin (2001).

15. See Woessner (2011) for a comprehensive account of Heidegger's reception in America.

16. See, for example, Rorty (1979, 1991); Taylor (1985, 1995); and Dreyfus (1991).

17. See, for example, Dreyfus (1992) and Haugeland (1998).

18. Kripke's (1982) creative interpretation of Wittgenstein has similarly been dubbed "Kripkenstein."

19. Murray (1978) provides a helpful anthology of responses, both constructive and critical, to Heidegger, ranging from Ryle and Carnap to contemporary American philosophers.

20. In an editorial footnote, McGuinness refers the reader to *Being and Time*, but this is surely mistaken. Wittgenstein was far more likely to be familiar with "What Is Metaphysics?" especially since he was in conversation with the Vienna Circle around the time that Carnap composed his response. Cf. Murray (1978, 81).

21. See especially a number of the essays in Taylor (1985, 1995).

22. See, among others, Haugeland (1982); Guignon (1983); Dreyfus (1991); and Carman (2003).

23. Our thanks to Denis McManus, Stephen Mulhall, and especially P. M. S. Hacker for responding to an earlier draft of this introduction.

2 The Meaning of Being and the Possibility of Discourse
Heidegger and Wittgenstein Converse

Stephen Mulhall

1 A GENEALOGICAL MYTH OF PHILOSOPHY

Human beings are creatures who comprehend the phenomena they encounter in the world they inhabit. When a man transfers the contents of the family laundry basket to the washing machine, sets it going, and then spends an hour or two ironing the clean but crumpled items of clothing that emerge, every aspect of his endeavors presupposes an implicit understanding of the various things he utilizes. Unless he was capable of correctly identifying the presence and location, the nature and the functional possibilities of the basket, the clothes, the washing machine, and the iron, he would be in no position to perform his domestic duties. Human beings are in this sense immersed in a world of comprehensible entities as fish are immersed in water; but they are also capable of reflecting upon their implicit comprehension of that world—that is, of thematizing it and putting it in question. Our laundryman might, for example, be struck by the efficacy of the washing liquid with which he loads the washing machine, and wonder exactly how it achieves its cleansing purpose; or he might, as he unloads the machine, wonder how exactly shirts are constructed, by whom, and in the light of a conception of what is needed to be respectably dressed. Any such moment of reflective questioning might be thought of as the beginning of an intellectual trajectory that typically culminates in the development of a systematic body of knowledge such as chemistry, textile design, social history, or economic theory—what Heidegger would call an ontic science, in which a particular domain or dimension of the world is delineated and made the subject of an appropriately specific kind of intellectual inquiry.

But our laundryman's capacity to question his own everyday comprehension of the world, and thereby to deepen that comprehension, can also be turned upon the more systematic bodies of knowledge that he now inhabits. For having established himself in the field of chemistry, he might ask himself what mode of understanding is implicit in the rigorous procedures of chemistry whereby he investigates the chemical aspects of the world with a view to building powerful theories of its nature. In theorizing about the chemical structure of a particular substance, for example, what is he presupposing about the essential nature of the elements from which any such structure must be composed, and their combinatorial possibilities? In assuming that all material entities are possessed of chemical structure, what is he presupposing about materiality as such? And in testing his theory, why does he presuppose that what he can establish about observed instances of the behavior of this substance will apply to unobserved instances?

In thus thematizing and questioning the conceptual and methodological resources deployed in any given ontic science, our laundryman-turned-chemist is now transforming himself into a philosopher. The purpose here is not to determine when the individual chemist must acquire membership of a different disciplinary union; it is to mark the introduction of a particular kind of question—the kind that naturally arises about the procedures internal to an ontic science (any answers to which can therefore be regarded as deepening our understanding of whatever kind of knowledge that science delivers), but that necessarily cannot be answered by utilizing those procedures (since their validity is exactly what is now in question). To raise and pursue such questions is to find oneself engaged in the kind of philosophical inquiry that Heidegger calls "regional ontology"—an inquiry into what it is for something to have a particular kind of nature, and into what makes it possible for us to acquire genuine knowledge of that nature. Another name for this particular regional ontology would be "the philosophy of science"; but such familiar branches of philosophical inquiry as "the philosophy of religion," "aesthetics," and "the philosophy of history" can also be thought of as regional ontologies.

Thus far, my mythical genealogy of philosophy (my account of its unaccountable origins) might not seem particularly Heideggerian—I suspect that most philosophers will have tried to explain the peculiar nature of their work to nonphilosophers in such terms (however radically they might wish to qualify them later). However, my myth implicitly invites us to take a further step that is often regarded as being distinctively Heideggerian, but that really emerges as naturally from the questions of regional ontology as questions of regional ontology emerge from those of ontic science. The myth thereby indicates that this Heideggerian step is in fact a development to which philosophy naturally subjects itself by reflexively reiterating exactly the same human tendency to question, and so deepen, our comprehension of the world that engenders philosophy in the first place. For if each regional ontology enhances our understanding of whatever the corresponding ontic science reveals to us by subjecting its presuppositions to productive questioning, must not whatever is presupposed in the acquisition of that enhanced understanding also be capable of being put in question, and to equally productive effect? How could we, in all consistency, avoid asking ourselves what exactly it is to engage in regional ontology?

Precisely because each regional ontological inquiry concerns itself with what we comprehend of a particular region or dimension of the world, what most immediately strikes us about it is its differences from other regional ontologies. The issues and problems that preoccupy philosophers of art or religion often appear very distant from those that predominate among philosophers of science or mind or language—unsurprisingly, given the obvious differences between the corresponding ontic regions and our bodies of knowledge about them (can we even say that they all generate systematic bodies of knowledge, or all concern themselves with a kind of entity or its properties?). On the other hand, each such branch of philosophy asks very similar questions about its particular region of human existence in the world. After all, each regional ontology is, precisely, an inquiry into the *ontology* of that region—an inquiry into what it is for phenomena to exist as, to be, phenomena of the relevant kind (material, aesthetic, linguistic, or mental), and what it is for us to grasp them as they are. To comprehend what regional ontological inquiries are, then, we have to inquire into both their "regionality" *and* their "ontologicality"—which means asking what, if anything, links inquiries in the philosophy of science to those in aesthetics or the philosophy of religion or the philosophy of language.

Such links appear to exist at two main levels. First, questions that emerge in one regional ontology often relate to those in another. For example, a philosophical understanding of religious beliefs and judgments involves establishing an understanding of distinctively religious language; and that understanding cannot be acquired independently of addressing broader questions about the nature of language as such—the domain of the philosophy of language. Neither of these regional ontological inquiries can assume its priority over the other: if philosophers of religion claim to establish certain conclusions about how language works in religious contexts, how exactly those claims might be aligned with claims made by philosophers of language, who may have very different kinds of language use in focus (whether either party should give ground in the light of the results of the other, and if so which), is and should be an open question—to be settled by a dialogue between the two parties. The crucial fact is that such dialogues are possible, for that exemplifies the dialogical openness of any one regional ontology to its others.

The second level of linkages may initially sound more distinctively Heideggerian. If (as he puts it) the philosophy of religion concerns itself with what it is for something to be divine, and the philosophy of mind with what it is for something to be mental, and the philosophy of science with what it is for something to be material, then one way of articulating the unity of these distinct enterprises is to say that all are concerned, in their different ways, with what it is for something to be: with what it is for a phenomenon to manifest itself, both as it is in itself and as being rather than not-being, and with what it is for us to be capable of comprehending it as such—as something in particular rather than something else or nothing. This is the meaning of the question of being, the question of the meaning of "being": it is what Heidegger calls the question of fundamental ontology. But my genealogical myth aspires to demonstrate that its emergence as a question is not an arbitrary "Continental" imposition on an otherwise perfectly rational and exhaustive cultural economy of knowledge, in which each legitimate ontic region or body of knowledge naturally incubates its own regional ontological discipline, and nothing else. For if the mere existence of a diverse array of ontic regions naturally engenders a diverse array of regional ontologies, that array of regional ontologies will as naturally engender the question of fundamental ontology, and for exactly the same reason—the natural tendency of human comprehension to thematize and question itself.

I just introduced the question of fundamental ontology as directing us toward linkages between regional ontologies at two different levels; but I don't mean to imply that the two levels are essentially distinct and self-sufficient. After all, if there is no such thing as something's being (as opposed to not-being) except as a particular kind of thing—if something can exist only as some specific thing or other—then the fundamental ontological question of what it is for something, or anything, to be is internally related to the question of what it is for something to be a particular kind of thing, and so is internally related to the business of some particular regional ontology. And that business is itself internally related to questions that arise in other regional ontologies—internal relations of the kind acknowledged in my earlier discussion of the first level at which the enterprise of regional ontology is unified. In this sense, to raise the question of fundamental ontology is, necessarily, to raise the question of links between regional ontologies on both levels at once; those two levels are simply different aspects of one and the same articulated field.

Note also that recognizing the reality and significance of the question of fundamental ontology does not require that we commit ourselves to the legitimacy or even the availability of a single, specific answer to that question—for example, to one mapping of any given regional ontology's relations with any other (or even to the idea of there being a single mapping), and so to a single exhaustive taxonomy of the various ways in which things may be, or to a specification of some feature (or some set of features) that all existent beings must exemplify or instantiate insofar as they exist. Some philosophers have thought it possible to give such a specification of what it is to be, and have disagreed with the specifications of others; others still have denied that any such specification is conceivable. Some have argued that work in certain regional ontological inquiries should be constrained by results established in others, while disagreeing with one another about which regional ontology should constrain and which should be constrained; others have argued against any, even provisional, assignments of relative priority; and others still have denied the existence of any significant relations between any such regions. For example, many analytical philosophers feel that theories of meaning constructed in the philosophy of language and logic should constrain the interpretative options available to aestheticians and philosophers of religion; some feel that attention to religious and aesthetic uses of language should rather constrain our choice between general theories of meaning; and others again may feel that, once specific accounts of language use in particular circumstances are established and given due weight, there may be nothing left for a theory of meaning to be a theory of.

Acknowledging the reality and significance of the question of fundamental ontology does not require us to adjudicate between these disagreements, or to deny that they may persist beyond any adjudication, thereby betraying a fundamental mutual incomprehension; the point is rather to thematize the sheer fact of their existence—the fact that it is so much as possible to have such intelligible discussions about whether and how the various regional ontologies relate to one another. For the reality of such debates, whatever their terminus in any particular case, serves to make manifest a horizon of intelligibility within which they are conducted. The various positions taken up in such debates adumbrate a determinable and endlessly redetermined categorial field of diversity-in-unity or unified diversity to which the articulation—more precisely, the sheer articulability, the simple comprehensibility—of the question of fundamental ontology bears witness.

And those who are struck by the articulability of that question are not committed to one particular way of articulating it; in particular, they need not regard themselves as posing a familiar kind of request for causal explanation, only one that (impossibly) aims to treat all that is as an effect of some cause. For to treat the question of fundamental ontology as articulable need not involve assuming that any particular way of making sense of things within the world might be used to make sense of the world as such, or as a whole; it merely involves acknowledging that there is something inherently questionable about the ways in which we do make sense of any and every particular kind of thing. For if we are capable of making sense of whatever we encounter, then that too (the validity, the diversity, and the interrelatedness of the ways in which things make sense) is something of which we can attempt to make sense (to thematize, to put in question, and so—we hope—to grasp more fully).

2   A WITTGENSTEINIAN VERSION OF HEIDEGGER'S VISION

Heidegger's articulation of the question of the meaning of being might seem to be of interest solely to philosophers, since its primary focus appears to be the internal dialogical structure of the discipline. This impression can be dispelled by comparing Heidegger's way of formulating the matter to that implicit in a certain reading of Wittgenstein's *Philosophical Investigations*, one that emerges from a certain tension implicit in the use he famously makes therein of the idea of a "language-game"—a term of art that emerges as follows:

> We can also think of the whole process of using words in (2) [the famous tale of the builders] as one of those games by means of which children learn their native language. I will call these games "*language-games*" and will sometimes speak of a primitive language as a language-game.
>
> And the process of naming the stones and of repeating words after someone might also be called language-games. Think of certain uses that are made of words in games like ring-a-ring-a-roses.
>
> I shall also call the whole, consisting of language and the activities into which it is woven, a "language-game." (*PI* §7)

This passage invokes at least four ways in which the term might be used—to pick out ways of teaching children to speak, ways in which words are woven into children's games, primitive kinds of language, and finally "the whole, consisting of language and the activities into which it is woven." Most commentators focus on the fourth way, and take Wittgenstein to mean the idea of a language-game to have a wholly general application to the phenomenon of language.

Perhaps so: but which kind of general application? Some of Wittgenstein's later general pronouncements suggest that he thinks we can often dispel our philosophical unclarities about our lives with words by imagining primitive versions of some aspect of them purely as objects of comparison (and hence not as revelations of essence). As he puts it, "Our clear and simple language-games are not preliminary studies for a future regimentation of language . . . [but] rather stand there as *objects of comparison* which, through similarities and dissimilarities, are meant to throw light on features of our language" (*PI* §130). However, other things that Wittgenstein says about his "language-game" methods have encouraged people to attribute to him two related and opposing ideas—that to speak is simply to make a move in a language-game, and that language should be thought of simply as a family of such games. Read this way, our actual, everyday uses of words are not simply to be compared with (and hence recognized as essentially distinct from) the uses of words in deliberately simplified, imaginatively constructed language-games, but are rather to be understood as themselves language-games, or at least as sets or arrays of language-games. Ordinary language would then be actually composed of, and so analytically separable into, a very large number of language-games with words: they make up the basic units or building blocks of language, and hence of linguistic competence—not a philosopher's artifact, but rather the *Heimat* of our words. Such a picture of language and speech is taken to be essential to Wittgenstein's vision of words, and so of philosophy, by many commentators—both those sympathetic to Wittgenstein's work, and those deeply out of sympathy with it. But according to Rush Rhees (one of Wittgenstein's students and friends), although that picture is sometimes encouraged by Wittgenstein's words, it runs counter to other strands of his thinking, and ought to be given up in their favor, for any such picture would make conversation impossible, and obliterate the very idea of a language (see Rhees 1998).

If understanding the meanings of words really was exhausted by grasping rules for their use, if words were equivalent to pieces in board games, they could not form the medium of conversational exchanges. For understanding how to converse—how to follow the development of a conversation, to make a pertinent or telling contribution to it, to redirect its focus, to acknowledge the relevance of another's contribution without agreeing with it, to recognize when it has reached a dead end or when a little further persistence will bring it to an illuminating resting-place—understanding all this is not something that can be reduced to the application of a body of rules, or fruitfully compared with learning how to make moves in a game. This kind of understanding is essentially responsive both to the subject matter of the conversation and to the individual contributions of those participating in it; but moves in chess do not have a subject matter, and could not give expression to what they bring to a game from their experience outside it. If being able to speak involves being able to converse, then it is not just a matter of applying words in accordance with criteria, of making linguistic moves, or of doing things with words.

Rhees is equally hostile to the idea that language as a whole is a family of distinct language-games, for then it might be thought that there must be something wrong with the question, "What does it mean to say something?" or, "What is the unity of language?" For why should we expect there to be any such unity in any given collection of language-games, in the fundamentally various ways we speak or do things with words? Wasn't this assumption precisely what led the author of the *Tractatus* astray, compelling him to seek the will-o'-the-wisp of the general form of the proposition, and to attribute to ordinary language the structural unity of a calculus? And doesn't the author of the *Investigations* repeatedly find that philosophical confusions result from a conflation or crossing of language-games—a failure to respect differences of use? By contrast, Rhees not only thinks that there *is* something that might be called the unity of language, and that Wittgenstein never lost his desire to thematize it; he also believes that trying (and failing) to get this unity into focus has been *the* characteristic business of philosophy since its inception, and hence that any conception of language that occludes the question thereby threatens philosophy's historical unity, its deepest concern, and even its ultimate point.

The notion of "conversation" as a center of variation here finds a second major point of application in Rhees's thinking; as well as bringing out certain crucial aspects of what is involved in an individual's ability to say something, it provides a way of conceiving of how language as a whole hangs together. Rhees claims that the various different forms of human discourse and practice relate to one another in the way that various contributions to a conversation relate to one another. In other words, the unity of language is the unity of a dialogue; the various modes of human discourse about things interlock intelligibly with one another, and the sense that each makes is both constituted by and constitutes the sense of these interconnections. As Rhees puts it: the generality or unity of language is the generality or unity of a form of life.

Part of what Rhees is driving at is already implicit in the ways in which we participate in specific conversations. Two builders discussing a construction problem will bring to bear an understanding not only of construction techniques but also of the economic and political contexts within which they are working (which option is cheaper, and how much additional expense matters), the kind of building under construction (a house, a church, a factory), and thereby an understanding of the particular activities that go on in such a building, and their relation to other activities in the culture more generally, and so on. The conversation is about this building project, but it will draw upon the participants' understanding of the bearing of a variety of other domains and concerns upon it; and without a grasp of those interlocking considerations, the conversation would lose its grip on its subject matter.

This interweaving of the various aspects or dimensions of human social life is also exemplified at what one might call the disciplinary level of culture, at which particular domains of human inquiry and activity are rendered systematic and reflective. On the one hand, especially since the Enlightenment and its concern for the autonomy of both individuals and cultural spheres, we have tended to think of the domains of politics, morality, religion, art, history, physics, biology, and so on as essentially distinct, possessed of a particular internal logic and purpose that separates them from even cognate domains, and that might itself be the subject of systematic study. On the other hand, whenever we try to make sense of a particular phenomenon, we find that any of these disciplines may contribute to that project.

Suppose we want to understand global deforestation. We will certainly need to acquire statistical information about its prevalence and rate of acceleration, and thus draw upon a variety of technological and computing resources, as well as developing a sense of its historical context. To understand why it is happening, we will need to grasp its underlying economic rationale, the ways in which local and international political systems react to it, and the ways in which a given country's climate, geography, social composition, and cultural expectations contribute to it. To determine its costs, we may need to range into the realms of botany, biology, and other environmental sciences, into aesthetic, moral, and religious conceptions of its significance—even perhaps into the domains of psychoanalysis, literary criticism, and cultural studies in order to grasp what kinds of imaginative and psychic meanings have informed our relations to the forest, and hence what—beyond economic and social forces—might be driving us to remove them, as well as what might be lost with their loss.

Like most other issues, then, the phenomenon of deforestation will have its historical, political, moral, technological and scientific, social, and cultural aspects and implications, and so can be properly understood only by seeing how each of these aspects and implications bear upon the others; and this means that it forms a fit subject for conversation between those well versed in a variety of forms of human inquiry—between historians, scientists, political theorists, sociologists, literary critics, and others. Each participant will bring her own particular understanding and expertise to the conversation; but each can learn from what the others bring, and may even alter her understanding of her own enterprise as a result; and each can in principle grasp that the others are capable of making a significant contribution to the task of better understanding the subject matter of the conversation. This is the individually mediated cultural analogue of what Rhees calls the kind of understanding that is capable of growth—of a deepening that finds expression in one's ability to see how things hang together: both the various modes of human understanding of our life in the world and the various aspects of that life itself.

Rhees's image of a conversation here foregrounds his sense that the various branches of human culture have a bearing on one another, that their distinctive concerns and methods nevertheless can and do interlock intelligibly with each other; and he sees this as both a reflection and an exemplary instance of the fact that their subject matter—any aspect of reality whatever that bears upon and is engaged by the forms of human life in the world—itself manifests a dialogical unity, with each of its aspects having an intelligible bearing on the others. This is why Rhees claims that language makes sense insofar as living makes sense.

3   PHILOSOPHY, SOPHISTRY, AND FORMS OF LIFE

We can now reformulate Heidegger's assumption that philosophical inquiry is essentially parasitic on the existence of the various forms of human understanding of, and inquiry into, reality; in Rhees's Wittgensteinian terms, it is a mode of discourse whose subject matter is the various forms of human discourse. But if those forms of human discourse manifest an essentially dialogical unity, then so must the various forms of distinctively philosophical discourse; if our life with language, and so language itself, has a dialogical unity, then so must the aspect of our (life with) language that takes that life as its distinctive concern. Conversely, if one holds that philosophical discourse has no dialogical unity, that amounts to saying that its subject matter has no such unity; it amounts to assuming that language, and hence our life with language, does not manifest any interlocking intelligibility of the kind that might be a possible object of the kind of understanding that can grow and deepen (or fail to). To adapt Rhees's words: if living makes sense, and hence language makes sense, then so must philosophy; and if philosophy does not have this kind of sense, then neither will language, or the human form of life with language. And this claim might both remind us of the institutions that reflect this vision of philosophy's cultural significance (or fail to), and recall us to philosophy's own mysterious origins.

In modern Western European culture, the exemplary institutional expression of the dialogical unity of reality, our knowledge of it, and our way of living is the university. The point of bringing a representative variety of ontic enterprises (by which I mean sciences, social sciences, humanities, and arts) under one roof is not simply to reduce overheads or to corral socially disruptive intellectuals; it is to create a context that embeds and embodies a vision of (the contributors to) each branch of human knowledge as conversing with one another. Each department certainly pursues its own ways of acquiring knowledge under its own direction; but each does so in a context that makes it as easy as possible for its members to encounter, learn from, and put in question the findings and queries of members of any other department.

Certain institutional arrangements may make this kind of intercourse more natural than others—and here the collegiate model of a university may have a particular value, since each college's self-governing membership amounts to a microcosm on a humane social scale of the university's aspiration to intellectual diversity-in-unity. But that is only one way of aspiring to facilitate this ideal of mutual conversibility in the face of explosively expanding bodies of knowledge, not to mention financial, political, and cultural pressures.

One university department will be of particular importance to the university's *raison d'être* so understood; and that is its department of philosophy. Its internal articulation reflects as broadly as possible the internal articulation of the university as a whole; and its inherent tendency to put in question the intelligibility of the relations between those branches—to reflect upon the significance of the fact that they are the internal articulations of a single subject—means that it is uniquely committed to bearing witness to the dialogical diversity-in-unity of human knowledge and of the reality it aspires to grasp. Philosophy itself is not an ontic science: it is rather the subject that aims to comprehend and question the very possibility of an ontic science, the subject for which the intelligibility of that possibility (the possibility of knowing something, anything, as it really is, hence as being rather than not-being) is an issue, an inherently questionable matter. Philosophy is the subject for whom that possibility matters because it is a way of posing the question of its own nature—the question of whether its own continued existence matters, or matters any longer.

And of course, sometimes philosophy finds that its own continued existence does not matter to anyone else. In Britain, for example, whenever the government significantly reconfigures university funding, many universities respond by closing their philosophy departments. They thereby demonstrate their inability to see the point of philosophy in the context of a university, and so their inability to see the point of their own existence as universities; and in refusing to contest these responses, the British government and the British people demonstrate their own inability to see the point of either philosophy or universities in and for the wider culture. And what are we to say of a culture that no longer sees any point in raising the question of whether its own particular formation, its internal articulations of intelligibility, have any point—whether it continues to make sense to inhabit the cultural forms through which its inhabitants are currently formed?

But philosophers shouldn't repress their own responsibility for this fate—for how many philosophy departments currently reflect in their internal structures a sense of the vital significance of the question of fundamental ontology? How far do our departments make room for raising the question of how their various activities relate to each other, as opposed to being an assemblage of self-sufficient enterprises, or a domain within which the relative importance of various branches of the subject is fixed, effectively put beyond question? If, on reflection, we cannot confidently say that our own ways of living as philosophers reflect the conviction that the question of whether philosophy makes sense is of such importance, then we should not heap all the blame for our present cultural irrelevance on either universities or governments, as if our fate could have been forced upon us only from without.

These issues also return us to the unaccountable origins of philosophy as a discipline. At the beginning of the *Republic*, Socrates is confronted by the sophist Thrasymachus, who claims that justice is best understood as whatever is in the interest of the stronger party. One might therefore take him to be offering one possible interpretation of our concept of justice; and indeed, Adeimantus and Glaucon later develop a similar view, and thereby induce Socrates to criticize their stance with a view to developing his own account. But Thrasymachus's position is in fact very different from that of Adeimantus and Glaucon, and in a sense far more consistent, for in suggesting that justice amounts to whatever is in the interests of the powerful, he is in fact doubting the reality of justice altogether. If what we talk of as "just" and "unjust" merely reflects the balance of power in a given social group, then there is in fact no substance or reality to that stretch of our discourse. All there is to talk about in this domain could be exhaustively expressed in terms of power, so language could suffer the loss of the concept of justice altogether without losing its ability to register the reality of our social world.

But even characterizing Thrasymachus as denying that our discourse about justice embodies any reality fails to capture the true reach of his skepticism, for it is part of the sophists' position as Plato understands it that they hold the same view of human discourse in general. Their characteristic view that mastery of discourse is a matter of understanding how to achieve rhetorical effectiveness—how to use words to achieve one's goals, that is, to move others to align themselves with the speaker—reduces all speech to a matter of practical efficacy or power (the view that twentieth-century emotivists held of all nondescriptive discourse). Thrasymachus's view about the true nature of talk about justice is thus merely a particular application of the general sophistic view about the true nature of human speech: it has no reality to it, it embodies distinctions and values to which nothing corresponds in reality, and hence it lacks any genuine substance.

This is why Thrasymachus (unlike Adeimantus and Glaucon) is rightly wary even of conversing with Socrates: for he knows that in so doing, he is merely entering an arena for the exercise of rhetorical power of which Socrates is a master. So he demands payment for his participation, tries to avoid answering Socrates' questions and criticisms, and (as far as possible) tries to avoid saying anything himself in explanation of his position; he also becomes abusive—asking why Socrates' nurse allows him to go around spouting drivel. Little wonder that Socrates characterizes Thrasymachus as springing on the group like a wild beast, as if he wanted to tear them into pieces; he rejects the epitome of human conversation that is dialectical philosophical discourse because his position amounts to a denial of the possibility of discourse of any kind.

This portrait of the sophist as an abusive wild animal utterly resistant to domestication in discourse is thus not simply a caricature, a way of making

Socrates' victory over his most intimate enemy far too easy; it is a dramatization of the sophistic view of language as such, and hence of our life with language. To view human discourse with the sophists is to reduce it to the brutish exercise of power, to void it of any genuine substance; it amounts to denying that there is anything to understand in what people say to one another in conversation—to view language as entirely failing to make any contact with reality. This is more than mistaking a particular appearance for reality, more even than losing one's grip on the very distinction between illusory appearance and reality in some particular domain; it amounts to rendering utterly unreal or empty the distinction between making contact with reality and failing to do so right across the board.

This is the threat Rhees sees in any attempt to understand what it is to speak in terms of an analogy with moves in a game, and to understand language as a family of self-sufficient language-games. Such attempts teeter on the brink of characterizing linguistic understanding as a matter of knowing how to do things with words, to achieve certain effects or practical outcomes; and in so doing they risk eviscerating human modes of discourse of any genuine substance, regarding them as akin to moves in a meaningless game rather than ways of being responsive to reality. They thereby deprive philosophy of any genuine substance by depriving it of its central subject matter (by denying that there is any such thing as human discourse) and by regarding its distinctive mode of dialogue as having no more genuine substance than any other. To present philosophical wisdom as one more commodity for sale in the agora, and to present it to one's paying customers as a matter of mastering rhetorical techniques, is not so much to mistake sham philosophy for the genuine article; it is to lose one's grip on the very idea that there is a real distinction to be drawn in this area. And that not only deprives philosophy of sense but also implies a corresponding lack of sense in language, and in our life with language, altogether. Hence, Rhees at one point claims that sophistry is not so much mistaken as evil, for to take it seriously is to empty human life of meaning or sense.

Rhees does not think that a thoroughgoing sophist will be converted simply by offering him a philosophical account of human discourse as having some bearing on reality; after all, a consistent sophist will claim that any such philosophical account is simply another exercise in rhetorical manipulation. In truth, however, the sophist is not really defending a coherent view of thought and language (to which another might be opposed) but rather inhabiting a self-subverting fantasy of them; she believes that she has grasped the truth about discourse, but her view empties the very ideas of discourse, truth, and reality of any content. Hence, there is no argumentative route from sophistry to a perception of human discourse as genuine; there are only sophistic ways of removing oneself from a life within the reality of human discourse (among which we might count talk of language-games), and hence ways of trying to prevent or discourage people in general, and philosophers in particular, from so exiling themselves.

But how exactly does the idea of language as having the unity of a dialogue or conversation discourage us from such damaging errancies? How does it allow us satisfactorily to acknowledge the reality of discourse? It must not do so by suggesting that human culture amounts to one big conversation, and hence that our various ways of discursively grasping reality constitute contributions to an overarching discourse that takes as its subject matter Reality as such—Reality as essentially One. The idea of conversation at this (or indeed any) level of Rhees's account is a center of variation, not a putative description; and although Plato might have been tempted by such a hypostasization of the Real, Rhees is not.

The image of a conversation rather suggests an account of any given mode of human discourse in terms of its own dialogical context or horizon—with the multiple bearings of each branch of that discourse on other branches giving substance to the thought that each individual branch gets a purchase on reality by showing how the purchase it offers hangs together with (that is, is fruitfully intelligible to, and can itself render fruitfully intelligible) the purchase offered by other branches. The same kind of account can then be given of the relations between these given modes of discourse: their various ways of interlocking with one another substantiate the claims of each to register some aspect of the reality of things.

We here return to the contextualizing Wittgensteinian thought from which Rhees implicitly orients his reading: that "to imagine a language means to imagine a form of life" (*PI* §19). The nature and reality of a given form of discourse are centrally constituted by its specific place in the interlocking unity of human discourse as such. In its proper place in this discursive context, each such mode of discourse really is a way of getting to grips with what is real; and apart from it, its claim to be a mode of discourse (and hence to articulate a way of distinguishing reality from illusion, a way of getting at the truth of things and of achieving a growth in understanding) loses its substance. One might say, then, that, for Rhees, all that can be milked out of the idea of Reality as such, Reality as essentially One, is the fact that our modes of discourse are dialogically articulated and dialogically interrelated. Hence, to show that and how those different modes of discourse are so articulated and bear upon one another in such ways just *is* to show that there is genuine reality in the different ways we talk to one another about our world. It doesn't give us good or bad grounds for believing this to be the case; it clarifies what the claim that it is the case—and hence what the possibility of discourse, of language that is open to reality, of speech—in fact amounts to.

4 PHILOSOPHY, FINITUDE, MYSTERY

I couldn't consistently conclude this discussion without acknowledging various ways in which the significance of the role I have been assigning my discipline—in the university, in the broader culture, and in (what one might call) the cosmos—might put itself in question.

While my genealogical myth is designed to capture the sense in which philosophy can be said to be rightly and intelligibly interested in everything, in all that is, it may also thereby create the impression that the philosopher must be occupying a position above or beyond all that is—a kind of God's-eye view on Creation from without (how else could he take it in as a whole?). But philosophy does and must occupy a position within the domain that it aspires to take in as if from the outside. Just as philosophy's claim to be the university department that uniquely aspires to acknowledge the articulated unity of the university as a whole must cohere with the fact that it is also just one more department within that articulated unity, so philosophy's claim to be the singular point within the culture at which its articulated unity is acknowledged must cohere with the fact that it is simultaneously one node in that culture. It follows that philosophy's various ways of putting the deliverances of other intellectual disciplines in question can themselves be put in question from the perspectives afforded by those disciplines. Practitioners of any ontic science can question the accuracy of any philosopher's characterization of their founding presuppositions; they might claim for themselves a field of inquiry that philosophers have long regarded as their own; they can even argue that philosophy can claim to be grappling with anything of any genuine intellectual substance only insofar as it regards itself as continuous with some ontic science or other.

I don't find the last of these claims convincing; but some of my colleagues do, and I can make sense of their sense of conviction. But one can surely acknowledge the way other intellectual disciplines might have a bearing on philosophy and its concerns without conceiving of this as a matter of usurpation or reduction. For example, one might think (as does Stanley Cavell) that aspects of the phenomenon that philosophy grapples with under the name of skepticism are engaged with in literature under the name of tragedy; or one might hope to learn something about the roots and the significance of philosophy's apparent aspiration to find a God's-eye view of reality and culture by drawing upon the lessons of psychoanalysis or theology; or one might be brought by the work of historians and sociologists to appreciate the cultural specificity of the terms in which philosophy understands any given aspect of its concerns, and so understands itself.

Such possibilities of interdisciplinary dialogue cannot be rejected a priori by any philosopher who recognizes the pertinence to their enterprise of the question of fundamental ontology, for it precisely depends upon acknowledging that a culture hangs together only insofar as any of its thematized modes of understanding can in principle intelligibly and fruitfully be engaged in dialogue by any other. Whether any such encounter will in fact be fruitful, or even mutually intelligible, can only be proven through its concrete working-out from case to case; but its bare possibility is surely something that anything worth calling philosophy is obliged (on pain of self-subversion) to acknowledge.

What this moment of humility or self-abnegation in my analysis really registers is the fact that any philosophical work is necessarily situated or conditioned by its place in the broader economy of a culture; and that directs us toward the more general point that philosophy is and must be thoroughgoingly conditioned or situated insofar as it is (in effect) one step in the reflexive unfolding of the distinctively human mode of comprehending the world.

To say that that comprehension of the world is distinctively reflexive—that is, that it is always capable of putting itself in question—is simply another way of saying that human comprehension is essentially finite (for if it were not, if it were absolute or unconditioned, it would be beyond any possible question). Any given body of knowledge or understanding has limits, it is always capable of and subject to further refinement (which will sometimes take the form of revolutionary reconceptualization), and it will always be conditioned by presuppositions that can themselves be the subject of inquiry—perhaps within its own precincts, certainly within the precincts of other branches or modes of human inquiry. In short, there can be no such thing as an absolute end or terminus to human knowledge of reality—nothing that is beyond further interrogation, hence closed to further enrichment or deepening.

Since my genealogical myth of philosophy is driven by a characterization of human comprehension as inherently produced by, and hence inveterately subject to, questioning, the conception of philosophy that emerges from it must be marked by that same acknowledgment of our finitude. What may now be clearer is that philosophy's way of being marked by, hence of bearing witness to, our finitude has to do with the fact that its defining aspiration (to articulate the question of fundamental ontology) is both undismissable and unfulfillable.

Insofar as philosophy is defined as an inquiry into the human capacity for comprehending inquiry as such, beyond any particular way of acquiring understanding of any particular domain of reality, it amounts to a kind of absolutely purified or intensified exemplar of this aspect of the human way of being (one in which questioning comprehension aspires to be both subject matter and means, with nothing other than itself involved). But insofar as any such inquiry must itself be questionable, because it is no less subject to condition and limitation than any other exercise of this capacity, it is destined to fail to fulfill its own defining aspiration. In the end, then, the sheer existence of philosophy makes it manifest that human beings aspire by their very nature to a completeness of understanding that they cannot realize. Philosophy is the place at which finite human understanding endlessly attempts, and as endlessly fails, to take itself in as a whole; and it thereby reveals that it is internal to the nature of finite beings to be subject to the mysterious, unsatisfiable desire to transcend their own finitude. Philosophy's unending struggle with the question of whether it makes sense even to try making sense of the many and varied ways in which reality does (and does not) make sense to us is thus the most fundamental way in which human beings manifest the essentially enigmatic finitude of their being.

3 Wittgenstein and Heidegger and the "Face" of Life in Our Time

Simon Glendinning

Concepts lead us to make investigations; are the expression of our interest, and direct our interest.

—Ludwig Wittgenstein

Perhaps one thinks that it can make no great difference which concepts we employ. . . . But . . . this is not true.

—Ludwig Wittgenstein

((Meaning is a physiognomy.))

—Ludwig Wittgenstein

What it is that we are talking about is shown in how we talk about it, and in how that talk enters our lives, the shape—the "face"—that life containing such talk has.

—Cora Diamond

Our ordinary language, which of all possible notations is the one which pervades all our life, holds our mind rigidly in one position, as it were.

—Ludwig Wittgenstein

In this chapter I attempt to develop a consistently Wittgensteinian reading of Heidegger's interest in the use of the expression "Being," and to do so in relation both to the Heideggerian interest itself and to Heidegger's discussion of the possibility of an investigation that explicitly pursues such an interest. The chapter thus aims to outline what can claim to be a distinctively Wittgensteinian way of coming to terms with, and of appreciating, both the content and the form of Heidegger's investigation into the meaning of "Being."

As the citations I am leading off with serve to indicate, my recommendation will be that we take up the Heideggerian interest in relation to a

Wittgensteinian question concerning the "face" of a life containing such talk. Although I hope to make this recommendation compelling, I am aware that a reading of Heidegger's interest from a Wittgensteinian point of view that is not through and through critical of Heidegger's interest is likely to seem implausible. Given the apparently extreme distance between Wittgenstein's ultra-mundane investigations of the logic of ordinary language and the vertigo-inducing heights of the Heideggerian question of Being—or indeed Heidegger's other equally extraordinary questions about Angst or the Nothing or the Worldhood of the World or Dasein—the very idea of pursuing a sympathetic reading of the latter via the former might be thought a nonstarter. I will identify a feature of Wittgenstein's recorded remarks on Heidegger that opens a reading of his interest in the meaning of "Being" that is anything but critical through and through. However, this should not obscure the fact that the Wittgensteinian point of departure that guides me here also exposes a sharp distinction between the two thinkers, and I will try to make some headway clarifying the differences too.

1   THE AUGUSTINIAN PICTURE OF NONSENSE

What might a reader committed to following Wittgenstein make of Heidegger's "weird and wonderful" ways of going on in philosophy?[1] P. M. S. Hacker, one of the most dedicated contemporary defenders of Wittgenstein, takes his bearings on this question from a discussion recorded by Moritz Schlick in the early 1930s when he was taking dictation for a book to be cowritten by Wittgenstein and Friedrich Waismann (Waismann 1997). Wittgenstein briefly considers what we might do if we want "to do justice" to a proposition like "the Nothing noths" (see Baker 2003, 69–71). Commenting on the passage, Hacker suggests that, for Wittgenstein, this task will be achieved by freeing someone who is inclined to advance such propositions from their confusion. In particular, he suggests that "Wittgenstein tries to imagine what *misconceived picture* underlies Heidegger's nonsense" (Hacker 2003, 18).

Central to Hacker's reading is a presumption of guilt: the proposition "the Nothing noths" is, as many philosophers since Rudolf Carnap have insisted, strictly nonsensical. The real question is how to free people from any inclination they may have to say such things. Hacker admits that a classical Carnapian logical decapitation of metaphysics lacks the more respectful attention to what someone is actually thinking that he finds in Wittgenstein. However, both are attempting to deliver us from nonsense, and so, ultimately, for Hacker, "The difference between Carnap and Wittgenstein on this issue lies largely in the bedside manner" (Hacker 2003, 19).

Giving Heidegger's propositions short shrift became something like a badge of honor for analytic philosophers in the postwar period, and it remains so for many who find Wittgenstein's ways of going on in and with philosophy congenial. On the other hand, there is another remark recorded by Schlick, from the year before the discussion just mentioned, in which Wittgenstein mentions Heidegger by name, and his generous comment on Heidegger's wanting to speak about "Being and Dread" [*Angst*] should give us pause for thought: "I can readily think what Heidegger means by Being and Dread. Man has the impulse to run up against the limits of language. . . . This running-up against the limits of language is *Ethics*" (Murray 1978, 80).

In my view, Wittgenstein's own conception of what philosophy can hope to achieve both respects and deflates the Ethical impulse he is talking about here. This is not just a point about his respectful bedside manner. At the end of his brief comment on Heidegger he suggests that a misfiring attempt to say something—the upshot of running up against the limits of language—may nevertheless be a sort of gesture that *"points to something*," and he cites St. Augustine finding those who make a point of *avoiding* all such misfiring talk as certainly *no less problematic*, and perhaps *even more problematic* than those who, without saying more, want to say more: "St. Augustine already knew this when he said: 'What, you wretch, so you want to *avoid* talking nonsense? Talk some nonsense, it makes no difference!'" (Murray 1978, 80).[2]

I intend to outline an approach to Heidegger's interest in the question of the meaning of "Being" that goes as far as possible in the direction of this Wittgensteinian reading of it. Framing the reading with reference to St. Augustine's admonition of the avoiders of nonsense will be central to this task. However, it will also help explain why the "what" of Heidegger's interest cannot be the subject of a bit of plain speaking or ordinary talk about things. I will then make an attempt to outline how we can, nevertheless, take this interest seriously and, indeed, philosophically. Doing so will shed new light on the distinctive way in which "we in our time" have come to avoid speaking about it today (see *BT* 1/19). I will begin with Heidegger's own framing of his interest.

2   HEIDEGGER AND THE MEANING OF "BEING"

In view of its leading off with a citation from Plato's *Sophist*, it has been remarked that *Being and Time* begins "in the middle of a Platonic dialogue" (Sallis 1986, 99; see also Mulhall 2001a, 185–96). However, what that *co-locating* of texts passes over is the insistence in Heidegger's opening words of a fundamental *dis*-location of times: a contrast between the situation that belonged to a certain "we . . . now" in Plato's time and a very different one that belongs to the "we in our time" in ours (*BT* 1/19). This opening contrast is elaborated as a puzzle: namely, that, unlike "the ancient philosophers" who found "what you mean when you use the expression '*being*'" "continually disturbing" and were "perplexed" by what it means, "we . . . today" are not puzzled by it at all. "Not at all" (*BT* 1/19). Heidegger begins then with a puzzle about the absence of a puzzle, an absence that marks our time as contemporary, as distinctively ours. It is a kind of "riddle" (*BT* 4/23)[3] that, as he puts it, "we already live in an understanding of Being"— and yet today we are utterly untroubled by the fact that the meaning of Being "is still veiled in darkness" (*BT* 4/23).

This is an intriguing but no doubt also perplexing opening for a reader today, for even if one accepts that Heidegger is right to say, "This question has today been forgotten" (*BT* 2/21), and even if one accepts that it "provided a stimulus for the researches of Plato and Aristotle" (*BT* 2/21), indeed, even if one accepts that "what sanctions its complete neglect" in our time is rooted in the very tradition of analysis of the concept "Being" that has come down to us from those noncontemporary Greek sources (*BT* 2/21), a contemporary reader might still wonder whether the absence of a puzzle is really so puzzling. That is, a reader in our time is likely to have concerns that it is not clear what the question means or even if it means anything at all: one might well think today that the so-called "question of Being" is itself, *as a question*, fundamentally *questionable*. And yet, right from the start, Heidegger is up and running, resolutely committed to what the title of the very first section of *Being and Time* dramatically calls "*The Necessity for Explicitly Restating the Question of Being.*" What, if we take our orientation from Wittgenstein, should we make of this?

3   THE AUGUSTINIAN PICTURE OF LANGUAGE

Hacker, as we have seen, draws on Wittgenstein to refer to "misconceived pictures" animating Heideggerian nonsense. Another Wittgensteinian blow might begin by recalling Wittgenstein's methodological recourse to the use, and perhaps especially the "ordinary use" (the dimension of intelligibility apparently conceived as simply opposed to a nonsensical "metaphysical use") of our words. So a Wittgensteinian philosopher might worry that Heidegger's launching headlong into the question of the meaning of "Being" without any preliminary attention to the use or uses of the ordinary little word "is" may itself be a sort of philosophical false start: a point of departure rooted in philosophical confusions. In his essay "Heidegger's Question of Being and the 'Augustinian Picture' of Language" Herman Philipse develops just such a response to Heidegger's interest. While acknowledging various ways in which Wittgenstein's and Heidegger's work have "structural similarities" (Philipse 1992, 251), Philipse pointedly asks whether the most basic steps of Heidegger's approach fall foul of a distinctively Wittgensteinian diagnosis of philosophical failure:

> If one accepts Wittgenstein's critique of the Augustinian picture of language, what should one think of Heidegger's question of Being to the extent that it is concerned with "the leading and fundamental sense of

> Being, that manifests itself in and through the amazing polyvalence of
> the single little word 'is' "? (Philipse 1992, 257–58)

Philipse's question opens out onto a claim that insofar as Heidegger retains
a commitment to a "leading and fundamental sense of Being" he does so in
virtue of being misled by the Augustinian picture of language. Bewitched by
the idea that the model of "name and its bearer" holds quite generally in
language, so that for each word there must be a corresponding "meaning,"
Heidegger assumes that an investigation into what we *mean* by "the single
little word 'is' " must disclose, at the bottom of its striking "polyvalence," a
fundamental "unity and simplicity of Being."

Central to Philipse's effort to dispel the fog around Heidegger's question
is recourse to a counter-analysis of "the polyvalence of the single little word
'is' " that he also derives from Wittgenstein. This counter-analysis plays an
important part in Philipse's readings of Heidegger more generally, and is
presented as a linguistic analysis that would challenge Heidegger's sense of
a "riddle" in this context (Philipse 1998, 36).[4] The Wittgensteinian counter-
analysis is that philosophical misunderstandings often arise when we fail
to see that "the same word [may have] different modes of signification."
Philipse cites Wittgenstein's identification of three such modes in the case of
the verb "to be": "[It] may be used as a copula, as a sign for identity, and as
an expression of existence" (Philipse 1992, 261). Arguing, then, from this
"Wittgensteinian point of view," Philipse suggests that Heidegger's question of Being shows a marked dissatisfaction with the diversity of uses, a
dissatisfaction based on the misleading but beguiling idea that "the various
meanings of the verb 'to be' must be rooted in one 'fundamental sense': 'the
sense [*Sinn*] of "*Being*" ' as such" (Philipse 1992, 262).

One can object to this reading in two related ways. The first objection is
that Philipse himself presents his discussion as taking up only one "pole"
identified in Heidegger's approach to the question of Being: the "pole of
unity." However, Philipse also acknowledges that this pole has another end:
a "pole of differentiation." Moreover, these poles are not poles apart; on the
contrary, they are somehow the same thing said in two ways: "The principle
of identity is *at once* a principle of differentiation" (Philipse 1992, 257),
Being is *always* "at once" the Being of beings. Hence a movement of "differentiation," what one might call, following Derrida, the *dissemination* or
the dispersal of the *seme* as unit(y) of meaning (what Heidegger refers to in
his own way as "amazing polyvalence"), is being thought here as entailing
a *meaning* of "Being" that is *a priori* irreducible to a single sense of Being
that one might attempt to grasp in abstraction from (or as having some
unity that is prior to) a subsequent dispersal. No: variety, variation, differentiation, amazing polyvalence cannot be held to one side, even provisionally. If there is a "pole of unity" to be *in some way* thought in this scene of
originary dispersal it cannot be the thought of a single basic meaning that
would be the radical root of all variations. Indeed, it is striking that what

Heidegger actually identifies as manifestly *singular* is not a meaning but "the single little word 'is.'" So it does not seem obvious that Heidegger is committed to the idea of a univocal "meaning of Being" that Philipse supposes he is.

4   WITTGENSTEIN AND THE MEANING OF "IS"

This point takes me to a second objection to Philipse's Wittgensteinian counter-analysis. The argument against Heidegger is that he is bewitched by the Augustinian picture of language. However, when Philipse draws on Wittgenstein to provide a linguistic analysis of modes of signification that disperses the fog around the verb "to be," it is not the Wittgenstein of the *Investigations* but the Wittgenstein of the *Tractatus* that is called upon (*TLP* 3.323). However, not only is "the author of the *Tractatus*" a common foil for the later Wittgenstein, but had Philipse attended to the *later* Wittgenstein's reflections on the use of the word "is" (which would have been in keeping with his deployment of the diagnosis of the Augustinian picture, similarly belonging to the later philosophy), he might have been struck that what the *early* Wittgenstein "would like to say" in relation to cases where we actually do "make use of this identity" of words across kinds of use that "do not yield a *single* meaning" is subject to critical questioning. Here (curtailed in the interest of brevity) is the relevant sequence of remarks from the *Investigations* on the uses of "is."

> Now isn't it remarkable that I say that the word "is" is used with two different meanings (as copula and as sign of equality)? . . . One would like to say that these two kinds of use don't yield a single meaning; the union under one head, effected by the same word, is an inessential coincidence.
>
> But how can I decide what is an essential, and what an inessential, coincidental, feature of the notation? . . .
>
> What's the point of using the same word? In the calculus we don't make use of any such sameness of sign!—Why the same piece for both purposes?—But what does it mean here to speak of "making use of the sameness of sign"? For isn't it a single use, if we actually use the same word? . . .
>
> If I understand the character of the game aright, I might say, then this isn't an essential part of it.
>
> ((Meaning—a physiognomy.))
>
> Language is an instrument. Its concepts are instruments. Now perhaps one thinks that it can make no *great* difference *which* concepts we employ. . . . But . . . this is not true. (*PI* §§561–68)

I have cut a lot out here, and leave it to the reader to reflect on the chain of remarks as they appear in the *Investigations*. However, I think I have cited enough to get into view both a sense of the significance that might attach to our finding it "part of the game" with the word "is" that we do "actually use the same word," and a distinctively Wittgensteinian suggestion that to "understand the character of the game aright" is akin to appreciating the singularity of a "*face*."[5]

One thing that is perfectly clear is that Wittgenstein wants to put pressure on the idea that "understanding the character of the game aright" is simply a matter of (or reducible to) "knowing the rules" that define it. Indeed, the interpretation of being-at-home-in-a-notation that construes it as "operating a calculus according to definite rules" is exactly what he wants to overcome (*PI* §81). Philipse, at one point, refers to Karl-Otto Apel's suggestion that Wittgenstein's comparison of language with tools "would prove that his later philosophy is just another expression of [what Heidegger diagnosed as] the purely technical relation of modern man to the world, a symptom of [what Heidegger had called] the 'technical era'" (Philipse 1992, 256). But what one might call "the spirit of technicity" that Heidegger finds so pervasive in our time, rapidly globalizing out of a European origin, belongs precisely to the one who thinks that "it can make no *great* difference *which* concepts we employ." And this attitude is exactly what Wittgenstein objects to as well. As long as it doesn't take too much time or trouble to do so, some may think it would be better if we were to employ two or maybe even three distinct concepts where currently there is this potentially misleading "union under one head." On such a view, it is simply a practical matter whether we decide to carry on as we do now or we switch over to a more perspicuous and less confusing notation. But this is not Wittgenstein's recommendation at all. On the contrary, what he emphasizes is the actual use that unites these uses under a single head. In other words, what he stresses is that in *wanting to use the same word here*, in our appreciation of the "face" of its meaning, *we are ourselves the pole of unity*. To be oneself the pole of unity in this case means: in some sense one appreciates the physiognomy, the singular "face" of the meaning of the little word "is." It means one finds it irreplaceably fitting to make use of the single little word "is" for a variety of purposes. It is not that there is a single, identifiable basic meaning subtending the various uses; but it remains a "single use" in that we do, in fact, use the same word.

Wittgenstein seems only to speak of the "face" of meaning in connection with single words. Heidegger, however, is not content to regard "understanding the character of the game aright" with regard to the use of "is" as just one sample or example of our understanding of the use of words among others. On the contrary, appreciation of the "face" of meaning, a pole of unity, in *this* case should be seen, in his view, to pervade and encompass *all the rest*. Indeed, Heidegger reads the entire history of philosophy (very persuasively, I think) as having an implicit if distorted appreciation of this too: the way we are inclined to construe our being-at-home-in-the-world *in general* is everywhere informed by our construal of the character of *this* game *in particular*. So, for Heidegger, decisions regarding "what is an essential feature of the notation" in *this* case are not on a par with others, but have been fundamentally fateful for us. Indeed, Heidegger's wager with regard to the meaning of "being" is this: the singularity of the "face" of the notation with the single little word "is" is not simply one "face" among others manifest in our life with words in general, but metonymically captures the "face" of a life—*our* life—with words *überhaupt*. In the next section I will pursue this contrast between Wittgenstein and Heidegger a little further.

5 RUNNING UP AGAINST THE LIMITS OF LANGUAGE

Wittgenstein suggests that the one who understands the game aright with the word "is" is the one who uses the same word for uses that do not yield a single meaning, and hence functions as the pole of unity in the meaning of the little word "is." Heidegger generalizes: that *Dasein is the pole of unity of the meaning of "is"* says something about *the "face" of our life as a whole.*

In my view, it is with this difference that we can begin to see what Wittgenstein has in mind when he says that Heidegger's interest runs up against the limit of language. Heidegger takes one feature, one "face" of our notation, and uses it to try to say something about the "face" of the whole. "Being," rather than being one concept among others, becomes what Wittgenstein calls a "super-concept." And yet, Wittgenstein will continue, if this word has any meaning then—like every word, any word—this is just the "humble" one that belongs to its everyday use and no more (*PI* §97).

Heidegger's generalization is not, however, without motivation. The fact that the multiple ways of speaking about "being" are united under one head is not simply one fact about our notation among others but, in its manifest pervasiveness in the notation that pervades our lives, makes of it a concept that expresses an interest that has a claim to unite *all* of our interests under one head. We are the pole of unity in the meaning of "being." *This is no longer simply a remark about the use of "is," but aims to say something about the essence of our existence, as a relation to Being.*

The attempt to say something *beyond* a remark about the use of "is" *with* a remark that really is just a remark about the use of "is" cannot, according to Wittgenstein, be made. Our interest in this concept is always and only an interest among interests. That is, what is and can only be an *example* of our interest is being taken to be *the* exemplary interest—the fundamental expression of interest itself, an interest through which we might try to say something about the essence of our life as a whole. For Wittgenstein, then, Heidegger's attempted generalization is a case of "running up against the limits of language." On the other hand, while he (Wittgenstein) insists that one really cannot say something *more* with our words than would be said by someone who *avoided* trying to say anything more at all, he also affirms St. Augustine's suggestion that the *desire* to say more is not to be ridiculed or rejected; indeed, it *"points to something."* This desire to say something more is, Wittgenstein suggests, a fundamentally (capital "E") *Ethical* desire, ("This running-up against the limits of language is *Ethics*"). It is the expression of a desire beyond any particular desire in life: it is the expression of what Emmanuel Levinas—who, of course, famously associates ethics with the encounter with the "face"—would call (capital "D") Desire (Levinas 1969, 34). In what follows I want to explore Heidegger's interest in this light.

6 THE SPIRIT OF TECHNICITY

As a prelude to a discussion of what, if anything, can be made via Wittgenstein of Heidegger's interest in the meaning of "Being," it is worth noting that, notwithstanding the contrast between Wittgenstein's particularistic approach to the "face" of our life with this or that word and Heidegger's effort to say something about the "face" of our life as a whole, both thinkers seem equally to stress that "the pole of unity" has a certain *fragility*. In Wittgenstein's case this is apparent in his acknowledgment that the very one who *in some sense* "understands the character of the game aright" is also the one who can come to experience the (undeniable) instrument-character of our concepts as implying that it makes no *great* difference whether we use the same word or different words for different uses of "is" (though he or she might well accept it is just too much bother to learn different words). In our time, in what both Heidegger and Wittgenstein figure as a distinctively "dark" time, we have come to a point where we, in fact, no longer regard it as of any special significance whether we use this word or that. Our appreciation of the "face" of a life with the little word "is" is being overwhelmed by the spirit of technicity.

I do not think this is a marginal concern for either Wittgenstein or Heidegger, and in each case it gives the ambition to come to terms with ourselves as users of language a quite specific kind of ethical dimension: a concern with the *ethos* of our time. Their perception of a "darkening of our world" or "the darkness of our time" is inseparable from their sense of obligation to become custodians of a spirit other than the one that dominates today. Whether this is experienced as a call to become a "custodian of grammar," as Wittgenstein once put it (*PhR* 85), or, with Heidegger, "the guardian of Being" (*BW* 217), both see their work in philosophy as an attempt to cultivate a *poetized* rather than a *technological* spirit. Both of these spirits belong, in an essential way, to deeply rooted European trajectories in our understanding of the world and the significance of our lives; indeed, they belong precisely to the trajectories already picked up on in the remark by St. Augustine that guides Wittgenstein's "Ethical" reading of Heidegger.

Seen in this way, Heidegger's methodological insistence on the question of Being is to be understood as an attempt to capitalize on the pervasiveness of the use of "is" in our life with language that hopes to call the Dasein of European humanity back to an understanding that in some sense it *is*, and hence to call Dasein back to care about a life with language in something other than a merely technological instrumental way. And this is a call uncannily paralleled in Wittgenstein's apparently opposing methodological refusal to capitalize on *any* word in our language: for this too is an effort marked by its resistance to the reduction of the use of language to the *technē* of "operating a calculus according to definite rules." Wittgenstein's concern with our life with language is characterized by his astonishing sensitivity to the manifold categorial (grammatical) differences that belong to the "depth grammar" of our language (*PI* §664)—and that will doubtless include an interest in the particulars of the use of the single little word "is." However, for reasons of its pervasiveness, Heidegger takes the latter interest as *the* leading interest, or, which is the same thing, as a particular interest that does not fall short of a totally general interest in our life with language.

"Concepts," Wittgenstein concludes in the sequence of remarks I have been highlighting, "lead us to make investigations. They are the expression of our interest and direct our interest" (*PI* §570). Heidegger insists that a philosophical investigation into the "face" of human life *in our time* must be led by an interest that has "today been forgotten." At issue with *this* disappearance would be a changeover in (let's say) the "spirit" of our life, which would singularly mark the "face" of "we . . . in our time." We would then have become the ones who understand themselves in such a way that, as far as giving a thematic analysis of who we are is concerned, *this theme*, the idea of ourselves as the pole of unity in the understanding of Being, "isn't an essential part of it." To put this rather boldly, the task here for both thinkers is not one of giving an analysis of language that is as rigorous and scientific as possible, but seeking a way to preserve a threatened sensitivity to a "*great difference*," which, in our striving for a scientific self-understanding, we have, in our time, all but lost.

In the *Blue Book*, Wittgenstein suggests that "our ordinary language, which of all possible notations is the one which pervades all our life, holds our mind rigidly in one position, as it were" (*BB* 59). Perhaps one thinks that it can make no *great* difference which notation "of all possible notations" we employ. Could it be just this difference—the difference between those for whom everything can hang on what we in our time regard as an essential part of the notation that pervades our lives, and those for whom it makes no great difference which notation we use beyond the practical "time and trouble" it may give us (*PI* §569)—that is at stake in the intervention in our time and the spirit of our time effected by both Wittgenstein and Heidegger?

7   THE "FACE" OF OUR LIFE

There is no suggestion in Wittgenstein's discussion of the use of "is" that those who *do* "make use of the identity" and so in fact do "use the same word" do so because they know the character of the game requires it of them or have some special interest in this way of going on. Indeed, as I have already suggested, the fact that someone actually does go on this way is entirely compatible with their wanting to give an analysis of the different uses of "is" that takes no real interest in the fact that they do. There is a distinctive disjunction here between how we express ourselves pre-reflectively and what, if anything, we are inclined to say when that pre-reflective way of going on becomes an issue for us. In this section I want to go back to the initial stages of Heidegger's effort explicitly to take up what he calls "the question of Being" with this disjunction in view. Doing so will show up a further striking affinity between Heidegger and Wittgenstein, this time concerning their way of handling this sort of disjunction, and its place in their understanding of the character of what they want to call a "philosophical" investigation. I will then return to the question of how Heidegger's investigation into the meaning of "Being" responds to the "face" of a life that finds that such talk "isn't essential to it," and hence what might call for an effort to say something that puts such talk back into circulation.

As we have seen, Heidegger's own understanding of *the kind of question* he is engaging with includes the idea that *our* starting condition is distinctive: "we . . . in our time" are the ones who are dead even to a puzzle concerning the meaning of "Being." Before returning to Heidegger's conception of this starting position, I want to take advantage of his holding back from leaping in concerning the meaning of "Being" to ask what justification one might offer for thinking that there is anything that one might legitimately call an *investigation* into the meaning of "Being" in the first place.

I intend this question to resonate with the quotation from Cora Diamond at the head of this chapter, in which she introduces the "physiognomic" theme that she takes to characterize "in a nutshell" a Wittgensteinian approach to meaning: "[W]hat it is that we are talking about is shown in how we talk about it, and in how that talk enters our lives, the shape—the "face"—that life containing such talk has" (Diamond 1991b, 60). It is this idea of the "face" of a life with such talk that is in view with Wittgenstein's reference to someone who understands the character of the game aright. The distinctively Heideggerian "limit" issue here concerns Dasein as the fragile pole of unity in the meaning of "Being," and hence the "face" of our life as pervasively, albeit vulnerably, marked by a relation to Being. What, he is asking, of a life that does *not* ask the question, a life that is content to *avoid* saying anything about Being? What is *its* "face"? These are Heidegger's questions of spirit, questions at stake in his taking up anew the question of the meaning of "Being." But how should we even begin an attempt to bring to concepts what is understood by the Dasein who is the pole of unity with the little word "is"?

Diamond's Wittgensteinian nutshell might be summarized in its own nutshell with this slogan: tell me how you are looking and I will tell you what you are looking for. The Wittgensteinian question I want to raise with respect to Heidegger's text in order to broach the questions of spirit is whether it provides any basis for the idea that there is some way of looking or seeking, some way of going about one's business, that might intelligibly be called undertaking an investigation into the meaning of "Being." Do we have *any idea at all* how to distinguish going about *that* investigation rightly and going about it in the wrong way altogether? Is there anything that one can call doing or failing to do *that*? And if not then the very idea of such an investigation, as yet, has no sense—and hence also (according to the summary nutshell) the idea that there is a distinctive "what" that we are inquiring about has, as yet, no sense either. The passages of *Being and Time* that I want to follow in this section are concerned precisely with the question of whether one can find a way (even) to begin with the question of Being.

Although Heidegger does not begin *Being and Time* with an analysis of the ordinary use of the word "is," questions concerning the meaning of the words we use and our understanding or nonunderstanding of them are, in fact, strikingly to the fore in his point of departure. Indeed, it is striking that Heidegger immediately identifies the question of Being in terms of what we *mean* and *understand* by "Being." The question Heidegger wishes to "raise anew" is precisely "*the question of the meaning* [Sinn] *of Being*" (*BT* 1/19). He is interested, therefore, in *what is understood* in "any understanding whatsoever of Being" (*BT* 1/19).

So Heidegger is concerned straightaway with issues of meaning and understanding. Nevertheless, with Philipse, one might still balk at the assumption that there is some singular "what" that is the "what is understood" in the particular case Heidegger is concerned with. Or, in the Wittgensteinian terms that I am urging we look at this in, one might still want to ask what sense there is, if any, to undertaking an investigation that would take up this question.

In the second section of *Being and Time*, and on the basis of little more than a previous and, of course, itself baffling assertion that "we already live in an understanding of Being," Heidegger outlines what would make it possible to get things going in the following terms:

> Inquiry, as a kind of seeking, must be guided beforehand by what is sought. So the meaning of Being must already be available to us in some way. As we have intimated, we always conduct our activities in an understanding of Being. Out of this understanding arise both the explicit question of the meaning of Being and the tendency that leads us towards its conception. (*BT* 5/25)

The questionableness of the question is held at bay here with a barely supported assurance that what is asked about in the question is, in fact, already "available to us in some way." But then that should be enough: we should still be able to tell "in some way" what will and what will not be "appropriate conduct" for an investigation in this case.

Yet Heidegger immediately goes on to state, or confesses on our behalf, that things are not nearly so simple:

> As we have intimated, we always conduct our activities in an under-standing of Being. Out of this understanding arise both the explicit question of the meaning of Being and the tendency that leads us to-wards its conception. We do not *know* what "Being" means. (*BT* 5/25)

Heidegger's first remarks about the conditions of an investigation suggest, however shakily, why he thinks he may be able to address the question of Being in an appropriately focused way. But then suddenly the road seems closed again: we do not know what "Being" means, and so we do not know what we mean by the question of Being. However, according to Heidegger, the fact that "[w]e do not *know* what 'Being' means" does not mean that in attempting to address the question we are simply talking nonsense and should give up. We may not *know* it but we are not, he thinks, in a condition of ignorance either:

> We do not *know* what "Being" means. But even if we ask, "What *is* 'Being?'," we keep within an understanding of the "is," though we are unable to fix conceptually what that "is" signifies. We do not even know the horizon in terms of which that meaning is to be grasped and fixed. *But this vague average understanding of Being is still a Fact.* (*BT* 5/25)

Rendering what is already in some way available to us conceptually trans-parent in the way that it shows itself (that is, *as something in this way familiar*) is the form of clarification that Heidegger attempts in *Being and Time*. What should be striking, however, is that this is also precisely what Wittgenstein attempts in *Philosophical Investigations*. Indeed, it is in view of just this *form of difficulty* that both Wittgenstein and Heidegger take a distinctively *philosophical* question to lie. The sense of a distinctive form of unclarity here is specified through a contrast with the state of *pre-theoretical ignorance* that comes before making discoveries or building theories in nat-ural science: it is *this* contrast that brings into view what they will both want us to acknowledge as the contour of a distinctively *philosophical* question.

When Wittgenstein gives an example of this he once more cites St. Au-gustine, here disorientated by a difficulty in regard to the question of time ("What, then, is time?"): *I know well enough what it is, provided that no-body asks me; but if I am asked what it is and try to explain, I am baffled.* "This could not be said about a question in natural science," Wittgenstein notes (*PI* §89). Heidegger's conception of our starting unclarity with respect to the question of Being has exactly the same shape: it concerns something that is, in one way, "closest and well known" but, in another way, "the farthest and not known at all" (*BT* 43/69). Heidegger's investigation is thus oriented toward bringing something that is, in what he calls "an egregious sense," "*hidden*" into clear view, to "let us see" it in the very way in which it shows itself (*BT* 35/59).[6] Significantly, the Augustinian reference that Wittgenstein draws on to illustrate the sense of something that can be "hidden" precisely because of its "familiarity" (*PI* §129) also belongs to Heidegger's elaboration of this point, although the issue has (apparently) shifted. Heidegger cites St. Augustine's sense of estrangement from his own being: "But what is closer to me than myself? Assuredly I labour here and I labour within myself; I have become to myself a land of trouble and inordinate sweat" (quoted in *BT* 43–44/69). The theme may appear to have changed but the avowal of estranged empuzzlement is the same.[7]

So there is if not knowledge then at least some pre-reflective *familiarity* that should make it possible to get an investigation started and, indeed, motivates doing so not "just casually" but on the basis of an "explicitly formulated" question (*BT* 5/24–25). On the other hand, however, if Heidegger really does not know what "Being" means, how can he *be* so sure that there *is* anything at all that *is* "what is asked about" in this question? How can he *be* so sure that an investigation of any kind could possibly be undertaken on this question? Heidegger's basic answer, his basic argument, is: look at the questions just posed, the very questions themselves can only be asked, you yourself can only ask them, from within an understanding of the meaning of the single little word "is." Of course, we have no problem with this understanding when no one questions us and no special difficulty when we are questioned just casually about what is understood in this understanding. The *problem* is, however, that when we come *explicitly* to ask ourselves about what is understood here, we are, if we are not already "infiltrated with traditional theories" concerning the meaning of the "is" (*BT* 6/25), far from surefooted and, in the face of being utterly unprepared to engage in an investigation with respect to an estranged empuzzlement of this "distinctive character" (*BT* 5/24), more than likely tempted to elaborate "ideas" based on a "picture" of Being, as Wittgenstein might put it, rather than to pursue an investigation that conceptually unfolds what it means to be the pole of unity in the meaning of "Being": an investigation of our all-pervasive pre-reflective *familiarity* with the meaning of the "is."[8]

8   HOW TO AVOID THINKING

According to Heidegger's "limit" argument, pursuing an interest in "Being" requires a turn in our investigation toward a testamentary interrogation of ourselves as that entity that *is*, in view of its familiarity with Being, the pole of unity of "Being." At issue, then, is a distinctively philosophical investigation of the entity "in which a pre-ontological understanding of Being is comprised as a definite characteristic" (*BT* 13/33).

But now note: this investigation does not aim at empirical knowledge of some being or other, not even of human beings. The kind of understanding one is trying to achieve is not scientific knowledge of any kind of being. There really is, in that sense, nothing "hidden" to be known. However, we have also come to the point in our cultural history or in the history of our culture where even the question concerning that with which we are so pervasively familiar—Being, and hence the originary dispersal of Being in the Being of beings in various domains—"has today been forgotten." Indeed, in our time, the pervasively dominant way of understanding the world and the significance of our lives is one that is devoted "solely [to] beings and beyond that—nothing" (*BW* 97). It is closed, therefore, to an interest, which, according to Heidegger, is *the* most fundamental for the being that we ourselves are.

We are the pole of unity of the meaning of "Being." Yet with the dominance of the spirit of technicity there threatens to disappear from human life even that willingness to speak more about which no more can be said, a willingness that belongs implicitly to the history of philosophy, and that, as responsive to our very being-what-we-are, "speaks in the destiny of man" (*BW* 437). Its loss is not therefore one among others for us. The "face" of our life, in our time, becomes correspondingly de-formed, de-faced—decapitated.

Heidegger does not pretend to know what an ordinary life "containing such talk" would look like. Certainly it was never his motivation for restating the question of Being that ordinary people would start engaging *en masse* in "original philosophy" (*IM* 10). On the other hand, however, it is precisely in view of the "face" of a life *without* such talk, indeed in view of *a life in which this theme-for-talk is increasingly encountered only—"you wretch"—as something to avoid* that "in the limits within which philosophy can accomplish anything" (*IM* 42),[9] Heidegger resolutely puts this talk *back* into circulation (see *IM* 20).

NOTES

1. Cora Diamond speaks about the "weird and wonderful" things Heidegger has to say about Nothing in Diamond (1991a, 87). I cite this, in part, in order to acknowledge my gratitude to Cora Diamond (and likewise to Stanley Cavell) for being among the first to make space within a faithful reading of Wittgenstein for a lively appreciation of Heidegger. I would like to extend this word of gratitude to the editors of this volume in recognition of their remarkable efforts to take this further, and for their extremely helpful comments on early drafts of this chapter.
2. The common translation of St. Augustine's remark (from the end of *Confessions*, book 1, chap. 4) runs: "Yet woe to them that keep silence, seeing that even they who say most are as the dumb." It seems to me that only the first part of Augustine's remark is actually cited by Wittgenstein here. Moreover, it is not entirely clear what Wittgenstein adds in his supplement to it. However, we can fill it out somewhat with reference to a conversation between Wittgenstein and Maurice Drury in which Wittgenstein returned to Augustine's

remark (cited in Friedlander 2001, 149–50). In that conversation Wittgenstein explicitly read Augustine's remark as one that chides those who take the rubbish spoken by others as a reason to avoid saying anything themselves. In particular, Wittgenstein claimed that the common translation, which renders Augustine's "*Loquaces*" as "they who say most," "misses the point entirely" since the word is "a term of contempt." Wittgenstein recommended using the English word "chatterboxes" instead, emphasizing that Augustine's point is that one is not excused from speaking up on important questions simply because of the arrant nonsense spoken by others. No, we are not excused from speaking for this reason. We are, one might say, called to Ethics; something is demanded of us and we should not refuse to respond, and it doesn't make a bit of difference if others respond inadequately.

3. *Rätsel*, translated by Macquarrie and Robinson as "enigma."
4. See also Philipse (1998, 331–35), where Philipse asserts that "we use the verb 'to be' in the different senses of existence, predication, and identity" and that it is a mistake to think that "one and the same question of Being" is at issue with the meanings of this verb, and hence that "we need to practice linguistic analysis and not phenomenology" (Philipse 1998, 332).
5. Physiognomy (from the Greek *physis* meaning "nature" and *gnomon* meaning "interpreter") is the assessment of character or personality from outward appearances, and especially from the *face*.
6. I discuss the significance of Heidegger's wanting to bring clarity to what is "hidden" "in the very way in which it shows itself," and its connection to Wittgenstein's (notoriously obscure) remarks in the *Investigations* on the impossibility of bringing philosophy *final* "peace" (§133), in Glendinning (2011).
7. In one respect the shift of theme is fairly superficial since Heidegger, like St. Augustine, regards a certain way of being in *time* as characterizing the *fundamental* meaning of a finite existence (see *BT* 17/38). On the other hand, as we have seen, the condition of empuzzlement that Heidegger is particularly concerned to voice relates to the *absence* of a felt puzzle, in our time, with respect to the question of the meaning of "Being." Hence while St. Augustine expresses reflective disorientation with respect to a question that, once raised, is immediately experienced as a problem, Heidegger's disorientation includes a certain bafflement at the absence of such immediate bafflement. The phenomenological problem in Heidegger's case has a relation to history (of forgetting) not experienced in St. Augustine's.
8. On Wittgenstein's use of the idea of a "picture" as a casual, pre-theoretical— and not in itself incorrect—response out of which theoretical "ideas" that are in various ways inadequate and distorting can readily grow, see Mulhall (2001a, 36–38).
9. While Heidegger regards restating the question as belonging to "the fundamental conditions for an awakening of the spirit" and "indispensable if the peril of world darkening is to be forestalled" (*IM* 50) he stresses, surely correctly, that "philosophy can never directly supply the energies and create the opportunities and methods which bring about an historical change" (*IM* 10). Nevertheless, he does think that original philosophical questioning can initiate a "profound transformation" (*IM* 10) and "a new beginning" (*IM* 39): "It spreads only indirectly, by devious paths that can never be laid out in advance, until at last, at some future date, it sinks to the level of a commonplace, but by then it has long been forgotten as original philosophy" (*IM* 10).

4   The Provocation to Look and See
Appropriation, Recollection, and Formal Indication

Denis McManus

All of the great philosophers are difficult to read, but Heidegger and Wittgenstein seem to be so in striking ways. The oracular quality of the *Tractatus* is often remarked upon, and the later Heidegger's work can seem to represent a descent into "windy mysticism" of the sort that Ryle foresaw for Heidegger's work ([1928] 2009, 222). Wittgenstein's later work is equally—if differently—puzzling; it isn't technically complex but one finds oneself asking: what is Wittgenstein getting at? What is he trying to do? If he is making particular philosophical claims, why can't he spit them out? Similarly, Edwards claims that the early Heidegger "never says anything simply and clearly if he can say it oddly, obscurely and ponderously": "and I have no doubt that the desire to sound esoteric and original is part of the reason" (1979, 37, 35). Edwards's reaction to what he calls Heidegger's "hideous gibberish" (1989, 468) is extreme, but there is a widespread sense that Heidegger's writing is somehow willfully contrary or—as Edwards would have it—"*perverse*" (1979, 37).[1]

A related worry is that Heidegger and Wittgenstein seem to have an oddly casual view of the need to present us with philosophical proofs: the *Tractatus*, for example, appears to be largely a body of assertions and, as Okrent observes, "[o]ne of the most striking things about the way in which the early Heidegger presents his views . . . is his seeming lack of concern for argument" (Okrent 1988, 110). Just as Heidegger and Wittgenstein can appear unable to spit out clear articulations of the views that they are taken to be offering, commentators often feel they must "reconstruct—in some measure, construct—the argument[s] implicit in what [they] say" (Okrent 1988, 110).

This chapter will explore a more radical response to the foregoing features of Heidegger's and Wittgenstein's texts. This response takes its inspiration from the claim found in the *Tractatus* that "[t]he result of philosophy is not a number of 'philosophical propositions'" (*TLP* 4.112),[2] a claim that the *Investigations*' disavowal of "*theses* in philosophy" (*PI* §128) might seem to echo. Were Wittgenstein not to be espousing particular philosophical theses, that certainly would explain the difficulty of identifying such theses—and arguments in their support—in his texts. One version of this response focuses on the claim that Wittgenstein's insights are, in some sense, incapable of being captured in propositional form, and section 1 of this chapter considers briefly some attempts that have been made to argue that the same may be true of Heidegger's insights. The rest of the chapter presents an attempt of my own. It draws on commonalities in Heidegger's and Wittgenstein's understandings of philosophical confusion (section 2), explores Heidegger's reflections on Platonic dialectic (section 3) and "formal indication" (section 4) in identifying how one ought to respond to such confusion, sketches a case for seeing *Being and Time* as illustrating that response (section 5), and identifies some questions with which that sketch leaves us (section 6).

1 HEIDEGGER AND "THESES IN PHILOSOPHY"

Dahlstrom (1994) has argued that Heidegger faces a particular reflexive problem in articulating his fundamental ontology. The problem arises out of the fact that Heidegger can appear to identify that which propositions reveal with what he calls "the present-at-hand," but also to see himself as revealing to us forms of Being other than the present-at-hand.[3] Dahlstrom argues that Heidegger's use of the propositions that make up his texts must, therefore, be seen as embodying another kind of self-expression, one that he attempts to explain through an allusion to the early Wittgenstein: "[Heidegger] must be able to kick away the very ladder ('worldly' or 'theoretical' assertions, 'objectifying' concepts, and so on) on which he is forced to make his climb" (Dahlstrom 1994, 788). Dahlstrom is only one of a number of commentators who have explicitly drawn inspiration from Wittgenstein in developing readings of Heidegger as presenting insights that cannot be captured in propositional form. To add just one more example here,[4] Adrian Moore finds it "increasingly difficult *not* to hear a Tractarian injunction to throw away the ladder" in the early and later Heidegger, and suggests that we consider the possibility that Heidegger's proposals "resist[] being construed propositionally" (2012, 484).

There is a textual basis for ascribing such a view to Heidegger. He rejects the notion that an answer to the Question of Being might be "a free-floating result," with "what it asserts propositionally . . . just passed along" (*BT* 19/40); he warns that "a phenomenological concept . . . may degenerate if communicated in the form of an assertion" (*BT* 36/60–61); and he claims that "[w]ith any philosophical knowledge in general, what is said in uttered propositions must not be decisive. Instead what must be decisive is what it sets before our eyes as still unsaid, in and through what has been said" (*KPM* 137). Philosophical knowledge presents us then with something to be seen: in grasping "Being-in," for example, "the issue is one of *seeing* a primordial structure of *Dasein's* Being" (*BT* 54/81). To such a seeing one might expect to find a corresponding showing—Wittgenstein's terms are "*zeigen*" and "*aufweisen*"—and we find this too in Heidegger: phenomenology's task is "let[ting] that which shows itself be seen from itself in the very way in which it shows itself from itself [*das was sich zeigt, so wie es sich von ihm selbst her zeigt, von ihm selbst her sehen lassen*]" (*BT* 34/58), this being a matter of "exhibiting [the phenomena] directly [*in direkter Aufweisung*]" (*BT* 35/59).

But some see the claim that Heidegger's own insights might not be expressible through propositions as hopelessly obscure. Okrent sees it as "desperate" (1988, 292); Philipse insists that, "if Heidegger did not assert anything, there is nothing to discuss either" (Philipse 1998, 302); and in the light of Wittgenstein's identification of "the inexpressible"—which "*shows* itself"—with "the mystical" (*TLP* 6.522), Ryle's suspicion of "windy mysticism" looms once again. The ideas within Heidegger's texts to which commentators have turned in developing readings that make this claim central might seem to confirm such worries. For example, Dahlstrom gives pride of place to the notion of "formal indication,"[5] and, as we will see ahead, even otherwise sympathetic readers of Heidegger find that notion deeply obscure.

But, for now, I merely want to note that there are other significant worries about the readings of Heidegger sketched earlier. I have argued elsewhere that there is reason to doubt whether Heidegger endorsed either the proto-idealist explanatory project that Moore sees in his work,[6] or the claim that propositions reveal only the present-at-hand, upon which Dahlstrom's reading rests.[7] So I will explore another view, one that develops rather different analogies between Heidegger's and Wittgenstein's thought.

2   PHILOSOPHICAL CONFUSION AND ITS CAUSES

I suggest we begin by considering Heidegger's characterization of philosophical confusion and its causes. It is a striking feature of his criticism of other philosophers' claims that Heidegger characteristically charges them not with asserting falsehoods but with using words whose meaning has descended into "indeterminate emptiness" (*HCT* 269). For example, Descartes errs in "accept[ing] a completely indefinite ontological status for the *res cogitans*" (*BT* 24/46); when we talk of "psychical processes" we leave their "kind of Being" "for the most part wholly indefinite" (*BT* 293/339); and our typical understanding of "knowing" "remains the source of all sorts of confusion as a result of . . . indeterminacy in regard to its Being" (*HCT* 166).[8] As he puts it in earlier lectures, such talk is marked by a "fading of meaningfulness" (*PIE* 26–27, 141); indeed Heidegger goes so far as to claim that the "basic concepts of philosophy" "amount to nothing more than the possession of words": in using them, one succumbs to "the great danger that one philosophizes . . . in words rather than about things" (*IPR* 7).

For Wittgenstein too, philosophers' characteristic failing is making claims that "are not false, but nonsensical" (*TLP* 4.003). Quite how one understands that charge immediately leads us into controversy, of course;

but there is a not-obviously-absurd construal according to which it is the charge that we fail to assign a determinate meaning to the words we utter. We run different senses of a particular term or terms together, flipping back and forth between different construals of a sentence, even if we believe we are not doing so.[9] As Heidegger puts it, there is an "indistinctness of . . . meanings" in our philosophical confusions, as "different meanings run confusedly through one another," "a multiplicity of meaning-directions . . . indicated" (*PIE* 24).

Heidegger and Wittgenstein also seem to agree on at least one of the causes of this "indistinctness" of thought: "[W]hat confuses us is the uniform appearance of words" (*PI* §11). As Wittgenstein's famous analogy puts it, "[i]t is like looking into the cab of a locomotive," where "[w]e see handles" that "are used to do a wide variety of things" but "all looking more or less alike" (*PI* §12; *PhR* 58); a certain "bewitchment" by that "look"—by "surface grammar"—leads us to an "assimilation of expressions" (*PI* §109, §664, §14).[10] Similarly, for Heidegger, we are apt to conflate the modes of Being of entities described by different propositions because these differences "need not necessarily protrude . . . in the linguistic form" (*BP* 212). We "never heed the variety of beings" because of "the evenness, the undifferentiatedness of asserting and talking about . . . ": "[t]he equal and regular possibility of an assertion about . . . stones, trees, dogs, cars, 'passersby' (human beings)" gives the impression "that all beings which can be spoken about are, as it were, of the same kind" (*EP* 82–83). This suggests that Dahlstrom is right in thinking that, for Heidegger, assertions play an important role in creating philosophical confusion; but they do so not by revealing only the present-at-hand but by tempting us to overlook the diverse forms of Being that characterize the entities they describe. For Heidegger, an "orientation towards the assertion and its indifference towards its levelled and levelling character" creates the impression that the "manifestness of beings [is] a universally even and regular one" (*EP* 82–83), hiding the diverse forms of Being-in-the-world within which these assertions are "founded" and their "objects" reveal themselves. From this perspective, philosophical confusion arises out of a failure to reckon with what one might call the "life" behind the words we use, the "activities" and "forms of life" (*PI* §23) within which those words have their meaning and a determinate subject matter.[11]

One might suspect that Wittgenstein and Heidegger understand this "life" in rather different ways. For example, while Wittgenstein insists that we eliminate philosophical confusion by "bring[ing] words back from their metaphysical to their *everyday* use" (*PI* §116, italics added) and *Being and Time* begins its work with an examination of *Dasein's* "everydayness," Heidegger insists that we ultimately "disentangle ourselves from our ordinary conceptions of beings" (*FCM* 296), the "everyday perspective" in this sense identified with "[t]he common sense of the 'They'" (*BT* 288/334). While I have no desire to assimilate our two thinkers—into a Heidgenstein to rival Kripkenstein—Heidegger's remarks about the "everyday" need to be seen in the light of the equally fundamental theme in his philosophy that, when combating our *Seinsvergessenheit*, "Being is never alien but always familiar, 'ours'" (*MFL* 147)). Although Heidegger claims that we are dealing with matters "concealed from the consciousness of everyday life," he also describes what that calls for as a "[r]eturning to self-evident things" (*Supp* 160). It is also less than clear how much—and what kind of—weight Wittgenstein himself wishes to place on "the everyday," and Cavell may be right to suggest that "[t]he notion of the ordinary in Wittgenstein's later philosophy is meant only to contrast with the philosophical."[12] To anticipate a later theme, the important point here may be one upon which these thinkers agree—namely, that the failure involved in philosophical confusion is a failure to set to work—to appropriate—an understanding we already possess.

So reassured to some small degree, let us now see if we can develop the foregoing connections further.

3   COMBATING PHILOSOPHICAL CONFUSION: DENIAL, ARGUMENT, *ANAMNESIS*, AND *AGNOIA*

How, according to the foregoing picture, does one combat confused philosophical "claims"? One thing is clear: one doesn't *deny* them or attempt to *refute* them. When Wisdom told Wittgenstein of a conversation with another philosopher having gone badly, Wittgenstein is said to have replied: "Perhaps you made the mistake of denying something that he asserted" (reported in Bambrough 1979, 51). If the meaning of one's interlocutor's "assertions" is indeterminate, what one would oneself be saying, in saying that "what she says" is the case is not the case, would be equally indeterminate—another move within the same confused game.[13]

The same considerations cast a new light on the possible significance of argument within attempts to combat such confusions. Heidegger insists that "the danger of every dialectic" is that, "as far as results are concerned," such a dialectic can "bring[] to light an abundance of conclusions," whether it "is clear and critical about its own interpretive origin and interpretive significance" or "works mechanically with propositions" that are "blind to themselves" (*PIA* 108). If the meaning of the terms from which one reasons is "faded" and "indeterminate," "deductions" from "claims" articulated using those terms will be too—further moves within the same ill-understood game. Striving to establish through such a process positive philosophical theses of one's own would then be to miss the central point of the conception of philosophical confusion sketched earlier.

I do not rule out a role for argument in Heidegger's texts, in particular of a destructive sort that might reveal how, in one's "faded" words, "different meanings run confusedly through one another."[14] To borrow from Heidegger's discussion of dialectic—to which I turn in a moment—such reasoning might lead the reader to "see[] the inconsistency within himself, the inconsistency within his own comportment": he is "shown . . . that he presents the matter at issue sometimes in one way and then again in another way" (*PS* 261). We see an illustration of such reasoning when Heidegger points to how a skeptic comes to think of the subject as "similar to a box," while simultaneously believing that "there still lurks a relational character" in its "contents"; the latter's being still somehow *about* the "reality" that lies "outside" is "already tacitly implied . . . when one takes the phenomenon of knowing as one's theme" (*Supp* 163; *BT* 225/267, 61/88). Nevertheless, one can already sense why one might claim, as Heidegger infamously did, that "the idea of 'logic' itself disintegrates in the turbulence of a more original questioning" (*P* 92): such "questioning"—in which our "destructive" reasoning might play a part—focuses on the possibility that the meaning of the terms we use, and in which an "abundance" of supposedly positive "conclusions" might be deduced, may, for all that, be indeterminate.

So it may not be the case that, "if Heidegger did not assert anything, there is nothing to discuss either." But Philipse is certainly right to insist that "[i]t is up to the Heideggerians to explain what kind of speech acts Heidegger is performing" (Philipse 1998, 302). What kind of "speech acts" would then be appropriate were one to be combating philosophical confusion as section 2 understands it—that is, as a failure to bring to bear an understanding that we already possess? It seems apt to think of such a failure as a form of "forgetting," one that one might combat by—following Anscombe's translation—"assembling reminders" (*PI* §127). The motif of "forgetting" and "recollection" appears again and again in the early Heidegger, most obviously in the notion of *Seinsvergessenheit*; indeed Heidegger claims that "Being is what we recall" (*MFL* 146–47). But, of course, neither he nor Wittgenstein introduced this motif into philosophy, and an interesting discussion of it can be found in Heidegger's explorations of Plato's notion of *anamnesis*.

Heidegger sees in that notion a "mythologized" vision of a philosophy not dissimilar to that embodied in the notion of a "phenomenological reduction," a leading back—a re-duction—to the understanding on the basis of which we grasp entities: such "a re-seeing" (*PS* 231) is a "drawing back" to the understanding that is always prior to our encounter with entities, to that "which was already once and already earlier understood" but that is now "forgotten" (*BP* 326–27).[15]

In *The Sophist* lectures, Heidegger identifies the sophist as the target of Platonic dialectic and characterizes this target in ways that echo our earlier discussion. He proposes that "the dialectician and the philosopher . . . take that about which they speak seriously"—they focus on its "content"—whereas the sophist is "simply concerned with speech itself" (*PS* 150). Her "intention" is not to "conceal the matters at hand" or to "deceive"; rather she is "unconcerned with substantive content" (*PS* 159). Indeed Heidegger identifies "the activity of the sophists" with *Gerede*—"idle talk"—and the latter with an "adhere[nce] to what is said," one's being "caught up in words" that are themselves "empty" (*PS* 284, 171, 159). In such a condition, I lose "an original relation to the beings of which I am speaking" (*PS* 18).

The connection suggested here between philosophical confusion and in-authenticity is, of course, deeply thought-provoking, and, although I discuss it elsewhere (McManus forthcoming b, §§6.4, 8.5, and 9.2), I won't do so here. Instead my concern is with parallels with our foregoing discussion. Note, for example, how Heidegger believes we ought to engage with the sophist's "idle talk." A denial of the sophist's claims would be marked by the same "emptiness" that marks it; "we cannot at all speak against" the Sophist's "empty" words because "someone . . . who formulates this nega-tion . . . incurs the same difficulty": the difficulty "in a certain sense reverts back onto the one who intends to refute the sophist" (*PS* 291–92). Our foregoing discussion of the significance of argument also finds echoes:

> Dialectic is not the art of out-arguing another but has precisely the op-posite meaning, namely of bringing one's partner to open his eyes and see. (*PS* 138)
> [I]n the field of such fundamental considerations even the greatest display of scientificity, in the sense of proofs and arguments, fails. The only work to be performed here is that of opening the eyes of one's op-ponent. (*PS* 327)

This may sound a simple feat: what could be easier than "opening your eyes and seeing," or, to echo Wittgenstein, "looking and seeing" (*PI* §66)? But "most men do not possess" this "readiness to see" (*PS* 240) and two factors help explain why. Firstly, the "reminding" that dialectic strives to induce is "not given immediately to man, but instead . . . requires an overcoming of definite resistances residing in the very Being of man himself," in particular, a "peculiar self-satisfaction at adhering to what is idly spoken of" (*PS* 231, 136). Secondly, this tendency is one of which we are unaware: "[I]t is part of the very sense of *agnoia*"—the sophist's "forgetting"—"to believe that it already knows" (*PS* 260). Such forgetting is "not mere ignorance, mere unfamiliarity, but a positive presumption of knowledge" (*PS* 259), the pre-sumption, one might say, that one does not *need* to "open one's eyes"—or perhaps that one's eyes are *already* open.

So the dialectician's reminders are ones for which no one *asks*, not least because they remind us of what we do not realize we have forgotten. This gives us the beginnings of a way of understanding why the experience of reading texts that offer such reminders can be expected to be difficult. "[T]he comportment which needs to undergo the purification" that dialectic offers, "by its very sense, shuts itself off from . . . instruction by considering itself dispensed with the necessity of purification in the first place" (*PS* 260). We also see why such texts may need distinctive "speech acts" of their own. Having recognized the character of this *agnoia*, "the question arises con-cerning a *techne* which . . . would bring about [its] elimination" (*PS* 259). It "cannot be eliminated through the infusion of definite bits of knowledge"—"a definite stock of objective knowledge"; rather "a special kind of speaking

[is] necessary . . . in order to develop [the] readiness to see" that the sophist lacks (*PS* 259, 240). "No one will learn anything about a subject he . . . thinks he is already thoroughly familiar with" (*Sophist* 230a6–7, quoted at *PS* 260), so the sophist must be taken aback, so to speak; in her "peculiar self-satisfaction," the sophist "coasts along in words [*an den Worten entlang läuft*]" (*IPR* 8) and so must be *provoked* into "looking and seeing."

How is this done? What are the relevant "speech acts"? Heidegger describes Platonic dialectic as "presenting the things spoken of in a first intimation" or "indication," an "*Anzeige*" (*PS* 136). The following section will show that Heidegger seems to envisage the notion of "formal indication [*formale Anzeige*]" as targeting philosophical confusion understood very much in line with the account that section 2 set out, and as meeting the demands on dialectic that the present section set out.

4 COMBATING PHILOSOPHICAL CONFUSION: FORMAL INDICATION

According to Lafont, the principal legacy of Heidegger's discussion of "formal indication" is "a great deal of speculation" on commentators' parts about a notion he "never fully developed" (Lafont 2002, 231), while for Blattner, " 'formal indication' is merely a name for [a] problem, not a solution" (2007, 239). Even Kisiel, who makes much of the notion,[16] concedes that it is "esoteric" and "[n]ever thoroughly explained" (1993, 172, 497); and it is easy to doubt the prospects for such an explanation when one hears proposals such as that, through a formal indication, "the object [is] 'emptily' meant: and yet decisively!" (*PIA* 26). Indeed, our earlier discussion may seem to have exacerbated the difficulties associated with this "slippery notion" (Philipse 1998, 257), inviting a version of a familiar worry about Wittgenstein's early work. In response to "nonsensical" philosophical propositions, Wittgenstein offers "elucidations" that—he tells us—the reader who understands him will "finally recognize[] as nonsensical" too (*TLP* 6.54). But how do such "elucidations" differ from that which they combat? And how can more such nonsense help us? Similarly, in response to the "indeterminate emptiness" of confused philosophical propositions, Heidegger offers "formal"—"empty"—"indications." How do such "indications" differ from that which they combat? And how can more such "empty" words help us? We will take some steps toward answering these questions in this and the following sections.

None of Heidegger's discussions of formal indication can be described as clear, but some themes are clearly prominent.[17] Formal indications are meant to stop us in our tracks: they perform a "prohibiting (deterring, preventing)" role (*PIA* 105) in that they are meant to "hold in abeyance" the ways in which we have come to understand the entities toward which they point (*PRL* 44). As formal—that is, as possessing a certain emptiness—and as indications—as mere pointings—they draw our attention to how our reflection on the entities to which they refer us must arise out of a recovery of our own basic comportment toward them, "out of the mode *in which the object is originally accessible*" (*PIA* 17). As Heidegger says of the sophist, the problem here is "not mere ignorance, mere unfamiliarity" (*PS* 259). Instead, according to "the formally indicative definition of philosophy," what is at stake is the "appropriation" of "the basic sense of the factical situation of [our] comportment" toward entities (*PIA* 48). This must be "re-appropriated" if our reflection on entities no longer embodies determinate—or "concrete"—claims about them but instead an "ontologically indifferent" (*HCT* 216) "idle talk." By "fending off" or "keeping at arm's length" the ways in which we have "fallen" into understanding the entities to which it points, the very formality of these indications presses upon us "that concretion is not to be possessed . . . without further ado but that the concrete instead presents a task of its own kind," "the *appropriation of the concrete*" (*PIA* 26, 47).

In the light of section 2's account of philosophical confusion, we can see the appropriateness of formal indication for the job in hand; or more cautiously—and to echo Blattner—we can see what an apt name it provides for the problem of addressing such confusion. There may seem something comical about the claim that, through a formal indication, "the object [is] 'emptily' meant: and yet decisively!": such an "empty" remark would seem to leave the work of entertaining a thought half-finished—if that. But in judging it so, "we must not make illegitimate demands on the indication!" (*PIA* 26). Such indications cannot represent an "infusion of definite bits of knowledge" because any remark that did would *fail* as a formal indication: to use an expression of Brandom's (1994), "uptake" of formal indications takes quite a different form. Their formality and their serving merely to indicate draw attention to the *need* to "look and see" and are what makes them a proper response to philosophical confusion. Heidegger talks of the "necessarily limited way of achievement of the formally indicating" (*PIE* 57): such concepts "can only ever address the challenge of . . . a transformation to us, [and] can never bring about this transformation themselves" (*FCM* 296). But if philosophical confusion is a matter of failing to *appropriate* an understanding one already has, then an "infusion of definite bits of knowledge" is not what we need. Instead, in the demand that we "fill" the emptiness that these indications open up, we are to be provoked into setting to work an understanding we already have.[18]

Formal indications leave the reader much to do then because their purpose is precisely to get the reader to do something.[19] "[T]he whole thrust of the work serves to implicate the reader into . . . working through the matters under investigation" (*HCT* 26), and we cannot "simply pull out results" (*HCT* 26) from such formally indicative texts. In what is surely a related context—one in which "appropriation is the main point"—Kierkegaard insists that "results are nothing but junk with which we should not bother one another"; "appropriation" is a feat "which a result hampers" and "wanting to communicate results is an unnatural association of one person with another" ([1846] 1992, 79, 242). For Heidegger, such a desire betrays a misunderstanding of how the philosophically confused and enlightened differ.

5   CAN WE READ HEIDEGGER'S TEXTS IN THESE TERMS?

One might well still wonder, with Lafont, whether Heidegger ever "fully developed this view"; and the fact that Heidegger contemplated the foregoing metaphilosophical complexities leaves open the question of whether his writings really show the vision they express at work. As is often the case with metaphilosophical debates—and as the recent debate about the *Tractatus* illustrates well—it is one thing to argue on a priori grounds that a particular philosophical vision should be at work in a particular piece of philosophical writing and another to show that it really is. So is *Being and Time*, for example, *really* formally indicative?

A straightforward answer to this question is impossible for at least two reasons. Firstly, the "formal indicative" vision is very abstractly specified. Indeed, if Heidegger's own writings and Platonic dialogues, for example, both illustrate it at work, then it must be so.[20] Secondly, one finds in Heidegger's early philosophy an ongoing metaphilosophical rumination that does not obviously ever find resolution. So that philosophy and its self-understanding are very much moving targets. I have argued elsewhere, for example, that *Being and Time* reinterprets Heidegger's early ideas within a particular philosophical project that he formulated around 1925 and abandoned certainly by 1929 (McManus forthcoming b, §9.1; McManus unpublished).

This project imposes upon those early ideas a very particular metaphilosophical spin, in attempting to rehabilitate the notion of a "science of Being" on the basis of an (attempted) demonstration that time is "the possible horizon for any understanding of Being" (*BT* 1/19). The concept of "formal indication" has a distinctly low profile here; but Heidegger did insist, in a 1927 letter to Löwith regarding *Being and Time*, that "[f]ormal indication . . . is still for me there even though I do not talk about [it]."[21] I believe a case can be made for taking seriously the possibility that *Being and Time* might indeed fit the "formal indicative" vision as I have specified it—admittedly abstractly—earlier. The case focuses upon our *experience* of that work, of how we find it difficult, and—if that difficulty does not simply lead to us close the book—how we end up reacting to it: that vision, I will suggest, makes a particular kind of sense of that experience, that difficulty, and that reaction. The vision suggests one should encounter in a Heideggerian text a disorienting challenge to the ways in which we have come to understand ourselves and our world, one that drives us to reflect again on our basic experience of those phenomena. That, I think, is not a bad description of what *Being and Time* is and does.

If formal indications are to destabilize our "self-satisfaction at adhering to what is idly spoken of" and to provoke us into "looking and seeing," they must positively *resist* assimilation to "results"—to "definite bits of knowledge"—about the (actually indeterminate) subject matter of the words in which we have come to "coast along." There clearly is a sense in which we experience such "resistance" when we open *Being and Time*. For those of us who have been around that text for a long time, let's attempt to recall what first encountering it is like.[22]

One finds there an examination of something called "the Question of Being," of whose sense we are unsure and that Heidegger himself indeed tells us we have forgotten. This is followed by an analysis not of—say—consciousness or matter but of what Heidegger calls "the present-at-hand," "the ready-to-hand," and "Dasein." So an attempt to assimilate Heidegger's descriptions to a set of "results" faces the question, "Results about what?" Dasein? But what is that? Heidegger does, of course, explicate the perplexing notions he introduces but not in terms in which we are any more "at home." Dasein, for example, is "the entity that understands Being"; but that "understanding" isn't, for example, knowledge; and the concept of "Being," of course, is "the darkest of all" (*BT* 3/23). Similarly, Dasein is "Being-in-the-world"; but "the world" in question is not, say, everything that there is or the entirety of space; and the "being-in" in question is not a spatial relation; rather it is a form of "familiarity" (*BT* 54/80), although—again—not a form that might be understood as a form of knowledge.

And so on. In this way, *Being and Time*'s description of our lives refuses to bottom out, as it were, through definition in terms of familiar concepts or as answers to familiar philosophical questions. His notion of "knowing as a mode of Being-in," for example, "stands neither this side nor on the far side of idealism and realism, nor is it either one of the two positions": "[i]nstead it stands *wholly outside of an orientation to them and their ways of formulating questions*" (*HCT* 167).

But Heidegger's descriptions do not merely resist—prohibit (deter, prevent)—they also indicate. Heidegger tells us that each of us is *Dasein*—identifying *Dasein* indicatively or indexically as "us"—and that his discussion begins with a description of *our* everyday life; there we encounter the ready-to-hand, examples of which, he tells us, are tools. As we continue to read, we find ourselves trying to see to what it might be in our lives that these descriptions are pointing. We do so because Heidegger's formally indicative remarks do not merely resist. As Pöggeler puts it, they are not only "provocative" but also "evocative" (1991, 220).

In his recent introduction to Heidegger, Wrathall (2005, 10) writes, "Heidegger offers a phenomenological description of the entity that each of us is. In trying to understand his description, you should make constant reference to your own experience of who you are." The "formal indicative" vision suggests that this isn't just what we should do, but what we *have* to do: Heidegger's formulations don't offer up any ready sense—any "results"—that might spare us the trouble of such "reference." Wrathall (2005, 10) tells us that we must "check [Heidegger's] description against [our] own experience"; but as with other indicative or indexical expressions, we must turn to "our experience" not merely to check the accuracy of Heidegger's descriptions but also in an effort to determine just what they might be saying. Indeed, eliciting this kind of turning back to our experience may actually be the point of the exercise: not a necessary expedient if we are to understand "results" we take Heidegger to be proffering, but instead the response that his writings are attempting to provoke.[23]

To return to some earlier Wittgensteinian themes, one might see in Heidegger's remarks an invitation to *see* something, an invitation that—if accepted—could be described as a showing. We can also now see why Heidegger's offering of formal—"empty"—indications is not, after all, quite the incongruous response to philosophical propositions—themselves meant in an "indeterminate emptiness"—that it might seem to be. First of all, the indeterminacy of the sense of the former is apparent, whereas that of the latter is not: Heidegger's formal indications resist understanding—"a quite definite task for the understanding of [their] content" is set for us (*PIA* 26)—whereas it is characteristic of our philosophically confused claims that we believe we understand them when we do not.[24] We "presume" to understand this "idle talk" in which we "coast" and that we believe articulates determinate claims about our world "without further ado," whereas Heidegger's formal indications force upon us a need to "re-appropriate" our "original access" to our world. Such remarks are "formal" or "empty" in requiring us to ask ourselves which aspects of life they might connote and, in addressing that question, we must "look and see." Much as Heidegger characterizes "formally indicative" "philosophical definitions," a typical claim from *Being and Time*'s existential analytic "is not one whereby the object presents itself fully and properly": "[o]n the contrary, it is precisely the decisive *departure-situation* for the actualizing movement in the direction of the full appropriation of the object" (*PIA* 27; cf. also *FCM* 296–97).

We can then perhaps give Edwards just a little more credit as a recorder of the "phenomenology" of reading Heidegger. Heidegger may want not to sound esoteric but to *be* esoteric, to make things difficult for us because we no longer see a difficulty we are evading. Heidegger's descriptions represent obstacles he deliberately places in our way but with a view to getting us to do something we don't realize needs doing. Heidegger wants to induce in us a "readiness" to "look and see," a "readiness" that "most men do not possess." Instead we are "caught up in words," without "an original relation to the beings of which [we are] speaking"; we are victims of a forgetting of which we are unaware, a forgetting "part of the very sense" of which is "to believe that [one] already knows"—that we already are "looking and seeing." A different kind of "*techne*"—other than the "infusion" of "a definite stock of objective knowledge"—is required if we are to be driven out of this "positive presumption of knowledge"—"a special kind of speaking," a distinctive kind of "speech act."

6   FURTHER QUESTIONS

Clearly much more needs to be said about this distinctive "*techne.*" The previous section may have encouraged the thought *that* Heidegger's descriptions do indeed deliberately resist—deter, prevent—and may also have given some feel for *how* they might do so. *That* Heidegger's descriptions are indicative—evocative—is also plausible, I think, but it is less than clear *how*. There is obviously something fanciful about the notion that a text like *Being and Time simply* points, such that one might expect all of its component sentences to instantiate a single—"indicative"—kind of "speech act." The case I have made here is better seen as a case for thinking of such a text as a whole as formally indicative, with its "indicative" work being done partly *through*, for instance, the kind of "destructive" reasoning that section 3 discussed, and through what are recognizably descriptions of our experience, though ones the purpose of which is to induce us to "look and see."[25] Such complications may mean that the motif of "formal indication" cannot generate a reading of Heidegger's texts all by itself, so to speak; but one might not think that Wittgenstein's comments on "assembling reminders" and—following Anscombe again—constructing "perspicuous representations" can—all by themselves—generate a reading of his, while still thinking that those comments tell us something important about those texts.[26]

What I have provided here is no more than a sketch of how an "indicative" power might be seen at work in *Being and Time*, and of a need that such a text might then be seen to meet. In filling out that sketch, we will surely need to explore, for example, what one might call the "literary qualities" of Heidegger's texts. I have in mind, among other things, Heidegger's "strange new language game of prepositional and adverbial schematisms" (Kisiel 1994, 178–79)—of the *Wovor*, the *Worumwillen*, and the *Woraufhin*—and the way in which he adapts words from ordinary usage and sets them to work in unprecedented ways in what is also clearly philosophically motivated reflection. Such co-opted terms make up much of the fabric of *Being and Time*: they include "care," "concern," "conscience," "guilt," "projection," "resolution," and indeed "Dasein" itself, its mundane origins hidden from the Anglophone reader by the (understandable) decision often made to leave this term untranslated. In what is, in our present context, a striking choice of words, Heidegger claims to "formalize" such terms (*BT* 283/328). But they manifestly are meant to bring—in some way or other—some of their original resonances with them: they are not "thought up arbitrarily" (*BT* 281/326), such that an "*x*" or a "*y*" might substitute for "conscience" or for "care." So this is surely among the places where one might begin to think about how such texts—and such terms—might be meant to be "indicative" or "evocative."

In doing so, we will also, of course, begin to think about how such thinking might possess a form of rigor—about why some would-be formal indications "mean" their objects "decisively," whereas others might fail.[27] This raises further and more pointed questions: do *Heidegger's* texts—understood as formally indicative—actually work? Is his particular *"techne"* the best way to do such work? To introduce one possible limitation, Wittgenstein once expressed the worry, "The seed I'm most likely to sow is a certain jargon" (*LFM* 293), a new set of words in which one might "coast." But that danger is surely more pressing still in Heidegger's case, as he would seem to have acknowledged when he reprimanded a student by saying, "There will be no heideggerizing here! We want to get at the topic!" (quoted in van Buren 1994b, 45).

So we see many difficult questions arising here; in closing, I will pose just one more: how might the issues discussed have worked themselves out in the later Wittgenstein's mode of writing? Might his "perverse" "lack of concern" to spell out what we might think of as "his results"—and the arguments that we assume are meant to support them—reflect a misunderstanding on our part of the kind of work his writings are meant to accomplish? His texts are not full of unfamiliar technicalities; their difficulty lies more in understanding the *significance* of the various "speech acts" we encounter there: the descriptions of ordinary use, the dialogues, the questions addressed to the reader and invitations to reflect on what one would say if . . . or to imagine that. . . . Might such a mode of writing exemplify a *"techne"* quite other than the "infusion" of "objective knowledge," a "special kind of speaking" that seeks to disorient those who "coast along in words" and elicit in them a "readiness" to "look and see"? The very peculiarity of Wittgenstein's texts encourages such cautious thoughts, and my concern here has been to suggest that we might profitably take the apparent "perversity" of Heidegger's texts in the same spirit.[28]

NOTES

1. Cf. Warburton on the perception of *Being and Time* as "a deliberately obscure piece of writing" (2011, 210).
2. I use the Ogden translation of *TLP* throughout.
3. Cf. Dahlstrom (2001). Blattner (2007) and Lafont (2002, 233) raise related worries.
4. Cf. Cooper (2002) and Witherspoon (2002). As we will see, also relevant here is Minar's discussion of "Heideggerian reminders" (2001, 209).
5. Kisiel sees "formal indication" as "the 'secret weapon' in Heidegger's methodological armoury" (1994, 178), providing a "nonobjectifying understanding" of "the full immediacy of human experience" and yielding "a philosophy that is more a form of life on the edge of expression than a science" (1993, 376, 455, 59).
6. See McManus 2007 (forthcoming b; forthcoming c, esp. n. 36).
7. See McManus (forthcoming b, chap. 4 and 8) and Schear (2007). There is a truth in passages that suggest that formal indications are specifically designed to prevent our understanding entities solely as present-at-hand (see, e.g., *FCM* 297). But chapter 8 of McManus (forthcoming b) argues that it is a truth consistent with the broader view I present here.

8. For further documentation of Heidegger's extensive use of such terms of criticism, see McManus (forthcoming b, chap. 9 n. 15).

9. McManus (forthcoming a) argues that "resolute" readers of the *Tractatus* share this view, despite their being sometimes drawn to the rhetorical insistence that nonsense "is only ever sheer lack of sense" (Conant and Dain 2011, 72).

10. McManus (2006) shows that this idea also plays a central—if slightly different— role in Wittgenstein's early thought.

11. For further discussion of the issues raised in this paragraph, see McManus (forthcoming b, chap. 8; forthcoming d).

12. Reported in Putnam (2001, 176). Similarly, I believe that there are no Cartesian— and, hence, un-Wittgensteinian—implications in Heidegger's call for "a return" to "original" or "basic experience" (*PRL* 50, *PIA* 16).

13. This is a theme in Phillips (1999) (e.g., pp. 8, 24–25, 41–42) and a truth in Hacker's insistence that "the negation of a nonsense is a nonsense" (1990, 55), which I have seen leave some philosophers unmoved.

14. McManus (2006) and McManus (forthcoming a) defend such an understanding of what it is overwhelmingly natural to call the "reasoning" that one finds in the *Tractatus*.

15. My concern here is not with how faithful an account this provides of Plato's thought but with how Heidegger was drawn to understand that thought.

16. Cf. n. 5.

17. See, for example, *PRL* 36–45; *PIA* 25–28, 87, 104–6; *FCM* 291–300; *PIE* 21, 47, 57, 59, 65, 77; *LQT* 234, 410–11; and *PM* 52, and for further useful documentation, Kisiel (1993) and van Buren (1994b). Discussions of this notion that I have found useful are Crowell (2001, chap. 7); Dahlstrom (1994; 2001); and Streeter (1997).

18. As Streeter nicely puts it, such responses are possible only "if they are left enough formal space" (1997, 427).

19. Hence, Dahsltrom is right to claim that such an indication is "not so much a statement . . . as it is a score or script to be performed" (1994, 790). Cf. Crowell (2001, 141); Grondin (1994, 353); Lafont (2002, 231); Streeter (1997, 413); and *PIA* 100 on "[l]eaving the retracing to the individual." One also might hear an echo of a remark of Wittgenstein's that Rhees reports: "I don't try to make you *believe* something you *don't* believe, but to make you *do* something you won't do" (Rhees 1970, 43). (I'd like to thank David Egan for reminding me of this remark.)

20. Note 26 suggests that the latitude that this abstraction leaves open mirrors disagreements in discussions of Wittgenstein over quite what his own project— of "reminding" us of the "life" behind our words—involves.

21. Quoted in Kisiel (1993, 19). Although sometimes hidden by Macquarrie and Robinson's translation, talk of "formal indication" can be found in *Being and Time* at, for example, *BT* 114/150, 116/152, 117/152, 231/274, 313/361, and 315/362.

22. Thomson appears to have forgotten—and, from my perspective, may be missing an interesting possible continuity in Heidegger's work as a result—when he claims that it is "the distinguishing feature of the later Heidegger's 'poetic' style . . . that, after *Being and Time*, he is no longer content simply to construct arguments in relatively straightforward philosophical prose, but also begins to try to lead his audience performatively to see the phenomenon ultimately at issue for themselves" (Thomson 2011, §3.2).

23. The reading of Heidegger that McManus (forthcoming b) presents could be seen as illustrating such a response. See chap. 6 in particular.

24. See Dahlstrom on Heidegger's philosophy "stand[ing] in conflict with the easy confidence that words in their customary usage are reliable"—that "we generally know what we are talking about" (1994, 785)—and representing "a

warning that genuine access to what [our words] point to is not at all common" (2001, 249).

25. Heidegger's descriptions being "empty" in the relevant sense does not deny them meaning—potentially including descriptive meaning—any more than the recognizable "emptiness" of "I," "here," and "now" does; and "pointing out [*Aufzeigen*]" plays a noteworthy role in Heidegger's more general account of assertion (*BT* 154/196). (On both of these issues, see Streeter 1997, §3.) But the latter, of course, complicates any story that might be told about formally indicative descriptions having a *distinctive* power.

26. Another crucial question is: isn't Heidegger more of a "constructive" philosopher than the above discussion suggests? Even if his texts do induce us to look back at our experience, isn't that merely a step to something further—our formulation of a correct ontological theory or a new "grammar" through which one might "grasp entities in their Being" (*BT* 39/63)? These are difficult issues that I can't resolve here, although I have taken some initial steps elsewhere (see §4 of McManus 2008 and §9.2 of McManus forthcoming b). What I think is worth noting here—given our present concerns—is that readings of Wittgenstein's own work raise much the same issues. See, for example, Hacker's account of the "*positive* task" of "logical geography" (Hacker 2007, 100), which he believes is overlooked in Baker's "*exclusively* therapeutic" Wittgenstein (Baker 2004, 152), and related debates over whether the early Wittgenstein "resolutely" rejected the "positive" task of intimating ineffable metaphysical truths, and over quite how purely "destructive" such a rejection would be. (On the latter, see, for example, Goldfarb 2011 and McManus forthcoming a.) Dahlstrom's Wittgensteinian Heidegger might be seen as ineffabilist, Moore's only in a nuanced sense, while Witherspoon (2002) is very much "resolute." The fact that we find these parallel issues might be seen as providing some support for this chapter's comparative thesis, but it also, of course, highlights its level of abstraction.

27. Both before and after *Being and Time*, Heidegger distinguishes the rigor of philosophy from that of science (see, for example, *TDP* 93 and *Basic* 235) and Julian Young proposes that "the ground" from which "the later (*and even, to a degree, the earlier*) Heideggerian texts" "spring lies . . . in poetic vision" (Young 2002, 21; italics added). Support for that thought might be found in Heidegger's characterization of " 'poetical' discourse" as a "disclosing of existence" (*BT* 162/205); but, as my comments on argument suggest, the story here is bound to be complex.

28. For helpful comments on material on which this chapter is based, I would like to thank Anthony Beavers, Katalin Farkas, Simon Glendinning, Paul Lodge, Stephen Mulhall, Herman Philipse, Joseph Schear, Tom Sorell, Andreas Vrahimis, Dan Zahavi, and, in particular, David Egan, Stephen Reynolds, Aaron Ridley, Aaron James Wendland, and Daniel Whiting. In addition, my work has benefited from the comments of members of the audiences at *The Cartesian "Myth of the Ego" and the Analytic/Continental Divide* conference, held at the University of Nijmegen, September 2010, and the *Wittgenstein and Heidegger* workshop, held at Christ Church, Oxford, May 2012. I would also like to thank the University of Southampton and the Arts and Humanities Research Council for periods of research leave during which work on which this chapter is based was done.

5   The Authenticity of the Ordinary

David Egan

1   INTRODUCTION

One of the most salient and original features of Wittgenstein's later philosophy is the appeal it makes to ordinary language: "What *we* do is to bring
words back from their metaphysical to their everyday use" (*PI* §116). This
appeal situates our language and concepts within the broader forms of life
in which we use them so as to dispel certain idealizations that creep into our
thinking. For instance, Wittgenstein links our use of the word "understanding" to the broader patterns of behavior into which it fits—the circumstances
in which we say we or someone else has understood, when we withhold
ascribing understanding, what sorts of sufficiently bizarre outcomes could
upset our normal use of the word, and so on—to clarify the criteria for using
the word. One result of his investigation is that "understanding" cannot denote a distinct inner state or process because the criteria for using the word
connect essentially with outward behavior (see *PI* §§138–55). Wittgenstein
insists that his investigation does not rely on explanations or discoveries but
simply on describing what we already know: "All *explanation* must disappear, and description alone must take its place" (*PI* §109).[1] Wittgenstein
aims to dissolve philosophical confusion not by telling us anything new but
by drawing our attention to features of our ordinary use of words that we
have overlooked or forgotten. This appeal to ordinary language is innovative precisely in its recognition that such reminders can be philosophically
fruitful at all, and that what is open to view may still elude us. We miss certain simple but crucial facts precisely because they are so obvious.[2]

Avrum Stroll (2002, 104) claims that Wittgenstein is the first philosopher
to recognize that reminders of ordinary and obvious facts can have powerful
and less-than-obvious philosophical consequences. However, Stroll seems
to have forgotten about Heidegger. Heidegger's phenomenology, much like
Wittgenstein's appeal to ordinary language, finds insight in drawing our attention to things we have passed over because they are already so familiar.
For Heidegger, the entities that are most familiar to us are the ones whose
significance is the most difficult to assess: "That which is ontically closest
and well known, is ontologically the farthest and not known at all; and

its ontological signification is constantly overlooked" (*BT* 43/69). Stroll's oversight is at least somewhat understandable. Not only does Heidegger write in a tradition that is remote from and opaque to many of the scholars interested in Wittgenstein, but also both his style and ambitions seem impossibly remote from anything we might recognize as "ordinary language." Nevertheless, the similarities between Heidegger and Wittgenstein are striking, the more so for the lack of contact or shared influence between them.

Within Heidegger scholarship, comparisons with Wittgenstein have found a certain currency in developing the normative and socially constituted aspects of Heidegger's analytic of Dasein.[3] My aim here is to extend that comparison in the opposite direction. Rather than ask how Wittgenstein informs our reading of Heidegger, I will investigate how Heidegger informs our reading of Wittgenstein. In particular, I will claim that extending the parallels between Heidegger and Wittgenstein allows us to unearth something like a Heideggerian appeal to authenticity in Wittgenstein's appeal to ordinary language.

Such an exercise amounts to more than adding to the list of similarities other authors have found between Wittgenstein and Heidegger. Rather, it constitutes a step toward clarifying what might be described as the moral fervor of Wittgenstein's work. On one hand, Wittgenstein has little to say about ethics and is dismissive of saying anything of much use about it. On the other hand, his writing carries a rare moral intensity, which only occasionally comes to the surface.[4] Drawing out the quasi-ethical import of Wittgenstein's appeal to ordinary language through its connection to Heideggerian authenticity clarifies the nature of this moral intensity.

I begin by sketching Heidegger's conception of the shared world of Being-with and *das Man* in *Being and Time* (section 2) before exploring how Wittgenstein helps us flesh out that shared world (section 3). Heidegger finds a too-ready absorption in this shared world to be a signal feature of inauthenticity, raising the question of whether Wittgenstein's emphasis on the ordinary betrays a flight into inauthenticity. But far from insisting on the unshakeability of our ordinary practices, I claim Wittgenstein emphasizes their ungroundedness (section 4). This emphasis on ungroundedness allows me to trace the moments in Wittgenstein's appeal to ordinary language that parallel Heidegger's description of anxiety, the uncanniness that it discloses, and the authenticity of owning up to this uncanniness (section 5).

2   DASEIN AS BEING-WITH

Of all Heidegger's coinages, the best known—*Dasein*—is not in fact a neologism. It is also one of the most likely to go untranslated in discussions of Heidegger. Literally rendered as "being there," it is most commonly translated in non-Heideggerian contexts as "existence," though here it differs from *Existenz* in referring not so much to the bare fact of being but rather to the mode or quality in which something or someone exists. I might assert the *Existenz* of a paternal aunt, but then talk about the misery of her *Dasein* and how I might alleviate it.

Heidegger picks up on this qualitative aspect of *Dasein* in yoking it to his phenomenological project, which places the lived quality of existence before abstract theorizing. Heidegger first introduces the term, saying that he will use it to describe "[t]his being which each of us is himself and which includes inquiring as one of the possibilities of its Being" (*BT* 7/27). Dasein is different from other entities in that its being can be an issue for it: rocks simply are, whereas Dasein always takes a stance on who it is, what it has been, and what it will become—even if it never formulates this stance explicitly—and it can inquire about its own being. Dasein is not simply just another entity to be encountered in the world, but is rather the being to whom all these entities are intelligible and matter. Heidegger calls Dasein a "clearing" (*BT* 133/171) because entities become intelligible as entities only within the space opened up by Dasein.

Heidegger's starting point, which constitutes the first division of *Being and Time*, is the analytic of Dasein in its average everydayness: he seeks to grasp Dasein's ordinary self-understanding.[5] The self-understanding that interests Heidegger is not the thematic self-understanding of human existence that we find in the work of philosophers, but the pre-theoretical understanding with which Dasein engages in the world proximally and for the most part.[6] Before giving any explicit answer as to how it understands itself and its world, Dasein already gives an implicit answer in its practical engagement with the world. Heidegger characterizes Dasein as Being-in-the-world: he begins, that is, by considering Dasein as embedded in and engaged with its world rather than considering it from a position of detached contemplation. "Sciences are ways of Being in which Dasein comports itself towards entities which it need not be itself. But to Dasein, Being in a world is something that belongs essentially" (*BT* 13/32). Our everyday comportment already presupposes the intelligibility of the world we engage in, and Heidegger investigates this basic intelligibility by examining Dasein in its "average everydayness" (*BT* 43/69). In other words, like Wittgenstein, Heidegger begins with the ordinary.

To understand how this everydayness can be "average"—and to consider the possibility of a non-average everydayness—we must come to grips with a crucial feature of Heidegger's analytic of Dasein: the fact that we are not Dasein alone but exist essentially in this world *with* others. We encounter other people proximally and for the most part as Dasein, and not as the sealed-off enigmas that the problematic of skepticism about other minds presents to us. The engaged world of everydayness finds us acting with and upon tools that were equally made for, and could equally be used by, other people like ourselves. And, more importantly, our own sense of who and what we are is shaped by our engaging with others whom we deem to be our fellows.[7]

Heidegger finds the traditional conception of the self as an isolated consciousness inadequate because Dasein comes into its Dasein-hood as Being-with-one-another: the "who" of everyday Dasein is not the isolated individual but the individual constituted by social norms. Being-with is a necessary and structural feature of Dasein—an existentiale in Heidegger's jargon—because it is a condition for the possibility of Dasein's articulated, intelligible world. Each of us makes sense of the world in our own way, but the very notion of making sense of the world in the first place and the concepts with which we make sense of the world are things we articulate together.

If Being-with is a constitutive feature of Dasein's existence, then Dasein's existence is largely constituted by features that are not uniquely its own. One feature of tools' readiness-to-hand is that they are ready-to-hand for others as well. A shoe is a shoe only if anyone with the same sized foot can wear it. My shoes are available to me *as* shoes only insofar as they are available as shoes to others as well. This promiscuous availability is part of what makes a shoe a shoe: it is available to many people indiscriminately because there is a way that *one wears shoes* that applies across the board. As Being-with, Dasein is constituted by a wide range of norms that dictate what *one* does, which Heidegger calls *das Man*.[8] *Das Man* does not simply articulate the norms according to which one wears shoes, but renders shoes intelligible as shoes in the first place: without these norms, shoes would not show up to us as shoes but as unintelligible assemblages of leather, canvas, and rubber. *Das Man* is not an individual, nor a group, but it "Articulates the referential context of significance" (*BT* 129/167). By highlighting the existential role of Being-with and *das Man*, Heidegger emphasizes that the intelligibility of Dasein's world involves sharing and shaping this intelligibility in concert with others. This claim is stronger than simply saying that I am inevitably a creature of my times. I am not simply *of* my times, but in an important sense, I *am* my times: the social norms of my milieu are a constitutive feature of who I am, even if I react against them. We might say that Heidegger has an externalist conception of the self.[9]

3 WITTGENSTEIN'S ATTUNEMENT AND *DAS MAN*

Hubert Dreyfus and others have found in Wittgenstein a valuable resource for fleshing out the nature of *das Man*, a concept about which Heidegger makes unclear and sometimes conflicting remarks. Just as Heidegger finds the shared nature of intelligibility a crucial and overlooked aspect of our everyday engagement with the world, Wittgenstein's appeal to ordinary language draws on the overlooked significance of our sharing our language and forms of life with others. In drawing out the shared practices of our common world, Heidegger focuses primarily on the readiness-to-hand of tools, but much of what he says about tools applies to language as well.[10]

First, language operates as part of a holistic network in which words take on significance in the way that they relate to and play off other words, and the various roles that they serve in human practices. Second, we usually use language unreflectively and transparently, thinking about what we want to say and not about the (upon reflection, quite mysterious) fact that these sounds or symbols manage to express anything at all. Third, the workings of language come to our attention only when we are not operating smoothly within language: we are far more conscious of the grammar of a language we speak poorly, for instance, because expressing ourselves in that language requires deliberation that draws our attention from what we want to say to the language itself. And last, we relate to language differently when we step back from it to examine it rather than use it transparently as a tool.

Communication essentially involves agreement in how we use words. For Wittgenstein, however, the agreement goes far deeper than simply the definitions of words. "It is not only agreement in definitions, but also (odd as it may sound) agreement in judgements that is required for communication by means of language," he writes (*PI* §242). We are able to communicate only because we already agree on a vast raft of matters that underwrite that communication. The "agreement" Wittgenstein speaks of here is *Überein-stimmung*, in contrast with *Einverständnis*: not agreement in the sense of a negotiated settlement, but agreement in the sense of a pre-reflective accord. We do not sit down over a negotiating table and choose what judgments we will reach agreement on, but, rather, we are able to sit down at a negotiating table at all because we already find ourselves in sufficient agreement that we are able to make sense to one another. In *On Certainty*, Wittgenstein discusses propositions like "The earth has existed for a long time," which have the form of empirical propositions, but play a role more akin to logical propositions: they are not themselves subject to doubt, but are the basis of agreement upon which other matters can be doubted, discussed, investigated, and so on. "We know, with the same certainty with which we believe *any* mathematical proposition, how the letters A and B are pronounced, what the colour of human blood is called, that other human beings have blood and call it 'blood'" (*OC* §340). Wittgenstein famously likens such propositions to hinges, writing: "If I want the door to turn, the hinges must stay put" (*OC* §343).

Wittgenstein recognizes that this emphasis on agreement can be mistaken for a dogmatic refusal to consider certain questions: "'So you are saying that human agreement decides what is true and what is false?'—What is true or false is what human beings *say*; and it is in their *language* that human beings agree. This is agreement not in opinions, but rather in form of life" (*PI* §241). Agreeing in forms of life means sharing at least enough common ground that our lives are intelligible to one another, such that communication, understanding, and learning are so much as possible between us. That we can exchange opinions at all, whether to agree or disagree, means we already share enough in common that we recognize each other's opinions as opinions, and share a sense of what it means to have an opinion, to form one, to shift one, and so on.

Stanley Cavell calls this kind of agreement "attunement":[11] what I say not only reaches you but also resonates in you. In an oft-cited passage, Cavell elaborates on this attunement as

> a matter of our sharing routes of interest and feeling, modes of response, senses of humour and of significance and of fulfilment, of what is outrageous, of what is similar to what else, what a rebuke, what forgiveness, of when an utterance is an assertion, when an appeal, when an explanation—all the whirl of organism Wittgenstein calls "forms of life." (Cavell 1976, 52)

This Wittgensteinian conception of attunement helps to flesh out the nature of the shared intelligibility of Heidegger's Being-with. Wittgenstein provides a detailed exploration of Heidegger's insight that sharing a world with others involves not just sharing a common language and tools but attunement on a deeper level of overall orientation and comportment. We share language and tools because we also share a sense of what is worth saying, what sorts of projects are worth pursuing, and how one goes about pursuing them.

Wittgenstein articulates the conformity of our general comportment, but Heidegger finds in *das Man* something more insidious than attunement.[12] Heidegger notes our tendency to conform with what *one does*, not because one has decided to do things this way, but simply because this is how things *are done*. The passive voice is revealing here: we accord ourselves with *das Man* passively, rather than actively choosing our own course. In our average everydayness, Heidegger suggests, we accord ourselves with *das Man* unthinkingly, allowing our actions and opinions to be dictated to us by what *one* does or thinks, stifling our own agency in the matter. This accord with *das Man* enables a great cover-up whereby we present our forms of life to ourselves as binding and necessary. In according ourselves with what *one does*, we do not simply choose not to find our own way of doing things, but we avoid acknowledging that there is even a choice there to be made. This cover-up is the keystone of what Heidegger characterizes as inauthentic existence.[13]

Dreyfus suggests that Heidegger's discussion of *das Man* fails to distinguish between conformity and conformism (see Dreyfus 1991, 154). Talking about the "dictatorship" of *das Man*, Heidegger describes the conformism it induces: "We take pleasure and enjoy ourselves as *one* takes pleasure; we read, see, and judge about literature and art as *one* sees and judges; likewise we shrink back from the 'great mass' as *one* shrinks back; we find 'shocking' what *one* finds shocking" (*BT* 126–27/164; translation modified). The sorts of judgments that involve conforming to the popular views on literature and art are a far cry from the sorts of judgments on whose agreement Wittgenstein takes us to conform. The latter kinds of agreement are what make discourse possible at all; the former are the sorts of matters over which we can debate, agree, and disagree because of the fundamental agreements of the latter kind. To use Wittgensteinian language, we might wonder whether Heidegger has confused the agreement of *Einverständnis* with the agreement of *Übereinstimmung*.

How best to make sense of Heidegger on *das Man* is a fraught issue, one not helped by inconsistencies in Heidegger's text, and I will not pursue this issue here.[14] Instead, I want to turn the spotlight on Wittgenstein and ask whether Heidegger notices an important aspect of our attunement that Wittgenstein misses. In his discussion of *das Man*, Heidegger identifies in our conformity to public norms an existential tendency toward conformism. We accord ourselves unthinkingly with public norms, and although this tendency might be a lifesaver when it comes to driving conventions, it shades over into the sort of groupthink that suppresses the possibility of an authentic existence. In emphasizing our attunement without remarking on the coercive nature of this attunement, a Heideggerian might suggest, Wittgenstein does not acknowledge the possibility of authenticity. Wittgenstein's appeal to ordinary language, it may seem, amounts to an appeal to inauthentic absorption in *das Man*. Indeed, Wittgensteinian comparisons with Heidegger tend to focus on Division I of *Being and Time*, where Heidegger analyzes Dasein only in its average everydayness. Only in Division II does Heidegger fully explore the possibility of authentic existence, and comparisons with Wittgenstein seem to run dry at this point.

Answering this challenge requires that we extend the comparison between Wittgenstein and Heidegger to include Heidegger's account of authenticity. Doing so uncovers an important aspect of Wittgenstein's later philosophy that might go unnoticed in the absence of this challenge. Wittgenstein not only emphasizes our attunement but also emphasizes the ungroundedness of this attunement. I will develop this point in the next section, and connect it to Heidegger's conception of authenticity in the one that follows.

4   THE UNGROUNDEDNESS OF ATTUNEMENT

The importance of shared practices and forms of life features prominently in the secondary literature on Wittgenstein, but the importance of there being nothing to guarantee these shared practices and forms of life receives less attention. For the most part, commentators on Wittgenstein take our attunement as a given, and explore the consequences of this given being a necessary condition for the possibility of communication, or as constitutive of a community. The most notable exception to this rule is Stanley Cavell, whose reading of Wittgenstein informs much of what follows.

Wittgenstein encourages us to examine language in the context of the broader life of which it is a part: "[T]o imagine a language means to imagine a form of life" (*PI* §19). Wittgenstein often uses the metaphor of a mechanism to show how our words and concepts are interconnected:[15] we understand a part of a larger whole by considering how it connects to other parts, and what these parts accomplish in moving together. Grasping the use of a word involves understanding the forms of life in which it finds application. This point may be clearer in the case of "judgment" or "understanding" than in the case of "cat" or "tree," but it applies generally. Examples involving chairs recur throughout the *Investigations*,[16] with Wittgenstein showing how this mundane concept relates to various other concepts—like sameness, simple/composite, belief, and so on—such that its use is embedded in our broader life with words.

If understanding a word also means understanding the forms of life in which it finds application, learning language is also a process of acculturation, where we are inducted into the forms of life that involve language. Wittgenstein shows a deep interest in what Cavell calls "the scene of instruction," where an act of teaching or learning takes place.[17] The *Investigations* open with St. Augustine's account of how he learned language, which treats language learning as primarily an activity of attaching names to things. Wittgenstein finds this account inadequate because it assumes that language learning is simply a matter of finding the right words to give voice to a thinking that is already in place (*PI* §32). Augustine's scenario imagines the pre-linguistic child as already sharing its elders' forms of life, so that all it must learn are the names attached to various things and practices, all the while presupposing a ready familiarity with these things and practices. By contrast, Wittgenstein emphasizes that we learn language together with the forms of life of which language is a part: in learning language, children do not simply learn to attach labels to things but also learn the things along with the labels. Cavell elaborates on this point in discussing Wittgenstein's vision of language:

> In "learning language" you learn not merely what the names of things
> are, but what a name is; not merely what the form of expression is for
> expressing a wish, but what expressing a wish is; not merely what the
> word for "father" is, but what a father is; not merely what the word
> for "love" is, but what love is. In learning language, you do not merely
> learn the pronunciation of sounds, and their grammatical orders, but
> the "forms of life" which make those sounds the words they are, do
> what they do—e.g., name, call, point, express a wish or affection, indi-
> cate a choice or an aversion, etc. (Cavell 1979, 177–78)

In Wittgenstein's view, learning what a thing is called also involves learning what that thing *is*.

Instruction depends crucially on attunement between the teacher and the learner. Most learning takes place within a framework that the learner already shares with the teacher. High school mathematics, for instance, follows a linear progression because topics build on one another successively. Students need a foundation in coordinate geometry before they learn trigonometry, and a teacher inducts students into the principles of trigonometry by drawing on that shared framework of coordinate geometry. The shared framework need not be so academically oriented: to teach someone to give and obey orders, the teacher and learner need to share a language, a sense of what a task is and why it is worth accomplishing, of teamwork, and so on (or we might manage to teach someone *this* set of commands because we already share a sense of what a command in general is, how it is taught, obeyed, and so on).

As the example of mathematics illustrates, what we learn can become the shared framework for further learning: trigonometry builds on the framework supplied by coordinate geometry, which in turn builds upon the framework supplied by Euclidean geometry, algebra, and the Cartesian coordinate system, and these frameworks in turn build upon more elementary frameworks, and so on down. But how far down? How, for instance, can we speak of learning the activity of learning without circularity? Eventually our ability to learn from or with one another reaches bedrock. Ultimately, our ability to learn from one another is a manifestation of our basic attunement, which is not itself something we can teach, and without which no teaching or learning would take place. The importance of attunement to understanding—and the fact that this attunement is not grounded in anything deeper than itself—is the central lesson of the parable of the wayward pupil, which motivates much of Wittgenstein's discussion of rule following:

> Then we get the pupil to continue one series (say "+2") beyond 1000—and he writes 1000, 1004, 1008, 1012.
> We say to him, "Look what you're doing!"—He doesn't understand. We say, "You should have added *two*: look how you began the series!"—He answers, "Yes, isn't it right? I thought that was how I *had* to do it."—Or suppose he pointed to the series and said, "But I did go on in the same way."—It would now be no use to say, "But can't you see . . . ?"—and go over the old explanations and examples for him again. (*PI* §185)

The scenario of trying to teach the wayward pupil reveals how quickly our explanations come to an end with a practice like basic arithmetic, and hence reveals the nature of the agreement that our mathematical practices presuppose. If you don't understand this, there is no deeper level of agreement I can appeal to in order to bring you back onside; if you don't understand this, I have no idea where I stand with you, I have no sense of what you might agree to. You are an enigma to me.

Wittgenstein's later work is peppered with bizarre parables like that of the wayward pupil, where things take a turn for the unexpected: we encounter a disappearing chair (*PI* §80), a growing and shrinking lump of cheese

(*PI* §142), a talking lion (*PPF* xi §327), and many, many more. Each parable serves its own particular purpose, of course, but a common thread is that each challenges our assumption that the forms of life that we inhabit are in some way fixed or absolute. Wittgenstein claims that his interest in the scene of instruction is not based in hypothetical speculations about the psychology of concept formation—he is not making an anti-Chomskian point against the innateness of our conceptual categories—but rather in revealing the logical relation between our concepts and our forms of life:

> I am not saying: if such-and-such facts of nature were different, people would have different concepts (in the sense of a hypothesis). Rather: if anyone believes that certain concepts are absolutely the correct ones, and that having different ones would mean not realizing something that we realize—then let him imagine certain very general facts of nature to be different from what we are used to, and the formation of concepts different from the usual ones will become intelligible to him. (*PPF* xii §366)

By exploring worlds where the facts are different than what they are, and where our common understanding fails us, Wittgenstein repeatedly emphasizes the ungroundedness of our attunement.

Wittgenstein wants us to recognize the importance of attunement, but he also wants us to be struck by just how remarkable it is that we are indeed mutually attuned. Enigmas like the wayward pupil bring this reminder into sharp relief. We could be enigmas to one another—we sometimes are—and if this were the rule rather than the painful exception, we would not share the forms of life that we do. If we could never be certain that others add as we do, we would not use addition in the ways that we do. The process of acculturation by which we come in to language and shared forms of life presupposes a basic attunement that is not itself taught or learned; indeed, our ability to teach and learn is one manifestation of this attunement. That for the most part we are sufficiently attuned that we make sense to others and they to us is essential to our being able to share a language and forms of life, but nothing guarantees this attunement. Throughout the *Investigations*, Wittgenstein seeks to undermine precisely the mind-set that assumes or insists that our attunement is justified by independent standards of correctness. On the contrary, the very practice of justification is one manifestation of our attunement. For me to be able to justify anything to you, we must already share enough common ground that you have a similar sense of what a justification is, how it works, and what sorts of things stand in need of what kinds of justification.

Wittgenstein explores the regularity of our attunement by considering how we teach, learn, and apply rules. Considering a rule on analogy with a signpost, he asks how the signpost tells us which way to go, considering the possibility that we could interpret an arrow like "→" as pointing left (say, the part on the right is not the point of an arrow but the opening of an aperture with the line flowing leftward out of it, signifying the direction one is meant to go; see *PI* §85). A second arrow, which tells us how to interpret the first, is no help here, since "every interpretation hangs in the air together with what it interprets, and cannot give it any support" (*PI* §198). The point here is not that the signpost is inescapably ambiguous, but that neither the signpost itself nor further instruction or interpretation can irresistibly dictate how we use it. We do indeed follow signposts and engage in a wide variety of rule-governed practices without a second thought—and if we did not, we would not share the common life that we do—but this regularity manifests an attunement that is itself ungrounded.

5   ANXIETY AND AUTHENTICITY

At the end of section 3, I asked whether Wittgenstein's emphasis on attunement constituted an inauthentic absorption in *das Man*. In the previous section, I tried to show that, far from taking our attunement for granted, Wittgenstein draws our attention to how remarkable it is that we make sense to one another at all. Wittgenstein acknowledges the importance of attunement, but also wants us to see this attunement as ungrounded. There is nothing insidious about following a rule in the way that everyone else follows that rule, but we get ourselves into trouble when we make the further step of assuming or theorizing that some independent standard of correctness compels our and everyone else's conformity to the rule. Conforming to what *one* does, then, is not so much the problem, but rather the problem lies with taking this conformity as grounded in a source more stable and absolute than our mutual attunement. Here Wittgenstein and Heidegger are agreed. For the most part, we tend to accept both our conformity to norms and the conformism of received opinion with an air of necessity and inevitability. Because this is the way things are done, surely they could not be done in any other way. Because just *this* is how we live, we want the security of seeing our forms of life as grounded on the most solid bedrock.

Of course, even the most solid bedrock is afloat upon a sea of magma. Even the firmest foundations are unstable. Recognizing this fact is, for Wittgenstein, a key measure in releasing us from the feeling of compulsion certain philosophical pictures force on us. For Heidegger, it is a requirement of authenticity. In Division I of *Being and Time*, Heidegger explores anxiety as a crucial mood that signals to us the ungroundedness of our forms of life. We find a similar mood of anxiety pervading Wittgenstein's appeal to ordinary language. Contrary to readings of Wittgenstein that emphasize the shared norms of an established community,[18] I have highlighted the ubiquity in Wittgenstein's work of scenes of instruction: Wittgenstein is interested not in established communities but in the probing by which we explore and discover whether and how we can establish common ground with others. Throughout these investigations, Wittgenstein rehearses the anxiety that things might not turn out as we expect or hope. In these passages, Wittgenstein enacts the anxiety that Heidegger describes. Investigating the scene of instruction induces the vertiginous discovery that our lives literally depend upon an attunement that comes with no guarantees.[19] For both Wittgenstein and Heidegger, the importance of attunement comes not just with the recognition that this attunement is ungrounded, but also with the recognition of the anxiety this ungroundedness induces.

Heidegger describes two ways we might respond to this existential anxiety. One is the inauthentic flight into the *Man-selbst,* or one-self. Inauthentic Dasein flees from its anxiety by absorbing itself in its everyday activities without reflecting deeply upon them: Dasein flees toward "entities alongside which our concern, lost in *das Man,* can dwell in tranquillized familiarity" (*BT* 189/233–34; I have left *das Man* untranslated). Inauthentic Dasein engages in everyday practices while turning a blind eye to their ungroundedness. It accepts social norms as fixed and absolute, not the result of human attunement but simply "the way things are."

By contrast, authentic Dasein confronts this anxiety as disclosing the fundamental uncanniness (*Unheimlichkeit*) of Being-in-the-world: "Uncanniness is the basic kind of Being-in-the-world, even though in an everyday way it has been covered up" (*BT* 277/322). The German *Unheimlichkeit* suggests homelessness, which captures precisely the sense of disorientation that comes with discovering the ungroundedness of our ordinary practices, and contrasts suggestively with the connotation of home (*Wohnung*) in the German word for "ordinary," *gewöhnlich.* On one hand, the ordinariness of our language and forms of life stems from our being at home with them. On the other hand, our shared attunement is itself ungrounded, and reflecting on this fact both undermines certain philosophical prejudices and leaves us with the uncanny feeling of not being at home in our practices in the way we had comfortably assumed.

Wittgenstein's appeal to ordinary language does not represent an evasion or suppression of this uncanniness. Instead, he sees uncanniness inscribed in our inhabitation of the ordinary. The ordinary is our home in the sense that ordinary language is the language that speaks to and from the particular situation we find ourselves in. The concepts of ordinary language articulate the interests and needs of the people that use them, and they are useful to the extent that they are usable. We find it useful to price cheese according to its weight, but this practice would lose its point if the weight of cheese were constantly fluctuating. If everything were in a continual flux of rapid growth and shrinking, our concept of weight would lose its point, or would have radically different applications, whereas other concepts would become useful to us. Our concepts are not absolute precisely because they are responsive to our circumstances in their particularity. The appeal to ordinary language thus acknowledges the impossibility of a godlike perspective for which, as Wittgenstein puts it, "certain concepts are absolutely the correct ones." Wittgenstein does not mean that, in our finitude, we fail to grasp the absolutely correct concepts, but rather that it is of the nature of concepts to belong to forms of life that are themselves not absolute. Acknowledging our language and forms of life as ordinary means acknowledging the uncanny fact that our being at home in them gives them no absolute grounding.

In this reading, the question of whether *das Man* denotes conformity or conformism becomes a bit of a red herring. What constitutes lostness in the one-self is not a vaguely defined conformism but rather the suppression of the uncanniness of Being-in-the-world. Rather than confront the uncanniness of existence, inauthentic Dasein takes comfort in affirming its stability. Inauthenticity does not stem primarily from conformism in judgment over the topic *du jour* but from suppressing the ungroundedness of all our agreement, whether in conformity or conformism. Such an attitude accepts the conformity of social norms no more than authentic Dasein, but relates to it differently, treating it as fixed and necessary. This attitude is also liable to fall into some sort of conformism. A Dasein that relates to itself and its world as fixed and unchanging has no need to develop opinions that differ from received wisdom. This sort of conformism is not so much a conformism to particular judgments, but rather an acceptance of the sorts of arguments that happen to be current on the topics that happen to be current.

If I am right in tracing these parallel trajectories through Division I of *Being and Time* and Wittgenstein's appeal to ordinary language, Heidegger's exhortation to authenticity that becomes the focus of Division II is no more a repudiation of the everydayness of Division I than Wittgenstein's reminders of the ordinary are repudiations of the ordinary. Indeed, Heidegger emphasizes that authenticity does not transfigure Dasein's world or its relation to others (*BT* 297–98/344), just as someone who is fully cognizant of the uncanniness of our ordinary practices need not engage with those practices any differently.[20] Stephen Mulhall emphasizes that Heidegger's analysis of inauthentic Dasein is an analysis of Dasein in its *average* everydayness, raising the question of whether there are other ways of inhabiting the everyday. Mulhall answers that authentic Dasein represents a repudiation of inauthentic Dasein's averageness—its subjecting of itself to the average—and not of its everydayness: "Authentic Being-in-the-world is not a transcendence of or escape from everydayness but a mode of everydayness; it is not an extraordinary mode of Being, but a mode of inhabiting the ordinary" (Mulhall 1994, 151). The contrast with average everydayness for Mulhall is authentic everydayness. Authentic Dasein does not move beyond the everyday but accepts the everyday without becoming lost in it.

The moral fervor we find in Wittgenstein, which I remarked upon in my introduction, has much in common with what might inspire fervor in Heidegger's appeal to authenticity. In much the same way as Heidegger, Wittgenstein sees most of us—especially those who embrace traditional methods of doing philosophy—as lost and needing recovery. This recovery is not a matter of providing us with new ideas, new truths, new theories, but of helping us inhabit where we are without self-deception. Wittgenstein describes his appeal to ordinary language in terms of "bringing us back" to the everyday use of words. If we are to find an analogy in Heidegger, Wittgenstein's calling us back to the ordinary resembles nothing quite so much as the Heideggerian call of conscience. Not coincidentally, Heidegger also characterizes this call in terms of bringing back: in heeding the call of conscience, "Dasein specifically brings itself back to itself from its lostness in *das Man*" (*BT* 268/312; I have left *das Man* untranslated). Philosophy, for both Wittgenstein and Heidegger, is not a matter of moving forward to the new discovery that will ground our practices, but rather a matter of calling us back to the ungroundedness that we have always already known and always already forgotten.[21]

NOTES

1. Cf. *PI* §§89–90 and 126.
2. Gordon Baker (2004b, 263) offers a "Provisional Typology of Remarks in the *Philosophical Investigations*," which identifies three different kinds of remarks: (1) remarks on grammar (e.g., *PI* §199: "It is not possible that there should have been only one occasion on which only one person followed a rule"), (2) extremely general facts of nature (e.g., *PI* §142: "The procedure of putting a lump of cheese on a balance and fixing the price by the turn of the scale would lose its point if it frequently happened that such lumps suddenly grew or shrank with no obvious cause"), and (3) pictures (e.g., *PI* §194: "The possibility of a movement is supposed, rather, to be like a shadow of the movement itself"). When I talk about "simple but crucial facts," I mean facts in the broader sense in which (1) and (3) as well as (2) constitute observations about fundamental but unnoticed-because-obvious features of our existence.
3. Heidegger scholars who make reference to Wittgenstein include Hubert Dreyfus (1991), Charles Guignon (1983), John Haugeland (1982), and Taylor Carman (2003). An early proponent of the Wittgenstein-Heidegger comparison is Karl-Otto Apel, a number of whose essays on the topic are collected in English in Apel (1980).
4. The foreword to the *Philosophical Remarks* is one of the most striking of such instances.
5. Dreyfus (1991, 28) cites three reasons that Heidegger gives for taking Dasein as a starting point—that Dasein relates to its being as a question, that Dasein understands itself in terms of its average understanding, and that Dasein's understanding of its being implies an understanding of all modes of being—while remarking that none of these reasons is fully convincing. I am not sure they are meant to be, or could be. Heidegger conceives of his project as a hermeneutic circle: no matter where we start, we must provisionally take some things for granted, but can then circle back to question those assumptions and reconfigure our project in light of this further questioning. If there were rock-solid reasons for taking just this starting point, there would be no reason to circle back and reinterpret it. And indeed, division 2 of *Being and Time* can be read as just such a reinterpretation.
6. This frequent Heideggerism is Macquarrie and Robinson's translation of *zunächst und zumeist*. Stambaugh has it as "initially and for the most part." *Zunächst* can mean either "initially" or "proximally," depending on context. As it is used in *Being and Time*, both translations are appropriate: Heidegger

emphasizes that we are ensconced in the world in an engaged manner *before* we can contemplate it in a disengaged manner, and we encounter the world in this way because the equipment and others in it are ontically *closest* to us (*das ontisch Nächste*) (*BT* 43/69).

7. This paragraph, and the next two, appears in a slightly different form in Egan (2012).

8. Both English translations of *Being and Time* render this term as "the 'They,'" which is an unsatisfactory translation of a term for which there is no good English equivalent. *Man* is the German impersonal third person singular, the same as "one" in English, but translating *das Man* literally as "the one," as Dreyfus and Carman do, carries confusingly Messianic connotations. I will leave *das Man* untranslated in this chapter, but will aim to bring out the implications of Heidegger's usage as often as possible by using verbs with either the impersonal third person singular or the passive voice: *das Man* speaks to what "one does" or what "is done."

9. Carman (2003, 137) describes Heidegger as a "social externalist."

10. In *Being and Time*, Heidegger treats language as ready-to-hand (see *BT* 161/204), and Wittgenstein also draws a number of analogies between language and tools (see *PI* §§11, 14, 15, 17, 23, 41, 42, 360). Stephen Mulhall (1994, 144–48) defends and explores the comparison of language to tools as a similarity between Wittgenstein and Heidegger.

11. See Cavell (1979, 32). The word "attunement" is also used to translate Heidegger's *Befindlichkeit*. Despite some similarities, the two uses of "attunement" are not the same, and the discussion of attunement in this chapter is not meant to cover *Befindlichkeit*. Cavell's Wittgensteinian conception of attunement is a relation between two or more people whereas Heidegger's attunement is a relation between Dasein and its world.

12. As a matter of fact, Heidegger disavows making any value judgments here or elsewhere about what he calls "deficient" forms of Being. I find this supposed neutrality very difficult to square with the language that he uses. As if "inauthentic" were itself not a term laden with negative value judgment, he also refers to inauthentic Dasein as "deficient," "lost," and "fallen," among other things, in language that ranges in its associations from psychoanalytic notions of repression and self-denial to theological notions of sin. The initial discussion of *das Man* in §27 of *Being and Time* uses particularly strong language. Heidegger refers to the "averageness" of *das Man*, saying it "keeps watch over everything exceptional that thrusts itself to the fore. Every kind of priority gets noiselessly suppressed. Overnight, everything that is primordial gets glossed over as something that has long been well known. Everything gained by a struggle becomes just something to be manipulated. Every secret loses its force. This care of averageness reveals in turn an essential tendency of Dasein which we will call the 'levelling down' of all possibilities of being" (*BT* 127/165). If Heidegger truly seeks to present the notion of *das Man* free from any condemnatory language, he does a spectacularly bad job of it.

13. This paragraph appears in a slightly different form in Egan (2012).

14. I consider *das Man* in more detail in Egan (2012).

15. For example, *PI* §§6, 12, 193–94, 270–71, 559. However, we have to be careful in reading Wittgenstein's use of the machine metaphor, as he also frequently uses it to exemplify a kind of thinking he wishes to criticize.

16. See *PI* §§1, 35, 47, 60, 80, 253, 356, 361, 368, 486, 575.

17. See Cavell (1991). Besides the opening sections of the *Investigations*, which consider Augustine's child and the tribe of builders, see also *PI* §§27, 31, 32, 35, 49, 53, 54, 77, 85, 86, 143, 144, 145, 156, 157, 159, 162, 179, 185, 189, 197, 198, 206, 207, 208, 223, 224, 232, 233, 237, 244, 249, 250, 257, 282,

308, 320, 328, 340, 361, 362, 375, 376, 378, 384, 385, 386, 441, 495, 535, 590, 630, 636, and 693. Cf. also Cavell (1989, 75): "In the culture depicted in the *Investigations* we are all teachers and all students—talkers, hearers, overhearers, hearsayers, believers, explainers; we learn and teach incessantly, indiscriminately; we are all elders and all justices."

18. I am thinking primarily of Wright (1980) and Kripke (1982).

19. McDowell (2000, 43–44) also discusses this experience in terms of vertigo.

20. Here we might see Heidegger's and Wittgenstein's shared influence from Kierkegaard, whose knight of faith could appear to all the world as a humble shopman. How exactly we should spell out Heidegger's conception of authenticity is obviously a topic of considerable debate in the secondary literature, where we find often radically conflicting interpretations. I want to remain as neutral as I can in this discussion while acknowledging the difficulty of interpreting Heidegger on authenticity. My main positive contribution to this debate lies in the suggestion that the comparison between Wittgenstein's appeal to ordinary language and Heidegger's appeal to authenticity can work both ways: this chapter mainly uses the latter to draw attention to features of the former, but I believe this "authentic" reading of Wittgenstein could also inform our reading of Heideggerian authenticity.

21. In addition to my fellow editors, I'm particularly grateful for feedback from Stephen Mulhall and Denis McManus.

6   Wittgenstein, Heidegger, and the Question of Phenomenology

Charles Guignon

Some commentators have noted similarities between the work of Wittgen-stein and Heidegger, especially Wittgenstein's post-*Tractarian* remarks and Heidegger's lectures and writings of the 1920s, with respect to the issue of phenomenology.[1] These similarities have led to speculation about whether Wittgenstein's use of the word "phenomenology" in the early 1930s gives us reason to suppose that he was familiar with the phenomenological tradition that, starting with Husserl's *Logical Investigations* in 1900–1901, evolved through the work of Heidegger and other major continental figures, and currently is influential among certain contemporary philosophers (see, for example, Gallagher and Zahavi 2008). Despite these similarities, however, I am inclined to agree with more recent findings that Wittgenstein's use of the word "phenomenology" springs from an entirely different tradition (see Park 1997). Nevertheless, some themes in Wittgenstein's later writings resonate with ideas that emerge from Heidegger's phenomenology. In what follows, my goal is to point out some similarities in the thought of these two philosophers insofar as they evoke major Heideggerian phenomenological themes. This comparison will also bring to light how Heidegger came to reject many of Husserl's ideas, thereby developing a distinctive phenomeno-logical point of view.

In the Husserl/Heidegger tradition, "phenomenology" is the name for a *method*: it directs us to *describe* what shows up for us in our encounters with things prior to theorizing and high-level reflection. Its aim is clarifica-tion or elucidation of what appears as it appears—in Heidegger's words, "'phenomenology' means . . . to let that which shows itself be seen from itself in the very way in which it shows itself from itself" (*BT* 34/58). What this method tries to bring to light, however, are not those items that typically do show up for us but rather "something that proximally and for the most part does *not* show itself at all: it is something that lies *hidden*," although it constitutes the "*meaning*" and "*ground*" of what typically shows up (*BT* 35/59). This "proximally and for the most part" unnoticed back-ground, which lets entities become manifest, is called the "being of entities." I hope to show that there is a similar move made by Wittgenstein. Although philosophy cannot identify any special *thing* above and beyond what we normally encounter in the world, we can discover that what shows up in our lives displays an order Wittgenstein calls a "grammar," and that elucidating this grammar can serve as the "legitimate heir" of what used to be called "philosophy" (*BB* 28, 62).

My procedure will have four parts. First, I will try to disentangle the Wittgensteinian and Heideggerian uses of the term "phenomenology" by showing how both philosophers, having started out from a somewhat similar conception of philosophy as essentially involved in "logic," went on to bypass traditional conceptions of logic in order to develop a new approach to philosophical problems. Though Wittgenstein briefly experimented with calling his method "phenomenology," it becomes clear that his use of the term has no relation to Heidegger's. Second, I will try to show that, regardless of whether there are causal connections between the two thinkers, both Wittgenstein and Heidegger developed parallel conceptions of the contextualism characterizing our being in the world, a contextualism expressly worked out in Heidegger's characterization of phenomenology. Third, I compare the two philosophers with regard to the fact that they tend to develop a constitutive view of language, a view that was central to Heidegger's conception of phenomenology in the 1920s.[2] Fourth, I will sketch out how the protophenomenological approach I cull from these two philosophers tends to transform our conception of the method and tasks of philosophy as such.

1   FROM LOGIC TO PHENOMENOLOGY

Born the same year, and so contemporaries until Wittgenstein's death in 1951, both Heidegger and Wittgenstein wrote almost entirely in German, and both initially wrote in response to problems arising in the German-speaking intellectual world. It is therefore not surprising that the orientations of their early works are similar in some respects. Like many philosophers at the turn of the century, both saw themselves as contributing to the field of logic, and both tended to see logic as the core of philosophy. As is well known, Wittgenstein's *Tractatus* was a seminal work in the development of what we might call "the pervasiveness of logic thesis," the view that the totality of propositions and the world they purport to represent are determined in advance by logical forms that predefine at once both the possible meaningfulness of cognitive discourse and the possible combinations of objects.[3] Less well known is the fact that the young Heidegger saw his primary direction of research in philosophy as being logic. In the *curriculum vitae* attached to his 1915 PhD dissertation, he wrote that, although he was "highly focused" on the study of theoretical mathematics, logic was "the philosophical discipline that still interests me the most" (*BH* 8). A quick survey of the titles of Heidegger's seminars and courses over his lifetime reveals that logic remained one of the primary subjects he taught again and again at least until the 1940s.[4]

It is important to keep in mind that the term "logic" was then used in a very broad way. Most philosophers of the late nineteenth century continued to think of logic as Kant had thought of it. The field of logic was seen as comprising three areas: the theory of concepts, the theory of judgments, and the theory of inference (called "*Konsequenzlogik*"). A typical philosopher in the nineteenth century would agree with Kant's claim that "logic has not increased much in content since Aristotle's times, and indeed cannot do so by its nature" (quoted in Käufer 2001, 459). What this means is that, because everything worth knowing about inference had already been established in ancient times, the subject of inference was of little interest to logic. Consequently, the prevailing view was that the subject matter of that field was concepts and judgments.[5] Moreover, if concepts are expressed by words and words have meaning only in the context of a sentence (that is, in a proposition or judgment), then the main focus of logic would be the formation and legitimation of concepts.[6]

Although Heidegger explicitly defines "logic" as a "speaking and thinking that defines and uncovers things," he clearly is sympathetic to Husserl's ([1929] 1969, 18) observation that the Greek word *logos* "in its pregnant sense" refers to "the idea of a rational norm" governing the formation of concepts. *Logos* refers to "the ability to form legitimate concepts; . . . [I]t signifies the rational concept-forming and likewise the correct concept itself" (*LQT* 6; see note 5). Implicit in this definition is the idea that "logic" refers to an underlying set of principles of order that ensures that concepts organize and articulate what-is in a coherent, meaningful way. Logic is the "hidden" background of meaning (*Sinn*) that gives order to the context in which things appear and thereby makes any intelligibility whatsoever possible.[7]

A second important similarity between Wittgenstein and Heidegger is found in the fact that, after a relatively short period of work in the fields they would have regarded as logic, both began to question some of their earlier presuppositions about the pervasiveness of logic. Wittgenstein's growing dissatisfaction with his own earlier conception of an all-pervasive logic is evident in his later seemingly sarcastic description of the belief that "[t]hinking is surrounded by a nimbus.—Its essence, logic, presents an order: namely, the a priori order of the world; that is, the order of *possibilities*, which the world and thinking must have in common. But this order . . . is *prior* to all experience. . . . It must rather be of the purest crystal" (*PI* §97). What he is putting in question here is his earlier confidence that there is one monolithic logical system or form inhabiting all of language and reality. Although Wittgenstein is still concerned with discovering the underlying principles of order in language (now more often called "grammar" than "logic"), his view tends to suppose that there is a plurality of grammars rather than one all-inclusive logic. The "ideal" of a universal, underlying system of order in every type of language use now comes to look like an unwarranted presupposition, "like a pair of glasses on our nose through which we see whatever we look at" (*PI* §103). It is something we read into language rather than something we find in an actual investigation of language use. When he asks, "[H]ow many kinds of sentences are there?" he answers, "There are *countless* kinds" (*PI* §23). Where before declarative sentences had been the paradigm of language, now all the "language-games" we play with words, symbols, expressions, gestures, and so on are examples of language use.

Heidegger, for his part, comes to describe his task as one "of *liberating* grammar from logic" (*BT* 165/209). In *Being and Time*, he comes to reject the idea that all language consists of declarative sentences of the sort Aristotle had called "apophantic." In Heidegger's view, more primordial (*ursprünglich*) than the "apophantic *as*" presupposed by sentences such as "The hammer weighs two pounds" are the sorts of "hermeneutic *as*" found in utterances such as "Too heavy! Give me the other hammer!" (*BT* §33). Far from thinking that language at the most basic level consists of assertions or propositions (*Sätze*), Heidegger suggests that "genuine" language is found in *silence* (*BT* 165/208). According to Heidegger, what imparts order and meaning to what we encounter in our everyday dealings is not a "pure" lattice-work of "logic"; it is instead the organizing framework of what he calls the "worldhood" of the world (*BT* §§14–24). Heidegger even seems willing to follow Wittgenstein in supposing that grunts, gestures, and signals can be examples of language. Although both thinkers, in their mature writings, continue to suppose that there is a background of order (or multiple backgrounds) that lets entities show up *as* such and such, they eschew any neo-Platonic or supernaturalist notion of an invisible yet ever-present logic whose ontological character can be taken as self-evident. Order in the world comes from the world itself, not from some extra-worldly source.

As representatives of different intellectual trends in early twentieth-century thought, there are, needless to say, profound differences between Wittgenstein and Heidegger. Nevertheless, there is one similarity between these two that seems both important and puzzling. Heidegger had used the name "phenomenology" for his philosophy as a consequence of the influence of Husserl's writings on his early thought. Indeed, most of the phenomenological tradition we know today has been motivated by Husserl's characterization of that method. What is puzzling, however, is that Wittgenstein also referred to his own thought as "phenomenology" for a brief time (from 1929 to around 1932) after returning to philosophy at Cambridge. The puzzle arises because, as already noted, it seems certain that Wittgenstein never read or knew about Husserl, the founder of phenomenology. So the question arises: Did Wittgenstein mean something by the term "phenomenology" that is similar to what appears in the work of the figures we associate with the movement called "phenomenology," and especially in the work of Heidegger, who transformed the conception of method he inherited from Husserl?

This question has stirred up a variety of opinions among scholars. The outcome of the discussion is, in my opinion, inconclusive. We know that

Wittgenstein remarked to Rush Rhees, "You could say of my work that it is 'phenomenology.'" We also know that a chapter of the *Big Typescript* entitled "Phenomenology" begins with a section titled "Phenomenology Is Grammar."[8] Moreover, the 1929–30 notebooks translated as the *Philosophical Remarks* start out with a discussion of the attempt to develop—and the ultimate decision to reject—a "phenomenological language" (sometimes called a "primary language"), where such a language would be one that expresses immediate experience without hypotheses about the metaphysical nature of what it describes. The advantage of such a language, Wittgenstein suggests, would be that it directly displays the grammar of any language that studies physical reality: "Thus, phenomenology would be the grammar of the description of those facts on which physics builds its theories" (*PhR* I §1). Later in that text we learn about "a theory in *pure* phenomenology in which mention is only made of what is actually perceptible and in which no hypothetical objects—waves, rods, cones and all that—occur" (*PhR* XXI §218). The goal seems to be a notation in which what is immediately experienced is captured, with no extra assumptions being added on. We are also told that a phenomenological description of the world we inhabit would be "unmanageably complicated" (*PhR* XXII §230), although it would have the advantage of making evident the logical multiplicity of the grammar of any languages in which statements about the world can be made. Because phenomenology directly displays grammar, where "grammar" refers to the multiplicity of combinatorial possibilities and restrictions there can be among objects, it is possible to say that phenomenology is grammar.

As to the question of whether there are connections between early Wittgenstein and Husserl, we might note that there are indeed some similarities between Wittgenstein's conception of phenomenology and Husserl's. Husserlian phenomenology instructs us to begin by bracketing or holding in abeyance all assumptions about the world we find around us, assumptions drawn from common sense or science (together called "the natural attitude"). Both Wittgenstein and Husserl are metaphysically abstemious. But with that, it seems that similarities end. Wittgenstein's phenomenological *language* is supposed to reveal the grammatical multiplicity of physical languages, whereas the phenomenological *method* devised by Husserl aims at showing how anything whatsoever comes to be encountered by consciousness. This emphasis on subjectivity later will be the source of a breach between Husserl and Heidegger. But all phenomenologists in the Husserlian tradition are primarily concerned with our modes of comportment to what there is and how anything can show up for us as counting or mattering in some way or other. It is not clear that this is what Wittgenstein was trying to get at.

As to the question of whether there could have been any influence between Wittgenstein and Heidegger, it seems likely that, with the exception of one passing reference to Heidegger in Wittgenstein's remarks, neither Wittgenstein nor Heidegger had heard of one another (*LWVC* 68–69). In fact, as Park (1997) points out, the word "phenomenology" was used by Ludwig Boltzmann, whom Wittgenstein studied, and was used by Ernst Mach, Einstein, and other physicists, not to mention the very similar idea indirectly used by Rudolf Carnap. Hence, the word played an important role in two unconnected traditions. However, in the absence of any causal connections between the two thinkers, the most we can do is note formal similarities. That will be my aim in what follows.

2   PHENOMENA IN CONTEXT

Even though Wittgenstein's and Heidegger's paths may never have crossed, there are interesting similarities in their mature thought. The similarities that appear can be understood in reference to what was "in the air" when they were writing. Both thinkers seem to have questioned ideas that were implicit in the thought of many logicians of the time. One widely accepted view they seem to have questioned might be called the "name-and-object model" of the relation of language to the world. The idea behind this view is that (1) the world consists of objects of various sorts and (2) where we find a noun there must be an object to which the noun refers. These claims suggest (3) that understanding a word must be in part at least a matter of grasping the object to which the word refers.

Another common idea that both philosophers might have questioned is the idea that the primary function of language is to convey information and that information is conveyed paradigmatically by declarative sentences— that is, by "propositions" or "assertions." On this view, other possible uses of language might be construed as variants or derivatives of propositions, and therefore may be analyzable into a propositional—that is, subject/predicate—form. This view of language gives us a reason to suppose that a general account of language can be developed that will see all forms of language in terms of one basic form, the "noun phrase/verb phrase" propositional form. In such a formally worked-out language, words gain their meaning by serving as names for the objects that make up reality.

Wittgenstein and Heidegger each focused his attack on different aspects of the standard view of language and world, but their combined attacks have the same direction and effect. With respect to the primacy of the proposition, we saw that Wittgenstein asks, "[H]ow many kinds of sentences are there?" and answers, "There are *countless* kinds; countless different kinds of use of all the things we call 'signs,' 'words,' 'sentences'" (*PI* §23). It would be in tune with Wittgenstein to add here that there are also countless ways that even nonverbal expressions may be *taken* as language in particular situations—gestures, moans, snorts, grunts, winks, finger flicks, clicks— and that there are also formulas found primarily at ritualized occasions, such as "I do" at a wedding or making the sign of the cross in church, that have nothing to do with conveying information. The conclusion to draw, according to Wittgenstein, is that "what we call 'proposition,' 'language' ['*Satz*,' '*Sprache*'] has not the formal unity that I imagined, but is a family of structures [*Gebilde*] more or less akin to one another" (*PI* §108). What determines whether something counts as language depends on a multitude of features and relationships in specific contexts, including regularized usages, specific purposes to be realized, analogues of standard linguistic forms, correlations with basic "animal" gestures and facial expressions, and natural acts with clear implications (e.g., spitting). What is needed for anything to count as linguistic is a "grammar" of some sort, where what can count as a grammar should be construed in a way sufficiently broad to delineate the boundaries determining what counts as meaningful for specific domains of language-games (*PI* §496, 499).

Wittgenstein also challenges the assumption that the word/world correlation can be fully accounted for in terms of the name-and-object model. Certainly there are cases where naming and using a name can serve as a model of how language hooks up with the world. But there are innumerable cases where the word/world relationship cannot be understood according to the one-to-one, objectifying name-and-object model. In order to understand a remark such as "This toothache is killing me," more is needed than grasping what the words "toothache" or "me" happen to name. The utterance is not so much a statement about objects in the world as it is an expression of pain and exasperation, where words do not exactly *refer* to anything at all. For example, the idea that "toothache" names or refers to a pain-occurrence, a pain-thing, which should be thought of as an item in the world, is attacked in Wittgenstein's extended criticisms of common philosophical assumptions about sensation words (e.g., *PI* §§404–8). In Heidegger's vocabulary, it presupposes that there is a present-at-hand thing where the very idea of a *thing* has no role to play. It should be obvious that the criticism made here is similar to Heidegger's claim that expressions such as "Too heavy!" cannot be adequately understood solely in terms of the name-and-object model. The boundaries that delimit meanings—the grammar—are determined not by the essences of objects but by our uses in real contexts.

What the foregoing observations suggest is that the Wittgensteinian and Heideggerian ways of criticizing standard philosophical accounts of phenomena such as language show that, even though the two philosophers are following different paths, both may be seen as employing, in their mature works, something very close to the phenomenological method developed by Heidegger. Their concern is with describing what shows up in our pretheoretical lives *as* those things appear. Heidegger claims that phenomenology is purely descriptive—it "does not do *any* proving *at all* by the rules of the 'logic of consistency' [*Konsequenzlogik*]" (*BT* 315/363). The persuasive force of phenomenology is grounded in its enabling one to see the "subject matter" in a way that elucidates what we are trying to grasp. What makes this approach different from Husserl's conception of phenomenology is that, whereas Husserl always supposes that what is described is how things show up for a "consciousness" or an "ego," the mature writings of Heidegger and Wittgenstein put such traditional Cartesian-derived notions as ego or consciousness in question. The distinction between subject and object as a rule has no real role to play in describing our average, everyday ways of being engaged in the world.

We saw that, on Heidegger's view, phenomenology reveals something that is for the most part *hidden* in our daily lives—namely, the all-pervasive background of meaning that lets anything stand forth and become manifest. What is a "phenomenon" in the deepest sense is the meaning-endowing contexts and activities that make up our shared public world. Although Wittgenstein no longer uses the term "phenomenology" in his writings from the mid-thirties onwards, the idea that philosophy can consist primarily of description is fundamental to his work. "All *explanation* must disappear, and description alone must take its place. . . . The problems are solved, not by coming up with new discoveries, but by assembling what we have long been familiar with" (*PI* §109). What we are concerned with is something we already know but usually overlook, partly because our sense of things is distorted by misleading pictures and analogies (see Braver 2012, esp. chap. 1). "Philosophy just puts everything before us, and neither explains nor deduces anything.—Since everything lies open to view, there is nothing to explain" (*PI* §126).

Wittgenstein agrees with Heidegger that we miss the most important things about our lives in the world not because they are covered up or concealed but because they are so omnipresent that they are always directly in front of our eyes—like our eyeglasses, which we do not see because we see everything through them. "The aspects of things that are most important for us are hidden because of their simplicity and familiarity. (One is unable to notice something—because it is always before one's eyes)" (*PI* §129). This tendency to have a muddled view of things explains why Wittgenstein issues his famous imperative: "[D]on't think, but look!" (*PI* §66). When we think about things, we tend to impose a conceptual net over what is there, a template that forces us to encounter things through a particular grid of interpretation. The only way to avoid this distortion is to hold in abeyance our philosophically conditioned concepts in order to just look at what we are trying to understand.

It goes without saying, however, that none of us can turn into a perfect *tabula rasa* with no frame of reference whatsoever for engaging in description. Both Wittgenstein and Heidegger accept the fact that we always bring with us some prior comprehension of what we are encountering, a "pre-understanding" that enables us to sort things out, make distinctions, and recognize possible combinations and incompatibilities in the field of intelligibility we bring to the world. For Wittgenstein, we always have an at least tacit understanding of the "grammar" of the language-games we are engaged in. The aim of a phenomenological approach, then, is to carefully look at what we want to understand (or to imagine alternatives to what we find) in order to *remind* ourselves of the underlying grammar we have come to grasp in becoming competent members of a speech community. The point is that we always already find ourselves in a space of meaning where a multiplicity of factors sketch out and sustain meaning of a particular sort. The proper job of philosophy, then, is to elucidate and explicate as much as possible of what that background of meaning is. The ideal outcome is to prevent grammars that might be appropriate for certain regions of our lives (for example, the ordinary object language for furniture or the language of ideal shapes for geometry) from being used where they are inappropriate.

For his part, Heidegger sees that, as human agents, we are always embedded in the context of meaning he calls the "worldhood of the world." In the examples he provides of this background of meaning, we see how entities in general can emerge as counting or mattering to us in familiar ways only by virtue of their place within one of the familiar contexts in which we dwell. So, for example, a hammer appears on the scene first and foremost as equipment for hammering within the meaningful, smooth functioning of a workshop. Pencils and paper show up *as* equipment for accomplishing business of certain sorts only within an office where things can have a place that endows them with a meaning. For the most part, we find ourselves ensconced in contexts of meaning that make it possible for anything to show up as significant in some way. Heidegger and Wittgenstein agree in seeing human intelligibility as always *contextualized* and *holistic*, a matter of being immersed in shared loci of meaningfulness that underlie and support our ability to make sense of anything.

3   PHENOMENOLOGY AND LANGUAGE

It is important to see that the method of phenomenology I am attributing to Wittgenstein and Heidegger is very different from the phenomenological approach developed by Husserl. Despite his originality and critical spirit, Husserl was inclined to hang on to the presuppositions that made up what mainstream philosophy understood as "logic" in the sense we discussed. Wittgenstein never was much impressed by Husserl, if he'd heard of him at all, and Heidegger quite explicitly separated himself from Husserl. In a telling remark in a letter to William J. Richardson in 1944, Heidegger admitted that it was not so much Husserl's conception of phenomenology that provided the basis for his approach in *Being and Time* as it was Aristotle's method, especially in the *Nicomachean Ethics*, that lay at the foundation of the phenomenology found in *Being and Time*. In a letter published in Richardson's *Heidegger: Through Phenomenology to Thought*, Heidegger says that conversations with Husserl "provided the immediate experience of the phenomenological method" that was used in *Being and Time*, but that the decisive role in the formation of his method was played by "a renewed study" of Aristotle. In his opinion, Husserl's phenomenology remained trapped in a specifically epistemological position "according to a pattern set by Descartes, Kant and Fichte," whereas Heidegger's own method followed the path laid out by Aristotle (*HR* 299–300). In a similar vein, in his short biographical piece, "My Way to Phenomenology" of 1963, Heidegger says that phenomenology "is thought more originally by Aristotle" than it is by Husserl (*TB* 79; *GA* 14:99).

Although we cannot always trust Heidegger's later accounts of his earlier motives and influences, we might nevertheless ask: What is the method of phenomenology Heidegger derives from Aristotle? We can get an insight into Heidegger's distinctive approach to phenomenology by looking at the lecture course he delivered in the summer semester of 1924 (just before he began writing *Being and Time*), a course titled Basic Concepts of Aristotelian Philosophy. This course covered a wide range of subjects in creative ways, but one of its primary aims was to show how Aristotle undertook the project of introducing and clarifying the basic concepts that appear and reappear throughout his philosophical works. At the beginning of book 7 of the *Nicomachean Ethics*, Aristotle says, "Here, as in all other cases, we must set down the appearances [*phainomena*] and, first working through the puzzles, in this way go on to show, if possible, the truth of all the beliefs we hold [*ta endoxa*] about these experiences. . . . For if the difficulties are resolved and the beliefs are left in place, we will have done enough showing" (*Nicomachean Ethics* 1145b1ff., quoted in Nussbaum 1986, 240). What is distinctive about Aristotle's method is to start by examining the ordinary beliefs of *hoi polloi*—that is, of ordinary people in a specific community—as things appear, which is to say, as they are sustained and circulated in the *endoxa* of shared beliefs and attitudes of those who make up the linguistic community. "These, then, are the things we say [*ta legomena*]" (*Nicomachean Ethics* 1145b8–20, quoted in Nussbaum 1986, 240). In Martha Nussbaum's words, "For Aristotle, *phainomena* must be understood to be our beliefs and interpretations, often revealed in linguistic usage. To set down the *phainomena* is not to look for belief-free fact, but to record our usage and the structure of thought and belief which [such] usage displays" (Nussbaum 1986, 243–44). What we want to make visible in the science of phenomena is "the world *as it appears* to, as it is experienced by, observers who are members of our kind" (Nussbaum 1986, 245).

For Aristotle, then, the main subject matter of phenomenology is what *we* say, how beings *of our kind* interpret and understand what shows up for us, and not some brute facts about "experiences" available only to a first-person standpoint. The "philological purpose" of Heidegger's lecture course, its purpose as a study of concepts, is to clarify and elucidate the fundamental concepts that give expression to the primordial understandings of things that emerged at the dawn of our civilization. The goal is to recover the "traditional content of ancient ontology until we arrive at those primordial experiences in which we achieved our first ways of determining the nature of Being—the ways that have guided us ever since" (*BT* 22/44). We are "demonstrating the origin of our basic ontological concepts by an investigation in which their 'birth certificate' is displayed" (*BT* 22/44).

In *Being and Time*, Heidegger makes it clear that this method of starting from what ordinary people say, and then testing it to find whether it stands up to "puzzles" we might pose, is the method of phenomenology he employs in this 1927 work. "All ontological investigations," he says, "must start with what the everyday interpretation of Dasein 'says' about them" (*BT* 281/326). Even when something is seen wrongly, "some injunction as to the primordial 'idea' of the phenomenon is revealed along with it" (*BT* 281/326). The ultimate goal of philosophy is to retrieve the primal force of the elemental words in which Dasein expresses itself. In Heidegger's words, "[T]he ultimate business of philosophy is to preserve the *force of the most elemental words* in which Dasein expresses itself, and to keep the common understanding from leveling them off to that unintelligibility which functions in turn as a source of pseudo-problems" (*BT* 220/262). As should be clear, phenomenology is concerned with providing elucidations of the ordinary words people use to express themselves; its goal is to display the origins of our "basic concepts," to disclose what lies at their roots, insofar as they arise from our linguistic interpretations of how things appear to us.

The "given" of phenomenology is therefore the plain, unadorned small talk or chatter that constitutes our shared understanding of the world. Heidegger uses the term *Gerede* to refer to the superficial grasp of things we all share by virtue of being participants in the "They" or "Anyone" of the public world. The shared sense of things that makes up idle talk carries and passes along a general sense of what and how things are. It sustains what Wittgenstein calls the "agreement in judgment" we have in common, an attunement (*Übereinstimmung* [*PI* §242]) that tunes us in and gets us on the same wavelength about the things we care about. For an example of idle talk (*Gerede*), we might consider the understanding most of us have of the Higgs boson particle: we chat about it and know it is somehow important, but we have only the vaguest grasp of what it is. Yet this vague and common understanding is what ties the complex formulae of physics to our ability to understand.

Heidegger considers how Aristotle was concerned to develop the superficial understanding in everyday small talk into a deeper comprehension that would then be expressed in the form of knowledgeable discursiveness (*Rede*). This project involves trying to develop a definition (*orismos*) of the basic terms used in the talk. We look at what we are "inclined" or "tempted" to say, and then revise those initial utterances in the light of "puzzles" that test our inclinations against possible alternative formulations and test cases.[9] A clarifying definition calls for a demarcation or circumscribing of the concept's boundaries (*perata*, from the Greek word *peras*, meaning "boundary" or "limit," which gives us our word "perimeter"). Such a definition makes it possible to fill in what the concept implies and presupposes relative to the contexts in which it is used.

Returning to our example, we can imagine how the concept of the Higgs boson might become clearer and more fully elaborated through the dialogical process of filling in and integrating it into an increasingly wide range of contexts where the concept might have a role to play. As we shift from *Gerede* to *Rede*, we move from "blowing smoke" and "faking it" to the possibility of genuine understanding and insight. A similar shift toward greater clarity is possible in the use of philosophical language: we come to grasp the origins of our basic concepts and appreciate the history of their changing meanings as they have evolved toward the ideal consummation (*telos*) of sense.

We have seen that Heidegger holds that, as participants in a public world of the "They," we are all initiated from the outset into the everyday interpretedness made available in idle talk or *Gerede*. This idle talk

> constitutes the kind of Being of everyday Dasein's understanding and interpreting. . . . In language, as a way things have been expressed, there is hidden a way in which Dasein's understanding has been interpreted. . . . Proximally, and with certain limits, Dasein is constantly delivered over to this interpretedness, which controls and distributes the possibilities of average understanding. (*BT* 167/211; translation slightly modified to avoid ambiguity)

Language provides us with our mode of access to anything, according to Heidegger. Because phenomena are always colored and shaped by language use, there is no way we could encounter brute, uninterpreted facts as they are in themselves, independent of linguistically articulated interpretations.

The everyday interpretedness of idle talk, Heidegger says,

> is one into which Dasein has grown in the first instance, with never a possibility of extrication. In it, out of it, and against it, all genuine understanding, interpreting and communicating, all re-discovering and appropriating anew, are performed. In no case is a Dasein, untouched and unseduced by this way in which things have been interpreted, set before the open country of a "world-in-itself" so that it just beholds what it encounters. (*BT* 169/213)

Ordinary language, which means the natural language a person is brought up into in becoming a participant in a world, contains a way of ordering and bringing to light the entities that make up the world as well as the Being of that world. This background of order that makes language intelligible can be made explicit though phenomenological elucidation. In the vocabulary of the Aristotle lectures, we might say that from *Gerede* it is possible to distill and make explicit the order of *Rede* or discursiveness, what the Greeks had in mind in using the word *logos*. *Logos*, the logic of a language, includes basic concepts and principles of order that pre-delineate a space of meaning (to use Steven Crowell's [2001] term). In terms of this *logos* or *Rede*, the world itself is given order and structure.

A similar picture of the role of language in imparting order can be found in the later Wittgenstein. The word "grammar" is a term Wittgenstein uses without attempting a precise definition. Nevertheless, we can approximate a definition based on how the term is used throughout Wittgenstein's writings. In a way parallel to Heidegger's conception of *logos*, "grammar" is used as a general term to refer to what imparts order and meaning to language and, thereby, to what we encounter in the world. As in the name for the discipline from which it is taken, the paradigm for the concept of "grammar" is first and foremost the rule-governed patterns of combination and syntax that impart regularity and intelligibility to what we say. But it also includes other meaning-determining features of language use, such as contextual factors, social practices, customs, institutions, features of the natural word relevant to our activities of making sense, the relation of words to learning and their origins (both actual and imaginary), and analogues in animal behavior. Wittgenstein also distinguishes "surface grammar" and "depth grammar" (*PI* §664) where the former refers to potentially misleading impressions of meaningfulness and regularity we might arrive at from false analogies or a superficial view, and the latter to underlying structures of language that reveal fundamental structures of the world as we understand it.

Features of grammar delineate structures of possible meaningfulness in our world, establishing what is possible and what is impossible in the field of what presents itself to us. For example, grammar makes it clear that I cannot be proud of the rings of Saturn, not because of some limitation in me or in the celestial bodies, but because a sentence such as "I am proud of the rings of Saturn" is ruled out as nonsense by the grammar of our language. What this shows is that distinctions of sense and nonsense, "this and that," what exists and doesn't exist, the totality of what Aristotle called *sunthesis* and *diairesis*, as well as the broader play of meaning and meaninglessness that organizes our field of intelligibility and lets things count for us in determinate ways, is an effect of the interplay of things we find around us together with the ways we talk about things. Wittgenstein goes so far as to put in question the very idea of there being *facts*—that is, something like the way things are in themselves—independent of their placement in a grammar of some sort. "But what things are 'facts?'" he asks concerning a purported mathematical fact, and he answers:

> Do you believe you can shew what fact is meant by, e.g., pointing to it with your finger? Does that of itself clarify the part played by "establishing" a fact?—Suppose it takes mathematics [or whatever grammar is relevant to the case under consideration] to define the character of what you are calling a "fact"! (*RFM* VII §18)

The point here is that it makes no sense to think that there are "facts as they are in themselves" independent of our ways of speaking and handling things. What we call "facts" always emerge into presence through the ordering system of a grammar.

The language we have mastered and use makes it possible for us to be in accord among ourselves in taking things *as* such and such. Items in the world, including perlocutionary impacts of language, become manifest and are realized through language. What we find around us and, indeed, that there is an *us*—a community of relatively like-minded agents in a social world—come to light through language. Language serves the function of establishing a footing with someone, as when we say, "Whew! Hot today, isn't it?" As a rule, such declamations are not taken as communicating information or as making inquiries. Even less do they seem to have, in the flux of ordinary life, the simple name and object form regarded as paradigmatic by traditional reflections on language. Their function is much more to open up a space of interaction with another person.[10] The fact that they *can be* construed as declarative or interrogative sentences for certain purposes does not entail that this is the sole correct way of understanding them (no matter how helpful it may be in regions of language use, such as explaining types of sentences).

4 PHENOMENOLOGY AS PHILOSOPHY

Both Wittgenstein and Heidegger turned their backs on the logic that had entranced them early on and tried to discover the principles of order in various regions of phenomena by exposing what is typically overlooked by much of traditional philosophy. Moreover, both continued to embrace a conception of a kind of philosophy based primarily on fresh descriptions of the world as it presents itself in our ordinary, everyday lives. Heidegger, as we have seen, calls his method "phenomenology," whereas Wittgenstein has no master term for his later method. The phenomenological dimension found in the later works of both philosophers is committed to preserving the understanding of things that inhabits our lives when the pretensions of technical sorts of philosophy have been stripped way.

Wittgenstein, as we saw earlier, suggests that ordinary language is in order as it is and so does not need any explanation. At other times, however, we get the feeling that he thinks this extreme hands-off stance is not sufficient and that some renovations are needed. Heidegger tends to be critical of the understanding embodied in our everyday ways of talking, although he is convinced that everydayness contains insights that should be respected and elaborated. This is one reason why he plays with etymologies and neologisms developed from plain speech.

Yet both philosophers are inclined to think that there is still a task for philosophy, whether it be called "justification" or "grounding." Wittgenstein rejects the project of foundation—philosophy "leaves everything as it is" (*PI* §124)—but he still feels that there are philosophical problems that call for elucidation and clarification. His point is not that philosophical justification is always impossible, but that it is often otiose: "Once I have exhausted the justifications [e.g., for following a rule], I have reached bedrock, and my spade is turned. Then I am inclined to say: 'This is simply what I do'" (*PI* §217).

Of course, to say that this is what we do is not to give a "naturalist" explanation for a phenomenon that genuine philosophy ought to say something about. Wittgenstein clearly sees the difference between *quid facti* questions and the sorts of *quid juris* questions that philosophy has always tried to answer. These questions of justification still are on the lookout for something like what the tradition has called "essence" and, in this sense, there is a genuine undertaking called "philosophy." What is distinctive about Wittgenstein's approach to philosophy, however, is the awareness that his sorts of phenomenological elucidations—observations that light up the grammar of what we say and do—are not an undertaking that can be done correctly only in one way, as argument-driven philosophy generally assumes. There are different approaches to clarification and perspicuous representation depending on the different purposes we may have. But insofar as those purposes are part of what makes up the stream of life we all flow in, "Philosophy only states what everyone admits" (*PI* §599; Anscombe's translation).

Although Heidegger's methodological considerations about how to do philosophy are much more complex, I believe he would have sympathy for some of Wittgenstein's thoughts on reenvisioning philosophy. We see his openness to a wide range of approaches to questioning in his later view of "thinking" (*Denken*) (*BW* chap. 8–11). Moreover, Heideggerian phenomenology is always coupled with a hermeneutics that tries to articulate the background of meanings that underlies and makes possible our understandings of things. It is typical of Heidegger's philosophizing to look at things under different aspects, from different viewpoints. Instead of arriving at a final answer, he circles back to the vocabulary of the plain. Both Wittgenstein and Heidegger are pluralists about philosophy, aware of how multiple contexts and tasks generate different views and approaches.

Those of us who recognize the contribution of these philosophers to the postmodern outlook, with its anti-essentialist tenor, may be surprised to see how often each of them uses the word "essence." But it is important to note that the word "essence" in their vocabulary is somewhat different from the way the word is traditionally used. In oft-cited passages, Wittgenstein says, "*Essence* is expressed in grammar," and "Grammar tells what kind of object anything is" (*PI* §371, 373). To speak of "essence" from a Wittgensteinian standpoint is to think of all language as structured by nets of combinatorial possibilities embedded in the usage of the language-games currently being played. Hence, to grasp what something is *essentially* is to see its place in the play of meanings and typical exclusions that determine the possible ways we can talk about anything. Because the grammar of language-games can change with circumstances, what counts as "essence" can also change. On Wittgenstein's view, if one thinks of an "object" as defined by whatever constellation of possible meanings various clusters of words in related language-games can have, then the "Being" of an object must be circumscribed by the underlying structures embedded in our languages. This is the constitutive view of language I have attributed to both Wittgenstein and Heidegger (see Guignon 1990a).

Heidegger, on the other hand, uses the word "essence" in a verbal sense, where it means not necessary attributes but something more like an inbuilt pathway of essential development of an entity whose mode of being is a becoming and unfolding into presence *as* a such-and-such. The nature of this unfolding is articulated in the natural languages people speak, and also (rather mysteriously) in language's "silent saying [*Sage*]" (*OWL* 126), where things first announce themselves. Heidegger's phenomenological conception of language as "expressing" (*Aussprechen*, literally, speaking out), like Wittgenstein's conception of language, is understood as a medium in which things come into their own and first become what they are.

In sum, we have found that Wittgenstein and Heidegger seem to be on the same page in their underlying conception of philosophy as phenomenology in the broad sense given to that term by Heidegger. For both thinkers, philosophy addresses a range of questions arising from traditional philosophical inquiries, and it looks for clarifying insights aimed at sidestepping or undermining those problems. For each, the appropriate method is description: a matter of diagnosing and treating the problems by calling attention to often unnoticed features of ordinary life. Both believe that there are certain underlying structures, deeply embedded although subject to change, that can be found either in the "worldhood of the world" or in the "grammar" of our language-games. Observing these enduring sorts of "essencing" can help us unravel some of the confusions that create philosophical puzzles in the first place.

It goes without saying that, in addition to these similarities, there are also profound differences between the methods and assumptions of the two philosophers. For example, Wittgenstein concentrates mostly on language, whereas Heidegger sees the linguistic ordering of being as going hand in hand with events arising from the interaction of earth, mortals, and gods. And Heidegger's diagnoses and redescriptions rely on metaphors of opening, concealing, emerging-into-presence, and so forth, whereas Wittgenstein's tries to stick to ordinary language. Nevertheless, the two philosophers can be grouped together in order to suggest a new and innovative way of doing philosophy.

NOTES

1. The most extensive study I have seen is Gier (1981).
2. My 1970s use of the term "constitutive" for this conception of language was influenced by talks with Charles Taylor, but it did not appear in print

until the publication of my 1979 dissertation, *Heidegger and the Problem of Knowledge*. I have expanded on the idea in several essays, including Guignon (1990b) and Guignon (1991).

3. The ancient idea that there is an underlying principle of order (*logos*) that shapes both thought and reality clarifies Hegel's ([1816] 2010, 29) claim that his *Science of Logic* is the "exposition of God as he is in his eternal essence, before the creation of nature and finite spirit." I am grateful to Richard Manning for help clarifying these ideas.

4. The last course Heidegger taught before beginning to write *Being and Time*, in the winter semester of 1925–26 at Marburg, was titled Logic: The Question of Truth. In the words of Thomas Sheehan, "As soon as the course ended, Heidegger went off to his cottage . . . and started writing out *Being and Time* by hand" (*LQT* ix).

5. In his 1925–26 lecture course, Logic: The Question of Truth, Heidegger gives a definition of "logic" as understood by the ancient Greeks, which probably would have been widely accepted at the time of these lectures: "Logic investigates speaking [*Reden*]—the thinking that defines things—inasmuch as speaking uncovers things" (*LQT* 6).

6. It should be noted, of course, that pointing out a common interest in logic in the case of Wittgenstein and Heidegger can be somewhat misleading, since the former had been influenced by Russell and Frege whereas the latter learned about logic through the Scholastics, Husserl, Hermann Lotze, and the Neo-Kantians.

7. The claim that there is a "hidden" meaning and ground that phenomenology is supposed to "let us see" is made at *BT* 35/59. The context makes it reasonable to suppose this refers to the *logos* in the "pregnant sense."

8. All quotes on these opening pages are from Park (1997, chap. 1).

9. Here, the similarity to Wittgenstein is quite striking: Wittgenstein says, "What we are 'tempted to say' . . . is, of course, not philosophy; but it is its raw material" (*PI* §254). The idea of what we are tempted to say has been developed by Stanley Cavell (1976).

10. Charles Taylor's papers (1985a, 1985b, 1995a, 1995b) are especially helpful on this subject.

7 Understanding the Being of the "We"
Wittgenstein, Heidegger, and Idealism

Edward Minar

[T]he anxiety that prevails today in the face of idealism is an anxiety
in the face of philosophy. (BP 167)

1 AFFINITIES

Both Wittgenstein and Heidegger describe their philosophical tasks in terms
of dialectics of forgetting and reminding. For the later Wittgenstein, "[t]he
work of the philosopher consists in marshalling recollections [*Erinnerun-
gen*, reminders] for a particular purpose" (*PI* §127). These bring to mind
"[t]he aspects of things that are most important for us" but "hidden because
of their simplicity and familiarity" (*PI* §129). Wittgenstein's aim is not "to
see right into [*durchschauen*] phenomena" (*PI* §90) as much as "to *understand* something that is already in plain view. For *this* is what we seem in
some sense not to understand" (*PI* §89). By asking "is the word ever actually used in this way in the language in which it is at home?" (*PI* §116),
and thereby reminding us of "the *kinds of statement* that we make about
phenomena" (*PI* §90), Wittgenstein's grammatical descriptions enact our
"struggle against the bewitchment of our understanding by the resources of
our language" by bringing together (somehow, occluded) aspects of our uses
of words with which "we have long been familiar" (*PI* §109).

Similarly, the Heidegger of *Being and Time* intends to respond to a forgetfulness characteristic of philosophy, forgetfulness of the question of
Being (*BT* 2/21). In the first instance, he seeks to understand what is "ontically 'closest' . . . and ontologically farthest but pre-ontologically . . . surely
not a stranger" (*BT* 16/37): Dasein or human being in its average everydayness. The goal is to recover an understanding of Being that philosophy
has "*passed over* in explicating Dasein" (*BT* 43/69). As phenomenologist,
Heidegger seeks to characterize Dasein in terms that are descriptive rather
than explanatory. "We must . . . choose such a way of access and such
a kind of interpretation that this entity can show itself in itself and from
itself" (*BT* 16/37). Phenomenology, then, will involve "letting something
be seen" (*BT* 44/70); "entities must . . . show themselves with the kind of

access which genuinely belongs to them" (*BT* 37/61). What appears "as that which shows itself," then, "is the Being of entities, its meaning, its modifications and derivatives." "Least of all," however, "can the Being of entities be anything such that 'behind it' stands something else 'which does not appear'" (*BT* 35–36/60). Starting from within, Heidegger reminds us of how we comport ourselves toward the world in which we exist. The need for reminders stems from a disorientation originating in particular features of our starting point—average everydayness. These distract us from the true character of Dasein, particularly when—as in philosophical reflection—we attempt to exercise a certain kind of intellectual control over everydayness, trying to ground it.

These are not accidental features of Heidegger's approach to phenomenology. Where Wittgenstein aims to "bring words back from their metaphysical to their everyday use" (*PI* §116), Heidegger seeks to unloose us from the tangles of philosophical confusion, allowing us to recuperate aspects of our ability to talk from which we have been alienated. Moreover, in pursuing his goals Heidegger draws on and draws out forms of self-knowledge akin to those elicited by Wittgenstein's methods.[1]

One way of trying to come to grips with the likenesses between Wittgenstein's and Heidegger's approaches is to consider how both court the suspicion, or shall we say the appearance, of idealism. They recognize that crucial aspects of their positions will appear to some readers to betray idealist sympathies, and their responses to these worries are internal to their philosophies. Wittgenstein emphasizes the reliance of what we mean on community agreement and the role of human needs, interests, and purposes in shaping our language-games. Heidegger's master thought is that Dasein is Being-in-the-world. He calls world "a moment in the structure of Dasein's mode of being" (*BP* 166). He delights in provocative formulations of the consequences: "Of course only as long as Dasein *is* . . . 'is there' Being" (*BT* 212/255). "*'There is' truth only insofar as Dasein is and so long as Dasein is*" (*BT* 226/269). What shows up in the world of our concern depends on a socially instituted background of significance rooted in practice.

For both thinkers, the world is home to *meaning*.[2] Things are given, constituted, as meaningful. There is a residual temptation to think that if so, things must be constituted *as* meaningful *by* a meaning-giving subject. If the world's hospitability to meaning requires a general, philosophical explanation, idealism will seem a prominent option. In my view, if we read Wittgenstein and Heidegger as advocating the *kind* of account of our relation to the world that they both are in fact most concerned to combat, the charge of idealism will appear not just natural but also inevitable. We can resist such readings only if we allow our authors to remake our expectations of what philosophy has to offer. If human agreement, or grammar, or discourse, or Dasein as Being-in-the-world, is interpreted as contributing to an account of our relation to the world in general that seeks to guarantee that our thoughts reach out to the world, both Wittgenstein and Heidegger show up as thinkers of an idealist cast. On this way of understanding them, each would *begin* philosophizing by stepping back from our place in the world. Each would *then*, on realizing that searching for a guarantee of contact with the world itself would require not only a stepping back but also a turning away from ourselves, propose strategies for coping with the resultant *limitations*, acknowledging them as such. We would be advised to be satisfied with what amount to idealist admonitions to settle for what we already have while accepting a particular conception of the meagerness and felt inadequacy of our everyday resources.[3]

The distancing step that initiates this dialectic is, however, neither obligatory nor plausible; idealist interpretations undo themselves.[4] Again, that is, reading Wittgenstein and Heidegger idealistically is symptomatic of the kind of philosophical confusion they mean to dispel. In working through the appearance of idealism, they draw us toward the realization that the descriptions they give of our lives in the world and in language are badly deformed by interpreting them as philosophical *theses* or explanations (see *PI* §§128, 109).

My aim is to call attention to specific ways in which Wittgenstein and Heidegger invite and try to allay the suspicion of idealism. In the end, I suggest that undoing the appearance of idealism helps locate the role of the "we" on whose "agreement in judgements" (*PI* §242) the very possibility of our having a world might be taken to depend. In the course of *our* philosophical activity we take on the *use* of this "we"—which at first blush might seem suited to signify a kind of transcendental subject. But in doing so, we do not specify a "something" that can serve as a ground for meaning in general, but rather express a recognition of the ground before us as the ground (*RFM* VI §31).

2 IDEALISM

How should we understand the issue of idealism here? There is reason not to try to be too explicit, as it is to Wittgenstein's and Heidegger's purposes to allow no definitive answer, as though "idealism" names a fixed set of doctrines with a stable sense. Suppose we ask how our thoughts and actions, on the one hand, and the world, on the other, must be constituted for the former to connect up to the latter in a meaningful way; in the case of thoughts, to represent it. Idealism points toward one kind of answer—namely, that "we, or our minds, or *the* mind, make up the world, to at least some extent" (Travis 2000, 11). The only world we have to do with is constituted or rendered intelligible by the ways our needs, practices, and interests shape how we go on with our concepts; any *further* question about how the world really is, about how it is in itself, fails fully to make sense.

Heidegger approaches the issue of idealism as it emerges in connection with his basic tenet, that Dasein is Being-in-the-world, quite straightforwardly:

The world is something Dasein-ish . . . . [Here] our inquiry comes up
against phenomena that are not familiar to the common understanding
. . . for which reason this understanding is compelled to set them aside
by arguments: . . . [viz.] If the world belongs to the being that I myself
in each instance am, to the Dasein, then it is something subjective. If it
is subjective and nature and the universe of being as intraworldly are
objective, then these latter beings—nature and the cosmos—are really
subjective. . . . [W]e have thus taken the stand of a most extreme subjective idealism. [According to the common understanding, then], [t]he
foregoing interpretation of the world [as "Dasein-ish"] is untenable [for
it appears as this idealism]. (*BP* 166–67)

Heidegger's prevailing attitude to the allegation that on his view the world
turns out to be subjective is that how seriously we should take it depends
on what is meant by "what and how the subject is" (*BP* 167)—a matter he
regards as altogether neglected in traditional debates between idealists and
realists. *His* conception of the subject, for these purposes, is made manifest
through his descriptions of Dasein as Being-in-the-world. These descriptions, he assures us, presuppose that "we, the Dasein, in apprehending beings, are always already in a world" (*BP* 166). This should prevent us from
conceiving of this subject as something prior, a locus from which the world
has been projected: "The world is something 'subjective,' presupposing that
we correspondingly define subjectivity with regard to this phenomenon of
world" (*BP* 168). Nevertheless, Heidegger decries straightforward dismiss-
als of idealism: "[W]e have to ask what . . . idealism—which today is feared
almost like the foul fiend incarnate—really is searching for" (*BP* 167). The
"extreme subjective idealism" with which the "common understanding" is
prone to confound Heidegger's own stance has inherited its notions of subject and world from its realist counterpart. It is committed to theorizing
the relation between two kinds of entities present-at-hand, thereby covering
over its own potential for opening up of the question of Dasein's Being.[5]
By opening the possibility that his thinking will be conflated with "an an-
thropocentric or subjectivistic-idealistic philosophy" (*BP* 224), Heidegger
forces us to recognize the centrality of the question of who *we*—we who are
philosophizing—are: "By means of fundamental ontology, which has the
Dasein as its ontological theme, the being that we ourselves are moves over
to the center of philosophical inquiry" (*BP* 224).

Some find similar strains of idealism in Wittgenstein. For Bernard Williams, the later Wittgenstein comes to the thought that "the limits of *our*
language mean the limits of *our* world," a plural version of Tractarian transcendental solipsism. Here "we" is not to refer to an empirical group to be
contrasted with the Hopi, cats, or Martians (to take the standard tropes
of otherness). Such contrasts would fall within the purview of our language and would not set limits to our world in the relevant sense. Instead,
"[W]hat the world is for us is shown by the fact that we can make sense of

some things and not others: or rather—to lose the last remnants of an empirical and third-personal view—in the fact that some things and not others make sense" (Williams 1976, 84). This factoring out of the "*fact* that we can make sense of some things and not others" is of paramount importance. On the one hand, the thought must be that in reformulating the issue in terms of what makes sense *punkt*, we are *identifying with* the "we" rather than identifying it, pointing it out. On the other, even with the disappearance of the "we," the world must still be viewed as *given* in *our* language (Williams 1976, 82). Here the Wittgensteinian standpoint remains, if not robustly, at least unequivocally, idealist:

> So *our* language, in this sense in which its being as it is has no empirical explanation, shows us everything as it appears to our interests, our concerns, our activities, though in the only sense in which we could meaningfully say that they determined everything, that statement would be false. The fact that in this way everything can be expressed only via human interests and concerns, things which are expressions of mind, and which themselves cannot ultimately be explained in any further terms: That provides grounds, I suggest, for calling such a view a kind of *idealism*. (Williams 1976, 85)

A form of *transcendental* idealism, with the attendant air of paradoxicality: if we try to say that our interests determine everything, we not only seem to step beyond the limits of intelligibility, but also appear to contravene something crucial that our interests have determined—namely, that our interests do not determine everything. We have, for example, *decided* that "it must be nonsense to say that anything about a number has been determined by our decisions" (Williams 1976, 95). Williams takes the tension here to represent a deep, inherent problem for the position.

Where is Wittgenstein in all this? What gives rise to the sense that there is an idealistic presence in his late writing? How does he deflect this suspicion?

3 AGREEMENT IN JUDGMENTS

As part of its complex dialectic, the rule-following considerations of *Philosophical Investigations* criticize a Platonist picture of meaning. On this picture, what is determined as the proper application of concepts is fixed by an underlying structure of rule-like entities or meanings, operating independently of our contribution and thus setting objective standards for how words are to be used. Wittgenstein reminds us that (ordinary) rules for using expressions are subject to interpretation, but when misunderstandings arise we endeavor to address them by giving examples or by adducing reformulations of the original rules. As with the original use of the expressions in question, this process of explanation relies for its successes on the responsiveness of those with whom we are trying to forge an understanding, with whom we share dealings with the world (see Diamond 1990). Appealing to a deeper level of rule-like entities to explain what is *really* going on when understanding is achieved is inert; such rules as we may have "had in mind" are themselves subject to interpretation. We are tempted to suppose that such underlying meanings are special in that they somehow bear the uses they determine on their sleeves, but we find that we have no right to take them to operate as they would have to serve as genuine norms. That is, insofar as they would be designed to be *available* to inform our uses of expressions but not *interpretable*, they would have to be *private*; what they determine would be the privilege of the one in whose mind they were laid up. Here, however, the picture gives out: "[T]o *think* one is following a rule is not to follow a rule. And that's why it's not possible to follow a rule 'privately'; otherwise, thinking one was following a rule would be the same thing as following it" (*PI* §202). At this point, we cannot make sense of the idea of the rule follower's actions according with *any* rule. The moral is that, counter to the picture, "there is a way of grasping a rule which is *not* an *interpretation*, but which, from case to case of application, is exhibited in what we call 'following the rule' and 'going against it'" (*PI* §201). Rules and interpretations "alone," by themselves, do not determine what counts as accord with them (*PI* §198). A whole background of contingencies— including "customs (usages, institutions)" (*PI* §199)—is in play when we count someone as going on in the same way as we do, when we count on his or her uptake.[6]

Coupled with the contingencies of responsiveness that are taken as foregone in our ways of following rules, the failure of an underlying structure of meanings to secure what counts as the correct uses of expressions might produce recoil into the idea that there are no genuinely objective standards of correctness.[7] At the end of the rule-following considerations, Wittgenstein seeks to counter this impression:

> "So you are saying that human agreement [*die Übereinstimmung der Menschen*, attunement of human beings] decides what is true and what is false?"—What is true or false is what human beings *say*; and it is in their *language* that human beings agree. That is agreement not in opinions, but rather in form of life. (*PI* §241)
>
> It is not only agreement in definitions, but also (odd as it may sound) agreement in judgements that is required for communication by means of language. This seems to abolish logic, but does not do so. (*PI* §242; cf. *RFM* VI §39)

It would seem that here Wittgenstein is confidently dismissing the suspicion that his commitments dissolve into a pernicious "subjective idealism."

Wittgenstein is clear that although "[o]ur language game only works . . . when a certain agreement prevails . . . the concept of agreement does not enter into the language-game" (*Z* §430). Accordingly, "[t]he agreement of humans that is a presupposition of logic is not an agreement in *opinions*" (*RFM* VI §49) but "a consensus of *action*: a consensus of doing the same thing, reacting in the same way" (*LFM* 184). Why is agreement in "reactions" agreement in *judgments*? What Wittgenstein has in mind is that we react to others *as* going on in the same way or not. These reactions to the intelligibility of others cannot be characterized as such independently of the facts involved in *our* being participants in a practice. It is critical to recognize that what lies behind the thought that the agreement in form of life that makes up agreement in judgments is not agreement in opinions. Until we determine what is said on the occasion of the use of a given form of words, there are no settled, determinate states of affairs expressed in our words, as it were "already," on which to agree or disagree; again, rules, definitions, meanings "*alone*" do not fix what is said. Rather, what is said is determined only where the relevant agreement manifesting our taking *this* as going on the same, *this* as doing something else, etc., holds sway. Our ability and willingness to count others as doing the same as we do provide the backdrop for the whole proceeding. "We talk and act. That is already presupposed in everything that I am saying" (*RFM* VI §17).

Whence the uneasiness that the role of agreement in judgments "seems to abolish logic"? On one level, the worry is fairly straightforward. If what one must do in following a rule—in adding, say—is dependent on contingent facts about the world, including facts about agreement, doesn't this introduce contingency into the determination of a particular course of action by the rule itself, undoing the force of the logical "must"? This train of thought casts the role of the relevant facts in the wrong place. Whatever determines what we are to do in adding comes from the practice of adding itself. The definiteness of any particular result is part of what it is for adding to be governed by determinate rules. These rules remain necessities, as is revealed in their role in the practice; the practice proceeds in such a way that the rules of addition do not leave open multiple courses of action, and they are not held open for revision, any more than in measuring, standards of measurement are always subject to being remeasured themselves. Generally, "the logical 'must' is a component part of the propositions of logic, and these are not propositions of human natural history" (*RFM* VI §49). What remains *contingent* is the fact that we have the practice of adding in the first place, along with whatever factors contribute to the practice playing its particular roles in our lives. Other, in some ways similar, practices might play somewhat similar roles in somewhat similar lives, but whether and in what sense these would count as *adding* is at best an open question. (The answer, for one thing, will depend on why we are asking.) Compare what Wittgenstein says in concluding *Investigations* §242: "[W]hat we call 'measuring' is in part determined by a certain constancy in results of measurement" (*PI* §242). This does not mean that how long something is depends on the contingencies involved in our reaching agreement in results; the existence of the practice or custom itself hinges on the relevant worldly conditions that normally do hold.

A deeper dimension to the apprehension about abolishing logic concerns not so much the necessity with which a particular course of action follows from a rule like "+2" as the very idea that such a rule can determine anything in the first place. On the Platonist picture Wittgenstein targets, it would be settled beforehand—prior to use—what our words mean; they "already" express determinate concepts or meanings making up the logical framework of language. Now suppose that the "problem of interpretation" broached in *Investigations* §198 and §201 leaves us with the following quandary: even given "determinate meanings," is there not always a further question about what words mean in their uses in particular contexts on particular occasions, about what *we* mean by them? After all, how these determinate meanings get *applied* remains up for interpretation. Suppose in addition that it appears that Wittgenstein's point is that the *further* question cannot be addressed in terms of still deeper meaning-rules (or the capacity of our candidate Platonic entities somehow to self-interpret), but only by *adding* the bare facts of human agreement. Then Wittgenstein's view would become that what we succeed in saying is always dependent on these sorts of facts. Now, however, it is unclear that this would be satisfactory, because at this point the applicability of the logical framework of language appears to depend on facts about the world (in particular, contingencies about *us*). Moreover, *which* facts will ground *which* applications must be determined by how the world is, in particular by those facts of agreement involved in determining what counts as going on in the same way. *Nothing*, it appears, is really settled beforehand.

Dissolution of the quandary comes in recognizing that it is indeed not settled prior to their being put to use what our words mean and that Wittgenstein is not appealing to agreement as an added "ingredient" that rectifies that situation. Agreement, in other words, is not an element that makes what our words *already* mean applicable. To think so would be a misunderstanding, one congenial to the picture with which he is struggling, of what Wittgenstein wants the notion of agreement to do. The misconstrual would be to take his appeal to agreement as a sort of (as it turns out, misfiring) attempt to complete the job that, as originally conceived, meanings alone were meant to do. But as we have seen, agreement manifests the capacity of our words *as put to use* to express anything intelligible in the first place. What Wittgenstein is worried about in scrutinizing the ways his appeal to shared practices "appears to abolish logic"—the position from which he feels he must labor to distance himself—is an idealistic reaction to Platonism, emphasizing as it does *our* role in determining meaning. This idealism shares with Platonism the demand that logic already operate beneath the bedrock of language as we use it. It threatens to have the consequence of abolishing logic in its implication that such a demand does not uncover genuine, independent norms; norms are conceived as always requiring help from us. At this point, they would become mere expressions of our (perhaps shared, but so far merely contingently so) subjectivity. Thus, we might say that idealism shares with its Platonist alter ego failure in that "difficult thing" of "recognizing the"—so to speak, everyday—"ground before us as the ground" (*RFM* VI §31).

4 ESSENCE AND GRAMMAR

Another way in which Wittgenstein courts and at the same time counters the suspicion of idealism emerges in *Investigations* §§371–73:

> *Essence* is expressed in grammar. (*PI* §371)
>   Consider: "The only correlate in language to an objective necessity is an arbitrary rule. It is the only thing which one can milk out of this objective necessity into a proposition." (*PI* §372)
>   Grammar tells us what kind of object anything is. (Theology as grammar.) (*PI* §373)

Now obviously §371 does not say that essence is *created* by grammar, but §372 indicates a problematic path toward thinking of the dictum in that way. Take what P. M. S. Hacker attributes to Wittgenstein, in the name of the "autonomy of grammar," in his commentary on §371: "Far from grammar reflecting the nature of things, what we conceive to be natures or essences are merely the shadows cast by grammar" (Hacker 1993, 236). This is misleading. Hacker's intentions notwithstanding, his late Wittgenstein here sounds suspiciously like he adopts a simple *inversion* of the picture conveyed by a metaphysical realist reading of the *Tractatus*, on which the rules of logical syntax show the logical form of the world by mirroring the possible combinations of objects. These determine the combinations of signs that the syntax allows as meaningful and so justify the syntax that permits them. On this view, recalling the Platonism targeted in the rule-following considerations, there are intrinsic necessities, out there, lying behind our use of concepts; they show in what counts as intelligible and what not, although the only way of *expressing* this in words is at best indirect; it is somehow shown in the "arbitrary rules" of the language. Once we have come this far, it appears impossible to suppress the question of *why* these rules manage to reflect the logical form of the world. The only viable alternative to said Platonism seems to be the idealist-sounding inversion that Hacker appeared to take as the message of §371, that conventions expressing our needs, interests, and purposes *project* the essences as "shadows" of themselves. But (as Hacker would no doubt agree), the inverted picture would still rest on taking seriously a question of explanatory priority that ought not to arise, and Wittgenstein's appeal to grammar is more complicated than it suggests. We ought not to think of essence and grammar as distinct and separately describable, but rather—in contrast to what the inverted, idealist-sounding picture invites—to read Wittgenstein as pushing against assigning priority to *either* language or world, conceived as separate realms. There is no sense to the idea of stepping back from our means of representation to ask whether they correspond to some independent reality; they embody or express the possibilities of meaning. A different grammar would mean different concepts, means of representing different essences.

Consider a passage that tempts Williams to read Wittgenstein as an idealist: "We have a colour system as we have a number system. Do the systems reside in *our* nature or in the nature of things? How are we to put it?—*Not* in the nature of numbers or colours" (Z §357). As Stephen Mulhall says, Wittgenstein's diffidence betrays reluctance about the either-or question (Mulhall 2008, 395). Wittgenstein has just suggested that without agreement in judgments about colors—agreement that depends in part on facts about us, in part on facts about world—our concept of color *would* not exist (Z §351). But these facts do not concern some preestablished essence of *color*. The role of the facts is not to guarantee a harmony between language and reality (which is already there in the uses that give language its life here); rather, they account for these particular linguistic practices finding application in our lives. Thus the ambivalence in *Zettel* §357, underscored in the next section: "Then is there something arbitrary about this system? Yes and no. It is akin both to what is arbitrary and to what is non-arbitrary" (Z §358; cf. *PI* §520). Not because the conventions governing the "system" are arbitrary but somehow manage to show the form of reality (either by reflecting it or projecting it), but because both our convening and our world have shaped the form of life in which the "system" finds a home.

As *PI* §373 indicates, giving grammatical descriptions is not simply reformulating verbal rules—it is telling us what kind of object something is. Describing the grammar of our concept of pain, for example, involves appreciating the role of the behaviors that are naturally expressive of pain. Pain can go unexpressed, of course, but what it is for *pain* to show itself is for it to be expressed in behavior in *these* ways. . . . What pain *is* is shown partly by calling attention to the connection between our talk of pain and our natural reactions to pain, others' and our own. *This* is what makes up our life with pain. "My relation to the appearances here [i.e., behavior] is part of my concept" (Z §543).

5   DISCOURSE

A fair Heideggerian rendering of "essence is expressed in grammar" would be "coming to presence (essence) is expressed in discourse (*Rede*; talk, telling)" (see *BT* 167–68/211). What is discourse? Heidegger tells us that "[d]iscourse is the Articulation of intelligibility [*Verständlichkeit*]" (*BT* 161/203–4), and that "[t]he intelligibility of Being-in-the-world . . . *expresses itself as discourse*" (*BT* 161/204). Although "[f]or the most part, discourse is expressed by being spoken out, and has always been so expressed; it is language" (*BT* 167/211), Heideggerian discourse is meant to be a *precondition* of particular linguistic expression; the "Articulation" on the basis of which we tell things apart, in the first instance in using them. Hubert Dreyfus (1991, 224) writes that discourse is "picking out the joints of the equipmental whole in the course of using equipment." As such, discourse enables us to bring particular things to language. In my view, discourse comprises largely implicit but articulable rules-in-use that constitute the particular meanings embodied in a practice against a background of worldly involvements. Such rules are not a ground for the practice as following these rules just is engaging in it with the appropriate mastery or understanding. Knowing what a hammer is called is based in knowing hammers, knowing how to use them, having mastery of the different ways hammers are uncovered in shared equipmental wholes. Discourse gives form to the space of meanings within which things show up, a nexus of agreed-in practices that makes representing things possible.

There are resemblances to the Wittgensteinian notion of grammar here.[8] Toward the end of §34 of *Being and Time*, Heidegger provides a complicated account of the relation between grammar and discourse. "Dasein has language," he writes; "man shows himself as the entity which talks" (*BT* 165/208). This is not because talking makes Being-in-the-world possible, but rather because "he [man] is the entity which is such as to discover the world and Dasein itself" (*BT* 165/208–9). Articulating world in dealing with particular entities (beings), Dasein can take its understanding into language.

But discourse—*logos*—first enters into *reflection* in connection with *assertion*, and here it gets interpreted as "logic," in particular, as that which provides norms of assertion. "Grammar sought its foundations in the 'logic' of this *logos*" (*BT* 165/209), Heidegger says; but distancing discourse (*logos*) by approaching it through assertion led to confusion: "The task of *liberating* grammar from logic requires beforehand a positive understanding of the basic a priori structure of discourse in general as an *existentiale*" (*BT* 166/209). In consequence, "this articulation [discourse] must not be confined to entities within-the-world which we cognize by considering them theoretically, and which we express in sentences" (*BT* 166/209). Although this crucial point is bound to be disguised in assertions *about* discourse, what is articulated in discourse is not a structure of representations, a conceptual scheme, but first and foremost the structure of world in which things first show up as having significance.[9] Behind what we put into assertions, there is an understanding of things expressed in practice. Grasping what a thing is by taking it up and thus relating it to the world of our concern prepares us for calling it by name.

6   HEIDEGGER AND IDEALISM

For Heidegger, the "we" constituting Dasein cannot be characterized independently of its disclosure of world:

> [U]ncovering . . . takes asserting out of the province of "subjective" discretion, and brings the uncovering Dasein face to face with the entities themselves. . . . "We" presuppose truth because "we," being in the kind of Being which Dasein possesses, *are* "in the truth." . . . It is not we who presuppose "truth"; but it is "truth" that makes it at all possible ontologically for us to be able to *be* such that we "presuppose" anything at all. . . . *"[W]e" must . . . presuppose "ourselves" as having the attribute of disclosedness.* . . . We must "make" the presupposition of truth because it *is* one that has been "made" already with the Being of the "we." (*BT* 227–28/270–71)

Here Dasein becomes who it is in the disclosedness of world to it; *before* this, there would be no "subject" to project its understanding onto the world.

Heidegger knows that we will be prone to thinking otherwise. We shall read him as exploring our conceptual scheme and then reflecting that, as we cannot get outside its limits, *our* world, the only world we have access to, must be formed by our practical and conceptual activity. It then seems as though the world as thus "intended" and structured can be contrasted with the world in itself; further, that the world in itself may be allowed to drop out of the picture. (This development could be regarded favorably or unfavorably.) Heidegger's immediate counter to such misreadings is that the constitutive determinations of Dasein cannot be described without reference to the fact that the world is always already disclosed to Dasein and is therefore not the result of its activity.[10] But even to say this raises the prospect of a kind of transcendental idealism:

> World exists . . . only if Dasein exists, only if there is Dasein. Only if world is there, if Dasein exists as being-in-the-world, is there understanding of being, and only if this understanding exists are intraworldly beings unveiled as extant and handy. World-understanding as Dasein-understanding is self-understanding. Self and world belong together in a single entity, the Dasein . . . in the unity of the structure of being-in-the-world. (*BP* 297)

Now it may appear that world and subject have been absorbed into Dasein; once one starts making *assertions* about how "[w]orld is a determination of the Dasein's being" (*BP* 296), an aspect of the structure of what sounds like a transcendental subject, idealism looms.

Practically every time Heidegger invites this worry, he wards it off by insisting that we have already taken for granted the picture of Dasein as discrete subject that he is trying to undermine. How does his response go?[11]

Heidegger tries to dismantle debates between realists, idealists, and skeptics over the existence and character of the external world in *Being and Time* §43(a). He begins by suggesting that we confuse asking what reality (the Being of the present-at-hand) means with asking what kind of access we have to real (present-at-hand) entities or beings—"whether the Real can be independent 'of consciousness' or whether there can be a transcendence of consciousness into the 'sphere' of the Real" (*BT* 202/246). We lack a clear understanding of the place of the concept of *independence* here: until we have clarified Dasein as Being-in-the-world, and thus located the Being of the subject, questions of the independence and reality of particular things remain ambiguous. We are prone to thinking that this independence (the independence of *world* as an *object*) should be settleable a priori by Dasein. Our relation to world would hang on Dasein's *first* being able to make such a determination about world as object—say, about whether *esse est percipi*.

Challenging the basic assumptions of this misleading picture, Heidegger maintains that access to what he calls "the 'world'" and "the Real"—basically, entities present-at-hand—is found in Being-in-the-world as care, which means that even such entities are ultimately intelligible to us in terms of the broad context or background within which Dasein comports itself toward them. The context is what Heidegger calls *Sinn*, "meaning," and it is Dasein that is meaningful; Dasein's Being is the background against which entities make sense, and not a subjective ground of it. Questions of the existence of "the 'world' and 'the Real'" cannot get raised as general, philosophical issues about the possibility or ground of our access to such entities. Most important here is that when world as a "determination" of Dasein's Being is disclosed, "the 'world' has in each case been discovered too" (*BT* 203/247). This implies that our ways of determining what is real are intelligible only in terms of how we actually deal with particular entities. Heidegger is adamant on this point: "Along with Dasein as Being-in-the-world, entities within-the-world have in each case already been disclosed" (*BT* 207/251). "Mere representing is in the genuine and best sense precisely with the entities themselves" (*HCT* 164). As a result, in trying to force the question of how things really are, we take the disclosure of Dasein's world, and with it the *discoveredness* of *some* real entities, as foregone. An important consequence is that our intra-worldly ways of determining what is real have not been exposed to the alleged global demand for grounding.

Thus the skeptical specter of confinement to the "'cabinet' of consciousness" (*BT* 62/89) arises only insofar as we have mistaken the being together present-at-hand of the "physical" and the "psychical" for the phenomenon of Being-in-the-world (*BT* 204/248). Accordingly, Heidegger declares that "[t]he 'scandal of philosophy'" is not that proofs of the external world are wanting, but that "the kind of Being of the entity [Dasein] which . . . makes requests for proofs has not been made definite enough" (*BT* 205/249). Once we uncover who Dasein is, the problem of the external world devolves into, on the one hand, ontical questions about what entities are real, to be settled if at all by our usual modes of inquiry, and, on the other, ontological questions about the Being of the real (reality). The former involve our modes of comportment and inquiry; the latter are addressed by describing our understanding of the world as revealed in these modes—for example, by putting the characteristics of our ways of dealing with reality on display. In neither case has the legitimacy of our ways of proceeding *or* their involvement with particular entities been brought into question.

Heidegger finds "a grain of genuine inquiry" (*BT* 207/250) in both realism and idealism. What is "doxographically, as it were" correct in "the thesis of *realism* that the external world is Really present-at-hand" (*BT* 207/251) is that the world of Dasein involves a "world" of entities present-at-hand. But realism thinks that proof of this is both necessary and possible; it isolates the subject from the "objective" realm of real, independent entities, leaving it trying to grope its way out toward them. Idealism harbors a deeper insight: "As compared with realism, *idealism*, no matter how contrary and untenable it may be in its results, has an advantage in principle, provided it does not misunderstand itself as 'psychological' idealism" (*BT* 207/251). It "expresses [albeit misleadingly] an understanding of the fact that Being cannot be explained through entities," which it tries to register by saying that "Being is 'in the consciousness'" (*BT* 207/251). The Being of something is correlative to our understanding of the thing. It is elucidated through laying out how understanding discloses the thing from out of the world of significance as articulated by discourse. As a result, we cannot bring to bear a prior grasp of the essence or nature of things to yield a legitimation of this understanding, because such a discovery of things would already presuppose that their Being has been disclosed. "Reality [the Being of the real] is possible only in the understanding of Being" (*BT* 207/251); and in particular, "only because [Being] is understandable in Dasein . . . can Dasein also understand and conceptualize such characteristics of Being as independence, the 'in-itself,' and Reality in general" (*BT* 208/251). Heidegger concedes, then, that idealism *as* "the understanding that Being can never be explained by entities"—as pointing to the crucial, ontological difference between Being and entities (beings)—"affords the only correct possibility for a philosophical problematic" (*BT* 208/251). Call it what one will, this is not much idealism; it contains no vindication of idealist *theses* about the dependence of Being or entities on an isolated subject, empirical or transcendental. Our understanding of the notions of dependence and independence, rather, operates within the context of world, always already disclosed.

To summarize: existence, reality, objectivity, independence are, Heidegger says, not possible without Dasein. This should not give us pause, for these are not *properties* of things but "determinations of Dasein," dimensions of assessment of how we relate things in the world. Do entities exist without Dasein? Let's look and see. Does reality exist as the Being of the present-at-hand? That question gets no grip; the way to reveal the character of Being here is by describing the structure of Dasein's understanding of itself as Being-in-the-world.

As we have seen, Heidegger puts his stance in a manner that both evokes idealism and points to its emptiness:

> Entities *are*, quite independently of the experience by which they are disclosed, the acquaintance in which they are discovered, and the grasping in which their nature is ascertained. But Being "is" only in the understanding of those entities to which something like an understanding of Being belongs. (*BT* 183/228)
>
> Of course only as long as Dasein *is* (that is, only as long as an understanding of Being is ontically possible), "is there" Being. When Dasein does not exist "independence" "is" not either, nor "is" the "in-itself." (*BT* 212/255)

The scare quotes are used advisedly. If one endeavors to inquire into and make assertions about how Being is, if one seeks an ontological ground of our understanding—if one tries to ask whether our concepts are the right ones, Wittgenstein might say—one risks treating Being like another entity or being. And then what one is asking—if anything—is no longer what one thought one wanted to ask. That is, again: On the one hand, matters of the reality and independence of entities may well be settled by our everyday procedures. Further questions about the objectivity and reliability of our ways of making determinations about reality that emerge as we make our way through the world are not inherently *deeper*; they, too, get settled in the same kind of way, by probing of our modes of inquiry. If something satisfies *our* (no doubt mutable and revisable) standards of objectivity, there is no need for it to satisfy some *other*, ostensibly deeper, standards operating from some transcendent perspective. On the other hand, if we were to put *Being* directly into question—for example, by asking whether it is dependent on Dasein—we try to treat it like a something that *is*. Direct assertions about Being in general are bound to misfire; we are reminded of the Being of entities through looking at the structure of Dasein's understanding. For Wittgenstein, we let contingency enter in the wrong place when we look for a grounding for our practices. Similarly with Heidegger: we forget the difference between Being and entities (beings) when we try to ground our understanding of Being, treating it not as always already engaging with an always already meaningful world, but as something like a conceptual scheme or set of representations to be evaluated as true or false.

7 "WE"

If, as philosophical habit inclines us, we read Wittgenstein and Heidegger as trying to give accounts of the relations of our practices to the world, we are apt to read them as idealists. Their appeals to how our practices are shaped by our needs and interests as well as their criticisms of realist attempts to legitimate what we do "from outside" will appear to show either that our practices shape the world or that there is nothing outside our practices that needs to be shaped. But once we mold the "we" into a *something*, we try to lend it an explanatory weight that it cannot, and is not meant to, bear. So how *are* we to understand this "philosophical we," the we of "our practices," the Dasein of whom Heidegger says "we *are* it, each of us, we ourselves" (*BT* 15/36)?

If we take Wittgenstein's appeals to our practices or Heidegger's insistence that Dasein is Being-in-the-world to be attempts to adduce facts that explain the ground of our capacity to make sense of things, it will seem natural to treat the "we" as a group that can be abstracted from its practices and distinguished by some definite, specifiable characteristics, independent of those practices. But on the other hand, as Williams emphasized, the relevant facts are not going to concern an *empirically* specifiable group, within the world; we need a transcendental "we" to serve as the condition and limit of the possibility of any intelligibility whatsoever. Now the "we" seems either to find its place, nonsensically, *outside* the world; or to disappear altogether and thus have no explanatory role to play.[12] Idealism leaves us with no place to stand. As we have seen, Wittgenstein and Heidegger want to prevent this movement of thought from getting started. We fall prey to it in thinking that the "we" is something to be specified *first*. But the community is not established beforehand by independently specifiable criteria any more than it is revealed once and for all by a philosophical discovery. "We" are those who are competent in language and who on particular occasions make sense of each other and the world in the ways that we do. With whom we do this is not for philosophy to ascertain or to decide. One finds what it is to make sense by making oneself intelligible to oneself and others, through the means of self-expression within one's reach, which means one must be responsive to who the others are and how one relates to them in present circumstances. Thus is the Being of the "we" uncovered. There are no guarantees that we shall succeed in making sense. Perhaps *this* is the anxiety with which idealism, trying to offer philosophical comfort by presenting us with a ground that could be no ground, where none could be, leaves us.

NOTES

1. On Wittgenstein's appeal to the everyday as a method of self-knowledge, see the writings of Stanley Cavell—for example, Cavell (1976a).
2. For Heidegger, meaning [*Sinn*] is "that wherein the intelligibility [*Verständlichkeit*] of something maintains itself" (*BT* 151/193). If, as Heidegger says, "*only Dasein can be meaningful [sinnvoll] or meaningless [sinnlos]*" (*BT* 151/193), the sound of idealism cannot simply be muted.
3. On philosophical dissatisfaction with our "position" with respect to the world and various ways of conceptualizing and coping with it, see the writings of Barry Stroud—for example, Stroud (2011), especially chap. 5, "Indispensability."

4. On Wittgenstein, see Williams (1976). My understanding (in apparent contrast with Williams's) is that this "deconstruction" is deliberately enacted in Wittgenstein's texts.
5. For Heidegger, idealism harbors, if not a truth, at least an expression of something philosophically fundamental (see *BT* 207/251).
6. My current views on the rule-following considerations are in Minar (2011). For a close reading of the train of thought in *PI* §§201–2, see Minar (1994).
7. See the skeptical reading of the rule-following considerations in Kripke (1982), which shares a picture of determination by rules with the Platonism it opposes and which is under diagnosis in *PI* §§198–202.
8. Compare treatments in Mulhall (1996, 93; 2001a, 241–42). These treatments are significantly different.
9. That is, the nonrepresentational and non-individualistic background emphasized by Dreyfus (1991).
10. That is, the structures of Dasein's Being-in-the-world show Dasein's involvement with *particular* entities:

> To care belongs not only Being-in-the-world but also Being alongside entities within-the-world. . . . In thrownness is revealed that in each case Dasein . . . is already in a definite world and alongside a definite range of definite entities within-the-world. Disclosedness is essentially factical. (*BT* 221/264)

No room is left to ask for a ground for our involvement; Heidegger's descriptions could be said to enable us to see the ground before us as the ground. Thanks to the editors for bringing this way of putting the point to my attention.
11. For more detailed assessment, see Minar (2001). For an important treatment of related themes, see McManus (forthcoming b).
12. For a comparable point, see Moore (2007, 193).

8 Heidegger and Wittgenstein on External World Skepticism

Herman Philipse

1 INTRODUCTION

Heidegger and Wittgenstein presented themselves as radical philosophical revolutionaries, claiming that traditional philosophy suffers from serious defects. They both held that prominent problems of the philosophical tradition have to be defused, dissolved, destroyed, or deconstructed, instead of simply solved or naturalized.

According to Heidegger in *Being and Time*, "the" central question of philosophy has been *forgotten* (*BT* 2/21).[1] In order to raise it properly again we have to engage first in a phenomenological or hermeneutical explication of human self-understanding, which takes our everyday existence as its starting point, and aims at developing an adequate conceptual structure for human life or Dasein, the holistic network of so-called *existentialia*. But such an explication cannot succeed, Heidegger says, without a destruction (*Destruktion*) of the philosophical tradition (*BT* §6).

In his mature works, Wittgenstein held that exemplary *deep* philosophical problems arise through a misinterpretation of our forms of language, and that they have to be dissolved by providing a perspicuous representation of the interconnected ways in which we use the key terms in nonphilosophical contexts (*PI* §§111, 122). As Wittgenstein stressed, the ultimate aim of his later philosophy is "*complete* clarity," which "simply means that the philosophical problems should *completely* disappear" (*PI* §133).

It will be disconcerting for followers of Heidegger or Wittgenstein to observe that in contemporary analytic philosophy a number of philosophical problems that their masters sought to defuse, deconstruct, or dissolve have not disappeared. Many of the traditional problems of metaphysics and epistemology re-emerged, and a host of new solutions have been proposed. One will wonder, then, who or what went astray. Have present-day philosophers forgotten, or not even learned, the methodological lessons of Heidegger and/or Wittgenstein? Or is it rather the case that the diagnoses of traditional philosophy and the philosophical methods proposed by these protagonists are inadequate? Or, finally, should we explain our present predicament by the sociological observation that in philosophy many different factions have always coexisted, which have never been able to convince each other because decisive empirical or argumentative tests for their views are lacking? Do Heidegger's and Wittgenstein's proposals for a novel philosophical method perhaps presuppose points of view that are somehow optional?

Within the limited space of a chapter it will not be possible to discuss the numerous philosophical problems that were dismissed or allegedly dissolved by Heidegger or Wittgenstein in order to provide an answer to these questions. I shall focus on one traditional problem only, the problem of external world skepticism, which has been revived in recent philosophy in various forms. As one scholar recently wrote, "There has been a dramatic re-emergence of interest in radical skeptical arguments in the recent literature" (Pritchard 2005, 37).[2]

The setup of the chapter is as follows. First, I shall remind the reader of the structure of the problem, offer an explanation of why it arose in modern philosophy, briefly recall why it became central to philosophy at the end of the nineteenth century, and sketch the logical space of its possible solutions (§2). Next, I analyze Heidegger's dissolution of the problem of the external world as a complex of meaningless (*ohne Sinn*) questions in section 43a of *Being and Time*, comparing it with Carnap's deconstruction in *Pseudoproblems in Philosophy* (*Scheinprobleme in der Philosophie*) of 1928 (§3). We will then move on to Wittgenstein's notes on G. E. Moore's articles "Defence of Common Sense" (first published in 1925) and "Proof of an External World" (1939), which were published posthumously in 1969 under the title *Über Gewissheit/On Certainty* (§4). Having summarized Heidegger's destruction of the problem and Wittgenstein's dissolution of it, I shall try to assess the fruitfulness of their methods in this particular case (§§4, 5).

The focus of my chapter is philosophical rather than historical or philological. This is why I shall not try to situate section 43a of *Being and Time* or Wittgenstein's *On Certainty* within the huge reservoir of their manuscripts, which has become available, in part or in its entirety, by the rather unscholarly *Gesamtausgabe* of Heidegger's writings on the one hand, and the controversial Vienna Edition or the Bergen Electronic Edition of Wittgenstein's manuscripts on the other hand.

2   THE PROBLEM OF THE EXTERNAL WORLD: GENESIS, IMPORTANCE, STRUCTURE, AND SOLUTION SPACE

When René Descartes introduced his hyperbolic doubt of a deceiving God or demon in the first *Meditation on First Philosophy*, this philosophical maneuver was merely meant as a device in a speculative method for attaining positive results. Descartes intended to make his readers receptive to his mechanistic physics by undermining the epistemic impact of sense-perceptual awareness and of traditional (Aristotelian) opinions. He also aimed to demonstrate the indubitability of the "cogito" as a first application of his rationalist criterion of truth, and thereby overcome the Greek skeptical tradition that had been revived in the Renaissance (*AT* VII 21–36; see Gaukroger 1995, 336ff.).

Yet one of the two topics with which this hyperbolic doubt was concerned, the existence of the material world, unexpectedly became a persistent problem that would haunt philosophers in the centuries that followed.[3] How can we explain the astounding fact that a skeptical problem concerning the material world originated at the very time of the scientific revolution, during which geniuses such as Kepler and Galileo, Descartes and Huygens, or Boyle and Newton made spectacular progress in explaining aspects of this world? And how can we account for the "scandal of philosophy" that this skeptical problem could not be resolved satisfactorily during the centuries to come? (*CPR* B xxxix, n.).

As I have explained elsewhere at length, the skeptical problem of the material (or "external") world was motivated, ultimately and paradoxically, by the mechanistic or corpuscular conception of matter that underpinned the scientific revolution, even though Descartes officially used the arguments from perceptual illusions, dreams, and the deceiving God or genius (see Philipse 2007b, 340–45).[4] In order to avoid circular or purely verbal explanations of qualities such as warmth or colors, and phenomena such as sounds and odors, it was argued by Galileo, Descartes, and many others that these qualities had to be explained in terms of constituting corpuscles and their interactions, which lacked such qualities. For example, Descartes accounted speculatively for different colors in terms of the ratio of the angular velocities to the translational velocities of colorless light corpuscles reflected by material surfaces.[5] Because it was assumed that the composition of macroscopic objects by particles that lack such qualities can never yield them at the macro-level, it was concluded that these *explananda* do not really exist in the perceived physical world. Galileo wrote, for example:

> Hence I think that these tastes, odors, colors, etc., on the side of the object in which they seem to exist, are nothing else than mere names, but hold their residence solely in the sensitive body; so that if the animal were removed, every such quality would be abolished and annihilated. Nevertheless, as soon as we have imposed names on them, particular and different from those of the other primary and real accidents, we induce ourselves to believe that they also exist just as truly and really as the latter. (Galilei 1842, 333; translated in Burtt 1954, 85)

Descartes, who reproached Galileo for having "built without foundations," argued that if secondary qualities (as they came to be named) cannot exist in perceived physical objects, they cannot exist in sensitive bodies either, so that they had to be sensations or impressions in our immaterial minds.[6] But because we never predicate colors, for example, of mental phenomena such as sensations but only of material substances, it was concluded that implicit in our perceptual experiences there must be a projective mental mechanism or "judgment," as Descartes called it, which explains the fact that we attribute these secondary qualities to perceived material objects.[7] Furthermore, it seemed plausible to generalize this theory of perception to primary qualities as well. Shouldn't we assume, for example, that our visual perception of the geometrical shapes of material objects consists in us having mental impressions that correspond to our retinal images, from which the visually appearing shapes are constructed by means of a "natural geometry"?[8]

Clearly, then, the mechanistic corpuscular physics of the seventeenth century seemed to imply a representational theory of sense perception that gives rise to skeptical worries even without the fanciful hypothesis of a deceiving demon. If perception is in fact some kind of projection, which structurally deceives us concerning secondary qualities, and is based upon "sensations" existing "in" our minds only, how can we come to know that these perceptual sensations or sense-impressions are really caused by physical objects, which exist independently of our mental life?[9] Most physically informed philosophers after Descartes agreed that what we are really conscious of in perception are subjective sense-data and not the physical objects themselves.[10] If so, what justifies the projective judgments implicit in each perceptual experience to the effect that we perceive physical things, which exist independently of us?

As became clear during the seventeenth and eighteenth centuries, the solution space to this traditional problem of the external world is limited, and no solution is satisfactory. Rationalists such as Descartes attempted to demonstrate deductively the existence of the physical world by a proof of God's existence and his benevolence. Empiricists tried to argue inductively from the presence of perceptual impressions in us to the existence of their alleged physical causes. But the rationalist arguments for realism concerning the external world were unconvincing, and Hume showed that one could never establish the existence of the external world by arguing inductively from our sense impressions to their causes, if at least laws of causality have to be established inductively as well. This skeptical result was compensated for, but not eliminated by, Hume's naturalism, according to which we cannot help believing that the material world exists because "Nature" has implanted this belief in our minds and rendered it unavoidable (Hume [1739/40] 1978, 183).[11]

Idealists such as Berkeley or, much later, Edmund Husserl concluded that no material world exists independently of minds, and that the material things we perceive are in fact composed of, or constituted on the basis of, subjective sense impressions.[12] Similarly, Kant attempted to eliminate the skeptical problem by arguing that the phenomenal world is constituted by our subjective sensations, and that we cannot doubt its existence because experience of it is a transcendental condition of our self-awareness (*CPR* B 274–79). But the problem reemerged with regard to the *Ding an sich*, which Kant had to postulate as a cause of our sense impressions in order to avoid the absurd conclusion that the empirical world is a completely subjective creation.

When continental philosophers sobered up from German Idealism in the second half of the nineteenth century, both realism or naturalism and Kantianism became popular again. Eduard von Hartmann and others argued that external world epistemology (and not metaphysics) plays the role of "first philosophy," because it investigates a crucial presupposition of all empirical sciences, to wit that the material world exists independently of the perceiving subject (von Hartmann 1907, 12). Unfortunately, however, none of the solutions to the problem of external world skepticism, such as the hypothetical realism of Franz Brentano, the transcendental idealism of Husserl, or Hume's skepticism, could convince the philosophical community. It is against this historical background that we have to situate the attempts by Heidegger, Carnap, and the later Wittgenstein to deconstruct or dissolve the problem. Weren't they right in concluding that something must be wrong with a philosophical problem if not even one of its logically possible solutions is convincing?

As I said, however, varieties of external world skepticism reemerged in contemporary analytic philosophy despite these deconstructions by Heidegger, Wittgenstein, and many others, such as J. L. Austin. Although contemporary versions resemble the classical paradigms to a large extent, they are less dependent than the classical versions on representational theories of perception, and they do not presuppose or imply a variety of Cartesian dualism. According to the standard formulation, the skeptical problem consists of three theses that are jointly incompatible although each of them clearly seems to be true (see Pritchard 2002 and 2005).

Let *rsh* stand for a radical skeptical hypothesis, such as the assumption that I am a brain-in-a-vat that is stimulated by computers in such a way that my mental life is exactly as it is now, including my perceptual experiences.[13] All radical skeptical hypotheses are such that the postulated scenario will not make any difference to our actual mental life, so that we cannot discover in principle by using our perceptual capacities whether the skeptical scenario does or does not obtain. Let p be any perceptual judgment that I claim to know for sure, such as that I am now sitting in front of my desk, but which is false if *rsh* is true and vice versa. Then we can formulate the following three propositions, each of which seems to be obviously true, although they are jointly incompatible (I am using "~" as the negation sign):

1. I know that p;
2. I do not know that ~*rsh*;
3. If I do not know that ~*rsh*, then I do not know that p.[14]

We might also construct radically skeptical arguments of the following form:

4. I do not know that ~*rsh*;
5. If I do not know that ~*rsh*, then I do not know that p;
6. I do not know that p.

As is easily seen, the solution space for skeptical problems of this kind is limited as well. Few of us will be radical skeptics, who endorse (6) and deny (1), or Pyrrhonian skeptics, who practice *epoché* with regard to all propositions (1–6). Because the skeptical argument has only two premises, we are left with three options. We may either deny (4), or deny (5), or, finally, claim that the argument is not deductively valid, even though it appears to be a sound *modus ponendo ponens*. There are several ways of doing each of these things. For example, epistemological externalists might deny premise (4) because they hold that we do not need access to the grounds, arguments, evidence, or epistemic sources that give us knowledge in order to have it, and that we know that ~*rsh* if the belief that ~*rsh* tracks the truth in nearby possible worlds.[15]

Underlying premise (5) is a principle of epistemic closure, according to which knowledge is "closed" under known entailments, and which may be formulated as follows:

7. For all subjects S, and all propositions q, r, if S knows that q, and S knows that q entails r, then S knows that r.

Applying this closure principle for knowledge (CPK), we may think it obvious that

8. If I know that p (e.g., that I am now sitting in front of my desk), I also know that ~*rsh* (e.g., that I am not a brain-in-a-vat),

because I know that p entails ~*rsh*. From this, lemma (5) follows by transposition.

So we might attempt to argue against premise (5) by limiting somehow the application of the CPK. Fred Dretske and Robert Nozick have done so, paradigmatically, by also requiring for knowledge that the belief involved tracks the truth in nearby possible worlds (Dretske 1970; Nozick 1981, 204ff., 227ff.).[16] This solution of the skeptical paradox seems to be plausible at first sight because most of us will hold that our knowledge of everyday perceptual propositions does not depend upon the anti-skeptical knowledge that ~*rsh*. Although the *truth* of p presupposes the truth of ~*rsh*, we would set our standards for knowledge too high if we required that *knowledge* of p presupposes knowledge of ~*rsh*.

Finally, those who want to show that the skeptical argument is deductively invalid might do so by "contextualizing" the knowledge operator while retaining the closure principle in each context.[17] One might claim, for example, that our epistemic standards are raised drastically when we change the conversational context from everyday life to a philosophical discussion of skepticism. Whereas in everyday contexts, (1) is true, (1) might be false in philosophical contexts, so that in these conversational contexts (6) is true. In other words, we should be skeptics when we philosophize, but we cannot and should not be skeptics in our everyday life, as Hume already suggested. Accordingly, the skeptical argument (4, 5, 6) is not deductively valid if (6) is meant to hold in everyday contexts.

Each of these solutions to the skeptical problem has serious drawbacks, and none is endorsed by the philosophical community as a whole. So we might be tempted again by the diagnosis that there must be something wrong with the problem, and that it should be dissolved rather than solved. Let us now investigate whether Heidegger or Wittgenstein succeeded in "destroying" or deconstructing the problem of external world skepticism, either in the classical versions of the seventeenth to nineteenth centuries, or in the contemporary more limited versions that became popular from the late 1970s onwards. It should also be elucidated what it means to "destroy" or "dissolve" a philosophical problem as contrasted with solving it. Heidegger and Wittgenstein both intended to argue, it seems, that the skeptical problem of the external world cannot be formulated meaningfully. But what does this mean, precisely, and why would it be the case?

3   HEIDEGGER'S "DESTRUCTION" OF THE PROBLEM OF THE EXTERNAL WORLD

Both Heidegger and Carnap argued that the problem of external world skepticism is *meaningless*, as are its traditional solutions. However, they came up with very different arguments for this conclusion, and it is instructive to compare them.

According to Carnap in 1928, both the realist and the idealist contention are devoid of "scientific meaning" (Carnap 1967, 332). They are mere pseudo-statements, because they do not express a state of affairs of which we can discover in principle by experience whether it exists. Because the skeptical hypotheses that generate the problem of the external world cannot be tested empirically either, these hypotheses are cognitively meaningless as well. Carnap's conclusion that the problem of the external world is a pseudo-problem survived his liberalization of the empiricist criterion of meaning. According to "Empiricism, Semantics, and Ontology" in 1950, the problem results from a confusion between empirical questions of existence *internal* to a linguistic framework and *external* questions concerning the pragmatic utility of such a framework (Carnap 1956, supp. A, 206–8).

In order to evaluate Carnap's dissolution of the problem of the external world, two separate questions should be answered. One is whether the philosophical instruments Carnap used in arguing that the problem is meaningless, such as (the various versions of) his verification criterion of meaning or his distinction between internal and external questions, have survived the numerous criticisms of these tools. I shall not discuss this issue here, but it is clear that contemporary authors who raise the skeptical problem again do not think so. The other question is whether Carnap's dissolution of the problem succeeds in *removing the rationale* for formulating it (at least its traditional versions) in the first place, to wit, the physicalist conception of secondary qualities and the resulting representational theory of perception (see §2). Because Carnap did not attempt to do this, his empiricist dismissal of the problem of the external world is at least incomplete (see Philipse 2007b, 372).

Heidegger's discussion of the problem of the external world in §43a of *Being and Time* aims at addressing this second issue. According to Heidegger, many of the perplexing problems of modern philosophy result from an inadequate ontological conception of ourselves and of our relation to the world. This is why a new regional ontology of human existence is needed, which will eliminate these traditional problems.[18] In particular, Heidegger argues that the traditional Aristotelian categories of form, matter, and substance are derived from the realm of artifacts, and as a consequence are inadequate for conceptualizing human existence (*BT* 24–25/46).[19] According to Heidegger's revolutionary project in *Being and Time*, adequate ontological categories for human existence (so-called *existentialia*) have to explicate structural features of the pre-ontological manner in which we humans understand ourselves *in our everyday life*, both authentically and inauthentically. The fact that in ordinary language we always speak about ourselves in terms that refer to items in the world (when we identify ourselves with reference to our parents, our native region, our profession, our year of birth, our partner, etc.) already indicates that human life essentially is "Being-in-the-world" (*In-der-Welt-sein*). It is the task of the first two divisions of *Being and Time* to develop the conceptual apparatus of *existentialia* in terms of which human existence as Being-in-the-world and its temporal structure can be articulated ontologically. Because our mode of existence is Being-in-the-world, it is *incoherent* to suppose that we might exist although the world does not, as external world skepticism assumes.[20]

This diagnosis yields Heidegger's conclusion in §43a of *Being and Time* that the problem of the external world is "impossible" (*unmöglich*):

> The "problem of reality" in the sense of the question whether there is an external world and whether the existence of such a world can be proved, turns out to be an impossible problem, not because its consequences lead to inextricable impasses, but because the very entity which serves as its theme, is one which, as it were, repudiates any such formulation of the question. Our task is not to prove that an "external world" is present or to show how it is present, but to point out why Dasein, as Being-in-the-world, has the tendency first to bury the "external world" in nullity "epistemologically" and then to prove its existence. The cause of this lies in Dasein's falling. (*BT* 206/250; translation modified)[21]

Heidegger's *existentiale* of falling (*das Verfallen*) characterizes among other things the fact that we tend to model our ontological understanding of ourselves primarily on things that are present to us (*Vorhandenes*) or on the things we use (*Zuhandenes*), such as physical objects or tools, respectively, instead of explicating hermeneutically the manner in which we humans understand ourselves implicitly in daily life (*BT* 206/250). Although Heidegger never traces in detail the genesis of the problem of the external world, his global diagnosis of its rationale is correct. It arose (see §2) when physicists such as Galileo argued that in reality perceived physical objects lack many of the properties we think to perceive, so that perception is structurally deceptive. Philosophers then wondered how physical objects could cause this deceptive awareness of secondary qualities in us, and generalized the resulting representational theory of perception to our perception of primary qualities. In this approach, the perceiving subject is understood as a passive part of a causal network, and our perceptions are conceived of as final links of causal chains. Heidegger would say that these philosophers fall prey to *Verfallen* because they conceptualize the perceptual relation between a thing in the world and us as a relation between entities that are all present-at-hand (*vorhanden*). However, in everyday life we understand perception as an activity of exploration in the world, by which we discover things as they are in themselves (see *BT* 217–18/260–61).[22]

One might object to Heidegger's "destruction" of the problem of the external world in *Being and Time* that even if his diagnosis of its origin and nature were globally correct, this does not show that the problem is meaningless (*ohne Sinn*).[23] Let us grant Heidegger that the problem of the external world cannot be raised meaningfully within the framework of our ordinary self-understanding, because we cannot conceive of our personal identity without reference to things in the world. This does not imply, however, that the problem cannot be raised meaningfully within some other context, such as that of a scientific or philosophical analysis of matter and perception. Perhaps we should conclude that in this respect the manifest image differs from the scientific image, to use the Sellarsian jargon (Sellars 1963). May we not prefer the scientific image to the manifest one, and conclude that the problem of the external world is a legitimate problem? Heidegger's use of the pejorative term *Verfallen* suggests that this would be a mistake.[24] But what is his argument? Shouldn't we always prefer scientific results and their implications to our everyday convictions in cases of conflict because of the reliability of scientific methods, even when we practice philosophical ontology?

Heidegger's answer to this objection is contained in §69b of *Being and Time* (cf. also *BT* §§3, 9, 44c). He claims *à la* Kant that scientific facts become accessible only on the basis of an a priori constitutive framework, which Dasein projects onto the world. For example, when we practice mathematical physics, *nature itself* is mathematically projected in a specific way. He concludes that without such a framework, there would be no scientific facts at all.[25] And because Dasein is the transcendental subject that projects this framework, Heidegger's ontology of Dasein allegedly is both more fundamental and more adequate than an ontology of human life informed by the natural sciences.[26]

However, as I argued in §17A of my book *Heidegger's Philosophy of Being*, there are at least two reasons why this transcendentalist answer to the objection is inadequate—an internal and an external one. First, Heidegger's theory of understanding (*Verstehen*) as projection (*Entwurf*) implies that the global structure of our everyday meaningful world is also a transcendental framework projected by Dasein (see *BT* §31). If this were otherwise, our meaningful world could not collapse into nothingness, which happens according to Heidegger in the experience of *Angst* (*BT* §40).[27] But if both the meaningful framework of the everyday world within which things may be apprehended as tools (*zuhanden*) and the frameworks of natural science within which things appear as merely present (*vorhanden*) are transcendental projections, it is not clear why one of these frameworks would prevail ontologically over the other. Admittedly, physicists are practically engaged in the world when they set up experiments and perform measurements. It does not follow, however, that the *content* of their discoveries is ontologically less profound than the ontology of Dasein as Being-in-the-world, even if it is Dasein that practices physics in the world. Heidegger's claim that the world of tools and everyday life is the world in itself (*an sich*), whereas the world as revealed by science is not, cannot be justified within the Kantian framework of his own philosophy.[28]

Second, Heidegger's view that scientific facts cannot exist independently of a projected transcendental framework of "Nature itself" is either trivial or confused. It is true, of course, that many facts can be *discovered* only in the light of a projected framework, such as Newtonian mechanics. The existence of the planet Neptune is a well-known example.[29] But it does not follow, and is simply false, that Neptune would not *exist* if Dasein had not projected a mathematical framework, or that the fact that Neptune exists does not obtain independently of Newtonian mechanics.[30] Consequently, there is no good reason to assume that in general discoveries of natural sciences are ontologically less fundamental than Heidegger's "fundamental" ontology, which is developed by explicating the way in which we understand ourselves in everyday life. Hence we cannot conclude from the (alleged) fact that the problem of the external world does not make sense within this latter context, that it cannot be raised meaningfully by philosophers on the basis of (alleged) physical discoveries concerning secondary qualities, such as the discovery that physically speaking the temperature of a gas is *nothing but* the average kinetic energy of its molecules.

4   WITTGENSTEIN'S DISSOLUTION OF THE PROBLEM OF THE EXTERNAL WORLD

Before discussing Wittgenstein's *On Certainty*, let me briefly remind the reader of G. E. Moore's response to external world skepticism, which Wittgenstein criticized in these notes. In contradistinction to Heidegger and

Carnap, G. E. Moore did not tackle external world skepticism by arguing that it does not make sense. On the contrary, he assumed that one can formulate the problem of the external world meaningfully, and argued that a straightforward solution can be provided.

In "A Defence of Common Sense" (first published in 1925), Moore tried to state "some of the most important points" in which his own philosophical position differed from those taken up by some other philosophers (Moore 1959a, 32). One of these points is the truism that each of us knows or has frequently known things such as that one's body exists and has never been far from the surface of the Earth. After a lengthy exegesis of the terminology Kant used in his "only possible" proof of the external world in the second edition of the *Critique of Pure Reason*, Moore argued in "Proof of an External World" (first published in 1939) that *indefinitely many* such proofs can be constructed easily—for instance, by holding up each of one's hands in turn and saying, while pointing to it with the other, "here is one hand." By doing so, Moore claims, one has proved "*ipso facto* the existence of external things," and this is what Kant intended to do (Moore 1959b, 144).

Elsewhere, Moore explains that he uses what one might call an Inversion Strategy against the skeptic. To skeptical arguments of the form:

4. I do not know that ~*rsh*,
5. If I do not know that ~*rsh*, then I do not know that *p*,
6. I do not know that *p*,

he answers by stressing that we *do* know that *p*, so that the *modus ponendo ponens* is transformed into a *modus tollendo tollens* with the conclusion that after all we know that ~*rsh*. The reason why Moore considers this to be a legitimate move is that our knowledge of things such as that I have two hands is much more certain than the credentials of any skeptical hypothesis concerning the nonexistence of the external world (Moore 1922, 228).

Let us suppose for a moment (a) that claims such as "I know that this hand exists" are both meaningful and as certainly true as Moore thinks they are. Let us also assume (b) that they contradict skepticism concerning the external world (as is argued by Stroud 1984, chap. 3). Will this be sufficient to eradicate this type of philosophical skepticism? As many critics have argued, this does not seem to be true, because Moore fails to address the source or rationale of the skeptical problem, which I reconstructed in section 2. Even worse, in "A Defence of Common Sense" he endorses a sense-datum theory of perception and claims it to be "quite evident that my knowledge that I am now perceiving a human hand is a deduction from a pair of propositions simpler still"—that is, from propositions about sense-data (Moore 1959a, 53).[31] In other words, Moore rejects direct realism and embraces what he calls a "theory of representative perception," according to which "I do not *directly* perceive *my hand*" but I rather perceive (in a strict sense) "something which is (in a suitable sense) *representative* of it"

(Moore 1959a, 54; his italics). But it was a sense-datum theory of perception, motivated by the seventeenth-century analysis of secondary qualities, that triggered external world skepticism in the first place. As a consequence, Moore does not attempt to remove the reasons for raising the problem of external world skepticism, even if he succeeds in refuting the skeptic. What is worse, he fails to understand how accepting a sense-datum theory of perception undermines the commonsense basis of his anti-skeptical arguments.

However, that Moore did refute the external world skeptic has been contested by Wittgenstein in *On Certainty*. This booklet contains the remarks Wittgenstein wrote during the last year and a half of his life apropos of the two articles by Moore I mentioned. Because it is "all first-draft material," which Wittgenstein "did not live to excerpt and polish," as the editors stress, there are many problems of interpretation, which I shall neither raise nor resolve (OC iv). Yet one central line of Wittgenstein's argument may be summarized as follows.

Saying things such as "I know that this hand exists" while pointing to one of my hands cannot constitute a meaningful claim to knowledge, because in normal situations *it would not make sense to doubt* that this hand exists. Indeed, one can meaningfully claim to know something only if one can meaningfully doubt it. The judgments Moore claims that each of us knows for sure are often called "hinge propositions."[32] We cannot doubt such propositions *collectively* because the words that express them would lose their meanings if we did not accept these judgments. Our linguistic "system" or "language-game" is possible only if we endorse large numbers of empirical judgments, because one cannot have agreement in linguistic rules without agreement in unproblematic judgments (see *PI* §242).[33] And because doubting something is a move *within* an existing language-game, it does not make sense to doubt collectively the empirical judgments the endorsement of which is in part constitutive of that language-game. Moore's mistake was to counter the skeptical assertion that one cannot or does not know such things by saying, "I do know it," instead of by pointing out that these skeptical doubts are meaningless (see *OC* §521 and passim).

In their arguments to the effect that external world skepticism is meaningless Heidegger and Wittgenstein use different philosophical tools: on the one hand the *existentiale* of Being-in-the-world and on the other hand the insight that one cannot share rules for using words without also endorsing many unproblematic judgments in which these words are used. Yet there is an interesting similarity between their dissolutions of the problem of the external world. Both Heidegger in *Being and Time* and Wittgenstein in *On Certainty* focus primarily on everyday contexts and deny that in such contexts it makes sense to doubt the existence of material entities in general.

However, as I argued in §2, the real rationale for traditional external world skepticism is not to be found in everyday contexts, but rather in the conception of secondary qualities and in the representational theory of perception, which were widely endorsed by physicists and philosophers from the seventeenth century onwards. We saw (§3) that Heidegger attempted unsuccessfully to play down the ontological importance of the scientific image in §69b of *Being and Time*. Does Wittgenstein's mature conception of philosophy as explained in his *Philosophical Investigations* allow us to address the grounds or rationale for raising the problem of the external world? And does it do so more successfully than Heidegger's conception, so that the reasons for mounting external world skepticism can be dissolved effectively?

In *Appearance and Reality*, the Wittgenstein scholar P. M. S. Hacker provides us on the basis of Wittgenstein's writings with an extensive overview of the interconnected uses of terms such as "perception," "sensation," "feeling," and predicates of secondary qualities such as "white" and "cold," in order to show that both the traditional assimilation of secondary qualities to sensations and the (philosophical) causal theory of perception are "a quagmire of confusion" (Hacker 1987, 96; see also Bennett and Hacker 2003, 121–47). He stresses, for example, that terms for secondary qualities are defined by reference to public paradigms or samples, so that it would be conceptually confused to assimilate secondary qualities to sensations such as pains or tickles (Hacker 1987, 89, 108–10). Whereas sensations are felt in one's body, colors or sounds are properties of, or produced by, things, stuffs, or processes in the world around us (Hacker 1987, 103). This is not an empirical statement but rather a grammatical observation. As a consequence, it does not make sense to deny, for example, that colors are properties of material things or stuff, as seventeenth-century philosophers did and many present-day philosophers and scientists still do.

A scientist who is interested in philosophy might happily endorse these grammatical criticisms of traditional accounts of perception and of secondary qualities, because they do not contradict results of empirical research. Instead of saying, for example, that, physically speaking, colors are sensations caused in us by the impact of electromagnetic radiation on our eyes, one might say that this impact is part of the process that is constitutive of our perception of colors. And instead of saying that, physically speaking, material objects are not colored, one might say that the color of a thing depends both on the reflectance properties of its surface and on the spectrum of the normal incident illumination. The physics and physiology of perception can be formulated without the conceptual confusions inherent in the traditional doctrines of the subjectivity of secondary qualities and the representational theory of perception.

It follows that conceptual criticisms à la Wittgenstein can effectively demolish the traditional grounds for raising the problem of the external world. It is less clear, however, that they also dissolve varieties of radical skepticism proposed by contemporary philosophers, such as the hypothesis of a brain-in-a-vat. This hypothesis can be formulated without presupposing the traditional doctrines of the subjectivity of secondary qualities or the representational theory of perception. Can it also be demolished by applying connective conceptual analysis à la Wittgenstein? That is not yet obvious.

For example, the Wittgensteinian philosopher might object to the brain-in-a-vat scenario that we cannot meaningfully attribute mental properties to this brain because the relevant behavioral criteria for attributing them do not apply. But the skeptic may respond that what is decisive here is the first-person perspective and not the third-person point of view. Indeed, the brain-in-a-vat is the brain of a human being, who learned to use mental predicates and a language in general before she underwent the devilish operation. Because *ex hypothesi* this operation does not make any difference to her mental life, her self-attributions of mental properties and of bodily behavior will make sense as before, even though all self-attributions of bodily behavior will now be false. So we should conclude that there is a challenge left for the Wittgenstein-inspired philosopher who is puzzled by external world skepticism. The same holds for Heideggerians. A brain-in-a-vat will continue to experience itself as a Dasein-in-the-world, even though after the operation the world is in fact very different from how it seems to be.

5   CONCLUSION

Given the "dramatic re-emergence of interest in radical skeptical arguments" in the recent philosophical literature, we wondered whether present-day philosophers have forgotten, or not even learned, the methodological lessons of Heidegger and/or Wittgenstein. How can it be that external world skepticism is raised again today, and discussed by many authors, even though both Heidegger and Wittgenstein argued that it cannot be raised meaningfully? To what extent are Heidegger's "destruction" of the problem of the external world in *Being and Time* and Wittgenstein's dissolution of it in *On Certainty* philosophically convincing?

We saw that even if Heidegger's dissolution of the problem is effective in everyday life contexts, he did not address adequately the real grounds for raising traditional external world skepticism. In §2, I argued that these grounds consist in two corollaries of the corpuscular philosophy endorsed by many philosophers and scientists from the seventeenth century onwards: the theory of the subjectivity of secondary qualities and the representational theory of perception. Although Wittgenstein does not address these issues in *On Certainty* either, his philosophical method can be applied to them fruitfully. For example, the Wittgenstein scholar P. M. S. Hacker has demolished both doctrines effectively in his *Appearance and Reality* and in *Philosophical Foundations of Neuroscience* (2003), written in cooperation with the neuroscientist M. R. Bennett.

130   *Herman Philipse*

It is less clear, however, that by using a method of connective conceptual analysis one can also dissolve contemporary external world skepticism. The radical skeptical hypotheses put forward since the 1970s presuppose neither the theory of the subjectivity of secondary qualities nor a representational theory of perception. Can one show by using a method of Wittgenstein-inspired conceptual analysis that the brain-in-a-vat scenario is conceptually incoherent, for example? Or should we rather return to Moore at this point? More research is needed to answer these questions.

NOTES

1. For a critical interpretation of Heidegger's question of Being, see Philipse (1998).
2. Of course, Pritchard means a dramatic reemergence since the works of Strawson, Stroud, Unger, and others.
3. The other topic of hyperbolic doubt, the truth of elementary mathematical propositions such as 2 + 3 = 5, never became popular, either because one considered such a doubt as incoherent, or because one rejected Descartes' voluntarist conception of God that it presupposed.
4. The notion of "external" presupposes Cartesian dualism and is a misleading spatial metaphor. Incidentally, it is striking that many contemporary reconstructions of the "grounds" of the problem, such as Stroud (1984), focus on arguments from dreams or illusions. In his first chapter, in which he reconstructs Descartes' external world skepticism, Stroud does not even mention the argument from the deceiving God or demon, and he does not discuss seventeenth-century physics.
5. See *AT* VI 91–92 (*La dioptrique*, Discours premier) and *AT* VI 329–36 (*Les météores*, Discours huitième).
6. See *AT* II 380 (letter to Mersenne, Oct. 11, 1638); *AT* VI 85 (*La Dioptrique*, Discours premier); *AT* XI 3–6 (*Le Monde*, chap. 1); and *AT* IX ii 312–13, 317 (*Les Principes de la Philosophie* IV §§191, 198).
7. *AT* IX 236–37 (*Réponses aux sixièmes objections*, §9).
8. *AT* VI 114–47 (*La Dioptrique, Discours cinquième et sixième*).
9. Both Berkeley and Hume also argued that this theory of perception should be generalized to primary qualities. See Hume ([1748] 1975, 154).
10. See Hume ([1748] 1975, 152): "[T]he slightest philosophy . . . teaches us, that nothing can ever be present to the mind but an image or perception, and that the senses are only the inlets, through which these images are conveyed, without being able to produce any immediate intercourse between the mind and the object."
11. For (alleged) similarities between Hume's naturalism and Wittgenstein's view in *On Certainty*, cf. Strawson (1985, 14–21).
12. On Edmund Husserl's transcendental idealism, see Philipse (1995) and Philipse (2007b).
13. See Putnam (1981, chap. 1), and for what follows Pritchard (2002, 217ff.).
14. See Pritchard (2002, 217). As Pritchard stresses (n. 6), it does not matter that the argument is formulated in the first person singular, since the argument is meant to apply to any subject S at any time.

15. In this case, "nearby" possible worlds are defined as worlds that do not differ much from our actual world.
16. Because this requirement is met for our belief that *p* but (allegedly) not for our belief that ~*rsh*, closure does not apply in this case (8). Here, "nearby" possible worlds relative to the world in which a proposition *p* is true are defined as worlds in which proposition *p* is false. So "nearby" to our ~*rsh* world is the possible world in which *rsh* is true, but our belief that ~*rsh* does not track the truth in this nearby possible world. Hence, it does not amount to knowledge, so that (8) is false.
17. DeRose (1995) and Lewis (1996). See Pritchard (2002, 224–30), for an overview and critical discussion.
18. This is one of the five meanings of Heidegger's so-called question of Being. See Philipse (1998) for an extensive historical interpretation and critique of this five-fold question.
19. See also *BT* 92/125; *PIA* 22; and *GA* 24, 147–48.
20. One may wonder, of course, whether this is not a fallacy of equivocation, because the meaning of the word "world" in Heidegger's existential "Being-in-the-world" differs from its meaning in external world skepticism. See Philipse (2007a) for an analysis of the many ambiguities in *BT* §43a.
21. See also *BT* 202/246–47: "The question of whether there is a world at all and whether its being can be proved, makes no sense if it is raised by *Dasein* as Being-in-the-world."
22. For an extensive summary of Heidegger's diagnosis of external world skepticism, see Rudd (2003, 55–71).
23. For a somewhat different objection to Heidegger, cf. Rudd (2003, 60ff.).
24. Cf. *BT* 306/496 n.ii, where Heidegger denies that his ontology of *Dasein* has anything to do with the Fall of man.
25. See *BT* 362/414: "Only 'in the light' of a Nature which has been projected in this fashion can anything like a 'fact' be found. . . . The 'grounding' of 'factual science' was possible only because the researchers understood that in principle there are no 'bare facts.'" Cf. Philipse (1998, 121ff.), on the transcendental theme in *Being and Time*, and Philipse (2007a) on the problem of the *Ding an sich* in *Being and Time*.
26. Cf. Philipse (2007a) for an extensive analysis of the ambiguities in, and various interpretations of, Heidegger's position.
27. For an analysis, cf. Philipse (2007a, §9).
28. For this argument in more detail, see Philipse (1998, 322–26); cf. Philipse (2007a). For Heidegger's view of the world in itself (*an sich*), see *BT* 71/101, 87/120, 106/141.
29. *BT* 362/414: "Only 'in the light of' a Nature which has been projected in this fashion can anything like a 'fact' be found." Neptune was the first planet found by mathematically based predictions rather than by purely empirical observation. After Alexis Bouvard had concluded from deviations in the orbit of Uranus that it was subject to gravitational influences by an unobserved planet, Johann Galle observed Neptune on September 23, 1846. In Philipse (1998) I used the discovery of "the planet Pluto" as an example (327ff.), but the new definition of "planet" adopted by the International Astronomical Union on August 24, 2006, excludes Pluto, which is now considered as a "dwarf planet."
30. *BT* 362/414: "[I]n principle there are no 'bare facts.'" See Philipse (1998, 327–30). Heidegger seems to admit, however, that *entities* discovered by scientific research exist independently of the transcendental frameworks projected by

Dasein, even though he adds that they "show themselves precisely *as* entities which beforehand already were" (*BT* 227/269, my italics; cf. *BT* 212/255). This seems to imply, however, that even "being independent of Dasein" depends upon Dasein as a transcendental subject. Of course this is trivial if Heidegger is referring to the *concept* of "being independent of Dasein," but it is false if he is referring to independence from Dasein. See Philipse (2007a) for an extensive analysis of various interpretations of these "puzzle passages."

31. Moore specifies the sense-datum in the example of perceiving my hand as "a certain part of its surface" (Moore 1959a, 54), so that his sense-datum view differs from traditional ones.

32. Wittgenstein does not use this term. He says in German that "unsre *Zweifel* beruhen darauf, daß gewisse Sätze vom Zweifel ausgenommen sind, gleichsam die Angeln, in welchen jene sich bewegen (*OC* §341; Wittgenstein's italics).

33. This crucial aspect of Wittgenstein's argument is completely overlooked by Pritchard (forthcoming).

9 What Science Leaves Unsaid

Taylor Carman

> *Everyday opinion sees in a shadow merely the absence of light, if not its utter denial. In truth, however, a shadow is the manifest yet impenetrable testimony of hidden illumination.*
>
> —Heidegger, "The Age of the World Picture" (1938)

There is an early and a late (and perhaps a middle) Heidegger, just as there is an early and a late (and perhaps a middle) Wittgenstein. Yet, notwithstanding their different styles and the well-known discontinuities in their intellectual paths, both (or all six) share a commitment to the idea that philosophy differs from science (*Wissenschaft*) in fundamental ways; that it requires a different way of thinking and of using language; that it employs different methods; that it has a different point and purpose. Philosophy, Heidegger and Wittgenstein both maintain, is not *about* what science (*any* science) is about—namely, objective facts or positive aspects of the world. Indeed, Wittgenstein sometimes suggests that philosophy, being merely a kind of technique, is not strictly speaking "about" anything at all. How deep is this apparent affinity between their respective views of the nature of philosophy and its relation to scientific knowledge and inquiry?

1 PICTURES AS FACTS

The *Tractatus* can at times sound remarkably similar to *Being and Time*. "The world and life are one" (*TLP* 5.621) is reminiscent of Heidegger's characterization of human existence as "being-in-the-world." Similarly, "I am my world" (*TLP* 5.63) very nearly approximates "Dasein *is* its world existingly" (*BT* 364/416).[1] And "The world of the happy man is a different one from that of the unhappy man" (*TLP* 6.43) can be read as a poignant expression of Heidegger's claim that moods are not most fundamentally mental states but rather modes of world-disclosure (*BT* §§29–30 and passim).

Such sentences, however, are clear cases of what Wittgenstein himself calls "nonsense" (*Unsinn*)—that is, pseudo-propositions that attempt to say what cannot be said, and so say nothing. And yet Wittgenstein maintains that such abortive sentences, although meaningless, can serve a clarificatory purpose. Near the end of the *Tractatus*, perhaps echoing Frege's ([1892] 1980b) admission that he could not define but only "hint" at logically primitive notions (such as object, concept, and truth), Wittgenstein writes,

> My propositions serve as elucidations in the following way: anyone who understands me eventually recognizes them as nonsensical (*unsinning*), when he has used them—as steps—to climb up beyond them. (He must, so to speak, throw away the ladder after he has climbed up it.) (*TLP* 6.54)

What and how do Wittgenstein's pseudo-propositional sentences "elucidate"? Interpreters disagree. On one standard reading, what the metaphysical-sounding pronouncements of the *Tractatus* fail to *say*, they nevertheless show (*zeigen*)—and so manage to convey, after all. This approach, however, comes dangerously close to supposing that there really *is* something definite, something substantive, that Wittgenstein's propositions fail to say, and that *that* something—something into which we can perhaps have intuitive insight—is what they show.

That's what Cora Diamond (1991c, 181) calls "chickening out," by which she means failing to take sufficiently seriously Wittgenstein's disavowal of his own pseudo-propositions as a kind of sophisticated nonsense.[2] Diamond is surely right that the putative unsayable *something* cannot, on Wittgenstein's view, elude expression owing to a merely contingent limitation peculiar to us or our language; that it cannot be the sort of thing a creature different from us, with a different kind of mind or language, might be able to say and think—as, for example, Kant supposed his "things in themselves" can be known by God, whose intuition is not, like ours, constrained by passive sensibility but instead intellectual and productive. For Wittgenstein, on the contrary, not even God could think or express an illogical thought, since there is no such thing as an illogical *thought*; there is only language that expresses thoughts and language that does not:

> It used to be said that God could create anything except what would be contrary to the laws of logic. The truth is that we could not *say* what an "illogical" world would look like. (*TLP* 3.031)[3]

On what has come to be known as the "resolute" or "austere" reading, advanced and defended by Diamond and James Conant (see, e.g., Conant and Diamond 2004), the nonsense sentences of the *Tractatus*, like the nonsense utterances and inscriptions of traditional philosophy, turn out not to be oblique hints or inarticulate showings of esoteric truths. Rather, as

Wittgenstein says in the Preface, it will "only be in language that the limit [of thought] can be drawn, and what lies on the other side of the limit will simply be nonsense" (*TLP* p. 3).

The austere approach, however, arguably has trouble making sense of the *importance*, the philosophical *significance* Wittgenstein evidently sees in what Diamond and Conant regard as in effect mere strings of words—that is, useless and disposable nonsense on the order of "2 + 2 at 3 o'clock equals 4" (*TLP* 4.1272). It would be absurd to say that that sentence shows or even hints at anything deep or important. Is the poignant remark about happy and unhappy people living in different worlds no more meaningful than that? After all, Wittgenstein says, again in the Preface to the *Tractatus*, "the *truth* of the thoughts that are here communicated seems to me unassailable and definitive" (*TLP* p. 4). That seems to suggest that at least some of the sentences in the book do manage to say something, after all—indeed, something *true*! But what? Is the famous concluding sentence, "What we cannot speak about we must pass over in silence" (*TLP* 7), just an empty tautology, or at best sound practical advice? In short, how are we to distinguish silly and insignificant nonsense from interesting or important nonsense?

The resolute interpretation also runs up against the evidence of things Wittgenstein said not in but about the *Tractatus*. For example:

> The book's point is an ethical one. I once meant to include in the preface a sentence which is not in fact there now but which I will write out for you here because it will perhaps be a key to the work for you. What I meant to write, then, was this: My work consists of two parts: the one presented here plus all that I have *not* written. And it is precisely this second part that is the important one. (*SP* 94–95)

Presumably, the ethical point of the book lies (somehow) in that second, nonexistent part—the *important* part—which Wittgenstein didn't write. And surely the reason he didn't write it is not that he merely failed to or chose not to, but that it was essentially unwritable. And yet *that* part was, he says, the "point" of the book.

Again, it would be a mistake to suppose that "the book's point . . . all that I have *not* written" must be thinkable or sayable by some other kind of subject, God perhaps. But it would also be a mistake to suppose that there is only one species of philosophical nonsense; that since nonsense neither expresses nor reveals deep truths, it can only be as sterile and frivolous as "2 + 2 at 3 o'clock equals 4." Surely there are degrees, shades, varieties of nonsense.[4] Wittgenstein seems to suggest as much near the end of the *Tractatus* in the two very different things he says about "riddles" and "the mystical." Riddles (*Rätsel*) are pseudo-questions, sentences that appear to pose questions with possible answers, but in fact do not: "When the answer cannot be put into words, neither can the question be put into words. *The riddle* does not exist" (*TLP* 6.5). A (seeming) philosophical riddle is an illusion, a mirage. In stark contrast, he writes, "There are, indeed, things that cannot be put into words (*Unaussprechliches*). They *make themselves manifest* (zeigt sich). They are what is mystical" (*TLP* 6.522). Translated more literally from the German (though with modified emphasis), the two passages say that although "*There is no* riddle," nevertheless "*There is* the unsayable."

This difference between mere riddles and the mystical is crucial, if we are to draw any distinction at all between, as it were, serious nonsense and frivolous nonsense—nonsense that somehow makes manifest and illuminates and nonsense that merely obscures and distracts. Years later, Wittgenstein referred again to a kind of *truth* inherent in metaphysical error, presumably in contrast to merely disposable nonsense: "In a certain sense one cannot take too much care in handling philosophical mistakes, they contain so much truth" (*Z* §460). Of course, not all nonsense harbors or hints at truth and so needs to be handled with such philosophical care; the *Tractatus* is not "Jabberwocky."[5] For nonsense to be somehow philosophically interesting or important, it must do more than just fail to mean anything. If we are to kick away Wittgenstein's ladder, we must first be able to climb up it.

For example, the *Tractatus* is famous, rightly or wrongly, for advancing (or seeming to advance) what has come to be called the "picture theory" of meaning, although as Hans Sluga (2011, 27) points out, the theory was Bertrand Russell's before it was (or seemed to be) Wittgenstein's. I say "seeming" and "seemed" because, as Sluga says, "Wittgenstein would not have accepted the characterization of this view of meaning as a 'theory' " (Sluga 2011, 37n14). This is because, like Kant, who famously said that one cannot learn philosophy, but "at best only *to philosophize*" (*CPR* A837/B865; translation modified), Wittgenstein writes in the *Tractatus*, "Philosophy is not a body of doctrine (*Lehre*) but an activity" (*TLP* 4.112).

To the extent that they look like statements of a doctrine or theory, then, the sentences seeming to advance and defend the picture theory of meaning are surely among the sentences to be discarded as nonsense by the end of the *Tractatus*. After all, the theory (so called) asks us to imagine the logically primitive constituents of propositions extending what Wittgenstein calls tendrils or "feelers" out to the simple objects whose configurations constitute the world of facts, or in the words of the famous opening sentence of the book, "all that is the case":

> The pictorial relationship consists of the correlations of the picture's elements with things. These correlations are, as it were, the feelers of the picture's elements, with which the picture touches reality. (*TLP* 2.1514–2.1515)

The picture conception of meaning thus invites us to take a kind of orthogonal, or what John McDowell (2000, 44) has memorably called a "sideways on," view of the relation between language and the world. It asks us, that is, to (try to) consider the relation between language and the world from a point of view somehow external to that relation, from outside of language.

Yet the upshot of the picture conception is precisely that language *cannot* in principle stand in such an orthogonal (second-order) relation to its own (first-order) relation to the world. The picture theory ought therefore to be, according to its own principles, unassertable. In the Preface to the *Tractatus*, Wittgenstein writes, "[T]he aim of the book is to draw a limit to thought, or rather—not to thought, but to the expression of thoughts," and it will "only be in language that the limit can be drawn" (*TLP* p. 3). There is no point of view outside of language from which to describe the relation between language and the world. And from the inside, the logical structure of propositions just *is* the logical structure of the world. There is no gap between language and reality, and hence no relation—of picturing or mirroring or correspondence or anything else—between them.

Wittgenstein thus urges us to dispense not just with his own colorful metaphors of "pictures," "feelers," "touching" reality, and "the great mirror" (*TLP* 5.511), but also with the very distinction between the logical structure of language and the logical structure of the world. Consider these three sentences in the *Tractatus*:

> A proposition is a picture of reality. (*TLP* 4.021)
> A picture is a fact. (*TLP* 2.141)
> A propositional sign is a fact. (*TLP* 3.14)

A proposition is a picture, a picture is a fact, and therefore a proposition (or a propositional sign) just *is* a fact. That is, as Wittgenstein defines his terms, the very distinction upon which the picture conception of meaning ought to thrive—the distinction between propositions and facts—collapses. Language and the world coincide: "*The limits of my language* mean (*bedeuten*) the limits of my world" (*TLP* 5.6).

What the *Tractatus* accomplishes, then, is a kind of exhibition of the world as "all that is the case" (*TLP* 1), a world that itself consists of facts, or existent states of affairs (*TLP* 2)—that is, the world as described by the natural sciences in propositional, fact-stating language. What Wittgenstein wants to have *shown* is the world *being* the world described by science. But only facts can be stated; the world *being* a world of facts cannot be stated. The true fact-stating propositions of science describe the world, but they cannot describe its *being* constituted by the logical form of language; they cannot describe it as *being* a world whose form coincides with the form of the propositional pictures that can be true of it. Wittgenstein's own sentences in the *Tractatus*, which seem to provide such a second-order or sideways-on description of the relation between language and reality, turn out not to say anything at all—that is, they fail to be fact-stating propositions belonging to a scientific description of the world. The picture theory is not a theory. "Philosophy is not one of the natural sciences" (*TLP* 4.11).

2 WORLD AS PICTURE

Heidegger offers a strikingly similar account of philosophy and its relation to science in his 1938 essay, "The Age of the World Picture." Like Wittgenstein, he has in mind not an ordinary but a quasi-technical concept of picture (*Bild*): a "picture" in the relevant sense is a representation (*Vorstellung*); it has nothing specifically to do with vision or visual images. Heidegger's critique of the modern understanding of what he calls "the world conceived as picture" (*OBT* 87/67) is not the familiar claim that visual metaphors have dominated metaphysics, although Heidegger does argue elsewhere that Plato conceived of the intelligibility of entities as consisting in a kind of view or aspect (*eidos, idea*).[6] The theory of forms was indeed the precursor of the modern metaphysics of the "world picture," Heidegger says, yet the kind of picturing or imaging definitive of modernity differs fundamentally from any of its ancient antecedents, including the Platonic conception of understanding as vision or contemplation (*OBT* 88–89/68–69).

The difference becomes clear once we realize that Heidegger's essay is a deliberate generalization of Kant's doctrine of schematism in the *Critique of Pure Reason*. Heidegger's careful reading of the Schematism chapter in the first *Critique*—culminating in his 1929 book, *Kant and the Problem of Metaphysics*[7]—permeates the argument of the "World Picture" essay. Modern thought, Heidegger argues, has obscured the question of being more thoroughly and systematically than ancient and medieval philosophy had done prior to Descartes. Despite the explicit prominent role Descartes plays in the essay, however, it is Kant who in fact stands center stage in Heidegger's account of the scientific construction of human beings as knowing subjects and of the world as the representation they survey and command.

What then is a "picture"? An image or picture is ordinarily understood to be a copy or likeness, something secondary to and parasitic on what it represents. Reflections, shadows, and echoes, for instance, are all effects flowing from their originals, and as such presuppose the things they represent. For Heidegger, on the contrary, the "world picture" definitive of modernity is the metaphysical precondition of the construal of entities as objects of knowledge. Our understanding of objects as susceptible a priori to explanatory experimental inquiry presupposes an interpretation of the world as a constructed image standing over against a knowing subject. This image, which orders the world and makes scientific research possible, *precedes* the objects it purports to represent. Heidegger therefore sees the distinctive institutional character of modern science precisely in "the precedence of method (*Verfahren*) over the entities . . . that in each case become objective in research" (*OBT* 82/64).

And whereas images in the ordinary sense are often (but not always) descriptive, the modern world picture is essentially normative. Objects of scientific knowledge are answerable to what Heidegger calls the projected "groundplan" (*Grundriß*) of scientific research (*Forschung*). This kind of world-*ordering*—indeed world-*constructing*—image is no mere copy or likeness (*Abbild*), but instead stipulates a measure or standard to which objects must conform in order to *be* objects at all, which is to say, objects of rigorous scientific knowledge.

Whereas images in the ordinary sense are parasitic on objects, then, modernity's metaphysical "world picture" has ontological priority and normative import. Heidegger draws both of these features—its primacy and its normativity—from Kant's conception of images and imagination (*Einbildungskraft*) in the *Critique of Pure Reason*.[8] Heidegger's essay thus amounts to a continuation of the phenomenological interpretation of Kant that preoccupied him in the 1920s.

What is an image, according to Kant? To begin with, he says, perhaps tautologically, "the *image* is a product of the . . . faculty of . . . imagination" (*CPR* A141/B181). What is the faculty of imagination? Kant uses the word "imagination" sometimes to refer simply to having images in one's mind, sometimes in the sense of delusion or error. More often, though, he means it in a technical sense, according to which "imagination is a necessary ingredient of perception itself" (*CPR* A120n). To say that imagination plays a constitutive role in all perceptual experience is to say that our experience is not wholly passive but saturated with a kind of content that goes beyond what is merely given in intuition. Perception is always surrounded by a kind of halo of background beliefs, assumptions, memories, and anticipations. To see a dog, for instance, is to see something that might in a moment run, bark, or growl. As Husserl would later say, to see any opaque three-dimensional object is to see a thing as having a back side, though we neither see nor even typically form judgments about the back sides of things (Husserl [1913] 1976, §§38–46). The back sides of objects, like all the possible canine-typical behaviors of the dog, are *there* for us in our experience, whether actually or potentially, in virtue of the imaginative anticipations that are a function of our very ability to apply concepts to intuitions.

This conception of the constitutive role of imagination in perceptual experience provides Kant with the solution to a problem posed by his own sharp distinction between sensibility and understanding. For if concepts and intuitions are strictly distinct and heterogeneous, he asks, "[H]ow is the *subsumption* of the latter under the former, thus the *application* of the category to appearances possible?" (*CPR* A137/B176). Number, possibility, causality, and substance are not things we can intuit. How then can we ever experience anything as *exhibiting* or *instantiating* them?

Kant's solution is to conclude that "there must be a third thing, which must stand in homogeneity with the category on the one hand and the appearance on the other, and makes possible the application of the former to the latter." The mediating representation that acts as a bridge or link between the category and the intuition is what he calls "the *transcendental schema*" (*CPR* A138/B177). The schema of a pure concept is the "representation of a general procedure (*Verfahren*)[9] of imagination for providing a concept with its image" (*CPR* A140/B179–80). Consequently, "the schema is to be distinguished from the image" (*CPR* A140/B179), since, whereas images are always particular, schemata must as it were sketch out in advance or anticipate *all* possible instantiations of a concept. "No image of a triangle," Kant says, for example, "would ever be adequate to the concept of it. For it would not attain the generality of the concept" (*CPR* A141/B180). The schema is not the image of any particular triangle but the rule or procedure for constructing *any* triangle—a rule that presumably says something like, *draw straight lines connecting any three nonlinear points*.

Like the image, Kant says, "The schema is in itself always only a product of imagination" (*CPR* A140/B179). But whereas "the *image* is a product of the empirical faculty of reproductive imagination, the *schema* of sensible concepts (such as of figures in space) is a product and as it were a monogram of pure *a priori* imagination, through which and in accordance with which the images first become possible" (*CPR* A141–42/B181). Schemata, then, are rules or procedures issuing from the faculty of imagination specifying the construction of sensible images adequate to pure concepts of the understanding. As such, they are essential to the application of categories to appearances. It is the faculty of imagination that carves out the space of possibilities within which objects can appear to us as objects of knowledge. Images are no mere shadows or echoes issuing from an experience that already hangs together prior to and independent of them; they are what satisfy the demands of the schemata constructed by the imagination in rendering the world epistemically accessible and intelligible to us as such.

What allows schemata to play this crucial mediating role between the discursive categories of the understanding and the passive intuitions of sensibility, moreover, is the fact that they exhibit the deep a priori condition underlying all representation, both conceptual and intuitive—namely, time. For time is at once the form of inner sense, to which all appearances must necessarily conform, and the sequence or duration that makes intelligible the implementation and execution of anything like a rule or procedure. Unlike the word "three," the Roman numeral III is as an image of the number, since it is a product of the rule for exhibiting the number three in the temporally extended procedure of counting.

Time is thus the bridging condition that allows the imagination to project and anticipate the application of concepts to intuitions. As Kant says, and as Heidegger quotes him saying, "[A]n application of the category to appearances becomes possible by means of the transcendental time-determination which, as the schema of the concept of the understanding, mediates the subsumption of the latter under the former" (*CPR* A139/B178). Heidegger regards this as an explicit precursor to his own "interpretation of *time* as the possible horizon for any understanding of being at all" (*BT* 1/19). It is Kant's emphasis on time as the ultimate condition for the intelligibility of entities that most impresses Heidegger, who therefore writes of the Schematism chapter, "[T]hese eleven pages of the *Critique of Pure Reason* must constitute the central core of the entire voluminous work" (*KPM* 89/63).

Yet Heidegger later came to regard his identification of Kant's insight into the essential finitude of reason with his own analytic of Dasein as an error that threatened to obscure the deep gulf that in fact lay between the Kantian schematism and his own account of existential temporality. In the preface to the second edition of *Kant and the Problem of Metaphysics* of 1950 Heidegger acknowledges the "violence" of his interpretation and admits to having "gone astray" in his attempt to establish a "thoughtful dialogue" with Kant's text (*KPM* xvii/xx). By 1973, in the preface to the fourth edition, he confesses that "Kant's text became a refuge, as I sought in Kant an advocate for the question of being that I posed" (*KPM* xiv/xvii), and that in truth, "Kant's question is foreign to" the problematic of *Being and Time*. In the end, he concludes, the *Kant* book amounts to "a questionable digression" from his own philosophical project (*KPM* xv/xviii).

In the "World Picture" essay, Heidegger offers a fundamental reassessment of the Kantian schematism and its place in Western metaphysics, which he now characterizes as a systematic forgetting of the question of being. Consider Heidegger's description of knowledge in its distinctively modern form—namely, scientific "research" (*Forschung*). First, building on his own earlier phenomenological account of understanding as a temporal "projection" (*Entwurf*) of possibilities (*BT* 145/185), he argues that scientific research issues from the projection of a normatively binding "groundplan" (*Grundriß*) onto some open sphere or region of objects:

> The projection sketches out in advance the way in which the knowing procedure (*Vorgehen*) must bind itself to the sphere opened up. This binding is the rigor of research. Through the projection of the groundplan and the prescription of rigor, procedure establishes itself in the region of being of its object-sphere. (*OBT* 75/59)

Heidegger then argues that modern physics is "mathematical" in the ancient Greek sense of the word, in virtue of the a priori status of its projected groundplan, for

> through it and for it something is made out in advance in an emphatic way as the already-known. This making-out has to do with nothing less than the projection of that which, for the sought-after knowledge of nature, nature must henceforth be: the self-contained dynamic configuration of spatiotemporally related point of mass. (*OBT* 76/59)

The role of the a priori groundplan in rendering nature explicable for modern mathematical physics, on Heidegger's account, thus recapitulates the role of the transcendental schema in rendering spatiotemporal objects cognizable in Kant's epistemology. But what Kant had ascribed to the cognitive powers of the individual subject Heidegger sees in the institutional structure of the scientific enterprise as such, which he describes as "industrious activity" (*Betrieb*). Like his notions of "falling" (*Verfallen*) and "idle talk" (*Gerede*) in *Being and Time*, his description of science as industrious activity has at least a semi-disparaging tone. Yet, just as "Falling is an existential determination of Dasein itself" (*BT* 176/220), not just some regrettable, avoidable lapse into inauthenticity, so too "modern science is defined by . . . industrious activity" (*OBT* 81/63), which is therefore no mere contingent liability or blemish on scientific practice.[10]

Another constitutive feature of scientific research is what Heidegger calls procedure or "method" (*Verfahren*)—which is, not accidentally, the same word Kant uses in describing the schema as the representation for the production of images adequate to the categories of the understanding. It is in virtue of its procedural or methodical character, Heidegger suggests, that scientific knowledge can take the form of rule and law (*OBT* 78/61–62).

Only with the advent of modern science, Heidegger suggests, do human beings become "subjects" in the distinctively modern—that is, Cartesian—sense of the term. As a result of the projection of a groundplan for rigorous scientific research in the form of industrious activity, "man becomes that entity on which all entities are grounded in the mode of their being and their truth. Man becomes the relational center of entities as such" (*OBT* 86/66–67). Asking about modernity's understanding of being in general then leads Heidegger to the question concerning the "world picture" peculiar to the modern age, in contrast to antiquity or the Middle Ages. And it is this question that Heidegger famously subverts, proposing instead that the conception of the world as a kind of image or picture is itself unique to modernity's understanding of being. The very expression "modern world picture" presupposes

> something there could never be, namely an ancient and a medieval world picture. The world picture does not change from an earlier medieval one to a modern one, rather the fact that the world becomes a picture at all is what distinguishes the essence of the modern age. (*OBT* 88–89/68–69)

The metaphysical construction of the world as image or picture on the basis of an a priori groundplan for rigorous scientific research thus recapitulates the transcendental schematism in the first *Critique* and the temporal production of images that render objects intelligible to us by linking pure concepts of the understanding (which would otherwise remain empty) to bare intuitions (which would otherwise be blind). The concept of picture that informs Heidegger's essay has as little to do with vision and visual images as Kant's own conception of the pure rule-generating work of the transcendental imagination. Like the Kantian schema that inspired it, the "world picture" in Heidegger's sense is something more like a network of practical and theoretical commitments constituting a massive, institutionalized system of actions, procedures, assumptions, and anticipations that render the world objectively knowable—a system that underlies our seemingly self-evident interpretation of ourselves as rational subjects, or more specifically autonomous agents able to believe, to value, and to will.[11]

3   SAYING THE UNSAYABLE

Wittgenstein's *Tractatus* and Heidegger's "Age of the World Picture" essay thus offer parallel accounts of the modern scientific conception of the world. For both, scientific knowledge is correlative to an objective world of facts susceptible to being pictured in true propositions. For both, the framework of objective representation itself—the logical structure of language for Wittgenstein, the groundplan of rigorous research for Heidegger—cannot in principle picture its own position vis-à-vis the world it pictures. Instead, objective scientific discourse is locked into a direct, internal relation to the domain (or domains) of fact to which its theoretical propositions are restricted in principle.

Wittgenstein and Heidegger share a conviction that philosophy does not belong to that species of scientific discourse, that it is not in the business of stating facts in the way science does—namely, by prescribing a normative framework that demarcates a domain of possible facts and draws a sharp distinction between true and false propositions. What philosophy does instead, for both the Wittgenstein of the *Tractatus* and for the Heidegger of the "World Picture" essay, is to *show* the objective world captured in scientific thought and language *as* the world it is—namely, *as* a domain of objective fact susceptible to theoretical representation. Science represents facts; philosophy shows what the world must be in order to *be* a world of facts susceptible to representation.

What distinguishes the early Wittgenstein from the later Heidegger is that while the *Tractatus* embraces a hypermodernist conception of the world as strictly correlative to the propositions of science, Heidegger regards scientific objectivity as just one among many possible interpretations of the world—or more precisely, of what it is for a world to *be* a world, and for entities to *be* entities. Wittgenstein's dogmatic affirmation of what Heidegger calls the metaphysics of the world picture commits him to what I think can only be called neurotic scruples concerning what can and cannot be said since, as he sees it, only objective, fact-stating propositions can be said to "say" anything.

Heidegger insists that the conception of objectivity underlying scientific discourse and knowledge is neither false nor illegitimate, although neither can it be strictly speaking correct or right. Rather, he regards it as one in a series of historically contingent interpretations of being, none of which can be true or false as such, but which function instead as transcendental conditions of the distinction between truth and falsehood in a variety of discursive contexts. Since, unlike the Wittgenstein of the *Tractatus*, Heidegger does not take for granted a priori any stipulation of what can and cannot be said, he is free to say—in avowedly nonscientific language—what the language of science does not and cannot say, and what Wittgenstein, at least in his early philosophy, regarded as unsayable in principle—namely, *what* the world of objective facts stated in scientific propositions *is*, over and beyond (or beneath) those facts themselves. Wittgenstein might well reply that what Heidegger takes himself to be "free to say" nevertheless misfires and devolves into nonsense, just as all traditional metaphysical discourse has done. But this presupposes that the kind of saying at issue is precisely the kind of propositional, bivalent (true/false), fact-stating discourse characteristic of objective knowledge—and of science in particular. But language works in myriad different ways beyond the mere statement of facts: it evokes, expresses, attunes, caricatures, mimics, highlights aspects, draws attention, and focuses thoughts and feeling.

It remains to say how we ought to understand Heidegger's famously evocative and elusive language. He was adamant, in any event, that it was not the language of science, or of objective knowledge at all. However we construe it, Heidegger himself thought it allowed him to say precisely what Wittgenstein evidently wanted but could not allow himself to say—namely, that the world understood as a domain of facts assertable in scientific propositions has the character of a picture.[12]

NOTES

1. All translations from Heidegger in this chapter are my own. References to *OBT* give the page number in the original German (*Holzwege*, 6th ed. [1950; Frankfurt: Klostermann, 1980]) followed by the page number in the standard English translation, and likewise with *KPM* (*Kant und das Problem der Metaphysik: Gesamtausgabe 3*, ed. F.-W. von Herrmann [Frankfurt am Main: Vittorio Klostermann, 1991]); *IM* (*Eisnführung in die Metaphysik* [Tübingen: Niemeyer, 1953]); and *PM* (*Wegmarken*, 2nd ed. [Frankfurt: Klostermann, 1978]).
2. "To chicken out," Diamond writes, "is to pretend to throw away the ladder while standing firmly, as firmly as you can, on it" (1991c, 194). One could fairly reply that for it to be a ladder at all, there must be some way of climbing it.
3. "In a certain sense, we cannot make mistakes in logic" (*TLP* 5.473); "What makes logic a priori is the *impossibility* of illogical thought" (*TLP* 5.4731).
4. I don't here have in mind such things as patent falsehoods and non sequiturs, which are often called "nonsense." Nor am I referring to the distinction Wittgenstein draws between tautologies and contradictions on the one hand, which are "senseless" (*sinnlos*) and merely "show that they say nothing" (*TLP* 4.461), and metaphysical (nonformal) pseudo-propositions that somehow

generate an illusion of meaning, but are in fact "nonsensical" (*unsinnig*). The question is how metaphysical nonsense can even *seem* to say something and yet fail, and what or how, in so failing, it might yet be said to *show* or make (something) manifest.

5. I am grateful to the editors of this volume for drawing my attention to George Pitcher's illuminating essay on the affinity between the nonsense in Lewis Carroll and the almost wholly diagnostic character of Wittgenstein's later philosophy. One of the attractions of the austere reading, of course, is that it brings the *Tractatus* into such close contact with the writings from the 1930s and 1940s. And yet the relation between the early work and the later work is precisely (part of) what's at issue in debates surrounding the austere reading. I sympathize with Pitcher when he confesses, "I can detect no intimate connection between Carroll and the early Wittgenstein" (Pitcher 1965, 596).

6. See *IM* 80/111, 139/194 and *PM* 212/164, 223/173.

7. See also *Phenomenological Interpretation of Kant's* Critique of Pure Reason (*PIK*).

8. Heidegger never mentions Kant by name in the main body of "The Age of the World Picture"—only in the appendix (§6), where he remarks that the essential systematicity of the critical philosophy lies in "the transcendental essence of finite reason rooted in the imagination" (*OBT* 99/76).

9. As we shall see, it is no accident that Heidegger himself uses the word *Verfahren* to describe the kind of scientific research constitutive of "the age of the world picture." For just as the Kantian schema is a rule or procedure governing the production of images adequate to the pure concepts of the understanding, so too, Heidegger says, the procedure or method of research sketches out a "groundplan" (*Grundriß*) constitutive of the modern understanding of the world itself in terms of—or indeed *as*—a kind of image.

10. Heidegger's conception of scientific research as industrious activity anticipates Thomas Kuhn's (1962) notion of "normal science," which maintains itself before and after major theoretical paradigm shifts.

11. Heidegger's interpretation and critique of modernity of course apply no less to Nietzsche's conception of world in terms of value, and of human being in terms of the will to power.

12. I am extremely grateful to the editors of this volume for their thoughtful critical feedback on an earlier draft of this chapter.

10 Disintegrating Bugbears
Heidegger and Wittgenstein on Basic Laws of Thought

Lee Braver

I want to object to the *bugbear* of contradiction, the superstitious fear that takes the discovery of a contradiction to mean the destruction of the calculus.

—*LWVC* 196

The destiny of the reign of "logic" in philosophy is thereby decided. The idea of "logic" itself disintegrates in the turbulence of a more original questioning.

—*BW* 105

How should we think? There is a sense in which this is the first philosophical question since all further inquiries, themselves forms of thought, ought to conform to the rules of proper thinking. But any answer concerning *how* we should think raises the deeper question of *why* we ought to think this way rather than any other. Wittgenstein and Heidegger take on this slippery question with surprising, and surprisingly similar, conclusions.

Wittgenstein's early work treats logic as not just transcendental but transcendent, essentially independent of thinkers: "Logic takes care of itself; all we have to do is to look and see how it does it" (*NB* 11).[1] His later work, however, eschews all transcendence, focusing entirely on "the spatial and temporal phenomenon of language, not . . . some non-spatial, atemporal non-entity" (*PI* p. 52).[2] Just as he "bring[s] words back from their metaphysical to their everyday use" (*PI* §116),[3] so he returns the act of thinking to its mundane settings. Reasoning is that which happens when we reason.

Heidegger's phenomenological background allows him to start at the place that Wittgenstein arrived at only in the latter part of his career. Fundamental ontology examines subjects in light of Dasein's nature, so Heidegger insists on viewing even the most abstruse philosophical topics in terms of the role they play in our "average everyday" lives. In particular, he criticizes the idea that assertions are the primary locus of truth, arguing that they are actually derivative of more basic ways of living and acting.[4] Making logic immanent to human thinking profoundly changes its usual meaning.

Neither thinker rejects logic, but rather "the reigning and never-challenged doctrine of 'logic' " (*BW* 97)[5]—that is, its claim to govern all thinking with absolute authority. Heidegger states that " 'logic' and 'the logical' are simply not *the* ways to define thinking without further ado, as if nothing else were possible" (*IM* 127).[6] For Wittgenstein, "Aristotelian logic brands a contradiction as a non-sentence, which is to be excluded from language. But this logic only deals with a very small part of the logic of our language" (*LWPPI* §525; see also *LWPPII* 44). They also reject the idea that these founding rules can themselves be founded, each subjecting a specific law to extended analysis: the Law of Non-Contradiction for Wittgenstein, and the Principle of Reason for Heidegger. Let us take these up in turn.

1 WITTGENSTEIN ON CONTRADICTIONS

In Wittgenstein's early work all propositions must obey the same logical form in order to be capable of describing the world—that is, in order to function as language at all. His later work gives up such notions as the singular essence of language, which he comes to see as the result of a narrow focus on a limited range of examples,[7] to be cured by reminders of the great diversity that actually exists. "I had the mistaken idea that propositions belong to just one calculus. There seemed to be *one* fundamental calculus, viz., logic, on which any other calculus could be based. . . . The idea that logic gives the general form of a mathematical statement breaks down when one sees there is no such thing as one idea of a proposition, or of logic" (*AWL* 138).[8] Wittgenstein now finds that "what is called 'language' is made up of heterogeneous elements and the way it meshes with our lives is infinitely various" (*PG* 66).[9] In his adaptation of Hamlet, "there just are many more language-games [than] are dreamt of in the philosophy of Rudolf Carnap and others" (*RPPI* §920; translation modified). Instead of an absolute division between legitimate propositions and nonsense, there are only different games. "For me one calculus is as good as another. . . . If the games are really distinct from each other, then one game is as good, that is as interesting, as the other. None of them is more sublime than any other" (*PG* 334).[10]

He applies this strategy of using diversity to break the spell of an ideal essence to some very basic ways of behaving by imagining people speaking or thinking or acting fundamentally differently. "Don't think that our concepts are the only possible or reasonable ones: if you imagine quite different facts from those with which we are continually surrounded, then concepts different from ours will appear natural to you" (*RPPI* §643).[11] The vast array of possible language-games relaxes the natural assumption of our own ways of doing things as *the* way: "the value of such games is that they destroy prejudices; they show that 'it need not always be this way' " (*AWL* 139).

De facto plurality does not by itself prove that a variety of valid ways of thinking are possible, for the alternatives may be illegitimate. A master code of logic could invalidate these bizarre tribes as violating inviolable laws of reasoning, the way Wittgenstein thinks J. G. Frazer discounts "primitive" rituals as bad science.[12] "Reason—I feel like saying—presents itself to us as the gauge *par excellence* against which everything that we do, all our language games, measure and judge themselves. . . . We are used, as it were, to 'dismissing' [other patterns] as irrational, as corresponding to a low state of intelligence, etc." (*PO* 389).[13] By making logic thoroughly immanent, however, Wittgenstein rules out rules that, transcending all usage, can judge them authoritatively, from the outside, so to speak.

Wittgenstein does not shy away from applying this view to the deepest rules of thinking, those that seem fundamental to any kind of reasoning: "The laws of logic, e.g., excluded middle and contradiction, are arbitrary. This statement is a bit repulsive but nevertheless true" (*AWL* 71).[14] Wittgenstein had firsthand experience of logicians' dread of hidden contradictions upon which their systems could founder—Russell's discovery of set theory's implicit paradox brought Frege to despair, and Gödel did roughly the same for Russell.[15] While logicians feel compelled to painstakingly scour their work to prevent such a catastrophe, like a programmer combing through their code for bugs, Wittgenstein dismisses paradox-hunts as a "profitless" game akin to "thumb-catching" (*RFM* II app. III §12),[16] ridiculing "the *bugbear* of contradiction, the superstitious fear that takes the discovery of a contradiction to mean the destruction of the calculus" (*LWVC* 196).[17]

The idea of a hidden contradiction is based on the picture of a system that may be working fine now, but is actually rotting within, which somehow undermines its present effectiveness.[18] But, Wittgenstein argues, this concern makes sense only on the Platonist conception of meaning as an already existing kind of ideal object, sometimes called a meaning-object,[19] where rules contain all of their correct applications in advance.[20]

While the early Wittgenstein considered this absolute determinacy necessary to the very possibility of meaning, he came to see it as just a picture. The fact that, once trained, most of us follow rules the same way without thought or effort suggests certain images to us, such as that we are simply following rails already there, wholly independent of us, which anticipate all applications. But this is just a picture that not only explains nothing but also creates confusions when taken seriously: "When we do philosophy, we are like savages, primitive people, who hear the way in which civilized people talk, put a false interpretation on it, and then draw the oddest conclusions from this" (*PI* §194). A set of rules no more "contains" an undiscovered contradiction than the complete decimal expansion of pi already possesses "7777" within it, lying invisibly beyond the horizon of all the calculations that have actually been undertaken.[21] A rule's applications do not exist "out there" until we apply them; hence there cannot be an undetected contradiction lurking amid a set of rules or propositions. Contradictions are as contradictions do.

Contradictions can present practical difficulties—conflicting instructions confuse, for example[22]—but this is easily remedied by creating a new rule to determine which trumps which in such circumstances.[23] Using conceptual duct tape to keep logic chugging along, the way Russell appended an ad hoc rule to avoid his paradox, offended Wittgenstein's early austerity, but it fits his later embrace of the messiness of human affairs perfectly. "They do this. And they get along all right. What more do you want?" (*LFM* 203–4).[24] It is up to us to decide whether a system is broken; our hand is not forced by Meaning or Reason or anything metaphysical or capitalized. This is why Wittgenstein frequently claims that mathematics and grammar are inventions rather than discoveries.[25] Mathematics exists only in our calculations so "there is nothing there for a higher intelligence to know—except what future generations will do. We know as much as God does in mathematics" (*LFM* 104).[26] If math and logic are not independently existing entities but rather consist in our performance, then we determine their status.

> Suppose among the rules there were two that contradicted each other, but I had such a bad memory that I never noticed this and always forgot one of these two rules or obeyed alternately the one and then the other. Even then I would say, Everything is all right. After all, the rules are instructions for playing the game, and as long as I can play, they must be all right. It is only when I *notice* that they contradict each other that they cease to be all right. . . . Thus the conflict appears only when I notice it. There was no problem as long as I was able to play the game (*LWVC* 125).[27]

It is we who apply the rules, and if we do so unproblematically then, well, there is no problem. The only thing we have to fear about contradictions is the fear of contradictions itself.

2 HEIDEGGER ON REASONS

Heidegger's later work breaks the history of thought into epochs organized around individual "understandings of being" or basic conceptions of what it means to be that comprehensively shape a culture for a time. In the Middle Ages, for example, to be was to be the creation of God. This ontology implies a cosmology—the world exists because God made it; an ethics—being a good person means living up to God's expectations; and ultimately an entire worldview. "Metaphysics grounds an age in that, through a particular interpretation of beings and through a particular comprehension of truth, it provides that age with the ground of its essential shape" (*OBT* 57).[28]

Like Wittgenstein's strange tribes,[29] these epochs show us that our own way of understanding and interacting with the world is not inevitable or simply the way things are, but just one possibility. "What did we seek from this 'historical reflection'? To obtain a *distance* from what we take as self-evident, from what lies all too close to us" (*ET* 6).[30] Studying history combats our natural tendency to take our own way of thinking as the obvious, exclusive truth. We may not be able to step entirely outside our epochal understanding, but neither need we inhabit it naively.

The great achievement of metaphysicians is to put their epoch's understanding into words;[31] their great failing is to stop there without asking why or how this particular understanding came about. Metaphysicians ascend from individual beings to their beingness—that is, to what it means to be for that age—but they stop there as if this definition "just [fell] absolute from heaven" (*WT* 40).[32] Heidegger wants to move up another level from beingness to being itself or the truth of being, which is the "sending" or "giving" of these epochal forms of beingness. Although being itself is nothing outside or beyond historical manifestations, neither is it exhausted by any particular instantiation. To the question why we understand things the way we do, the answer is that being has sent this way of thinking to us.

Now this looks like just the kind of foundationalist vindication philosophy has always dreamt of. Thoughts sent by being must surely be synchronized with reality as it really is, cutting her at the joints. These laws would not be just what comes naturally to us but what comes from nature. But this is not at all what Heidegger means. The language about being "sending" ways of thinking to us means, as I understand it, that we did not, and could not have, created the ways we think. Any such endeavor would have to take place on the basis of an already operating way of thinking. This is his fundamental argument against modernity's dream of total autonomy.[33] Being is not a separate entity that devises and blesses us with the right way of understanding it; it is just the manifestation of beings to us in an intelligible way. If beings appear in fundamentally different ways then, for Heidegger, they simply are in different ways, each of which needs to be understood on and in its own terms rather than sifted through for the one true way.

Heidegger's candidate for an apparently universal law of thought, the Principle of Reason, is relevant here. The idea that everything that is has a reason for being rather than not being, and for being the way it is rather than some other way, seems to require these epochal understandings to have explanations that, if properly decoded, can teach us the master plan of history, reality, and reason. But Heidegger rejects this approach, which he was recorded as attributing to Hegel: "for Hegel, there rules in history necessity. . . . For Heidegger, on the other hand, one cannot speak of a 'why.' Only the 'that'—that the history of Being is in such a way—can be said" (*TB* 52).[34] Ultimate intelligibility stops at the bedrock of brute fact.

The view of history as explainable all the way down breaks down because any explanatory account must obey the rules of a particular way of thinking—what Foucault (1972, 224) calls being "within the true"—to be acceptable. However, what counts as a sensible explanation varies through history.[35] "Because it is God's will" might have been a perfectly satisfactory answer to why winter follows fall or why my daughter is sick some centuries ago, but it would be grounds for dismissal in professional meteorology or medicine today. Attempts to justify particular understandings depend on a particular understanding of justification, which places being "beyond explanation, for all explanation here necessarily falls short and comes too late, since it could only move within, and would have to appeal to, something that was first encountered as unconcealed" (*BQ* 147).[36]

In fact, the Principle's demand that everything have a reason "immediately propels us into groundlessness" (*PR* 13) because it requires a reason for the Principle itself.[37] But there can be no reason why everything must have a reason without already presupposing the Principle.

> We find ourselves in a peculiar situation with respect to the laws of thought. For whenever we attempt to call the principles of thinking to mind, they inevitably become a theme of our thinking—and its laws. Behind us, in back of us as it were, the laws of thought lie ever ready and guide every step of our thinking about them. This directive is immediately evident and appears to check every attempt to properly think the laws of thought in a single move. (*PT* 47)[38]

Like in his early discussion of guilt, we can never get "behind" all our ways of thinking in order to determine them. Being grounds our interactions with beings by "sending" us a way to think about them. But as that which determines what counts as a ground within that epoch, being cannot itself be grounded. "Man in his very nature belongs to that-which-regions [i.e., Being], that is, he is released to it. Not occasionally, but—how shall we say it—prior to everything. The prior, of which we really can not think . . . because the nature of thinking begins here" (*DT* 82–83).[39]

Heidegger agrees with Kant on what I have called the Framework Argument: Kant places our transcendental faculties beyond the realm of the explicable or justifiable since any justification of these specific forms and categories must employ them, and so cannot achieve the escape velocity for a genuinely independent legitimation.[40] Heidegger applies this argument to Dasein's existence, which "stares it in the face with inexorability of an enigma" (*BT* 136/175)[41] in the early work and to the epochal understandings of being in the later. Wittgenstein applies it to the rules of a game: "'Reason' only applies within a system of rules. . . . It is nonsense to ask for reasons for the whole system of thought. You cannot give justification for the rules" (*LWL* 88).[42] The categories of right and wrong apply only *within* a game but not *to* the game itself; while a chess move can be illegitimate, it's a category mistake to say a chess rule is wrong. It can be impractical or undesirable, but "a rule is not true or false" (*AWL* 70).[43]

Instead of accounting for why we have these concepts, tracing our understandings back to being actually seals them off from explication, bringing us face-to-face with their unyielding, spade-turning resistance to comprehension the way Silenus's rose that "blooms because it blooms" represents an anti-explanation, despite employing the explanatory "because" (*PR* 42–43). Heidegger frequently claims that, although being grounds our thought, it does so with a groundless ground ("*ein abgründlicher Grund*") that cannot itself be given any deeper foundation (*N* IV 193).[44] Wittgenstein agrees that "the danger here, I believe, is one of giving a justification of our procedure where there is no such thing as a justification and we ought simply to have said: *that's how we do it*" (RFM III §74).[45] For Heidegger, "The 'because' withers away in the play [of being's sendings]. The play is without 'why'" (*PR* 113), while Wittgenstein writes, "Why do I not satisfy myself that I have two feet when I want to get up from a chair? There is no why. I simply don't. This is how I act" (*OC* §148). Both philosophers ground our thoughts and actions in the way we actually think and act, in the ground beneath our feet rather than a metaphysical ideal in the heavens above.

3   ABYSSAL FRAMEWORKS

Wittgenstein's and Heidegger's arguments follow the same steps: they describe alternate ways of thinking in order to shake our tacit absorption into our own as the only legitimate one. Then they rule out the idea of fundamental rules of thought that could adjudicate among these incommensurable language-games or epochal understandings of being. Reasons occur only within particular ways of thinking, which themselves cannot be explained or justified. In Heidegger's term, which Wittgenstein occasionally approaches,[46] they are groundless grounds. They do ground our thinking and acting, but not in the metaphysical sense that would show that this way is absolutely necessary and all others illegitimate.

Seeing this abyss (*Ab-grund*) beneath our feet can be disturbing. We cannot justify our language-games by appealing to a wholly independent reality because it is only through some game or understanding that we can compare reality with our thoughts about it. "I cannot use language to get outside language. . . . Grammatical conventions cannot be justified by describing what is represented. Any such description already presupposes the grammatical rules" (*PhR* 54–55).[47] Heidegger makes the point in terms of conceptions of truth: correspondence can take place only on the basis of an unconcealment that lets beings show up in a particular way.[48] In a version of the *Angst* that seizes Dasein when she realizes that there is no such thing as the right way to live, Wittgenstein's interlocutor worries: "But what becomes of logic now? Its rigour seems to be giving way here" (*PI* §108).[49] He can even be seen as "trying to undermine reason," a charge he doesn't entirely dispute (*LC* 63–64).

But this anxiety is based on a misunderstanding. At the end of all justifying must lie acceptance; no matter what we put in our foundation, we are still the ones who decide whether to accept it as grounding, and we must do so without further justification.

> But isn't it experience that teaches us to judge like *this*, that is to say, that it is correct to judge like this? But how does experience *teach* us, then? *We* may derive it from experience, but experience does not direct us to derive anything from experience. If it is the *ground* of our judging like this, and not just the cause, still we do not have a ground for seeing this in turn as a ground. (*OC* §130)[50]

Thus, "at the foundation of well-founded belief lies belief that is not founded" (*OC* §253; see also *PG* 110). These bottom-level ways of thinking and acting form the framework within which people live their lives, think their thoughts, and play their games. Although ultimately groundless, they give us all the ground we need or can have.

Rather than undermining reason, Wittgenstein is removing its traditional, fantastical justifications, which he considers to be no more than pictures that we do not, and cannot, actually use.

> At this point, our thinking plays us a strange trick. That is, we want to quote the law of excluded middle. . . . "In the infinite expansion of ϖ either the group '7777' occurs, or it does not—there is no third possibility." That is to say: God sees—but we don't know. But what does that mean?—We use a picture: the picture of a visible series, the whole of which one person can survey and another can't. . . . So really—and this is surely obvious—it says nothing at all, but gives us a picture. . . . And this picture *seems* to determine what we have to do, what to look for, and how—but it does not, precisely because we do not know how it is to be applied. (*PI* §352)[51]

We have never had the cosmic reassurances we feel we need but, rather than showing how rickety our support has been, this actually shows how little we need them.

Lacking transcendent criteria, reasons and truth become relative to particular language-games or epochal understandings: "a *reason* can only be given *within* a game. The links of the chain of reasons come to an end, at the boundary of the game" (*PG* 97). Although Truth has been taken off the table, particular truths within smoothly functioning games work as well as ever. Semantic nihilism worries us only when we spurn such humble fare as unworthy imitations of true Truth, and suffer withdrawal symptoms from metaphysics.

> "But is there then no objective truth? Isn't it true, or false, that someone has been on the moon?" If we are thinking within our system, then it is certain that no one has ever been on the moon. . . . Our whole system of

physics forbids us to believe it. . . . But suppose that instead of all these answers we met the reply: "We don't know *how* one gets to the moon, but those who get there know at once that they are there; and even you can't explain everything." We should feel ourselves intellectually very distant from someone who said this. (*OC* §108)[52]

As some commentators have noted,[53] Wittgenstein is playing two perspectives against each other. Within our system, it is as true as true gets that (to change the unfortunately outdated moon example) 2 + 2 = 4 or this cup is grey. But we misconstrue the nature of knowledge if we take this to mean that anyone must admit this no matter what, on pain of irrationality or betrayal of their own nature or contradicting Reality. The most we can say is that they would be thinking along very different lines than we are, differences that cannot be adjudicated from a neutral, transcendent perspective. "Somebody may reply like a rational person and yet not be playing our game" (*RFM* I §115).[54] Wittgenstein cites as examples actually existing incommensurable language-games such as the clash between religious and scientific outlooks.[55]

To indicate the fact that they cannot be rationally mediated, Wittgenstein speaks of "conversion," "persuasion," or "combat"[56] among language-games, whereas Heidegger calls epochal changes "leaps" brought on by a "god" or "sent" from being. Their incommensurability means that we cannot get conceptual foreigners to start acting normally (that is, as we do) by reasoning with them, since the very thing we're trying to impart is our way of reasoning. Bringing others to reason as we do must perforce happen through arational means. A child, for example, isn't rationalized through arguments—were she susceptible to arguments, she would already be rational—but through training and socialization.

> Supposing we met people who did not regard [the propositions of physics] as a telling reason. Now, how do we imagine this? Instead of the physicist, they consult an oracle. (And for that we consider them primitive.) Is it wrong for them to consult an oracle and be guided by it?—If we call this "wrong" aren't we using our language-game as a base from which to *combat* theirs?
>
> And are we right or wrong to combat it? Of course there are all sorts of slogans which will be used to support our proceedings.
>
> Where two principles really do meet which cannot be reconciled with one another, then each man declares the other a fool and heretic.
>
> I said I would "combat" the other man,—but wouldn't I give him *reasons*? Certainly; but how far do they go? At the end of reasons comes *persuasion*. (Think what happens when missionaries convert natives). (*OC* §§609–12)[57]

The converted may very well look back on their conversion as shedding superstition to become maturely rational (or conversely as escaping a coldly materialistic viewpoint to find God's loving embrace). Indeed, accepting such a meta-narrative of progress may be an important part of a full conversion. But they will acknowledge the data or arguments as relevant and obviously true only in retrospect. We must first compel them to start thinking like us before they will find our reasons for thinking this way compelling, "brainwashing" them into rationality.

In Wittgenstein's terms, particular claims get their justification within a language-game, which in turn depends upon a form of life and cultural upbringing; for Heidegger, specific ideas and practices appear reasonable in a clearing or epochal understanding of being. Wittgenstein writes:

> All testing, all confirmation and disconfirmation of a hypothesis takes place already within a system. And this system is not a more or less arbitrary and doubtful point of departure for all our arguments: no, it belongs to the essence of what we call an argument. The system is not so much the point of departure, as the element in which arguments have their life. (*OC* §105)[58]

The relationship between system and argumentation is not arbitrary but internal, making justifications of other systems impossible and of one's own redundant. Using a similar image, Heidegger calls science's adherence to the Principle of Reason "the element within which its cognition moves, as does the fish in water and the bird in air. Science responds to the demand. . . . Otherwise, it couldn't be what it is" (*PR* 30).[59]

This bottom layer is not justified or grounded, nor can it be. It cannot be true or false, rational or irrational, both because it is not epistemic and because it determines what truth or rationality are. Besides, justification must come to an end somewhere, inevitably leaving the last step unjustified. It is here that Wittgenstein's pointing statements take over: "*This* is how we think. *This* is how we act. *This* is how we talk about it" (*Z* §309).[60] "Why do we do this sort of thing? This is the sort of thing we do do" (*LC* 25).[61] Whereas Wittgenstein's early work used tautologies as conceptual fence posts marking the borders of intelligible thought, he comes to use the stressed indicative to indicate the inevitable spade-turning moment: "Somewhere we must be finished with justification, and then there remains the proposition that *this* is how we calculate" (*OC* §212).[62] These apparently empty statements resist philosophy's drive to explain where no explanation can be. "The difficult thing here is not, to dig down to the ground; no, it is to recognize the ground that lies before us as the ground. For the ground keeps on giving us the illusory image of a greater depth, and when we seek to reach this, we keep on finding ourselves on the old level. Our disease is one of wanting to explain" (*RFM* VI §31).[63] Heidegger uses tautologies like "the world worlds" or "the thing things" because, unlike explanations that reduce phenomena to something else like defining heat as motion, tautologies focus attention onto the phenomenon, the whole phenomenon, and nothing but the phenomenon.[64] This applies above all to being as the event of beings manifesting themselves to us: "What the propriating yields through the saying is never the effect of a cause, nor the consequence of a reason. . . . What propriates is propriation itself—and nothing besides" (*BW* 415; see also *DT* 67). For Wittgenstein, "What has to be accepted, the given, is—one might say— *forms of life*" (*PPF* xi §345).

The demand for grounds creates an infinite regress since any reason cited must itself be grounded, so Wittgenstein prefers to stop the chain before it gets started: "Why do you demand explanations? If they are given you, you will once more be facing a terminus. They cannot get you any further than you are at present" (*Z* §315; see also *PO* 86, 217). Although seeking reasons or explanations makes perfect sense within a game—indeed, it's an important part of many games—we cannot do this for the game as a whole, as the Framework Argument states.

> *What* counts as a reason for an assumption can be given *a priori* and determines a calculus, a system of transitions. But if we are asked now for a reason for the calculus itself, we see that there is none. . . .
>
> "Surely the rules of grammar by which we act and operate are not arbitrary!" Very well; why then does a man think in the way he does, why does he go through these activities of thought? (This question of course asks for reasons, not for causes.) Well, reasons can be given within the calculus, and at the very end one is tempted to say "it just is very probable, that things will behave in this case as they always have"—or something similar. A turn of phrase which masks the beginning of the chain of reasons. (The creator as the explanation at the beginning of the world). (*PG* 110–11)[65]

Heidegger makes the same point: "Here questioning already counts as knowing, because no matter how essential and decisive an answer might be, the answer cannot be other than the penultimate step in the long series of steps of a questioning founded in itself" (*BQ* 7; see also *OWL* 12).

Just as Wittgenstein in his early work praised primitive belief in the gods over modern science because the former highlights the limits of grounding that the latter hides (*TLP* 6.371–6.372; *NB* 72), so Heidegger welcomes the Principle of Reason's revelation of the abyss beneath our feet. Heidegger shifts the inquiry from particular questions to the fact of questioning, asking "why then the 'why'?" (*M* 237/§74),[66] not in order to answer it but to confront the impossibility of any answer. It "is, as the supreme fundamental principle, something underivable, the sort of thing which puts a check on thinking" (*PR* 45). Coming face to face with the abyss beneath our ground can create anxiety but it can also instill wonder and gratitude, restraining the technological attempt to arrange all of reality around maximizing the satisfaction of our desires: "Everything depends on our inhering in this clearing that is propriated by Being itself—never made or conjured by ourselves. We must overcome the compulsion to lay our hands on everything" (*N* III 181). Ultimately, Wittgenstein's basic human reactions and Heidegger's sendings of being escape rational justification or evaluation. Just as Wittgenstein calls our form of life or language "akin both to what is arbitrary and to what is non-arbitrary" (*Z* §358), so Heidegger says that "one cannot inquire into the 'correctness' of a projecting-open at all—and certainly not into the correctness of *that* projecting-open through which on the whole the clearing as such is grounded. . . . Is then the projecting-open pure caprice? No, it is the utmost necessity, but of course not a necessity in the sense of a logical conclusion" (*CP* 229–30/§204). They are the source of all reasoning and hence, by the Framework Argument, can be neither rational nor irrational themselves: "The grounds that essentially determine humans as having a [destiny] stem from the essence of grounds. Therefore these grounds are abysmal" (*PR* 37).

4   CONCLUSION

So we have one of the founders of modern logic who comes to tolerate contradictions, and a historian of philosophy who deems the epochs of metaphysics inexplicable. These ideas represent an essential step in weaning philosophers from the perennial attempt to overcome human finitude, an overarching goal for both philosophers. Metaphysics has always promised to peel back the skin of the world, exposing the skeleton so that we may capture its intrinsic articulation. This dream was shattered by Kant yet, as Nietzsche said of the shadows of God, fully disentangling ourselves from it is a long, slow process.[67] In fact, Wittgenstein and Heidegger frequently characterize the mind-set they are attacking as the attempt to take up a divine perspective.[68]

While Heidegger's talk of being easily invokes theological associations, that reading commits the central sin of metaphysics—ontotheology—by representing being as if it were *a* being, especially as the Great Being in the Sky. Rather, "if we are inquiring about the meaning of Being, our investigation does not then become a 'deep' one, nor does it puzzle out what stands behind Being. It asks about Being itself in so far as Being enters into the intelligibility of Dasein" (*BT* 152/193). He speaks of sending to emphasize an ineliminable passivity to thinking: "To think is before all else to listen, to let ourselves be told something" (*OWL* 76).[69] Being's sendings are what make thinking possible at all, and what guide its particular forms. We think about the things and details of our experience that attract our attention, and in the way that they occur to us, which cannot be up to us on pain of infinite regress. "We will have to rely on Being, and on how Being strikes our thinking, to ascertain from it what features essentially occur" (*N* IV 214).[70] In logic, for example, we do not decide what can and should be negated; propositions present themselves to us as negatable.[71] Even the basic impulse to explain and understand is something we respond to rather than choose: "We are constantly addressed by, summoned to attend to, grounds and reason" (*PR* 3).[72] This is why Heidegger compares thinkers with poets who, eschewing clichés, listen intently to the connotations of words that have been dampened by idle usage.

Although thinking is entirely a human affair, it is largely a matter of our responses rather than our choices, or choices that are themselves responses. Not just perception and physical activity but thinking too should be modeled on J.J. Gibson's notion of solicitation—where a chair "invites" me to sit on it—rather than detached, deliberate ratiocination.[73] This is an important clarification of the notion of decision here. On the one hand, nothing wholly independent of humanity forces us to reason in any particular way; on the other hand, lots of factors like basic features of human nature and our particular socialization make certain ways of thinking or following rules natural and automatic. "What is it that compels me?—the expression of the rule?—Yes, once I have been educated in this way" (*RFM* VII §27).[74] This means that while it is not up to me to choose what the answer to a mathematical problem is—"what is a telling ground for something is not anything *I* decide" (*OC* §271)[75]—neither is there such a thing as our collectively making mistakes about, say, basic multiplication as if it were independent of humanity. The way we do it just is what multiplication is: "*The point is that we all make the SAME use of it*. To know its meaning is to use it *in the same way* as other people do. 'In the right way' means nothing" (*LFM* 183).[76] This is how Wittgenstein "solves" what has been called the rule-following paradox: one way of following the rule automatically solicits us once we've been trained, and this is the "way of grasping a rule which is *not* an interpretation" (*PI* §201), and so not vulnerable to the vast number of other possible interpretations.

Logic cannot escape the human, as Wittgenstein dearly wanted it to do in his early work, nor can studying the history of being allow us to rise above it, as Hegel tried to do. Both Heidegger and later Wittgenstein come to accept our ways of thinking as just that—*our* ways, which cannot be justified by appeals to anything transcendent. Wittgenstein and Heidegger explore these projects in order to free us of them, so that we may understand and accept being finite.[77]

NOTES

1. See also *TLP* 5.473, 6.124.
2. See also *BB* 1, 16; *PO* 321; *LFM* 231; and *OC* §47.
3. See also *PI* §190; *OC* §260; §406; *Z* §448; and Stern (1995, 12–13, 70, 92).
4. *BT* 33/57, 156/199, 160/203, 217/260, 226/269, 231/274, 357/408; *BP* 210, 227; *IPR* 14–15, 26; *MFL* 216–17; *PS* 125; and *LQT* 134.
5. See also *BT* 129/166–67, 165/209 and *IM* 27, 201.

6. See also *PM* 235; *Zo* 217; *PIA* 17, 123–24; *PS* 174–75; and *BP* 206–7, *Supp* 144.
7. *PI* §3, §304, §593; *RPPI* §38; *Z* §444; *AWL* 12–13, 46–47, 88, 107, 110, 115; and *PO* 418.
8. See also *AWL* 12–13; *PG* 211; and *RPPI* §38.
9. See also *PG* 106, 179; *PhR* 118; and *PI* §18, §65, §304.
10. See also *PG* 111, 116, 322; *LWVC* 124, 132–33, 202; *PhR* 321; *PI* §§23–24; Medina (2002, 152); and Staten (1986, 21).
11. See also *PPF* xii §366; *Z* §351; *RFM* IV §24; *RC* II §10; *RC* III §§121–24; and Malcolm (1982, 254, 257, 261–62).
12. *PO* 106, 119, 141; *LC* 58–59; Drury (1984a, 119); Drury (1984b, 93); and Monk (1990, 310–11).
13. See also *LC* 64; *OC* §498, §609, §611, §667; and *RPPI* §587, §622.
14. See also *LWL* 19; *RFM* IV §57; *LWPPI* §525; *OC* §670; and Dummett (1978, 168, 178).
15. See Russell (1959, 76). Frege warns his readers of undiscovered contradictions (Frege [1884] 1980a, 87, 105–6, 108, 112, 119), foreshadowing just the kind of disaster that befell him: the failure to find a contradiction among one's definitions, he writes, "shall, at bottom, never have achieved more than an empirical certainty, and we must really face the possibility that we may still in the end encounter a contradiction which brings the whole edifice down in ruins" (Frege [1884] 1980a, ix; cf. Frege 1980c, 234). If logic can accommodate tragedy, this is surely what it must look like.
16. See also *RFM* III §82; *RFM* VII §11; and *LFM* 206–7.
17. See also *LWVC* 119, 131, 141, *Z* §687; *RPPI* §1132; *RFM* I app. III §17; *RFM* IV §56; and *LFM* 209, 211.
18. *PG* 303; *LFM* 28, 124; *RFM* III §84; and *PhR* 319, 338.
19. *RPPI* §42, §349; *PI* §559; and *LWL* 59.
20. *BB* 39–40, 73–74, 142–43; *NB* 89–90; *TLP* 5.2523; *Z* §§138–39; *PI* §193, §197, §334; *PO* 399; *LFM* 196–99; *RPPI* §40, §139; *PG* 55, 481; *PI* p. 155; and *AWL* 83. This is one of the dominant topics of his later work, as I argue in chapter 2 of Braver (2012).
21. *LFM* 47, 66, 83, 95, 103–4, 107, 126, 131–32, 138–39, 171, 179, 235, 258; *RFM* V §9, §20; *RFM* VII §41; *PI* §352; *LWVC* 174, 199–200; *AWL* 67, 84; and *PG* 303–4.
22. *LWVC* 119–20, 125; *LFM* 176, 179, 213; and *RFM* IV §57.
23. *LWVC* 194, 201; *LPP* 116; *LFM* 206–9; *Z* §§685–88; and *PG* 303.
24. See also *LFM* 159, 201, 207, 209, 220; *Z* §320, §322; *OC* §131, §287, §359, §474; *RC* III §317; *CV* 64; and Bouveresse (2008, 5).
25. *LWVC* 34–35, 63; *RFM* I §32, §167; *RFM* I app. II §2; *RFM* II §38; *RFM* V §9, §11; *RFM* VII §5; *LFM* 22, 39, 82–83, 138–39; Wright (1980, 240–41); Baker and Hacker (1985, 10); and Dummett (1996, 446, 451).
26. See also *LFM* 255, 271; *PI* §208; *LPP* 69; *PG* 321, 480; *AWL* 192; *LWL* 89–90; *PhR* 149, 212; *RFM* VII §41; and Marion (1998, 181–92).
27. See also *LWVC* 120; *RFM* I app. III §11, §17; *RFM* III §21, §78; *RFM* VII §15, 16, §34; *LFM* 210, 217; *PO* 437; *RPPII* §290; *AWL* 71–72; and Monk (1990, 545).
28. See also *OBT* 79; *N* II 80; *N* II 131; *N* IV 7, 100, 205; *WT* 95–96; *BW* 330; *PR* 55, 87, 94; *CP* 169/§122; *ET* 150; *FS* 61; *WCT* 66; Edwards (1990, 93); Schürmann (1990, 4); and Thomson (2005, 55, 147).
29. Glock (2008, 97, 100); Williams (1976, 87); Malcolm (1982, 254, 257, 261–62); Baker and Hacker (1985, 240, 243, 328, 335); Apel (1998, 129, 143; 1980, 22); and Janik and Toulmin (1973, 245).

30. See also *M* 91; *PR* 89, 100–1, 105; *PT* 69; *Zo* 286; *QT* 37, 176; *HR* 257, 306; *WT* 42; Schürmann (1990, 7, 50); Young (2002, 86); and Thomson (2005, 8, 23, 39, 142).
31. *M* 300, 322–23, 375; *TB* 37; and *ITP* 5, 15, 58.
32. See also *EGT* 60, 99, 122; *BQ* 170; *QT* 115; *PM* 232, 278, 287–88; *N* IV 7, 211–12; *OBT* 57; *BW* 232, 247; *AM* 8, 102; *ITP* 16; Young (2002, 23–29); and Zimmerman (1986, 23).
33. *WCT* 46, 65; *WT* 97, 100, 106; *IM* 123–24; *CP* 179/§134, 221/§193; *P* 103; *DT* 58–59; *N* IV 28, 86, 103; *PM* 300; *QT* 128, 151; *PR* 76–77; *BW* 332; Polanyi (1967, xi, 60–62, 80, 91); and Braver (2007, 314–25).
34. See also *TB* 6, 33; *BW* 433; *IM* 30; *FS* 9; *CP* 171/§125; *M* 17, 206; *PR* 91, 108; *WIP* 63; and *QT* 39.
35. *WT* 39–40, 50, 52, 65, 78–79, 90, 121, 129, 135; *HH* 33–34; *IM* 56, 110; *PT* 69; *PIK* 22; *QT* 117, 176; *BQ* 48; *AM* 67; *PR* 79; and *EGT* 43.
36. See also *HH* 90; *Zo* 266; *BW* 415; *DT* 67; Malpas (2007, 194, 222); Rorty (1991, 15); and Schürmann (1990, 41).
37. *PR* 6, 11; *KPM* 199; and *IM* 5–6.
38. See also *WCT* 65; *BW* 324; *FS* 67; *M* 133, 350; and *MFL* 104. Aristotle similarly argues that the law of non-contradiction cannot be proven since any such proof would necessarily presuppose the law itself (*Metaphysics* 4.3.1006a5–11).
39. See also *DT* 65 and *PR* 62, 75, 84.
40. Kant ([1783] 1950, 65, 99); *CPR* B145–46, B 421–2; and Braver (2012, 194–96).
41. See also *BT* 228/271, 276/321.
42. See also *LWL* 104–5; *AWL* 4–5; *PG* 97, 110–11, 184–85, 303–4, 322, 334; *LFM* 95, 107; *RFM* I §19; *RFM* VII §18, §30, §35; *LWVC* 124, 133; *PO* 352, 418; *OC* §81–83, §105, §108, §110, §140–42, §144, §150–51, §167, §205, §248, §253, §307, §358–59, §514, §603; *BB* 89; Baker and Hacker (1985, 54, 105, 180, 163); Genova (1995, 44); Stroud (2000, 93); Medina (2002, 152); and Malcolm (1982, 254, 259, 262).
43. See also *AWL* 129, 162, 178; *LC* 59; *LWVC* 103–5, 126; *LFM* 138–39; *PI* §242; *RFM* I §5, §156; *RFM* III §75; *PG* 352, 401; Wright (1980, 61, 69); Hacker (1996, 121); Glock (1992, 77, 81); Pears (1988, 437, 446); Rouse (1987, 62, 124, 160, 210); O'Neill (2001, 3, 7); Gier (1981, 42); Stern (1995, 49); and Trigg (1991, 215).
44. See also *N* III 90; *PR* 68, 94; *BQ* 53; *PM* 232; *BaT* 204; and Schürmann (1990, 19–20, 34).
45. See also *RFM* I app. I §2; *RFM* III §78; *RFM* VI §21; *OC* §212; and *PI* §217.
46. *OC* §166, §253; *Z* §301; and *PI* §482.
47. See also *PG* 255, 283–84; *OC* §145; *Z* §333; *RPPI* §644; *OC* §§196–98, §292; *PG* 224–27, 443; *AWL* 28, 98n; Pears (1988, 462); Guignon (1990b, 665–68); and Wright (2004, 34). See especially *LPP* 49–50.
48. *BQ* 82, 174; *MFL* 127–28; *BW* 122, 176; and *BT* 220/263.
49. See also *OC* §108; *LC* 64; and *PO* 73, 408. See Michael Dummett: "If Wittgenstein were right, it appears to me that communication would be in constant danger of simply breaking down" (1978, 176–77). Compare with Heidegger: "Because we are speaking against 'logic' people believe that we are demanding that the rigor of thinking be renounced and in its place the arbitrariness of drives and feelings be installed. . . . We are so filled with 'logic' that anything that disturbs the habitual somnolence of prevailing opinion is automatically registered as a despicable contradiction" (*BW* 249–250).

50. See also *Z* §331 and *Z* §357.
51. See also *PI* §222; *RFM* I §22, §72; *RFM* V §§9–11; *PO* 94, 435; *PG* 481; *LFM* 131–32; Wright (1980, 220, 275–76, 312, 372); Baker and Hacker (1985, 236); and Dummett (1978, 185).
52. See also *RFM* III app. III §§7–8; Kober (1996, 424–25); and Stroud (2000, 93).
53. Lear (1998, chap. 11–12); Williams (1976, 76–95); Bloor (1996, 375); and Kober (1996, 428–29).
54. See also *RFM* III §70; *RFM* VI §45; *LFM* 110, 243, 261; *OC* §217; and *PI* p. 60.
55. *OC* §336; *RPPI* §366; and *LWL* 104.
56. *OC* §92, §233, §262; and *LC* 27–28; see also Rhees (1984a, 206).
57. See also *OC* §138, §292, §495, §498; *Conv* 4–5, 37, 57; *Z* §318, §352; *LFM* 58, 236; *Z* §461; *PI* §144; *LC* 64; and *LWPPII* 53.
58. See also *OC* §146, §167, §292, §337, §603; *PO* 437; Malcolm (1982, 254–55, 259; 1994, 76–78); Hintikka and Hintikka (1989, 237n5); Wright (1980, 373–76); Williams (1996, 4); Priest (2002 210–12); and Rouse (1987, 62, 124, 160, 210).
59. See also *PR* 3, 20, 22, 33, 37, 123; *FS* 67; and *STF* 98. Gadamer (1997, 22) uses the same metaphor to compare his work to Wittgenstein.
60. See also *PI* §71, §217, §483, §654; *OC* §28, §39, §128–29, §148, §254, §294, §551; and *PO* 121. As Robert Fogelin puts it, "The italicized demonstrative is the *leitmotiv* of Wittgenstein's later philosophy" (Fogelin 1995, 206).
61. See also *RPPI* §49; *Z* §700; and *LWPPI* §878.
62. See also *RFM* I app. I §2; *RFM* III §74, §78; and *RFM* VI §21.
63. See also RFM VI §21; *Z* §314; *RPPII* §314, §402, §453; and Braver (2007, 290–91).
64. Heidegger calls "tautological thinking . . . the primordial sense of phenomenology" (*FS* 80; see also *WCT* 153, 172, 233; *PR* 43; *TB* 42; *PLT* 179–80; *CPC* 60–61, 90–91; *BaT* 71; and Malpas 2007, 194, 222).
65. See also *PG* 94, 184–85, 322, 334, 401; *PI* §§654–56; *PPF* xi §161; *PPF* xi §345; *RPPII* §453; and *LWL* 104–5.
66. See also *MFL* 214–15; *IM* 5; *BCAP* 39, 178; and *KPM* 199.
67. Much of Braver (2007) traces this process.
68. For more on this, see the conclusion to Braver (2012).
69. "To think 'Being' means: to respond to the appeal of its presencing. . . . The responding is a giving way before the appeal and in this way an entering into its speech" (*PLT* 183–84; see also *PLT* 6, 209; *PM* 236, 279; *DT* 71, 74; *PR* 23–24, 47, 50, 53, 67, 87–88, 92, 96; *P* 49; N III 5, 187, 188, 214; N IV 181, 200; *PT* 25, 27, 53; *WIP* 75–79; *EGT* 19, 55; *BW* 104–5, 220, 328, 330, 361, 372, 409–11, 418, 423; *CP* 325/§265; *WCT* 6, 46; Zo 217; *QT* 54; *HR* 330; and *CPC* 62). Note that, strictly speaking, Heidegger rejects the distinction between acting and thinking (*BW* 217–18, 262; *QT* 40), as well as between activity and passivity.
70. See also *PR* 55, 94; *BW* 217, 384; *WCT* 115, 126, 132, 151, 232; and *LQT* 96.
71. *BT* 285–86/331–32; *BW* 104–5, 260; and *ID* 26–27, 39.
72. See also *PM* 293; *ID* 35; *PLT* 112; and *CP* 88/§61, 92/§67.
73. For more on this topic, see Braver (forthcoming; 2012, chap. 4).
74. See also *RFM* I §116; *PG* 109, 126; *LFM* 66, 107, 139; *LWL* 8; and *OC* §344, §358.

75. See also OC §317. "Do you *decide* how to apply the rule for multiplication? No; you just multiply" (*LFM* 238). The exception would be in cutting-edge math where no path has yet been cleared.
76. See also *LFM* 97, 101, 223, 235–37, 275, 290–91; *PO* 352, 395; *PI* §145, p. 155; *OC* §304, §496–97, §637, §651; *RFM* I §136; *RFM* II §74; *RFM* V §16; *LWVC* 134; and *AWL* 179.
77. I would like to thank David Egan, Stephen Reynolds, and Aaron James Wendland for their helpful suggestions. My *Groundless Grounds* (2012) was a source of material for this chapter and I thank MIT Press for permission to use it.

11 Understanding as a Finite Ability

Joseph K. Schear

Heidegger and Wittgenstein both characterize human understanding as an *ability*. They also both suggest that this ability is *finite* in nature. In this chapter I want to survey the different ways each of them respectively investigates the idea of understanding as a finite ability—first, to make some progress on what such an idea might come to, and second, to use it to shed light on each of their projects.

Consider first Kant's distinction between the finite intellect and the infinite intellect. This contrast is characterized by Kant in a number of different ways. According to one prominent characterization, an infinite intellect, possessed of a capacity for intuition that is the source or cause of its objects, produces its objects. Let me call this the productive intellect. By contrast, the intuition of a finite being, such as a human being, is *given* its objects from without, and therefore must be affected by objects to cognize them (see *CPR* B72, among other places).

According to a second characterization, an infinite intellect comprehends in one fell intuitive sweep the totality of whatever it comprehends. Let me call this, for reasons that will soon become clear, the "single gulp" intellect. Contrast a form of intellect that must successively "synthesize" the parts or aspects of what it comprehends. Such an intellect is in no position to cognize its object in one stroke—that is, swallow it all down in a single gulp.[1]

In what follows, I will put forward the following exegetical claim: whereas Wittgenstein explores the finitude of human understanding by juxtaposing it to the infinitude of the single gulp intellect, Heidegger explores the finitude of human understanding by juxtaposing it to the infinitude of the productive intellect. As a secondary claim, I will suggest that this difference in senses of finitude is coupled with a difference in the sense in which both are respectively anti-Cartesian philosophers. Whereas Wittgenstein's primary Cartesian target is a thesis in philosophical psychology—namely, that understanding consists in a mental state—Heidegger's primary target is a Cartesian thesis in ontology—namely, that the subject of understanding is a special kind of *thing*. I begin with Wittgenstein, and then turn to Heidegger.

1   WITTGENSTEIN ON UNDERSTANDING AS AN ABILITY

At *PI* §150, Wittgenstein explicitly introduces the idea of linguistic understanding as a kind of ability, set in contrast to the idea of understanding as
a mental state, or a state of consciousness. Consider an ordinary English
word, "chair." "Are there enough chairs for everyone?" "This chair is good
enough." You've just read three sentences (now four) containing the word
"chair." Would you call your understanding of this word a "mental state"?
If so, did you just enjoy four mental states? How long did each state last?
As long as it took for the word to be uttered? Or did the mental state, like
an echo, carry on but fade as the relevant sentence concluded? Can we determine the duration of each state by means of a stopwatch?

Wittgenstein writes in *PI* (p. 65):

> "Understanding a word": a state. But a *mental* state?—We call dejec-
> tion, excitement, pain, mental states. Carry out a grammatical investi-
> gation as follows: we say
> "He felt dejected the whole day"
> "He was in great excitement the whole day"
> "He has been in pain uninterruptedly since yesterday."—

We also say, "Since yesterday I have understood this word." "Uninterruptedly," though?

The question that concludes the passage is supposed to sound confused.
One could read it as marking the conclusion of a *reductio* of the thought
that understanding is a mental state, at least in the sense of a mental state
that is a conscious experience that takes time, that has genuine duration.
At *PI* §154 we are instructed, "[D]on't think of understanding as a 'mental
process.'" Call Cartesianism in the theory of understanding the claim that
understanding is a conscious mental state or process.

Compare the sense of confusion of "uninterruptedly, though?" with the
strangeness of the question "*when* do you understand the word 'chair'?"
And then note the kinship of this seeming confusion with the following
when-question. Wittgenstein writes:

> What if one asked: When *can* you play chess? All the time? Or just
> while you are making a move? And the whole of chess during each
> move?—And how odd that being able to play chess should take such a
> short time, and a game so much longer!" (*PI* p. 65)

Wittgenstein's alternative to Cartesianism, promising to avoid such queer
consequences, is the suggestion that the grammar of "understands" is closely
related to that of "can" or "is able to" or "know how to" (*PI* §150 and
§182). The respective grammars of this series of words and phrases "belong

in one investigation." Or in *PG* (47): " 'Understanding a word' may mean: *knowing* how it is used; *being able to* apply it."

A natural worry to have about the idea of understanding as an ability is the phenomenon of sudden understanding, as in: "Now I understand!" Recall the "since yesterday I have understood this word" in the first passage earlier. At *PI* §151 Wittgenstein considers this use of "understand," which serves as an entrée to the following illustrative scenario. A writes down a number series, and B, in the pupil position, is to figure out the formula that expresses the law of the sequence of numbers: "Now I understand!" and B proceeds to continue the series on his own. Surely *here*, if anywhere, understanding is a mental state—for example, the formula itself might very well occur to one, prompting the claim to understand. The familiar sense of understanding here imagined is something that *happens*, a moment of occurrent awareness, and so well captured by Cartesianism about understanding.

One might accommodate sudden understanding by conceding that the word "understanding" is ambiguous. Sometimes we use it in the ability sense; sometimes we use it in the state sense. Compare the word "bank." Sometimes we use it to refer to a pile of dirt by a river; sometimes we use it to refer to an institution that holds money and charges fees (among other things). But that can't be right. To lift a remark Wittgenstein offers in a different context: "Then has 'understanding' two different meanings here?—I would rather say that these kinds of use of 'understanding' make up its meaning, make up my *concept* of understanding. For I *want* to apply the word 'understanding' to all this" (*PI* §532). Suppose I hold up a picture of a pile of dirt by a river, and a picture of a branch of HSBC. You wouldn't want to apply "bank" to all this, at least in the same sense that you want to apply "understanding" to the state of sudden understanding and the ability to understand.

So how *do* the two uses of "understanding" go to "make up" one concept? The broadly Cartesian way to proceed here would be to start with understanding as an act or state of occurrent awareness. This is the fundamental use. And then the question is: How can we get from *this* to something with the shape of an ability? What glue holds together those four states of your understanding of the word "chair" so they can be seen to be something like actualizations of one fertile capacity—that is, your understanding of the word "chair"? An answer: the mental states are modifications of a single substance.

Wittgenstein's alternative to Cartesianism, at least on one reading, inverts the order of proceeding. This reading starts with understanding construed as an ability. That is the fundamental use of the word "understanding," expressive of the basic category in terms of which the concept of understanding finds its home. One then accommodates sudden understanding by construing it as the onset of an ability. "Now I can go on!" is one expression of this onset (among others). Does the formula *have to* come before B's mind for something like that expression to come out? We can easily imagine nothing whatsoever occurring in the pupil's mind when he says he can go on: he just finds himself able to go on, perhaps with a feeling of relief, a releasing of his breath, an unhesitating stroke of his pencil, as he struggles to hold back a smile. If the formula does occur in his mind, does that *suffice* for him to be able to go on? We can easily imagine a case of the formula occurring without being able to go on. And it is not hard to imagine, further, the shrillness of the inspired type whose insistent reports of "Now I can go on!" make no connection with actually being *able* to go on.

Wittgenstein accordingly says at *PI* §180 that "[i]t would be quite misleading . . . to call the words ['Now I know how to go on'] a 'description of a mental state.'" We are encouraged, as an alternative, to call the expression of those words a "signal" and to judge whether the signal was rightly employed by what the pupil goes on *to do*. With the case of sudden understanding so accommodated, as signaling the onset of an ability, its support for the truth of the claim that understanding is a mental state is disarmed. An occurrence of the formula (or what have you) coming "before the mind" is accordingly put in its place as, if not a piece of ornamentation, at least not integral to understanding as such. Understanding, Wittgenstein teaches us, is *not* a mental state.[2]

On a second reading, Wittgenstein's alternative to Cartesianism does not *deny* that understanding is, or at least can be, a mental state. His remarks on understanding rather amount to the effort to disabuse us of a *mythical* conception of mental states. The real problem with the Cartesian construal, according to this reading, is that the mental state of understanding is pictured in complete abstraction from its surroundings—for example, the stage-setting of B having learned algebra, having used such formulae before, and so on (*PI* §179). It is only in the context of this cropped picture that the problem arises of how to get a self-contained state to open up into the fertile ability to go on. However, if we acknowledge the occurrence of a state of consciousness in which the formula comes before the mind, but we do so in a way that recognizes its place in a wider context, then we can recover an innocent idea of understanding as a determinate mental state. Indeed, the occurrence of the formula, when it does occur, can suffice to be able to go on. "Now I can go on," in such a case, *is* an expressive signal, but also, at one and the same time, the self-ascription of a determinate mental state. On this reading, if we call the idea of understanding as a mental state a fly, Wittgenstein is letting the fly out of the fly-bottle.[3]

While the second reading may enjoy stronger textual support, it is not clear how much ultimately hangs on the difference between them. Either way, whether "Now I can go on" is best understood as merely signaling the onset of an ability, or rather, in doing that, expressing (at least sometimes) the self-ascription of a determinate mental state within the wider context of the flowering of an ability, the very fact that the text makes both readings available testifies to Wittgenstein's crusade against the Cartesian thesis that understanding *consists in* an experiential state or process.

2   WITTGENSTEIN ON UNDERSTANDING AS FINITE

Wittgenstein's characterization of understanding as, or as akin to, an ability of course raises many questions. For example, what sets understanding apart from other abilities, such as the ability to ride a bike? Wittgenstein likens not just understanding but also knowledge to an ability. What distinguishes the ability to understand from other broadly intellectual abilities to which it is clearly linked? My question in this chapter is: In what sense is the ability to understand, for Wittgenstein, finite? Wittgenstein's aims and methods generally tend to discourage the use of straightforward assertion. One suspects that if he did allow himself the force of assertion in this area, he would have said something like, "Understanding is *akin* to being finite." Or perhaps he might have said, "We are prone to think of understanding as infinite," followed by some imaginary scenario that makes that temptation somehow or other uncomfortable to discharge.

What would it mean to say that understanding is infinite? And why might we be tempted to say such a thing? In Wittgenstein's remarks on rule following, one of the temptations explored is the idea of understanding, or meaning, as a kind of act or state that has "already taken all those steps" (*PI* §188). In a characteristic scene of instruction, this temptation is attributed to the one occupying the teacher position, having encountered the pupil who, when he reaches 1000, continues to follow the order "+ 2" with 1004, 1008, 1012. The teacher, the voice of the interlocutor, wants to insist that he *meant* the order "+2," that the pupil ought to write 1002 after 1000. The "voice of correction" reminds the teacher that he doesn't want to say that he (the teacher) *thought* of the step from 1000 to 1002 when he meant his order, and that even if he did, there were surely other steps that he didn't think of. At *PI* §188, Wittgenstein's narrator steps back for diagnosis:

> [Y]our idea was that this *meaning the order* [+2] had in its own way already taken all those steps: that in meaning it, your mind, as it were, flew ahead and took all the steps before you physically arrived at this or that one.
>
> So you were inclined to use such expressions as "The steps are *really* already taken, even before I take them in writing or in speech or in thought."

Using the number series here as a trope for the "whole use of the word," Wittgenstein then returns (at *PI* §191) to the theme of sudden understanding—the grasping in a flash—that had earlier been set in tension with the notion of understanding as an ability. The flash understanding, construed now as a temptation, is imagined to determine all the steps in advance in such a way that there could be *no* possibility of misinterpretation. Such an act is called an "inordinate fact" or a "philosophical superlative" (*PI* §192).

Wittgenstein elsewhere warns against such a philosophical superlative: "[We] mustn't think that when we understand or mean a word what happens is an act of instantaneous, as it were non-discursive, grasp of grammar. As if it could all be swallowed in a single gulp" (*PG* 49). The non-discursive grasp is precisely the idea of the *intuitive* grasp characteristic of Kant's second sense of infinite intellect, the *single gulp intellect*. In understanding or meaning (say) the word "chair," hence grasping the concept of chair, the single gulp intellect grasps all the possibilities of something susceptible to being called out as a "chair," *in one fell swoop*. Accordingly, the totality of possibilities is grasped by the non-discursive intellect as *actual*, laid out before it, in a comprehensive intuiting.

By warning us not to think that when we understand a word what happens is an instantaneous grasp of grammar, Wittgenstein is in effect recognizing that our understanding is not of the form of a single gulp. It is not in that sense infinite; it is finite. And while the *assertion* of the finitude of human understanding is generally incompatible with Wittgenstein's methods, one might say that by participating in the temptation to be infinite, Wittgenstein is in effect *showing* human understanding to be a finite ability.[4]

Two further points are worth making before turning to Heidegger. First, there are materials here for a diagnosis of the attractions of Cartesianism about understanding. Throughout the *Investigations*, Wittgenstein is clearly concerned to debunk the idea that meaning or understanding something by a word is a matter of an experience or state of consciousness enjoyed at the time of speaking or hearing. One reason that the phenomenon of the "Now I understand!" receives so much attention, I think, is that Wittgenstein is attuned to the sense in which the eureka-like power of this particular kind of experience can pull one toward an experiential conception of understanding. But another reason the phenomenon is of such interest is that it is a concrete experience that, suitably inflated, is well adapted to the demands of the single gulp intellect. For here understanding does indeed involve a felt moment of insight, an instantaneous grasp of meaning that, under the pressure of certain philosophical temptations, can be construed as a reaching out and taking in of every possible use of the word at issue, from *here on out*. Wittgenstein's anti-Cartesianism accordingly targets a view of understanding as a kind of act or experience that is easily exploited by the fantasy of single gulp infinitude—hence Wittgenstein's almost obsessive concern with the phenomenon of sudden understanding.

Second, it is worth stressing the link between the single gulp intellect and the effacement of the distinction between actuality and possibility. I opened this chapter by distinguishing two Kantian characterizations of the infinite intellect, as the productive intellect and as the single gulp intellect. A third characterization offered by Kant is negative—namely, that "the distinction between the actual and the possible does not enter into the representation of this intellect" (Kant [1790] 2001, 273). Let me call this the modal characterization of the infinite intellect. We can see how the modal characterization follows from the single gulp characterization. For a single gulp intellect, the actuality of its object coincides with the totality of the object's possibilities: to grasp something in a single gulp is for all its possibilities to be actual, made present to the unlimited intuition of an infinite intellect. Accordingly, the single gulp intellect is a form of intellect that has no place for a distinction between the actual and possible.

One consequence of this is that the infinite intellect, however penetrating, is in no position to do grammatical investigation. In a well-known passage, Wittgenstein says: "We feel as if we had to *see right into* phenomena: yet our investigation is directed not towards *phenomena*, but rather, as one might say, towards the *'possibilities'* of phenomena" (*PI* §90). Contrasting our form of understanding to that of a single gulp intellect is a reminder that the distinction between the actual and the possible *does* enter into the representation of the human intellect. Whether any form of understanding that does not appreciate this distinction is truly intelligible is a difficult question (to which I will briefly return in my conclusion). What is clear, at any rate, is that any being bereft of the distinction would not engage in the philosophical enterprise of directing itself toward the possibilities of (actual) phenomena.

I have so far argued that Wittgenstein's remarks on understanding as an ability belong in opposition to a broadly Cartesian position according to which understanding consists of a mental state or state of consciousness. I have further argued that Wittgenstein depicts our understanding as finite, in contrast to the comprehensive intuitive power of the infinite intellect. Let me now turn to Heidegger.

3   HEIDEGGER ON UNDERSTANDING AS AN ABILITY

While the issue of mental states is *a* target in *Being and Time*, it is certainly not pursued in the unrelenting (ever returning) manner one finds in Wittgenstein's *Philosophical Investigations*. In the preface to that book, Wittgenstein announces the subjects that have occupied him in the form of a short list, which include the concepts of "understanding" and "states of consciousness." Heidegger's introduction of the concept of understanding, by contrast, is set within the context of reawakening the question of the sense of being. Indeed, the whole idea of the inner, the private, or the hidden gets nothing close to the attention in Heidegger's work that it enjoys in Wittgenstein's confessional *tête-à-tête*. Heidegger is simply not all that gripped by problems around the idea of a mental state.

The most sustained critical discussion of Descartes in *Being and Time* concerns his conception of space, and his conception of the world as *res extensa*. Of course part of the moral about Descartes' inadequate conception of the world is that if meaning is always already in the world, as Heidegger's phenomenology suggests, you don't need an inner space of mentality to "cook it up." And there are some appearances of Cartesianism in philosophical psychology, mostly as a fly to be swatted away. Heidegger's dismissal, in the provisional stages of the book, of the idea of the human as a "cabinet of consciousness" is one such (*BT* 62/89), followed by several reminders throughout the Division I account of being-in-the-world (e.g., *BT* 136–37/176 and 165/205). In Division II, the Dilthey-Husserl notion of an *Erlebnis* is sufficiently prominent in his tradition that Heidegger finds it necessary to guard against his idea of the voice of conscience being construed as an inner *Erlebnis*; hence "[T]he phenomenological structure of existing is not anything like experiencing" (*BT* 279/324).

However, Heidegger's resistance to Cartesianism in philosophical psychology is eclipsed by, or rather finds its place within, Heidegger's resistance to Cartesianism *in ontology*. His primary target is not the idea of understanding as a mental state but rather the Cartesian conception of the *subject* of understanding. According to this conception, the subject is a *res*, a special kind of *thing*—an entity whose mode of being is *Vorhandensein*. The modern fascination with consciousness and inner psychical conditions, on Heidegger's view, is ultimately one expression of a deeper ontological commitment to the subject of understanding as a present-at-hand thing.

Identifying this level of engagement with Cartesian philosophy puts us in a position to see the sense in which Heidegger in fact seeks to *recover* a certain form of Cartesian thinking about understanding. This is the Cartesianism that, with the *cogito ergo sum*, rightly took what Heidegger calls "the turn to the subject" (*BP* 123; cf. *BT* 24/45), but neglected to make the *sum* an issue. Hence the following introductory characterization of the project: "Our analytic raises the ontological question of the being of the '*sum*.' Not until the nature of this Being has been determined can we grasp the kind of Being which belongs to *cogitationes*" (*BT* 46/71–72). Heidegger's idea of understanding as an ability, then, has its place in this broader investigation of what it means for Dasein, for the subject who understands, *to be*.[5]

Being "is," as Heidegger makes clear, the intelligibility of what is. *This* is the notion of being that interests Heidegger (*BT* 152/193). "Entity" (*Seiend*) is Heidegger's term of art for that which is, all and only what there is: "[E]verything we talk about, everything we have in view, everything towards which we comport ourselves in any way" (*BT* 6–7/26). "Being" (*Sein*) is thus "that which determines entities as entities, that on the basis of which entities are already understood (*verstanden*)" (*BT* 6/25–26). The question, then, asks about what it takes to understand entities *as* entities—that is, what it takes to make sense of them in terms of their being.

The use of "as" here is meant to mark a contrast. Lizards and, for example, babies obviously interact with entities in all sorts of ways—and in the case of lizards, in all sorts of quite agile ways. But they do not, Heidegger must confess, comport toward entities *as* entities. Heidegger says if we use the "as" with lizards, we need to qualify the "as" by putting a line through it, as if to cross it out. The difference that makes the difference between we who are *Dasein* and the lizards, in Heidegger's view, is the possession of ontological understanding. And his question is: What does it take to have *that*?

To be a Dasein, then, is to be a sense-maker, to understand being. Dasein's understanding of being (*Seinsverständnis*) is a capacity or an ability, a *Können*. This, however, is not one ability among others that Dasein might happen peculiarly to have. For unlike being able to tie one's shoes or being able to speak (say) English, understanding being is an ability that is definitive of Dasein as the kind of entity that it is. Hence Heidegger's characterization of this fundamental ability not as an ability one "has" but as an "ability-to-*be*" (*Seinkönnen*).

So what is it to understand the being of an entity? To understand the being of an entity (including oneself) is to understand the ways that entity can be—and no less, cannot be. Heidegger characterizes the understanding at issue as the projection of entities onto their possibilities.[6] He writes, "In the projecting of the understanding, entities are disclosed in their possibility" (*BT* 151/192). This understanding is a matter of appreciating what is possible and not possible with the actual entities toward which it comports. More precisely, the human adult comports itself toward entities *as* actual or real thanks to understanding the possibilities in terms of which those entities are what they are, and whether they are. This prior understanding makes possible, in the sense of enables, comportment toward entities as entities.

We can approach Heidegger's conception of ontological understanding by reminding ourselves that we, unlike lizards and babies, hold things to standards.[7] Consider the following two examples to illustrate the phenomenon. To be a hammer is to be able, when well wielded, to drive in nails (among other things). The field of possibilities for being a hammer has developed through history by human agents engaging in the practice of carpentry. If one picks up a hammer to discover it wilt like a flower, one has been taken in. It is a gimmick, or maybe a work of art. The "hammer" is flouting the functional standards that make hammers what they are, and so *could not* be a real hammer. Those who understand carpentry, and so make sense of hammers *as* hammers, appreciate this fake hammer for what it is, and would acknowledge its unreality if challenged. To be a real or actual hammer, after all, is to accord with certain ontological—in this case, functional—standards.

Or take a more generic example: to be an ordinary, perceptible thing is to behave in more or less stable and predictable ways. The "laws" of ordinary, medium-sized things lay out the field of possibilities for being such things. For example, if one were to see an object—say, a rock—that pops in and out of existence before one's eyes, something would be awry, and would be recognized as such by any competent perceiver. The "rock" would be flouting the standards of substantial independence and persistence that hold for objects, and so *could not* be any such thing. Those who understand objects, and so make sense of them as such, would find themselves compelled in this situation to look again, and might very well worry that they have been drugged, for to be an ordinary, perceptible thing is to accord with certain ontological standards.

Heidegger is suggesting then, with great plausibility, that entities must "live up" to standards in order to count as being. Such standards are accordingly ontological standards, standards concerning what it is for entities *to be* as opposed to *not* being. Ontological standards are, one might say, the "ground rules" of the real. To comport toward actual entities oriented by the standards that frame their possibilities—an orientation without which, Heidegger claims, there would be no comportment toward entities *as* entities—is to understand being. The ability to appreciate, and look after, the distinction between the being and non-being of entities is what constitutes human understanding.

We can draw out this conception of ontological understanding by considering Wittgenstein's case of the disappearing chair at *PI* §80. Wittgenstein starts the imaginary scenario with: "I say, 'There is a chair over there.'" This utterance is, for Heidegger, a paradigmatic case of comportment toward an entity *as an entity*—that little word "is" expresses our understanding of being in action. Wittgenstein continues:

> What if I go to fetch it, and it suddenly disappears from sight?—"So it wasn't a chair, but some kind of illusion."—But a few seconds later, we see it again and are able to touch it, and so on.—"So the chair was there after all, and its disappearance was some kind of illusion."—But suppose that after a time it disappears again—or seems to disappear. What are we to say now? Have you rules ready for such cases—rules saying whether such a thing is still to be called a "chair"? But do we miss them when we use the word "chair"? And are we to say that we do not really attach any meaning to this word, because we are not equipped with rules for every possible application of it? (*PI* §80)

Wittgenstein's concern with the temptation to picture our life with language in terms of the single gulp intellect—always already equipped with rules for every possible application—is here on display. The strategy in the passage is to present a case in which, according to Wittgenstein's implied answers to his questions, we don't quite know what to say about whether the word "chair" is appropriate for this kind of thing. Realizing that we don't miss a rule for this strange case in our more ordinary uses of the word "chair" is, I take it, supposed to help disabuse us of the idea that genuinely understanding or meaning the word "chair" requires being equipped with rules for every possible case.[8]

How would Heidegger respond to Wittgenstein's questions in the passage? As I read him, his answer to Wittgenstein's first question would in fact be "yes," we do have a rule for this case (though talk of rules is not Heidegger's idiom). Supposing the use of the word "chair" at issue is the application of a concept to an object, purporting to home in on something in the world, a *real* chair, one way to put the rule would be: one doesn't use the word "chair" to pick out something that *could not* be a chair, for to be a chair is to accord with the standards that hold for chairs as such—the kind of thing one can sit in, like *this*. To comport toward chairs *as* chairs, to understand them in terms of their being, is to be prepared to rule this disappearing "chair" out as a genuine chair.

Does this mean that Heidegger is insisting that we are equipped in advance with *every* possible application of the concept of chair? Understanding chairs, Heidegger suggests, is a form of commitment to the bounds of possibility for being an actual chair. However, to possess this understanding is not to close off any possible novelty or vertigo in our life with chairs. Heidegger is not insisting that we are possessed of a single gulp intellect. We do not, in one single stroke, take all things in chair-wise. Heidegger's answers to Wittgenstein's questions, then, do not amount to denying the finitude of understanding that primarily preoccupies Wittgenstein. Heidegger firmly acknowledges the partiality and unfinishedness of human understanding (see *BT* §68 (a)).

But Heidegger *does* urge that, in so far as we are onto chairs as chairs, we hold chairs within the space of possibilities for being a chair. The relevant notion of the whole here is not the whole of *every* possible application. The whole, rather, is the framework in terms of which chairs are intelligible as chairs—in terms of which, that is, the otherwise unpredictable and dynamic life of chairs takes its course. This prior orientation, on Heidegger's view, far from closing our engagement with things down, is what *enables* our openness to things—hence his characterization of understanding as "fore-structure" (*BT* 150/191). This prior orientation does not preclude the possibility of contexts, real or imagined, in which we encounter something for which it is not clear whether "chair" is the right word.[9] Nor does it preclude a context of conversation in which using "chair" to refer to the disappearing chair might find of a kind of figurative, or playful, or hallucinogenic use. The claim is that the intelligibility of any such use presupposes the basic case in which chairs, *actual* chairs, are understood to be the kind of thing that they are: the kind of thing, for example, one can reliably sit on. Heidegger says:

> In German we say someone can *vorstehen* something—literally stand in front or ahead of it, that is, stand at its head, administer, manage, preside over it. This is equivalent to saying that he *versteht sich darauf*, understands in the sense of being skilled or expert at it (has the know-how of it). . . . If understanding is a basic determination of existence, it is as such the condition of the possibility for all of the Dasein's particular manners of comportment, not only practical but also cognitive. . . . Dasein, as existent, is itself an intrinsically understanding entity. (*BP* 276)

I cite this passage to register Heidegger's link between *vorstehen* (to preside) and *verstehen* (to understand). In colloquial German a *Vorstehe* (noun form) is, for example, the foreman on a construction site, the one who presides over the whole workspace. A *Vorstand* (different nominalization) is a presiding committee, like a board of directors, that is responsible for the whole of a company. In Heidegger's vision of us as understanding beings, understanding is the ability to orient oneself within a whole—a unified space of possibilities—in terms of which entities make sense as the entities that they are. And those of us possessed of this understanding are, one might say, "in the business" of looking after, or sustaining, the whole space of intelligibility in which we find ourselves. We are all (each of us), in Heidegger's picture, foremen, or custodians, of intelligibility.[10]

4   HEIDEGGER ON UNDERSTANDING AS FINITE

What, then, does it mean for the subject possessed of such ontological understanding to *be*? What consequences of the foregoing are to be drawn out, rather than neglected, regarding the *sum* of the *I understand*? How does all this put us in a position to offer an adequate ontology of the subject?

Here we are in a position to turn to Heidegger's conception of the finitude of understanding.[11] Heidegger considered Kant's distinction between finite sensible intuition and infinite intuition a decisive insight. But the sense of the infinite intellect that Heidegger focused on is not the single gulp characterization but rather the productive characterization. Whereas an infinite intellect, as the source of its objects, is wholly self-sufficient, a finite intellect is dependent on existing objects that are *other* than it and *already there*. Expounding Kant, Heidegger says:

> The finitude of human cognition does not lie in humans' cognizing quantitatively less than God. Rather, it consists in the fact that what is intuited must be given to intuition from somewhere else—what is intuited is not produced by intuition. The finitude of human cognition consists in being thrown into and onto entities. (*PIK 59/GA 25*, 86; translation modified)

Heidegger proceeds to appropriate this Kantian distinction as a notional contrast. His interest is not at all in the question of whether a divine intellect possessed of infinite intuition actually exists. Nor is the interest in whether we are required to postulate a divine intellect by the demands of reason in either its theoretical or practical application (or both). And the interest is not in measuring the power of a finite intellect according to a standard set by a divine intellect. Heidegger's primary interest in the Kantian distinction lies in its promise as a kind of explanatory contrast—that is, an illuminating *entrée* into appreciating the basic metaphysical condition of human understanding.[12] The condition of divine understanding is to produce or create its objects, and thereby be conditioned by nothing other than itself; its condition is to be unconditioned. The condition of human understanding, by contrast, is to be dependent on, and therewith conditioned by, objects that exist independently of it.

Kantian finitude so understood has to do with objects in our relation to them. Heidegger wants to place Kantian finitude in this sense within a more comprehensive finitude, a finitude to do with being and our understanding of it. For Kant, the basic framework of possibilities for making sense of the world is fixed and invulnerable. The contours of intelligibility delivered by critique are advertised as "complete" and "certain" (*CPR* A13). The fragility of ontological understanding—the liability of the basic possibilities in terms of which things make sense to failure—is foreign to Kant's thought. The finitude of death, in other words, has no official place in Kant's thought.

Death, in Heidegger's systematic ontology, marks a sense of radical futurity characteristic of existence, and therewith characteristic of human understanding. Death is officially the "horizon," in the sense of limitedness, of understanding. While Heidegger is not the first to draw a constitutive link between death and human understanding—Hegel is one notorious predecessor— no philosopher has given death a more fundamental place. By "death" Heidegger does not mean biological death or croaking ("perishing"). Nor does he mean the biographical death of the obituary ("demise"). Death is no impending storm, for it is not an event at all: "[Dasein] does not have an end at which it just stops, but it *exists finitely*" (*BT* 329/378). Death for Dasein is "a way to be, which Dasein takes over as soon as it is" (*BT* 245/289).

Death, that is, is no more and no less than "being-towards-death." To be toward death is to live in a manner that is oriented by the possibility of one's own impossibility, the possibility of "no-longer-being-able-to-be-there" (*BT* 250/294). Being *able* to be there, in Heidegger's technical use of that phrase, is being able to render the entities *there*, in the world, intelligible in their being. So the possibility of one's own impossibility—the possibility of being *unable* to be—is the possibility of the comprehensive breakdown of the understanding in terms of which entities make sense. This would coincide with a breakdown in one's self-understanding, for the shape of who one is, the sense of one's life as meaningful, is given by the possibilities of making sense that one's ontological understanding makes available. Death, then, is the essentially threatened character of human understanding. The threat is one of unintelligibility, of a wholesale failure or loss of sense. To be *toward* death is to live in the acknowledgment of the *fragility* of the understanding embodied in one's form of life. Heidegger characterizes this fragility as the possibility of having to "take it back," to "give up" on one's ontological understanding, rather than sustain allegiance to it as a basis for pressing on (*BT* 308/355 and 391/443). Death, so understood, is the *riskiness* of any understanding embodied in a form of life: any projection of a space of possibilities for making sense of things stands *exposed* to being disabled by the course of a recalcitrant reality, and hence brought down as a sustainable form of understanding. So the ontological understanding that enables our

engagement with entities is an ability that, paradoxically, affords an openness to encounter the materials for its own undermining.

From the finitude that Kant rests content with, the finitude of intuition,
there is but a short step to the finitude of death. This is so even if death, so
construed, does not figure in Kant's thought. Kantian finitude as contrasted
with the infinitude of the productive intellect is in effect the recognition of
the distinction between the sensibility through which objects are intuitively
given and the understanding that thinks those objects. An intellect for which
there is no such distinction is an intellect for which the distinction between
the possible and the actual does not apply. The latter distinction "would not
enter into the representation of such a being at all" (to return to the negative modal characterization of the infinite intellect introduced in section 2).
After all, for such an intellect, to think something possible just is for that
something to be actual; the realm of the possible and the realm of the real
coincide. Since anything that is thought possible is thereby *guaranteed* to
be actual, there is no sense to actuality *thwarting* this intellect's sense of the
space of possibilities. And since the productive intellect is not in a position
to be thus threatened by unintelligibility, the burden of its possibility is not
to be shouldered. Things are otherwise for the finite intellect, for whom the
distinction between the recognizably possible and the actual, and the threat
that distinction engenders, is, in Heidegger's vision, the medium of its existence. This is the finitude of a being bent on a sustainably intelligible form
of life, and so uniquely capable of fundamental change.

5   CONCLUSION

Wittgenstein's conception of the finitude of our understanding, its partiality,
is shaped by a contrast to the infinite intellect, cast as a single gulp intellect. We saw how a comprehensive intuiting leaves no room for the distinction between the actual and the possible. Heidegger's conception of the
finitude of our understanding, its liability to transformative reconfiguration,
is shaped by a contrast to the infinite intellect, understood as a productive
intuition. Here too, the distinction between the actual and the possible finds
no place. The single gulp power of intuition is logically distinct from the
productive power of intuition, but either power is sufficient, on its own, to
efface the distinction between the actual and the possible. Producing objects
and intuiting objects as a whole in one stroke of course come together in
the traditional idea of God. And just as the divine intellect, cast as a single
gulp intellect, may "see right into" phenomena, but is in no position to do
grammatical investigation, Heidegger puts his correlative point, about the
divine intellect's productive power, as follows: "God does not do ontology"
(*KPM* 318).

Can we really make sense of these infinite powers? For Heidegger, one
might think, there is some pressure for productive intuition indeed to make

sense. After all, it is meant to serve as one side of a contrast that helps illuminate the finitude of human understanding. For Wittgenstein, one might think, the fact that the power of single gulp intuition functions largely as an object of temptation, or fantasy, lessens the demand for it to be a coherent possibility. But the first thought may overestimate the demands of Heidegger's explanatory contrast, or at least the sense that can be made of an infinite intellect by the end of the investigation, while the second thought may underestimate Wittgenstein's sense of the power of the temptations to which he gives voice. These are difficult issues, and must be left for another occasion. This much, however, seems clear: if appreciating the distinction between the possible and the actual, as both Heidegger and Wittgenstein suggest, is fundamental to any recognizably human understanding of things, then the very idea of an infinite intellect, even if coherent, could doubtfully serve as our measure.[13]

NOTES

1. This sense of the infinite intellect is prominent in §77 of Kant's ([1790] 2001) *Critique of the Power of Judgment*. I have formulated this sense sufficiently liberally to allow for its object to be "all things" (as in the traditional notion of the divine intellect) or, more limitedly, a comprehensive grasp of a determinate object of cognition (for example, what it is to be a chair). For a discussion of Kant's different senses of the powers of an infinite intellect, and the claim that they do not cohere, see Gram (1981). The "single gulp" intuition has a long history in classical rationalist philosophy, from Descartes' clear and distinct perception, to Leibniz's "adequate" cognition, to Spinoza's *scientia intuitiva*.
2. This is the style of reading one finds in the work of G. P. Baker and P. M. S. Hacker, and Bede Rundle. See Baker and Hacker (2005, 367) and Rundle (2001, 110).
3. This is a style of reading one finds in the work of John McDowell, most recently in McDowell (2009), as well as in Finkelstein (2003).
4. Doing justice to Wittgenstein's notion of perspicuous representation (*PI* 122) as a finite but intuitive form of intellection is an important task that extends beyond the scope of this essay.
5. Would Wittgenstein recognize sense in such a question? The closest analogue to his vicinity would be something like: What does it mean to be a speaker? One suspects that Wittgenstein would hear this as one of those big metaphysical questions that needs dissolving, not solving.
6. See especially §31 and §32 of *Being and Time*.
7. For a reading of the Heidegger of *Being and Time* centered on this notion of understanding, see Haugeland (2013).
8. Compare Warren Goldfarb (1997b), who reads the disappearing chair passage as a brief against what he calls the fixity of meaning, following Wittgenstein's own discussion of "fixed meaning" (*feste Bedeutung*) in the preceding section.
9. If to provoke such hesitation is the point of Wittgenstein's disappearing chair scenario, then the example Wittgenstein offers, so presented, is not convincing for the point he is trying to make. Cavell's case of the saddle peg chair strikes me as a better case to provoke such hesitation (see Cavell 1979, 71).

10. On Heidegger's notion of understanding as correlated with a unified space of possibilities, see *BT* 145/184.
11. The material that follows draws on my "Historical Understanding" in *The Cambridge Companion to Heidegger's Being and Time*, ed. M. Wrathall, Cambridge University Press, forthcoming.
12. Heidegger: "The essence of finite human knowledge is illustrated by the contrast between it and the idea of infinite divine knowledge, or *intuitus orginarius*" (*KPM* 17).
13. Earlier versions of this chapter were presented to audiences at the Post-Kantian European Philosophy Seminar in Oxford and the 2012 meeting of the International Society of Phenomenological Studies in Maine. I am grateful to both audiences for their questions and reactions. Special thanks to the editors of this volume for their helpful comments and suggestions, and to David Cerbone, Max Edwards, and Adrian Moore for instructive conversation.

12 Human Activity as Indeterminate Social Event

Theodore R. Schatzki

This chapter joins ideas of Heidegger and Wittgenstein to create a unified conception of action. Its starting point is that each philosopher's writings—Wittgenstein's "later" remarks and Heidegger's *Being and Time*—contain a profound intuition about human activity. Not only does each philosopher exhibit sympathy for the intuition present in the other's work, but also these intuitions are complementary: combined, they are central pillars of a wider account of human activity. Heidegger's intuition is that human activity is an indeterminate, three-dimensional temporal event. Wittgenstein's intuition is that human activity is a social phenomenon—that is, something socially constituted. Combined, these intuitions suggest that activity is an indeterminate social event.

This conjoint view on activity remains vital today. In both men's estimation, human activity—as opposed to consciousness, mind, perception, or reason—is primary in human experience. Being-in-the-world is centrally, though not exclusively, acting in practical contexts. Wittgenstein now and again writes such things as—quoting Goethe—that "in the beginning was the deed" (*OC* §402). The idea that human activity is an indeterminate social event represents a further step in the development of the post-Cartesian thesis of the primacy of activity. Both philosophers, in different ways, advocate this thesis. Today, amid resilient Cartesian intuitions, it remains a still insufficiently explored general orientation to human existence.

Before beginning, I should acknowledge that this chapter is a two-leveled construction. To begin with, my interpretations of Wittgenstein and Heidegger are constructions. What I mean is that the interpretations do not purport to articulate only what these philosophers actually thought about some subject matter. They base themselves on and seek compatibility with the texts of Wittgenstein and Heidegger. But they formulate ideas that are suggested, intimated, or pointed at in the text. These ideas, as a result, are to varying degrees mine and not just theirs. In the case of Heidegger, moreover, I lean on an intuition that dominates a stage of his philosophical career different from the one my discussion principally draws on, although I am also careful to indicate how the intuition concerned is present at the latter stage.

The acceptability of this sort of creative interpretation is well established in the Heidegger literature, where interpreters attempt to do all sorts of things with his work. Among certain interpreters of Wittgenstein, however, creative interpretation is highly disreputable. This sentiment is strongest among readers who, stressing the therapeutic character of Wittgenstein's remarks, insist on respecting strict interpretations of certain methodological and metaphilosophical comments of his. Examples of such comments are his claim that the job of the philosopher is to marshal recollections (*PI* §127) and to state what everyone concedes (*PI* §599), as well as his statements that the point of his investigations is to seek peace from philosophy (*PI* §133), and to prevent language from going on holiday (*PI* §38). These interpreters, who have enjoyed an ascension in the past decade, narrow the sorts of inspiration that readers can "legitimately" draw from Wittgenstein's texts.

I do not want presently to enter a detailed discussion of this factious ground. My interpretive approach is nurtured by the well-known hope that Wittgenstein expresses in the preface to the *Philosophical Investigations* that his writing might "stimulate someone to thoughts of his own." I also have a more specific riposte. Regardless of Wittgenstein's understanding of the ultimate point of his investigations of psychological concepts and the phenomena coordinated with them, these investigations—above all, the straightforward but acute descriptions and observations of everyday experiences in their contexts that he provides when giving overviews of the use of words—are replete with insights into the actional (and mental) dimensions of ongoing human life. For instance, the insight that human action and mind are socially constituted *shows* in his analyses of the experiences and circumstances on the occasion or in the face of which concepts for actions and mental conditions apply. This insight is not a theoretical point but an aspect of human life that comes to light as Wittgenstein methodically explores concepts and the phenomena tied to them. There are also many occasions when Wittgenstein reflects on what his investigations reveal. These insights and reflections are there for the interpreter to articulate, think about, and develop further. To do so is to construct ideas on the basis of Wittgenstein's texts.

The second level of construction in this chapter is the act of joining Wittgensteinian and Heideggerian ideas to form a broader account of action. Any joining of insights from different sources is a construction, especially when, as in this case, these insights are won in pursuit of different problems, through different methods, and in the contexts of different predecessors. The wider account of action I construct, however, is not an arbitrary fabrication. Many philosophers have believed that Wittgenstein and Heidegger are kindred souls. Indeed, I argue that each thinker has affinities for the deep intuition that I attribute to the other. I submit further that, independent of textual evidence of affinity, their intuitions are complementary.

1   ACTIVITY AS INDETERMINATE TEMPORAL EVENT

When Heidegger began as a philosopher in the 1910s, the flow or flowing character of human life had captivated some of the most incisive philosophical minds of the era, including Henri Bergson, William James, Wilhelm Dilthey, Edmund Husserl, and A. N. Whitehead. Heidegger's lectures of the late teens and early 1920s are replete with passages that think and ask about the flowing character of experience. With time, however, he came to think that the notion of event (*Ereignis*) has priority over that of flow in understanding human being. This change became patent by the mid-1930s in the *Contributions to Philosophy*, in which "the event" names the happening of the clearing of Being,[1] the happening of that open realm into which humans stand, in which anything that is shows itself as such. Intimations of the centrality of the notion are also found, however, in *Being and Time*, the book on which most of my interpretation of Heidegger's views on activity is based.

Three intimations are presently pertinent. The first is Heidegger's indication that Dasein happens (*geschehen*; BT 371/423, 384/435). The second is his explication that the term *Geschichtlichkeit* (historicality, historicity) means the ontological constitution of the happening of Dasein (*BT* 20/41). The third is his statement that "we name the specific being-on-the-move (*Bewegtlichkeit*) of the stretched-out self-stretching [of Dasein] the happening of Dasein" (*BT* 375/427; my translation). This final quotation is of particular significance. Just as in the thirties "the event" names the happening of the clearing of Being, in *Being and Time* the happening of Dasein is the opening of the clearing as Heidegger understands the clearing in that book: as Dasein's temporal field. Heidegger did not, at the time of *Being and Time*, conceptualize the happening of Dasein—which is the same as the opening of the clearing—as the event (*Ereignis*). Yet he already made the sense of happening captured in the concept of the event central to his understanding of human being.

Dasein, human life, happens: it is an event, not a substance, state, or process. Since, furthermore, the Being of Dasein is existence, it follows that existence, or Being-in-the-world, happens. As I understand Heidegger, Being-in-the-world centrally consists in acting in worldly contexts. On my interpretation, consequently, acting (in worldly contexts) happens: it is an event. One sign that activities are events is that they assume places in successions of events: both baking a cake and solving a math problem occur before and after other events. Note that nothing in the following depends on the claim that Being-in-the-world centrally consists in acting in worldly contexts. It is enough for my discussion if Being-in-the-world is sometimes acting.

On Heidegger's account, the event of activity has a temporal structure. Examining this structure in some detail will lead to the important idea—not explicitly noted by Heidegger—that human activity is indeterminate. The claim that activity has a temporal structure falls out of the wider thesis that temporality (*Zeitlichkeit*) is the meaning of Dasein's Being (*BT* 17/38, 234/277)—hence the meaning of existence, or of Being-in-the-world. Setting aside interpretive issues about Heidegger's conception of meaning and intelligibility, it suffices for present purposes to interpret this thesis as stating that all the structures of existence are modes of temporality. Temporality, Heidegger further claims, has three dimensions: past, present, and future. He analyzes these three dimensions as, respectively, having beenness (*Gewesenheit*), making present (*Gegenwärtigen*), and coming toward (*Zu-kunft*).

By *temporality* Heidegger clearly means something different from what most people mean when they speak of time. Most people construe time as an objective phenomenon in the sense of something that persists independently of human apprehension and action. On most modern construals, moreover, time *qua* objective phenomenon is identified as succession, the before and after ordering of events. One key difference between objective time so construed and the temporality that Heidegger takes to be the meaning of human existence concerns succession.[2] Objective time, as indicated, is succession. The three dimensions of temporality, by contrast, are not successive (see *BT* 327/375). The past, present, and future of human existence occur together at once. To avoid misunderstandings, note that events in objective time can also be assigned to the past, present, and future, where the objective past and future are defined as the events or moments that occur, respectively, before or after an event or moment arbitrarily chosen as the present (for example, the moment this parenthetical remark is being read). The past, present, and future to which events can be assigned likewise form a succession: the past precedes the present, which precedes the future. By contrast, the past, present, and future of human existence occur all at once. Having been (the past) does not precede making present (the present), and coming toward (the future) does not follow having been and making present. Rather, all three are so long as a person exists: so long as someone exists she has been, makes present, and comes toward something.

Acting is a mode of Being-in-the-world. According to Heidegger, consequently, it must be a form of temporality. In Division One of *Being and Time* Heidegger elucidates existence *qua* Being-in-the-world as (1) thrown, projecting-Being-amid entities and (2) being-ahead-of-itself-already-in-the-world as having to do with entities encountered in the world (*Sich-vorweg-schon-sein-in-(der-Welt-)als Sein-bei (innerweltlich begegnendem Seienden)*; *BT* 192/237, translation revised). Each of these formulas has three components, and each of the three components of the second formula reinterprets one of the three components of the first. According to Heidegger, moreover, each set of three components is a specification of temporality, and each pair of components from the two formulas corresponds to one of the three dimensions of temporality. For example, thrownness, which is reinterpreted in the second formula as already-in-the-world, can be further interpreted as having beenness—thus as the past. Similarly, projecting, reinterpreted in the second formula as being-ahead-of-itself, can be understood as a coming-toward (toward, namely, what it is projected)—thus as the future. And Being-amid entities turns out to be a making present (the present).

These two formulas elucidate the temporal form of activity. Thrown-ness is already-being-in-the-world. I understand this as follows: whenever a person acts, she is always already involved in a particular situation, which is immersed in a particular historical context. What she does reflects or is sensitive or responsive to particular aspects of this situation. These aspects are givens, from which she departs in acting: they are what matters (*BT* 137–38/176–77) to her in the situation. Projection, meanwhile, is being ahead of oneself: it is putting ways of being before oneself and acting for their sake. Whenever a person acts, she acts for the sake of some way of being (for example, winning a competition, getting home on time, being a good sister), toward which she comes in acting. Being-amid, finally, is having to do with entities encountered in the world—that is, acting toward, with, and amid (*bei*) them. Heidegger sometimes describes this as falling into the world. All told, a person, when acting, falls into the world stretching out between that toward which she is coming and that from which she is departing. This falling stretching out is the opening up of the past, present, and future of activity.

Most importantly, this structure can be described teleologically. The future dimension of activity, coming toward something projected, is acting for an end. The past dimension of activity, departing from aspects of a historical situation, is reacting to things or acting in their light—that is, being motivated.[3] The present of activity is acting-encountering entities. The temporality of activity is, thus, acting amid entities toward an end from what motivates. It is a teleological-motivational phenomenon. Because temporality is the meaning of Dasein's Being, it follows that human activity is inherently teleological and motivated.

So described, the future and past dimensions of activity harbor the determination of what people do. People act *for the sake of* something and *because of* this or that. By "determination," I do not mean causation. That for the sake of which and that because of which someone acts do not cause activity. Rather, they specify *what* to do. In §18 of *Being and Time* (*BT* 87/120), Heidegger writes that that for the sake of which someone acts (his or her end) signifies (*bedeutet*) an "in order to" (a purpose), which in turn signifies a "toward this" (a project), which itself signifies an action—which the actor proceeds to perform. Heidegger does not write this, but it makes sense to think that such a chain of signification specifies an action that the actor can carry out without further ado through the performance of a bodily action.[4]

Heidegger does not make a parallel claim regarding motivation, my narrowing gloss on the temporal past, but something similar holds. Like teleology, motivation determines action by shaping what is signified to a person to do. Indeed, an end picks out a particular action only in conjunction with matters in response to or in light of which the person acts: it is only in light of aspects of an actor's current situation that a particular action can be identified as how to proceed for a particular end. Hence, what is signified to someone to do rests on something for the sake of which she acts and matters in response to or in the light of which she does so.

As noted, a key feature of activity that follows from its character as three-dimensional temporal event is indeterminacy. Activity is indeterminate in the sense that it is not laid down in reality prior to a person acting either what that person will do or what teleological and motivational factors will determine what she does. Prior to t_n, in other words, nothing in reality requires, necessitates, or makes it the case that an actor perform a particular action at t_n or that any particular teleological or motivational factor determine what she does at that time. Something like indeterminacy dates back to Fichte and has been advocated by such thinkers as Hegel, Bergson, Sartre, and Derrida. Note that indeterminacy is not the same as lack of determination. Whatever a person does at t_n is determined by teleological and motivational factors. It is only with, and *as a feature of*, the performance that occurs at t_n, however, that it is specified, or determinate, which factors these are.

Indeterminacy follows from Heidegger's account of the temporal structure of activity. As discussed, the future and past dimensions of activity, which determine action, do not follow or precede the present dimension—that is, acting. Rather, they occur simultaneously with it. Because of this, both that for the sake of which and that given which a person acts are not determinate until she acts: the determination of action occurs along with, and not prior to, the acting itself. What the actor does is similarly indeterminate. Even when everything speaks for and nothing against a given activity, nothing can guarantee that it will occur. Action is irredeemably vulnerable to what philosophers call "weakness of will."

Heidegger's anchoring of indeterminacy in the event character of activity has a further notable consequence concerning the nature of performance. Human activity is often opposed to what philosophers call "mere events" (or "mere happenings"). Mere events are events, or happenings, that are free of intelligibility, teleology, and normativity and exhaustively woven into the web of material causality. The point of calling these events "mere" is to emphasize the utter difference between them and activities, which are also events. Philosophers differ as to the difference involved. Performance, meaningfulness, purposiveness, intentionality, normativity, and free will are among the features most commonly cited as characterizing activity events but not mere happenings. Actions are performed, meaningful, purposive, intentional, subject to normativity, or the result of free will. Other events, by contrast, just happen.

According to Heidegger, a clearing—whether it is construed, as in *Being and Time*, as Dasein's temporal field (existence) or, as in the *Contributions to Philosophy*, as an open realm into which humans stand—just happens. It befalls, moreover, the humans tied to it, either the individuals whose temporal fields are the clearing or the peoples (*Völker, Sterblichen*) who stand into historical clearings. Since acting is a mode of existence, acting likewise befalls people: acting, that is, befalls those who act, those who perform actions. It is people, of course, who perform actions. These performances, however, are not themselves performed. Performances of actions instead happen to, or befall, those who perform actions. A performance befalling someone *is ipso facto* that person performing an action.

This claim might seem confused: it might seem to hold that something people do—namely, perform actions—is something that befalls them—that is, is something that they do not do. It is important to see, therefore, that performance and befalling characterize different aspects of the event of activity. A person performs an action. The performance is the carrying out of the action. As noted, however, the performance itself is not performed. It, instead, befalls the person who acts. Yet even though the performance befalls her, it is *her* performance: *she* performs the action. What's more, because she does it, she is responsible for the action she performs: it is because it is her performance that a person is responsible for the action, the performance of which befalls her. In short, action combines something done and something that happens. Note that the fact that performance befalls a person does not exclude the possibility of free will. This is because free will can be understood, not, say, as something that initiates performance, a mental trigger, but as a condition implicated in the nature of activity events as performances. What I mean is that it follows, from what performance is, that if a person performs an action, she acts freely.

In sum, for Heidegger human activity is an indeterminate, three-dimensional temporal event that implicates human freedom.

2   WITTGENSTEIN AND INDETERMINATE ACTIVITY EVENTS

Wittgenstein interpreters of a therapeutic bent might claim that because Heidegger's phenomenological analysis of activity violates Wittgenstein's methodological directives there is no point to joining their ideas. Examples of the pertinent directives are returning language to its everyday use, providing reminders, giving overviews of the use of words, and not presuming that every noun designates a thing. It is worth emphasizing, therefore, that Heidegger's account does uphold another key directive of Wittgenstein's—namely, "[D]on't think, but look!" (*PI* §66). More precisely, Heidegger's method is a version of the phenomenological dictum, "To the things themselves," of which Wittgenstein's admonishment—I claim without argument—is a different version. It might be, moreover, that Heidegger's hermeneutic version of phenomenology accomplishes something that Wittgenstein advocates—namely, the provision of reminders. Heidegger's technical appropriation of the German language might even not be subject to Wittgenstein's strictures. In short, whether *Being and Time* violates Wittgenstein's directives is a complicated issue. *Pace* therapeutic interpreters, however, the issue is not germane to my present concerns—namely, the analysis of action—for Wittgenstein's remarks suggest convergence with the ideas that activity is indeterminate and an event.

Wittgenstein occasionally states that action underlies some aspect of human life that philosophers have treated as preeminent in or essential to it. Two such aspects are reason and language. Wittgenstein holds that human activity is not, ultimately, governed by reason and language. Rather, it itself undergirds them. Reasons (considerations) do explain, and linguistic normativity does govern much, if not most, of what people do and say when playing language-games. At a deeper level, however, the very existence of reasons and linguistic normativity in these games, as well as the specific shapes that they assume there, depends on how people spontaneously react and go on. Ultimately, consequently, that and how reason and normativity govern action depend on how people proceed. "I want to regard man here as an animal; as a primitive being to which one grants instinct but not ratiocination. . . . Any logic good enough for a primitive means of communication needs no apology from us. Language did not emerge from some kind of ratiocination" (*OC* §475, cf. §477). Or, "I really want to say that scruples in thinking begin with (have their roots in) instinct. Or again: a language-game does not have its origin in *reflection*. Reflection is part of a language-game. And that is why a concept is in its element within the language-game" (Z §391; translation improved). Both Wittgenstein's idea that how reason and normativity govern action depends on how people proceed and Heidegger's idea that human activity is indeterminate hold that activity underlies something often thought to govern it. In this sense, they are versions of the primacy of action in human life. The idea that human activity is rooted in spontaneous reacting thereby converges with indeterminacy.[5] It is also Wittgenstein's view that all language-games ultimately depend on how people spontaneously proceed (cf. the idea that the spade hits bedrock, that at a certain point we have to cease looking for an explanation and simply say this language-game is played—e.g., *PI* §654). Henry LeRoy Finch (1977, 218) formulates matters even more strongly in writing that "Wittgenstein's philosophy . . . rejects in principle the notion of any ultimate control over human action by ideas, . . . nature, causality, reason, will, or, indeed, any authority or external standard understood as a determinant of value." Wittgenstein certainly shows that reason, willing, and normativity do not accomplish this.

Wittgenstein's remarks on rule following provide closely related evidence of his sympathy for the indeterminacy of acting. Wittgenstein famously shows that a rule, by itself, cannot determine what it is (correctly) to follow it. A pervasive conception of rule following had held that a rule, by virtue of its content, makes fully determinate which actions do and which actions do not conform to it. Wittgenstein shows that whether an activity does or does not conform to a rule depends not just on the rule but also on the context of activity. An important feature of this context is what people do when conforming to the rule. Although considerable controversy has attended full treatment of the relevant context(s), it is clear that it is how people go on that determines what following particular rules is.

The pertinence of these remarks to indeterminacy rests on the fact that rules—treated either as formulations or as expressed in formulations—predate the actions that follow them. What these remarks demonstrate, consequently, is that a rule, something that preexists activity, cannot, before the fact, determine or fix what a person who follows it does. This conclusion has narrower scope than does the idea of indeterminacy, but it still illustrates the idea. Incidentally, the wider notion of indeterminacy applies to rule following: prior to acting it cannot be settled whether a person will conform to any particular rule or to any rule at all.

Wittgenstein's remarks likewise harbor sympathies with the ideas that human activity is an event and, more broadly, that lived human experience is composed of events. At *PI* §620, Wittgenstein writes, "*Doing* itself seems not to have any experiential volume. It seems like an extensionless point, the point of a needle. This point seems to be the real agent. And the happening in the appearance merely a consequence of this doing. 'I *do*' seems to have a definite sense, detached from every experience" (translation modified). The view expressed here (and criticized in the surrounding sections) is that the real acting that occurs in the performance of an action is a willing, an act of will, something not itself experienced. For Wittgenstein, by contrast, willing is not some extra thing "detached from every experience." It is, instead, the acting itself: "speaking, writing, lifting a thing, imagining something" (*PI* §615). Doings such as these are "the happening in the appearance." More precisely (see next section), such "happenings" are performances of bodily behaviors (*Benehmen*), in which these doings consist. These performances and the activities they constitute are events.

Wittgenstein similarly describes ongoing, lived experience as composed of events. When combating, say, the idea that the (mental) activities of thinking or reading are processes, Wittgenstein often asks his reader to examine his or her own experience and to consider what is going on when the reader is thinking or reading. Wittgenstein repeatedly suggests that what one finds are sensations, images, and actions (the latter, in this context, bodily doings). To the interlocutor who exclaims that these items are not the thinking or reading, Wittgenstein replies, "but they are what happens." The experiential items in which activities, in this case mental activities, consist happen; they are events. An example of this implication from a section that is part of a cluster of remarks focused on action is *PI* §642: "'At that moment I hated him.'—What happened here? Didn't it consist in thoughts, feelings, and actions?"

At the same time, Wittgenstein's remarks evince little support for the idea that activity as an event bears the temporal structure Heidegger attributes to it. The closest they come is in pointing out that activities that occur before or after given bodily doings can help determine that these doings constitute particular activities (see the impending discussion). Nonetheless, as the following section discusses, Heidegger's attribution complements a particular feature of social constitution as Wittgenstein conceives of it.

3   ACTION AS SOCIALLY CONSTITUTED

A very frequent but little commented on expression in Wittgenstein's corpus is the common German *bestehen in*. Wittgenstein repeatedly marshals this term to name what is in effect the central relationship between acting and being in mental/cognitive conditions, on the one hand, and experiential happenings on the other: acting and being in mental/cognitive conditions *consist in* such-and-such goings on in particular contexts. The types of goings-on that Wittgenstein routinely mentions in this context are actions (*Handlungen*), or behaviors (*Benehmen*),[6] sensations, feelings, images, and thoughts. Of these, behaviors take priority vis-à-vis activity: acting centrally consists in voluntary bodily movements (and pauses, *Z* §597) taking place in certain contexts. These behaviors, I hold, are those bodily actions, through the performance of which, on Heidegger's account, actors carry out the actions that are signified to them as ones to perform for the sake of such-and-such given this-and-that.

What is responsible for which particular activities it is that are constituted by given bodily doings on particular occasions?[7] It is not the behaviors by themselves; a given bodily doing, taken for itself, can constitute the performance of different actions.[8] Rather, it is the contexts in which the voluntary bodily movement takes place. Four relevant sorts of context can be discerned in Wittgenstein's remarks. The first is the past and future behaviors of the person involved. Wittgenstein offers multiple examples of a particular behavior constituting a particular performance (or expressing a particular mental/cognitive condition) because it occurs in the context of this or that other bodily doing. The second context is the other mental and cognitive conditions the person is in. To build on an example of Wittgenstein's (*PI* §581, *Z* §67), a person's nervous pacing at a train station might express expectation that an explosion will occur if he had overheard a stranger say to a compatriot the previous day, "Tomorrow at five o'clock the fuse will be lit." The third context is what is going on in the setting of action. To vary this example, a person's running from the station platform might express fear that an explosion is imminent if smoke is rising from an abandoned backpack near to where he had been standing. The fourth context is the practices and traditions that traverse the actor's world: the fact that particular bodily doings express particular activities or mental conditions in particular circumstances depends on cultural practices. This idea comes out in those passages where Wittgenstein remarks that familiarity with a culture is a condition of recognizing what something expresses (e.g., *LWPPII* 89). A final sort of context is an instance of the fourth—namely, the concepts of action that are carried in the practices the person carries on—that is, the conceptual understandings of actions that are alive in that person's world.[9] These understandings enable the occurrence of a particular bodily doing amid other doings in particular circumstances on the background of certain cultural practices to amount to the performance of such-and-such an action (and not another).

Society enters this story in three ways. First, many of the situations in which bodily movements constitute performances of particular actions are social ones, or depend on or presuppose social phenomena. Other people might be part of these situations, for example, or the situation might have come about on the background of social life. Second, cultural practices and traditions are social phenomena in the sense of gestalts of human coexistence. Third, action concepts are social in the sense that they are shared.[10] To the extent that contexts of these three sorts are ineliminable from the contextual determination of expression, this determination is inherently social. I believe that society is absent from the determination of very few, if any, expressions.[11]

Notice that this type of social determination differs from a sort often attributed to Wittgenstein on the basis of his remarks on rules—namely, that what counts as following or not following a given rule rests upon community agreement on the matter.[12] This kind of community agreement does not enter the foregoing account of social determination: it is not community agreement on the matter that determines what activity a given piece of behavior constitutes, but (social) circumstances, cultural practices and traditions, and shared conceptual understandings, among other things. In theory, a community—in the sense of a contingent group of people—could err in taking a given piece of behavior to express the performance of certain actions (or being in particular mental or cognitive conditions).

An additional aspect of the social constitution of action concerns actors. Being an actor is not a condition that falls to a human being merely by being human. It is, instead, a social status. To be an actor, someone who performs actions (for which he or she is responsible), is to be granted presumptive authority about what he or she is doing and why (see Johnston 1993). A human being acquires this authority through social interaction, by taking up and carrying on complex patterns of interaction by which people become, and remain, mutually intelligible and responsive to one another. Prominent such patterns include explaining what one is doing and why and subsequently acting consistently with self-ascriptions of actions and reasons. If a person is unable to extend such patterns, either as an infant or as an adult, he or she is not accorded the status of actor.

One consequence of Wittgenstein's ideas about the constitution and determination of expression is that activity is a worldly phenomenon. The behaviors in which activity chiefly consists are publicly present and available. This consequence might be thought unremarkable; after all, activity has often been thought of as outer in opposition to its sibling, mind, which is supposed to be inner. It is worth mentioning, therefore, that in Wittgenstein's texts there is another, less familiar reason why action is a public phenomenon. Wittgenstein claims that associated with many concepts for mental conditions are life patterns (*Lebensmustern*) that repeatedly appear in life. These patterns consist of behaviors, utterances, and their occasions and are completed by a picture of the inner (see *RPPII* §§650–52). Such patterns are not simply behavioral regularities; they are, instead, patterns of behaviors and utterances in the circumstances in which they occur. For Wittgenstein, in other words, behavior is essentially behavior-in-particular-circumstances (*RPPI* §314, *RPPII* §148). It is an arrangement of public items. Wittgenstein draws on this idea to differentiate voluntary activity from involuntary activity. What differentiates them is not the movement involved, nor the presence or absence of some mental phenomenon such as alleged acts of trying or willing, but rather the contexts—earlier and later behavior, circumstances—in which they occur. "What is voluntary is certain movements with their normal *surrounding* of intention, learning, trying, acting. Movements of which it makes sense to say that they are sometimes voluntary and sometimes involuntary are movements in a special surrounding" (*Z* §577; cf. *Z* §594).

The previous section cited evidence of Wittgenstein's sympathies with the Heideggerian idea that activity is an event. As just explained, meanwhile, Wittgenstein construes activity as consisting in the occurrence of bodily doings and so forth in particular contexts. Appropriating the idea of activity as an event in the context of interpreting Wittgenstein implies that these bodily doings happen to people. Wittgenstein's thought seems to converge with this conclusion when he writes:

> Writing is certainly a voluntary movement, and yet an automatic one. . . . One's hand writes; it does not write because one wills, but one wills what it writes. One does not watch it in astonishment or with interest when writing; does not think "What will it write now?" But not because one had a wish it should write that. For that it writes what I want might very well throw me into astonishment. (*Z* §586)

Indeed: the voluntary movement just happens. *Z* §586 concerns automatic movement. But the point that such movement just happens iterates. When one knows how to write and concentrates on what is to be said, the movements just happen. Similarly, when one learns to write and pays close attention to performing the correct hand movements, the movements in which paying close attention consist (furrowing the brow, staring intently) just happen. The bodily doings in which activities consist happen. In this sense, activity befalls people.

Wittgenstein's attention to bodily doings fills out a lacuna in Heidegger's account of Being-in-the-world. Activity, in Heidegger, is not just a temporal event but a spatial one too (see *BT* §§22–24). Activity is spatial in the sense that people always act attuned to a region of differentially near and far places and paths anchored at material objects. (A place is a place to *x*, where *x* is an action, while a path is a way from one place to another.) The fact that activity is spatial implies that activity occurs in the world—that is, in a common world of objects (Arendt's [1958] public). Although activity is not itself a material phenomenon, to be in such a world it must have material form or manifestation. Heidegger, however, is not very clear on this point. Wittgenstein, by contrast, conceptualizes the material form of activity as behaviors, or bodily doings, and thereby makes good Heidegger's neglect.

Just as Wittgenstein harbors sympathies for the idea that activity is an indeterminate event, Heidegger agrees with Wittgenstein that human action and mind are socially constituted. He claims, for instance, that Being-with is just as constitutive of human existence as is Being-in-the-world: the two, he writes, are equiprimordial (*BT* 114/149). It is true that Being-with is radically under-described in *Being and Time* (and related works) in comparison to the elaborate treatment lavished on Being-in-the-world. Nonetheless, Heidegger's claim, as well as the chapter in *Being and Time* on Being-with, reveals a deep-seated inclination to understand human life socially.

Being-with, or coexistence, has four basic aspects (see Schatzki 2005): (1) encountering others within the world, (2) acting toward others, (3) acting in the same world (the same organized practical contexts) as others do, and (4) the sameness of normative teleological organization (worldhood) of this world for whomever acts in it. Of present interest is (4). The normative teleological organization of a world comprises the ends, tasks, and actions that are enjoined of or are acceptable for people proceeding in that world. It is a common normative framework for anyone acting there. According to Heidegger, this common normativity fills out both the temporal structure of the activities of participants in the world and how they engage entities within it. Heidegger famously designated this common framework *das Man*: *das Man* is the social normativity that governs proceeding in particular worlds, particular organized practical contexts (see Dreyfus 1991, chap. 8). This is the sense in which the actions of those who proceed in these worlds are socially constituted. The role that *das Man* here plays corresponds to the contribution that practices and traditions make to the constitution of activity in Wittgenstein.

Indeed, I have elsewhere (Schatzki 1996) argued that each thinker's writings point toward the contribution that social practices make to constituting individual lives. Understanding this contribution requires a rich account of practices that encompasses the normativity denoted by *das Man*, the shared conceptual understandings revealed by Wittgenstein's remarks, and the teleological character of action. (Heidegger clearly affirms that action is teleological; this is not as clear in Wittgenstein.)

4   WITTGENSTEIN + HEIDEGGER

In *Being and Time*, activity is an indeterminate, temporal(-spatial) event. In Wittgenstein's later texts, activity is socially constituted in the sense that what action a bodily doing is the performance of depends on social circumstances, social traditions and practices, and shared conceptual understandings. Combined, these intuitions construe activity as an indeterminate, socially constituted event. As indicated, this conception of activity is a construction. My discussion of Heidegger departed from his texts in narrowing thrownness to motivation, importing a prominent concept from his later work into *Being and Time*, connecting signification to bodily actions, and highlighting an implication of his account of temporality that he does not discuss (indeterminacy). My discussion of Wittgenstein systematized the contexts in which behavior constitutes particular activities. Combining their intuitions adds a new level of construction. Doing this, however, is not arbitrary. Although he has a thinner notion of what this involves, Heidegger, like Wittgenstein, thinks of human existence as fundamentally social. Wittgenstein, moreover, develops thoughts close to the idea that activity is indeterminate, while also holding that the behaviors-in-circumstances in which activities consist are events. Indeed, each can be seen as providing something missing from the other's ideas.

To show this, I will borrow Aristotle's schema of the four causes as a heuristic (the four causes are the factors responsible for something being the entity it is). Heidegger and Wittgenstein can be construed as specifying different causes of activity *qua* indeterminate event. That for the sake of which and that in response to or in the light of which a person acts are spelled out in the future and past dimensions that Heidegger attributes to activity. These dimensions thus contain the final cause of activity (*telos*, end, purpose). Wittgenstein, meanwhile, explicates the formal cause of action, its whatness: which action it is, a performance of which is constituted by the happening of particular behaviors (and sensations, thoughts, images, etc.), depends on the contexts in which they occur, including the practices, traditions, and understandings of actions alive in the actor's worlds. The formal cause of activity thus arises from context. Wittgenstein also provides insight into the material cause of activity. For Aristotle, the material cause of something is its composition, what it is made of. An activity is not something of the sort that Aristotle imagined has composition. But although activities do not have the composition that material objects do, the behaviors and so on in which an activity consists are something like its composition. The relationship between an activity and what it consists in is close to that between an object and its composition (what it consists of). Hence, the bodily doings, sensations, images, and the like in which an activity consists can be treated as the material cause of activity.

Aristotle, finally, construed the efficient cause of an artifact (what produces something or brings it about) as the person making it. Because activities are events they do not have efficient causes of this sort. Performances happen to people. People, consequently, do not produce performances or bring them about. In the modern era, however, efficient causality has often been assimilated to physical causality. In the wake of this transformation, the question of whether human activities are caused, say, by neurophysiology has taken center stage. Heidegger writes nothing about whether activities have efficient neurophysiological causes, whereas Wittgenstein appears doubtful that physiological explanations will be found of psychological phenomena (see Z §§605–14). I am skeptical that Wittgenstein's considerations on this point militate against neurophysiological causes of the bodily movements, sensations, images, and so on, in which activities consist (versus the activities themselves). I will not, however, address the issue presently. It is fair to say that neither thinker attends much to efficient causality.

A final undiscussed point of complementarity between Wittgenstein and Heidegger concerns complexity. The event that Heidegger construes activity to be is not simple. It has a three-dimensional temporal structure, which contains its determination. This temporal structure is matched by the complexity and breadth of the consists-in relationship in Wittgenstein. The behaviors (and images, thoughts, sensations, etc.) in which activities consist constitute not just activities but also mental and cognitive conditions. The utterance, "Please respond right away," in which an instance of the activity of making a request consists, might simultaneously express irritation, resoluteness, hopefulness, or any of a range of other conditions.[13] It is not too great a leap from this fact to the idea that the behaviors that constitute a given activity also help constitute the mental and cognitive conditions—above all believing and desiring—that are implicated in the temporal structure of that activity.[14] It is not incompatible with Wittgenstein's texts to write that the believing and desiring that are implicated in the temporal structure of an activity *consist at least partly in* the occurrence of the very behaviors-(and sensations-and images)-in-their-circumstances, in which this activity consists. In short, the temporal complexity of the event of activity in Heidegger is matched by the complexity of the consists-in relation in Wittgenstein. One might say that these two complexities are different sides of the same coin.

I wrote in the introduction that the conception of activity as an indeterminate social event remains vital today. It counters the full range of causal theories of action in philosophy while leaving open the role of neurophysiology in bodily doings. It also joins cause with the radical wing of contemporary externalism regarding action and mind in emphasizing the social constitution of what we do. Wittgenstein + Heidegger thus offers new vistas on the compatibility of material causality and social constitution. This conception also joins the venerable minoritarian front against the primacy of the individual in philosophy and social theory. It opposes the widespread invocation of tradition, norms, cultures, roles, social structure, and the like to explain activity. And it points toward the centrality of social practices in human life. Their ideas remain at the forefront of theory today.[15]

NOTES

1. I will follow Macquarrie and Robinson's practice of capitalizing "being" when it is used to translate the noun *Sein*.
2. Heidegger marks the difference between existential and objective time by consistently using the term *Temporalität* for the temporality of human life and *Zeit* for objective time. In regimenting his language so, Heidegger signals that temporality is not a rival or substitute for time but a distinct, fundamental sort of temporal phenomenon. Human life exhibits a type of temporality that differs from the sort of time familiar in everyday and scientific contexts. For an overview of modern conceptions of such a temporality, see Hoy (2009).

3. In highlighting motivation, I de-emphasize that thrownness also connotes historical contextualization.
4. Heidegger's ideas here connect with those of Arthur Danto; see Danto (1965).
5. In his last writings, Wittgenstein writes of the indeterminacy (*Unbestimmtheit*) of concepts, life patterns, and rules (e.g., *LWPPI* §21, *LWPPII* 86). By "indeterminacy" he means imprecision (vagueness) or irregularity. There is no connection to the spontaneous reactivity to which his remarks point.
6. By a "behavior" Wittgenstein means a bodily doing, a type of action—for example, raising one's arm. When discussing activity, he also often uses the term *Bewegung* (movement). A movement is the physical displacement of (a part of) the body. The movements Wittgenstein has in mind are the ones involved when people do things (*PI* §612). They are voluntary movements. A behavior, consequently, is a voluntary physical movement.
7. I might add that Wittgenstein sometimes refers to the contextualized items in which activities and, especially, being in mental conditions consist as expressions (*Ausdrücke*). At times, he also speaks of these items as expressing (*ausdrücken*) or manifesting (*äussern*) actions and states of mind. Wittgenstein here uses a term with a dense philosophical history—fully deployed in the Vienna in which he grew up—to characterize the relation between mind/action and world.
8. This is one reason why the multiplicity of expression belongs to the essence of the mental (*LWPPII* 65). Another reason is that the performance of a given action, like being in a given mental/cognitive condition, can consist in different behaviors.
9. This sort of claim has been familiar in analytic circles since Burge (1979). For development in a Wittgensteinian vein, see Schatzki (1996, chap. 3 and 4).
10. The existence of shared concepts is highly contested in contemporary philosophy, but there can be little doubt that Wittgenstein thought that ordinary concepts are shared (see *PI* §242).
11. For a Wittgensteinian account of the social character of normativity (rule following) that is compatible with this account of the social character of action constitution, see Williams (1999).
12. For a version of this idea that derives it from Hegel instead of Wittgenstein, see Pippin (2008, chap. 6).
13. On the complexity of expression, see Rudd (2003, §7.2).
14. What I mean by mental/cognitive conditions being implicated in the temporal structure of activity is that the use of terms for such conditions articulates the past and future dimensions of activity. For example, a person who acts for the sake of winning a game can be said to *desire* winning it. A person who retreats in the face of a grizzly bear can be said to *believe* a bear is there or threatens him. In the text I write "helps constitute" because behaviors other than the ones in question might also help constitute (being in) the mental/cognitive conditions concerned. For discussion, see Schatzki (2010, 119–21).
15. I would like to thank the editors, and especially David Egan, for their very helpful comments on two earlier versions of this chapter.

13 Heidegger's Religious Picture

Stephen Reynolds

A *picture* held us captive. And we couldn't get outside it, for it lay in our language, and language seemed only to repeat it to us inexorably.

—Wittgenstein, *PI* §115

[T]he being of God is always conceived of as *verbum* [word], and the fundamental relation of man to him as *audire* [hearing].

—Heidegger's reading of Luther in 1924, *Supp* 110

The theologian Rudolf Bultmann famously claimed that *Being and Time*'s analytic of Dasein "appears to be nothing more than a secular philosophical presentation of the New Testament insight into human existence" (quoted in McGrath 2006, 185). We should be shocked, he wrote, to find that philosophy can discern the truths of Christianity all on its own. In this chapter I suggest that Heidegger's existential analytic remains religious in a peculiarly Wittgensteinian sense.

My contention is twofold: it is that Heidegger's analysis of the call of conscience articulates a Lutheran conception of human existence, and that this conception operates in such a way as to satisfy Wittgenstein's (admittedly loose) definition of a religious "picture." The chapter thus proceeds in two stages, each concerned with a particular analogue. First, there is a substantive analogue between the *content* of Heidegger's thought and the content of Luther's, the claim being that for both thinkers we are essentially powerless to initiate our own "salvation." Second, there is a formal analogue between the way in which this idea *functions* in Heidegger's thought and the way in which religious pictures function according to Wittgenstein. The claim here is that the role played by Heidegger's Lutheran view of humanity corresponds to that which Wittgenstein ascribes to religious pictures.

Section 1 addresses Wittgenstein's comments on religious belief in order to explain what he means when he says that faith consists in holding a religious "picture." Section 2 looks at Luther's understanding of grace, before turning to the young Heidegger's endorsement of it. Section 3 moves on to *Being and Time*, focusing on that phenomenon that most clearly exhibits this religious picture: the call of conscience. Finally, in section 4 I offer some concluding thoughts.

1 WITTGENSTEIN'S RELIGIOUS PICTURES

The majority of Wittgenstein's remarks on religious belief are to be found in his "Lectures on Religious Belief" (from 1938; in *LC*) and *Culture and Value* (compiled over a number of years). Before addressing the texts themselves, it is worth clarifying what Wittgenstein is—and is *not*—doing.

The focus of Wittgenstein's comments is the character of religious belief itself (and specifically, Christian belief). He is not advancing arguments for or against the existence of God, nor is he assessing the veracity of Christianity's historical narrative. Rather (as we might expect), he is looking at religious discourse and drawing from it a conclusion about the nature of religious belief. The crux of this conclusion is that religious belief is something quite different from "ordinary" or scientific belief. This conclusion has a critical as well as a clarificatory dimension: Wittgenstein wants to clarify the practice of believing, and doing so involves criticizing the prevailing understanding of that practice. In short, Wittgenstein contends that the "surface grammar" (*PI* §664) of our language confuses us; it leads us to suppose that the claims of faith are on a par with those of science, thereby obscuring the fact that one kind of belief is radically different from another. And his task, as always, is to help us to see aright.

Wittgenstein's remarks on religion can helpfully be distilled into four related propositions. (*a*) Because the meaning of a word is bound up with its use in a language (*PI* §43), a proper understanding of religious terms requires familiarity with the broader context of behavior into which they fit—that is, with the form of life to which they pertain. (*b*) One consequence of this is that the atheist and the theist are not—surprisingly—contradicting one another. (*c*) The theist's treatment of religious claims shows that, despite appearances, they do not articulate empirically verifiable propositions. (*d*) Finally, what such claims actually articulate is an interpretation of the world—a "picture"—that cannot be expressed in alternative, non-religious terms. And it is holding this picture that constitutes religious belief. I shall address each proposition in turn.

(*a*) The first proposition invokes what we might call the "standard" later Wittgenstein: the meaning of a word is so bound up with its use that to imagine a language is to imagine a form of life (*PI* §19). Consequently, understanding a word is not a discrete mental process (*PI* §§143–155) but a matter of mastering that word's application within the context of our broader practices.

The upshot of this is that, for Wittgenstein, religious terms cannot be properly understood when isolated from the religious life to which they belong. And this means that we cannot "first establish the truth of that belief and then use it as a reason for adopting" a religious life (Mulhall 2001b, 101)—for until we are familiar with that life, we will not understand what the terms of the belief *mean*.[1] Thus Wittgenstein offers us a peculiar model according to which religious *life* is the prerequisite for religious *belief*, not—as we might expect—the other way around. We do not believe and on the basis of that commit to religious practice; rather, we make that commitment and only then understand what it means to believe. This is why Wittgenstein describes belief as a "last result—in which a number of ways of thinking and acting crystallize and come together" (*LC* 56), and it is why he asks: "Why shouldn't one form of life culminate in an utterance of belief in the Last Judgement?" (*LC* 58; see also *CV* 32). I shall return to this ahead.

(*b*) All of this sheds light on the second, related point: that the atheist and the theist do not in fact contradict one another. Wittgenstein contends that he, as someone who is not religious, cannot contradict the person who claims that illness is a punishment, or who believes in Judgment Day:

> In one sense, I understand all he says—the English words "God," "separate," etc. I understand. I could say: "I don't believe in this," and this would be true, meaning I haven't got these thoughts or anything that hangs together with them. But not that I could contradict the thing. (*LC* 55)

Wittgenstein's point, then, is that he cannot contradict the theist because he lacks a proper grasp of what the theist is saying: he understands the terms "atomically" in that he could offer an abstract account of what they ordinarily denote, but he is not familiar with the way in which the theist uses them. And the reason he is unfamiliar with the theist's use of religious terms is that he does not share the theist's life. Until he does, the two will be speaking on different planes (*LC* 53, 56). As Wittgenstein puts it, he would have to live "*completely* differently" for the word "Lord" to "say something" to him personally: the practices that invest the word with religious significance are alien to him (*CV* 33).

But what is that added level of meaning that words such as "God" have for the theist? This brings us to the third and fourth of the foregoing claims.

(*c*) A recurrent theme throughout Wittgenstein's remarks on religion is his insistence that religious claims do not concern empirically verifiable entities or events, and it is here that the critical dimension of his view emerges. In "Lectures on Religious Belief," he takes issue with a certain Fr. O'Hara, a man who "cheats himself" (*LC* 59) by making religion a question of science (*LC* 57). If Fr. O'Hara is right, religion is all superstition (*LC* 59), but Wittgenstein insists that it is not: superstition is a "false science" borne of fear, whereas religion is "a trusting" (*CV* 72).

For someone such as Fr. O'Hara, religious terms denote entities and events whose existence and occurrence is empirically verifiable. But Wittgenstein maintains that those who hold religious beliefs do not—in fact—treat those beliefs as they do empirical propositions, for anything that they would normally call evidence has not the slightest effect on them (*LC* 56). For such people, historical proof of Christianity's narrative "is irrelevant" (*CV* 32), "[t]he best scientific evidence [amounting to] nothing" (*LC* 56). Indeed, if someone did believe in Judgment Day on the basis of a convincing scientific proof, Wittgenstein insists that her belief would *not* be properly religious: such evidence "would destroy the whole business" (*LC* 56). Certainly, the theist may talk of reasons, but her reasons "are entirely different from normal reasons" (*LC* 56). Religious beliefs play a role that is radically different from empirical claims, such that no level of empirical certainty would achieve the "religious" effect: "indubitability wouldn't be enough to make me change my whole life" (*LC* 57).

We might say, then, that the non-empirical nature of religious claims is indicated by the theist's approach to standard notions of evidence and certainty. But it is also indicated by the way in which she responds to such claims, by the conclusions she draws from them. So for example, when it is said that "God's eye sees everything," she is unlikely to envisage God's having eyebrows (*LC* 71). Similarly, when told of the kingdom of heaven, she is unlikely to search for it on a map.[2]

Finally, in an oft-cited remark Wittgenstein notes that the very notion of the ontological argument tells us "that what is at issue [in religious belief] is not the existence of something," such as a white elephant or an Olympian god (*CV* 82). In other words, the tendency to formulate arguments for God's *necessary* existence demonstrates that what is at stake is not the existence of a physical object. The very idea that God's essence should guarantee his existence distinguishes the concept of "God" from that of any empirical entity by highlighting the fact that its grammar does not allow for the question, "what would it be like if there were [or were *not*] such a thing as God?"—something we certainly could ask of white elephants.

(*d*) If a theist's assertions are not to be understood as empirical claims, then how are we to take them? This leads to the fourth point: that religious language articulates an interpretation of the world, painting a *picture* that only it can paint. In *Culture and Value* he has this to say:

> It strikes me that a religious belief could only be something like a passionate commitment to a system of reference. Hence, although it's a *belief*, it's really a way of living, or a way of assessing life. It's passionately seizing hold of *this* interpretation. (*CV* 64)

The first point to make is that, despite appearances, Wittgenstein is *not* advancing a non-cognitivist account of religious belief: he is not claiming, *à la* Braithwaite, that "believing" ultimately amounts to having a certain attitude, and that religious language serves merely to express it.[3] Although it occasionally looks as though this is his position—such as when he says the doctrine of predestination "is less a theory than a sigh or a cry" (*CV* 30)— he regularly insists that it is not. Hence in the foregoing quote he assures us that what is in question *is* a belief, and in his conversation with Lewy he explicitly denies that his position is non-cognitivist (*LC* 71). Certainly, he thinks that religion involves adopting particular attitudes, but that is not the end of the matter; there is also the *object* of such attitudes. *What it is* that the theist commits herself to passionately, "lovingly" (*CV* 32), and trustingly is a "system of reference"—an interpretation or picture of life.

Talk of pictures pervades Wittgenstein's remarks on religion. David Egan characterizes Wittgenstein's religious pictures as *conceptual pictures*: they are ways in which we conceive of things (Egan 2011, 57). More than that, they are foundational ways of conceiving of things—hence Wittgenstein's claiming that such pictures "regulate" and "guide" the theist's life (*LC* 54), and his referring to the possibility of a picture lying "at the root of all our thinking" (*CV* 83). As Egan puts it, such pictures are "organizing myths," conceptions that form the bedrock of our thought (where our spade is turned: *PI* §217). As such, they engender expectations and guide our inquiries (Egan 2011, 68–70). This is why Wittgenstein stresses that the *reasons* for adopting religious belief differ radically from our ordinary justificatory norms (*LC* 56): organizing myths are not subject to these norms because they lie at their base, providing us with interpretations of the world that shape our normative practices.[4]

Another central feature of Wittgenstein's *religious* pictures (as opposed to other types of pictures) is that the interpretation they articulate cannot be articulated in alternative, non-religious terms. "The whole *weight*" of a religious claim is in the picture, in the sense that "[a] picture tells me itself" (*LC* 72; *PI* §523). Whatever is expressed by the phrase "God's eye sees everything" cannot be expressed in any other terms, just as the meaning of a poem can be expressed only "by these words in these positions" (*PI* §531).

There are two outstanding issues to address. First, if a religious belief *qua* picture is not a belief in the "normal," empirical sense, how is it arrived at?

Clearly, we cannot adopt a religious picture unless we understand its terms, and as commentators have pointed out, this requires a kind of "conceptual reorientation."[5] The individual must adapt her use of familiar terms to fit unfamiliar practices, extending their application to satisfy the norms of a new milieu. She must master new uses for an old stock of words—"lord," "father," "kingdom"—in order to transform her "ordinary" way of seeing and discoursing about the world.

Yet this raises a query touched on earlier: if a condition for understanding religious language is familiarity with religious life, then such a reorientation of our concepts will not be possible without our adopting religious practices. But this seems to be a perverse way of viewing things; surely our grasp of these concepts comes *before* our commitment to religious life, motivating that commitment to begin with. If conceptual reorientation comes only *after* we have committed to certain practices, what reason would we have for committing in the first place? Wittgenstein's model suggests that religious life precedes our grasp of religious terms—but that is the very opposite of what we would expect.[6]

Wittgenstein writes that experiences such as suffering can engender faith (CV 85), and that we acquire religious pictures gradually, moving through different "levels of devoutness" (CV 32). These remarks indicate that pictures develop as follows. We begin with an impoverished, "atomic" understanding of religious terms: a picture-book notion of "God," for example, rather than that of the fully fledged believer. An experience of some kind, *combined with that "ordinary" understanding*, then edges us toward the boundaries of religious practice—spurring us, perhaps, to explore religious literature. As we touch those boundaries, we begin to reorient ourselves, extending our application of the relevant concepts to novel referents. As we do this we move further into the religious sphere, closer to the life and language of the theist we could not previously contradict. And with every step our "level of devoutness" heightens—our picture becomes increasingly sophisticated. The important point is that we do not commit to religious practices for no reason; rather, we do so on the basis of an "ordinary" understanding of religious terms, and we develop our picture from that point on. We may well hear of "God" from Fr. O'Hara, but we do not stop there: we act upon the concept he conveys to us, carrying it into a new form of life, and we refine it as we go.

The second outstanding issue is this: Wittgenstein insists that religious claims do not denote empirically verifiable entities or events, but if that is so, just what do they denote? There are three reasons why he cannot answer this question.

First, because he is not religious: we cannot grasp a term outside the life to which it belongs, and since—by his own admission—Wittgenstein does not live a religious life, he can do little to shed light on the non-empirical sense of "God." Second, because "God" is untranslatable: even if Wittgenstein were religious, the irreplaceable nature of religious pictures means that he could not explain "God" by employing alternative terms. And third, because *we* ourselves cannot grasp its use outside religious life: even if Wittgenstein were religious, and even if the terms could be translated, a written explanation would do little good. To understand any explanation he gave, we would have to join him in his religiousness.

Wittgenstein's central point is that religious belief has a distinctive character: it consists in espousing an interpretation of the world that organizes expectations, resists translation, and requires us to rethink familiar notions. In short, those who are "truly" or "properly" religious "believe" in the sense that they possess a picture that (i) sits at the root of their thinking, (ii) cannot be replaced, and (iii) demands a conceptual reorientation in order to be understood.

Wittgenstein is clear, then, that straightforward assent to certain meta-physical or historical claims is not sufficient to render an individual truly religious. That is why he regards Fr. O'Hara's Christianity as a sham. But although assenting to such claims is not *sufficient*, Wittgenstein is unclear as to whether it is *necessary*. Two divergent readings of his comments yield two divergent answers to this question.

On a "narrow" reading, someone whose picture makes no reference to Jesus, for example, is not properly Christian—however passionate her commitment to that "frame of reference." On this view, a believer is someone who possesses a picture that satisfies conditions (i)–(iii) *and* that makes some reference or appeal to transcendence (although the referring terms do not carry their ordinary, empirical sense). What makes her picture religious, then, is both its form ((i)–(iii)) and its content (it appears to involve assent to standard religious claims). Both are necessary, and together they are sufficient.[7]

But on a "broad" reading, a picture can be "religious" without any reference to transcendence. On this view, what matters is not so much the terms that make up the picture but its form—the way it operates. Religiousness consists not in sharing stories or teachings but in living by a picture that satisfies the foregoing criteria. And this means, of course, that an interpretation of existence that makes no reference to divinity but *does* meet those criteria *is* "religious."[8]

2   HEIDEGGER AND LUTHER

2.1   Luther on Grace

My central claim is that in *Being and Time* Heidegger is "held captive" by a Lutheran picture of existence, according to which we lack the means to "save" ourselves. I shall now outline Luther's conception of grace, before looking at how it manifests itself in Heidegger's thought.

Luther's understanding of grace stems from his understanding of sin. For Scholasticism, we have a natural capacity to know God, and prior to the Fall enjoyed an original intimacy with him. That capacity is part of our essence, but the intimacy was a gift added on. The effect of the Fall was to strip us of that gift, yet leave our essence intact—to disrupt our *present* relationship with God, yet leave us capable of finding him again. So for the Scholastics the Fall did not *totally* corrupt our nature; it merely deprived us of something that was *in*essential to it. Following the Fall we can still access God directly because our will and intellect remain oriented toward him.

Luther, however, sees things rather differently. On his view, our original intimacy with God *was* our natural state of being, so its loss represented a total corruption of our nature. The Fall did not simply strip us of a gift; it transformed our very essence. It did not simply disrupt our present relationship with God; it deprived us of the ability to relate to him at all. As Heidegger puts it in his 1924 seminar on Luther, Luther views sin as "a concept of existence" (*Existenzbegriff*) (*Supp* 108); he conceives of the disruption caused by the Fall in *ontological* terms.

For Luther, the Scholastic position amounts to idolatry, the construction of a God to suit our intellect. Worse, it renders the incarnation redundant: if the Fall had left us capable of knowing God and meriting his favor, God's saving act would have been superfluous—since we would be capable of saving ourselves (*Supp* 106). This opposition to Scholasticism leads Luther to an understanding of grace underpinned by four key characteristics.

(*a*) *Grace is unmerited*.[9] First, our corruptness means that we are incapable of earning grace, and as such, incapable of controlling its bestowal. Grace does not depend on faith, strength, or human works—on the contrary, they depend on it. We do not receive grace as a result of having faith, but have faith as a result of receiving grace. Similarly, good works arise from rather than cause justification: the Christian performs good works to thank God for his favor, not to bargain for it (McGrath 2009, 114).

(*b*) *Grace is external*. Second, our corruptness also means that any righteousness is *God's* righteousness, not ours. The justification God bestows through grace originates beyond us, in God himself. It is thus external to the believer: she is "clothed" (Ezekiel 16:8) in righteousness *in the sight of God*, but remains a sinner at heart (McGrath 2009, 120).

(*c*) *Humanity is passive*. Third, our corruption—again—entails that our role in justification is entirely passive. The Scholastics hold that reason and will enable us actively to ascend toward God, to know him through our own endeavors. But Luther holds the opposite: there is nothing we can do but *receive* grace. God makes himself known to us, and we are brought to him.

(*d*) *The means of grace is the Word of God*. Finally, the Word of God is the means by which the sinner receives justification. And the Word itself is mediated by the sacraments, in that they testify to God's promise of salvation. In short, the Scripture embodies God's Word, and the sacraments *speak* it to us (McGrath 2009, 172–74).

The "vocal" nature of grace is noted by Heidegger in his 1924 seminar. Here he reiterates Luther's observation in his *Lectures on Genesis* that after the Fall God's grace is manifest in speech: he *calls* Adam back from his sin rather than turning him away. To this Heidegger adds: "[T]he being of God is always conceived of as *verbum* [word], and the fundamental relation of man to him as *audire* [hearing]" (*Supp* 110, 192).

Grace, then, is an unmerited gift that comes from without, is passively received, and is conveyed by God's Word—his call to Adam, his promise to humanity. As such, it sits at the heart of Luther's theology, the *theology of the cross*. This is a theology of revelation rather than speculation, where God's righteousness is revealed not in the natural or moral world but in the cross of Christ.

2.2 The Young Heidegger

Luther's impact on the young Heidegger is impossible to deny and difficult to exaggerate. In 1919 Heidegger wrote to Engelbert Krebs announcing his personal dissatisfaction with the "system" of Catholicism, and it was around that time that his interest in Luther intensified.[10] In the winter of 1920 he commenced his "Introduction to the Phenomenology of Religion,"[11] a series of lectures in which he addressed Pauline Christianity. Luther's influence pervades Heidegger's reading of Paul—despite Heidegger telling his students that they must free themselves from Luther's perspective (*PRL* 47). At the outset he emphasizes that Paul's Christianity is revelatory, explaining that Paul came to faith through experience rather than teaching (*PRL* 49). And he regularly emphasizes that Pauline Christianity is characterized by strife—impliedly associating it with Luther's theology of the cross (*PRL* 66, 70, 90). What is most important for my purposes, though, is the Lutheran notion of grace that emerges toward the end of the course. Heidegger claims:

> The Christian is conscious that this facticity [i.e., the Christian life] cannot be won out of his own strength, but rather originates from God—the phenomenon of the effects of grace. . . . What is available only to us Christians is not sufficient for the task of arriving at Christian facticity. . . . The enactment exceeds human strength. It is unthinkable out of one's own strength. (*PRL* 87)

So like Luther, Heidegger's Paul sees grace as a prerequisite of faith, which is external to us, passively received, and not something we can achieve by our own means. "God alone acts," notes Heidegger; "not the works of human beings, but rather grace!" (*PRL* 90). Indeed, Heidegger even cites Luther (along with Augustine) when the issue of grace arises (*PRL* 87).

Heidegger's fascination with Luther continued long after these lectures. The following year he used a line from Luther as the motto for his class (*PIA* 137);[12] the year after that he explored Luther's understanding of sin (*OHF* 22); and the year after that he gave a seminar on that very topic (referred to earlier).[13] What makes these lectures significant, though, is that they represent the culmination of Heidegger's own phenomenological-theological project. Here, phenomenology and religion coexist, with primordial Christianity performing a phenomenological function by disclosing what Heidegger terms the "historicality" of existence. Only a year later Heidegger disrupts this marriage, claiming that philosophy must be "atheistic" in the sense that it must bracket all religious commitments. Philosophy, he now declares, has "its own task to fulfill"—namely, the engendering and maintaining of radical questioning. Because religion offers answers, it is inimical to that task; its speculations foreclose philosophy's most pressing inquiries (*PIA* 148).[14]

In section 3 I shall show that, however much Heidegger insisted on bracketing religion, the conception of grace to which he appeals in the "Introduction" lectures resurfaces in *Being and Time*, bringing with it a particular understanding of human existence.

3   THE CALL OF CONSCIENCE

3.1   The Call

In his bid to capture Dasein in its totality, Heidegger begins Division Two of *Being and Time* by analyzing Dasein's relation to its own end. He explains that Dasein's Being is Being-towards-death, a constant projection into the possible impossibility of its own existence. *Authentic* Being-towards-death consists in Dasein grasping this existential characteristic through an anxious "forerunning" of its mortality. Heidegger then asks whether authenticity thus understood is *practically* achievable. If so, then, given that Dasein is typically immersed in average everydayness, there must be something that brings the possibility of authenticity to Dasein's attention—something that "attests" to its potential. The "call of conscience" is the existential phenomenon that does just that (*BT* 267/312).

So the call testifies to the possibility of authenticity. But because authenticity consists in Dasein's fully realizing its own Being, testifying to the former is really a matter of pointing to the latter. Thus the call discloses the possibility of authenticity by disclosing the possibility of Dasein's Being-its-Self—the two are one and the same. And it does this by "summoning" Dasein *forth* to its "ownmost" Self (*BT* 269/314). That is, it calls Dasein's attention to the way in which it *could* be by appealing to the way in which it fundamentally *is*. This explains Heidegger's insistence that the caller is Dasein itself (*BT* 277/321): *this* call must come from *this* Dasein because what it discloses is *this* Dasein's ownmost Being—something no other entity could disclose.[15]

The "ownmost Being" that is disclosed by the silent call is a Being shot through with nullity: a "Being-guilty." Having been thrown into the world, Dasein's *origin* is a nullity in the sense that it is utterly unchosen—something reflected in the fact that the call itself is neither sought nor expected (*BT* 284–85/330). And as a being defined by projection, "it is essentially null" in the sense that all projection is finite: to realize one possibility is to cancel another (*BT* 285/331), with all possibilities being cancelled by death.

Dasein can respond to this disclosure by falling back into *das Man* or by living "resolutely." Resoluteness is a way of existing in which Dasein comes to understand its nullity by "taking ownership" of it. It consists in seizing hold of possibilities while being prepared to relinquish them, in committing to decisions while being ready to "take them back" (*BT* 308/355). But Dasein only becomes *authentic* when resoluteness becomes *anticipatory*—that is, when it becomes constant, reaching ahead to Dasein's end. Anticipation, then, is the most fully developed form of resoluteness—an application of the resolute stance to Dasein's entire existence. If resolute Dasein stands ready to relinquish discrete possibilities, anticipatory Dasein stands ready to relinquish the whole. It "anticipates" death by preparing to take *everything* back (*BT* 308/356).

Heidegger refers to the voice of conscience as "an alien power [*einer . . . fremden Macht*] by which Dasein is dominated," but quickly warns against "explaining away" his findings by positing "a possessor for the power," or by taking "the power itself as a person who makes himself known—God" (*BT* 275/320). As he sees it, once we understand that and how Dasein calls itself, there is no need to search for an external caller. My contention in what follows is not that the notion of the call of conscience smuggles God into the existential analytic, nor that it leaves open the possibility of doing so. Given Heidegger's explicit disavowal of any theological interpretation of the call, and his insistence that the caller is Dasein itself, neither of these claims is convincing. Rather, my contention is (first) that Heidegger's analysis of the call of conscience exhibits a Lutheran interpretation of human powerlessness, and (second) that this interpretation amounts to a religious picture. I shall address these points in turn.

3.2   The Lutheran Picture

Heidegger's discussion of the call is replete with Christian motifs. At the start he refers to authenticity as "an existentiell modification" of *das Man*, recalling Luther's claim that we are merely "clothed" in righteousness. And just as Paul's Christian, once called, "does not step out of this world" but merely approaches it in a new spirit (*PRL* 85), Dasein, once called, "does not detach [itself] from its world" but merely discloses it resolutely (*BT* 298/344). What is perhaps most striking, though, is the extent to which Heidegger's explanation of the call accords with Luther's account of grace as *unmerited, external, passively received*, and conveyed by the *word*.

First, like grace, the call is entirely unmerited and beyond our control. It "will not let itself be coaxed" (*BT* 275/319), he writes. Quite the opposite: it "is precisely something which *we ourselves* have neither planned nor prepared for nor voluntarily performed, nor have ever done so. 'It' calls, against our expectations and even against our will" (*BT* 275/320). In short, Dasein cannot control the call of conscience. It is not sought, expected, awaited, earned—nor even suppressed when it arrives. Dasein may respond by returning to *das Man*, but cannot avoid the call's initial silent disturbance. And because it cannot be earned, there can be no guarantee that it will occur at all. That is, the call is not *necessary*: nothing Heidegger says indicates that we are destined to be called.

Second, the call's origin is *external* to Dasein. On the face of it, we may think that Heidegger directly contradicts this when he claims that Dasein calls itself. Indeed, the internality of the caller is necessary since what it points to is *this* Dasein's Being in its particularity. Yet Heidegger also writes: "The call comes *from me* and yet *from beyond* me" (*BT* 275/320), that it "is from afar unto afar" (*BT* 271/316), and that "it is something like an alien voice" (*BT* 277/321). In short, the caller is external in the sense that it *transcends* the Dasein that is called, here and now. That which calls me is not my present self, lost as it is in *das Man*, but something that lies beyond what, who, or how I currently am. It may not be the Christian God that calls me, but nor is it quite *me*.

Third, the call's foreignness accounts for Dasein's *passivity*. Because the call comes from what Dasein is not, from a Being that Dasein has not yet mastered, the power it wields is "alien" and able to dominate Dasein (*BT* 275/320). Throughout the chapter Heidegger speaks of Dasein in passive terms: Dasein is *summoned*, *pushed*, and *aroused* by the call; its casual listening to *das Man* is interrupted by it (*BT* 271/316); it is *called forth* to its possibilities (*BT* 274/319), with the onus upon it to act; and it is *brought back* out of its fallenness (*BT* 268/312). At every stage, something is done to Dasein by the caller through the call.

Finally, just as the *Word* of God is the means of grace, the *voice* of conscience is the means by which Dasein comes to recognize its authentic potential. The call is discursive in that it discloses, it "lets something be seen" or points something out (*BT* 32/56). And this "giving-to-understand" is met with a corresponding "hearing" (*BT* 269/314). These remarks resonate with Heidegger's observation, mentioned earlier, that Luther conceives of God's Being in terms of the *Word*, and of our relation to him in terms of *hearing* (the exemplary instance being God's calling Adam). So just as Lutheran grace is conveyed by a kind of divine speech act, Dasein's authenticity is prompted by a moment of discourse. In both cases, an unmerited word from a transcendent source heralds new life.

Once Dasein has been posited as both the caller *and* the called, there appears to be no room for God. Yet nonetheless these sections of *Being and Time* espouse a Lutheran picture. It is a picture not of God or divinity but of humanity. For Luther, the individual is powerless to save herself and relies instead on an occurrence that is neither merited nor guaranteed, has its origin beyond her, and in the face of which she is passive. And it is this conception of humanity that underpins Heidegger's account of the transition to authenticity in *Being and Time*. Although Dasein has the resources to choose resoluteness and master anticipation once it has been called, it lacks the resources to instigate the call. Dasein, when lost in *das Man*, is powerless; its attaining authenticity depends on its hearing an unbidden, unexpected, alien voice.

3.3   The Wittgensteinian Model

When discussing Wittgenstein's remarks on religious belief I concluded that a religious picture consists in an interpretation of the world that (i) sits at the "root" of our thinking, (ii) is not replaceable, and (iii) requires a "conceptual reorientation" in order to be understood. I shall now explain how the view of human powerlessness that we find in Heidegger's discussion of conscience satisfies each criterion, beginning with the third.

The reader of *Being and Time* is regularly reminded of the need to "reorient" herself conceptually, either by Heidegger's express instructions or by the sheer obscurity of his prose. His exposition of the call of conscience is a prime example. From the start he makes it clear that by "conscience" he is not referring to the "everyday" notion of a "voice of conscience" but to something "purely existential." What he has in mind, he claims, actually underpins such everyday notions (*BT* 269/313). The same goes for the term "guilt." He spends several pages exploring its "ordinary significations" before stripping it down to its most basic, "existential" sense: "Being-the-basis of a nullity" (*BT* 283/329).

So if we are to understand the picture of the call we must understand—among other things—that the "call" is not a call at all, that "conscience" is not a subjective moral guide, and that "guilt" has nothing to do with having committed an offense or being indebted.[16] We need to understand that Heidegger's ontological terminology draws upon our ordinary vocabulary but shifts the parameters of its terms, so that "death" no longer denotes an empirically verifiable event but a defining structural feature of human Being. Just as the Christian does not look for the kingdom of Heaven on a map, the reader of *Being and Time* does not ask for silence as she listens intently for the call. To adapt Wittgenstein's example, if the reader of *Being and Time* confessed that she was "guilty," and her friend—having never encountered Heidegger—claimed that she was not, they would not be contradicting one another.

What about the notion that religious pictures sit "at the root of our thinking"? For Wittgenstein this means that they regulate the theist's life, guiding her thought and engendering expectations. As such, they constitute "organizing myths." Heidegger's picture of Dasein as powerless to save itself and in need of something like grace is part of a broader picture that performs this "organizing" role—a picture of Dasein as being at the mercy of its own existence. This picture underpins Heidegger's treatment of "nullity," "guilt," "thrownness," and "death," and is integral to the fallenness that pervades *Being and Time*.

Throughout *Being and Time*, Dasein is presented as lacking control of its Being "from the ground up." This is the very "nullity" of its thrownness: the fact that its existence is not chosen. And of course, it cannot control its *telos* any more than it can its thrown origin. However it projects into the future, whatever possibilities it appropriates, it is limited by the possibility that ends all possibilities—the impossibility of existence. In short, in thrownness and death Dasein is bookended by powerlessness; both its origin and its end lie beyond its control.

This powerlessness first manifests itself—both in *Being and Time* and in Dasein's life—in the fact that Dasein "finds" itself in average everydayness. It does not place itself there having reflected on the merits of *das Man* and chosen to take up its company, but is there from the start, deprived of its

Self and incapable even of seeing that deprivation.[17] Take this powerlessness away and the existential analytic as we know it collapses. No longer does Dasein fall into *das Man*; it jumps—and clambers free of its own accord. No longer is it thrown into the world; it chooses its facticity from the very start.

Finally, religious pictures as Wittgenstein describes them are irreplaceable in the sense that what they articulate cannot be articulated in any other terms. As Wittgenstein puts it in *Philosophical Investigations*, "A picture tells me itself" (*PI* §523). The picture of the call satisfies this criterion too. It is not a picture of God, of course, but of humanity—the same picture of humanity Heidegger employs in his "Introduction to the Phenomenology of Religion." There he speaks of grace, and in *Being and Time that* is replaced. But what remains is the depiction of the recipient. To adapt Wittgenstein's claim, what the picture of the call tells us is *itself*: it says that if we are to exist in a way that is proper to what we are, we must be called, summoned, or brought to do so by something transcending our present state.

4   CONCLUSION: RELIGIOUSNESS

This chapter has advanced two theses. The first is that Heidegger's exposition of the call of conscience exhibits a Lutheran view of human existence, according to which we are powerless to initiate our own salvation and rely instead on a grace-like event. The second is that this view of existence constitutes a religious picture in the Wittgensteinian sense. Hence the content of Heidegger's thought corresponds with Luther's understanding of humanity and grace, while its form—its function and nature—corresponds with Wittgenstein's description of religious pictures.

When closing my exposition of Wittgenstein I noted that his remarks could be interpreted in one of two ways. On the broad reading, the religiousness of a picture and its holder consists not in its content but in the fact that it is fundamental, irreplaceable, and demands a conceptual reorientation. On the narrow reading, a picture and its holder are religious only if the picture has these characteristics *and* involves reference to theistic claims. In the first case, religiousness is a product of nothing but the picture's form; in the second, it is a product of form and content.

I hope to have demonstrated (in 3.3) that Heidegger's Lutheran conception of human existence is (i) fundamental to his thought, (ii) irreplaceable, and (iii) requires us to rethink hitherto familiar terms. If that is the case, then Heidegger's picture of human existence is at least religious in the broad sense. I want to close, however, by suggesting that it is also religious in the narrow sense. It is not just *broadly* religious in that it constitutes a foundational, irreplaceable, and reorienting conception of humanity; it is also *narrowly* religious in that its content is recognizably theistic.

The key point is that Heidegger continues to see Dasein as being *open to* and *in need of* an unfathomable transcendent "voice." Part of what is indispensable to Heidegger's picture is the very notion of the "call" itself (*der*

Ruf)—the idea of a summons to something that is proper to us (think of "vocation," *der Beruf*). But it is also the idea that Dasein is and *must* be the object of certain acts (Dasein is thrown, Dasein is called). This conception of human existence as receptive to and reliant on something "beyond" is what renders the call narrowly religious, despite the absence of any stock theistic terms.

Although Heidegger appears to counter the charge of religiousness by maintaining that the caller is Dasein, he also embraces its alien nature—and it is when he does so that its religiousness is most evident: "That which calls the call, simply holds itself aloof from any way of becoming well-known, and this belongs to its phenomenal character. *To let itself be drawn into getting considered and talked about, goes against its kind of Being*" (*BT* 274–5/319; emphasis added). To start with, this remark resonates with another made by Heidegger years before:

> God has to endure becoming a factor in human experiments. He has to respond to an inquisitive, pompous, and pseudo-prophetic curiosity, that is, a curious looking-about-oneself in regard to Him, which does not submit to his sense of objecthood, that is, which is non-sense. (*PRL* 167)

More specifically, though, Heidegger's insistence that the caller is utterly "un-worldly," that in worldly terms it is "*nothing* at all" (*BT* 277/321), evokes Luther's notion of "the hidden God" (*Deus absconditus*)—the God we will never know, whose intentions will always be mysterious (McGrath 1990, 165–66). Heidegger might just as well have likened those who seek the caller in the world to Luther's "theologians of glory," who arrogate to themselves knowledge of God, claiming to see his glory in creation.

Ostensibly, then, Heidegger recasts the Lutheran picture, with Dasein taking God's role as caller. But he continues to proclaim the mystery and transcendence of the voice that calls—and he has to, because if he did not, the entire picture would change. If the call were not from "beyond," Heidegger would risk arriving at a conception of Dasein as master of its own Being, utterly self-sufficient. Dasein may be just that, but if *Being and Time* were to say so, it would read very differently.

So, the call is narrowly religious in virtue of its emphasis on transcendence, something that goes hand in hand with human powerlessness. The crux of the issue is that for Heidegger, as for Luther, we need and are open to something beyond our control. It is as if Heidegger were saying: "only a god can save us."[18]

NOTES

1. Wittgenstein clearly maintains that we cannot understand religious beliefs in isolation from the practical context—the religious life—to which they belong. However, we might object that in making this claim he is conflating what it is to *hold* a belief with what it is to *understand* one. Thus he effectively claims *both* that I cannot understand *and* that I cannot hold religious beliefs without

210   *Stephen Reynolds*

being versed in the life to which they pertain. Of these two separate claims, we might accept the latter but not the former, insisting that even if I cannot hold religious beliefs in isolation, I can perfectly well understand (for example) that and why my neighbor goes to church every Sunday, and what she means by "the sacraments." But the possibility of such understanding is precisely what he denies, a denial stemming from the thought that understanding is embedded in practice.

2. To paraphrase Kierkegaard's Johannes Climacus, as quoted in Schönbaumsfeld (2010, 173).
3. See, for example, Braithwaite (1978, 72–91).
4. Egan points out that a single "myth" may itself be reviewed, but only on the basis of another—not from a neutral standpoint (2011, 69).
5. See Schönbaumsfeld (2010, 183) and Diamond (2005, 125).
6. This is the subject of a debate between John Hyman and Stephen Mulhall (see Hyman 1999 and Mulhall 2001b). In the following paragraph I explain how an individual might adopt a religious picture in a way that reconciles Mulhall's position with Hyman's.
7. This is the view espoused in Schönbaumsfeld (2010).
8. We might reject the broad view not only because it conflicts with our ordinary understanding of "religious" but also because it renders that term so widely applicable as to be empty. Yet arguably the broad view fits better with Wittgenstein's comments on the Christian narrative (*CV* 32) and the non-empirical nature of religious belief (*CV* 82).
9. Initially Luther followed the *via moderna*, according to which God's favor—and so salvation—*can* be merited or earned. So in Biel's *pactum* theology, for example, God agrees to save the sinner if she performs certain acts. These acts are not inherently valuable but are held to be valuable by God for the purposes of the pact. The result is that God saves on merit alone—but also that he is under an *obligation* to do so, a consequence that some found objectionable. Luther is thought to have broken away from this *via* at around 1515 (see McGrath 2009, 74–76, 107).
10. See van Buren (1994a, 160–62; 1994b, 149).
11. Published in English in the collection entitled *The Phenomenology of Religious Life (PRL)*.
12. *Statim enim ab utero matris mori incipimus* ("No sooner do we leave our mother's womb than we begin to die").
13. For recent commentaries on Heidegger's debt to Luther, see S.J. McGrath (2006) and Crowe (2006).
14. He repeats the point in his 1935 lecture series, *Introduction to Metaphysics*: "Anyone for whom the Bible is divine revelation and truth already has the answer to the question 'Why are there beings at all instead of nothing?'" (*IM* 7). A detailed analysis of this development is offered by Wolfe (forthcoming).
15. The requirement that the voice be internal poses a problem for Mulhall's alternative reading of the call in which Dasein is called by a friend (see Mulhall 2001a, 277).
16. Heidegger of course plays on the German *Schuld* and its cognates.
17. Similarly, for Luther, only once she has received grace can the believer perceive the depths of her corruption; while in that corruption, she cannot.
18. I shall not discuss it here, but there is a good case for arguing that this picture finds its way into Heidegger's later work too.

14 Words as Works of Art

Aaron James Wendland

In "The Origin of the Work of Art," Heidegger tells us "art is truth setting itself to work" (*PLT* 38). The truth that sets itself to work in the work of art is not what we traditionally understand by truth—namely, the accurate representation of reality through a certain idea, image, or sign—but rather the disclosure of reality that is achieved in the opening up of a world. Heidegger offers two key examples of this phenomenon in "The Origin of the Work of Art": a painting of a pair of peasant shoes by Van Gogh, and an Ancient Greek temple. According to Heidegger "the Van Gogh painting is the disclosure of what the equipment, the pair of peasant shoes, *is* in truth" (*PLT* 35), and in this instance truth sets itself to work in the work of art by directly disclosing the peasant shoes *as* the peasant shoes that they are in relation to other aspects of a peasant woman's world.[1] Of the Greek temple Heidegger remarks:

> It is the temple-work that first fits together and at the same time gathers around itself the unity of those paths and relations in which birth and death, disaster and blessing, victory and disgrace, endurance and decline acquire the shape of destiny for human being. The all-governing expanse of this open relational context is the world of this historical people. . . . [And through the temple-work,] tree and grass, eagle and bull, snake and cricket first enter into their distinctive shapes and thus come to appear as what they are. (*PLT* 41)

Whereas the Van Gogh painting explicitly presents the peasant shoes by making them stand out against other features of the peasant woman's world, the Greek temple serves as a reference point that constitutes a world and all that appears in it. Speaking of the temple, Heidegger says that "the work opens up a *world* and keeps it abidingly in force," and it is precisely "the temple, in its standing there, [that] first gives to things their look and to men their outlook on themselves" (*PLT* 43, 42). Here truth sets itself to work in the work of art by creating a context in which entities, aspects, and dimensions of reality are concurrently determined and disclosed *as* the entities, aspects, and dimensions that they are. Despite the subtle difference between the examples Heidegger cites, "The Origin of the Work of Art" concludes with the assertion: "*All art*, as the letting happen of the advent of the truth of what is, is, as such, *essentially poetry*" (*PLT* 70). The reduction of painting, architecture, and the plastic arts to poetry is related to their symbolic form,[2] and a function of their ability to "bring beings into being" through a "poetic projection" that "sets itself into the work as figure" and "thrusts up the unfamiliar and extraordinary and at the same time thrusts down the ordinary and what we believe to be such" (*PLT* 72–73). Although Heidegger considers it an open question whether traditional art forms exhaust the essence of poetry,[3] he says that "language itself is poetry in the essential [disclosive] sense," and he claims that "language alone brings what is, as something that is, into the Open for the first time" (*PLT* 72, 71). As a totality of signs organized in a system of reference relations, "language, by *naming* beings for the first time, first brings beings to word and appearance" and "only this naming nominates beings *to* their being *from out of* their being" (*PLT* 71). In fact, Heidegger goes so far as to cite the final line in Stefan George's poem, "The Word," which reads: "Where the word breaks off no thing may be" (*OWL* 60), but in "The Origin of the Work of Art," Heidegger never shows us what enables signs, names, and words to bring beings into being. Therefore, this chapter looks back to *Being and Time*, forward to Heidegger's later essays on language, and laterally to the writings of Wittgenstein to see how truth happens, how words work, how words open up a world, and how words might work as works of art.

1   THE HAPPENING OF TRUTH

Heidegger begins his discussion of truth in §44 of *Being and Time* by saying that his "analysis takes its departure from the *traditional conception of truth*, and attempts to lay bare the ontological foundations of that conception" (*BT* 214/257). The traditional concept of truth treats assertions as the *site* of truth and claims that the *essence* of truth lies in the agreement of an assertion with its object. Heidegger, however, wonders "[w]hat . . . *is tacitly posited in this relational totality of the* adaequatio intellectus et rei? *And what ontological character does that which is thus posited have itself?*" (*BT* 215/258). Heidegger's answer to the first question is *aletheia* or unconcealment: if aspects of the world were concealed, then our assertions would never be able to correspond to them in an intelligible way. Hence, Heidegger calls unconcealment the "primordial phenomenon of truth," and he sees the agreement between assertions and other aspects of reality as parasitic upon it (*BT* 215/258). As for the second question, Heidegger identifies the ontological character of *aletheia* with those features of human existence that enable humans to disclose the world. "Only with Dasein's *disclosedness*," Heidegger writes, "is the *most primordial* phenomenon of truth attained," and he goes so far as to say "entities are uncovered only *when* Dasein *is*; and only as long as Dasein *is*, are they disclosed" (*BT* 226/269). Characterizing the unconcealment achieved in our particular way of being-in-the-world as a condition for the agreement of an assertion with its object vaguely resembles two remarks in Wittgenstein's *Philosophical Investigations*: "[T]he fact that the *speaking* of language is part of an activity," and "[T]o imagine a language means to imagine a form of life" (*PI* §23, 19). But before making this connection clear, it is worth analyzing Heidegger's conception of correspondence and unconcealment in detail.

In *Being and Time*, Heidegger rejects traditional correspondence theories of truth, which treat truth as an agreement between an ideal, mental, or linguistic representation and reality (*BT* 216/259). The problem with these theories is their inability to explain the way representations and reality agree: that is, elucidating truth in terms of a relation between ideal content and real objects doesn't amount to an account of the truth relation itself. In short, for a correspondence theory of truth to do any work, it cannot simply assert that *intellectus* and *res* correspond; rather it must specify the content of that correspondence.

Although Heidegger dismisses classical correspondence theories of truth as empty, he *is* concerned with offering a phenomenological account of our experience with the way assertions relate to the world. For Heidegger, "correspondence" is a characteristic of our engagement with reality. "Asserting," Heidegger writes, "is a way of being towards the thing itself that is" (*BT* 218/260). And far from identifying propositions as a kind of ideal, mental, or linguistic representation, Heidegger suggests we experience assertions as a set of tools or "ready-to-hand" signs that work by directing us toward specific aspects of our environment (*BT* 83/114). Take, for example, the assertion, "The board is black." This assertion corresponds to reality not by *representing* a fact, say, the board being black, but by providing us with a certain direction or orientation to the board that *presents* a fact about it: that it is black (*MFL* 125–26). Heidegger calls the orientation that enables an assertion to indicate its object as a kind of "uncovering." Through assertions, "the entity itself which one has in mind shows itself *just as* it is in itself; that is to say, it shows that it, in its selfsameness, is just as it gets pointed out in the assertion as Being—just as *it* gets uncovered as Being" (*BT* 218/261). The being-true of an assertion as being-uncovering is, however, "ontologically possible only on the basis of Being-in-the-world" (*BT* 219/261). And, Heidegger says, "this latter phenomenon, which we have known as a basic state of Dasein, is the *foundation* for the primordial phenomenon of truth" (*BT* 219/261): *aletheia* or unconcealment.

Aletheia, on Heidegger's account, is the expression Ancient Greeks used to capture the phenomenon of "unconcealment." Unconcealment is a privative notion that consists in "taking entities out of their hiddenness and letting them be seen in their unhiddenness" (*BT* 212/262). Hiddenness, for Heidegger, "has a dual sense: 1. having no awareness of; and 2. having no possible context" (*GA* 36/37, 188).[4] Sense (1) refers to a kind of ontic or inner-worldly concealment in which something is manifest but we lack an explicit understanding of it, whereas sense (2) refers to a kind of ontological or worldly concealment whereby the context through which something can manifest itself is lacking. The dual sense of concealment suggests that unconcealment comes in two forms: the unconcealment involved in making what is manifest explicitly understood, and the unconcealment that creates the context by which entities can be manifest in the first place.[5] The being-uncovering of assertions is the kind of unconcealment that makes what is explicit. Through assertions, Heidegger says, "that which is manifest may be made *explicitly* manifest in its definite character" (*BT* 155/197). The disclosure achieved in our distinct way of being-in-the-world is the kind of unconcealment that creates the context through which entities can be manifest in the first place. "The uncoveredness of entities within the world is *grounded* in the world's disclosedness. But disclosedness is that basic character of Dasein according to which it *is* its 'there' " (*BT* 220/263). Breaking *aletheia* down into unconcealment as making explicit and unconcealment as making manifest highlights the extent to which the truth of assertions presupposes our disclosedness—for again if no entities or aspects of the world were manifest, then there would be nothing for our assertions to direct us toward or make explicit—and it suggests that Heidegger was committed to what Charles Guignon calls an instrumentalist view of language whereby

> our ability to use language is grounded in some prior grasp of the *non-semantic significance* of the context in which we find ourselves. It is only because we have first understood the nature of reality that we can then come to comprehend the meanings of words. Language is seen as a tool for communicating and ordering this prior grasp of reality. Although language may play a very important role in making the world intelligible, it is itself possible only against the background of an understanding that is *non*linguistic. (Guignon 1983, 117–18)

Yet treating the truth of assertions as based on a non-semantic background significance that discloses the world raises doubts about the extent to which "language alone brings what is, as something that is, into the Open for the first time" (*PLT* 71). And alternatively, if this non-semantic significance is in principle expressible, then the extent to which it is actually non-semantic (as opposed to implicitly semantic) is an open question. But before these concerns can be addressed, we need a better sense of how what Heidegger calls the "formal structures" of our existence or what Wittgenstein dubs our "form of life" discloses the world and enables our words to work.

On Heidegger's account, our disclosedness "embraces the whole of that structure-of-Being which has become explicit through the phenomenon of care" (*BT* 221/264), and Heidegger's care-structure is made up of a series of interrelated phenomena—including worldhood, understanding, discourse, and *das Man*—that enable us to present the world and make that presentation explicit through our use of signs. Similarly, Wittgenstein sees our ability to use language as bound up with our mode of living-in-the-world—"to imagine a language means to imagine a form of life" (*PI* §19)—and although there are numerous ways to interpret Wittgenstein's use of "*Lebensform*," it is possible to read it in a Heideggerian vein where there are some structural or formal features characteristic of a human being.[6] Indeed, it seems Wittgenstein's appeal to context, practical activity, grammar, custom, and agreement as aspects of our meaningful use of words roughly reflects the various features that make up Heidegger's care-structure; but again all of this will be clearer when we take a closer look at the background significance that, for Heidegger, discloses reality and facilitates the correspondence of an assertion with its object.

In an attempt to come to terms with the background significance that grounds our meaningful use of words, Heidegger offers an account of the worldhood of our work environment and the practical understanding that that environment entails.[7] The worldhood of the world is the referential totality that determines the meaningful presentation of its component parts and helps define the identity of human beings. Hammers, in other words, are the entities that they are in relation to wood, nails, tape measures, other such tools, and ultimately our ability to engage in the activity of carpentry. Likewise, a given human being is the carpenter that she is by engaging in the act of carpentry and immersing herself in the equipmental whole that makes that activity possible. Of course, carpentry is carpentry if and only if it is directed to some sort of end, say that of building a house, and Hubert Dreyfus (1991, 223) defines the significance that grounds our linguistic activity as "the relational whole of in-order-tos and for-the-sake-of-whichs in which entities and activities that involve equipment have a point." On Dreyfus's reading, we disclose the component parts that make up a particular activity by engaging in that activity. He writes, "[T]he whole current situation is Articulated by coping" (Dreyfus 1991, 217), and also, "[W]hen I pick up a hammer and hammer with it, I pick out or Articulate one of its significations, i.e. the fact that it is used to pound in nails; if I use it to pull nails, I Articulate another" (Dreyfus 1991, 215). Put otherwise, our primary disclosure of entities and aspects of the world is achieved in our practical engagement with that world in a specific, holistic context.

Once dimensions of the world have been disclosed through our practical activity, Heidegger says, "to significations, words accrue," and here he treats "language as a totality of words" that "as an entity within the world we may come across as ready-to-hand" (*BT* 161/204). As a tool, language does its job in the context of practical activity by pointing out characteristics of the work in progress, providing predicates for subjects involved in the referential whole, and allowing expression to take place in the course of communal activity. As an example of this phenomenon, take the assertion "The hammer is heavy." Clearly, a hammer cannot be heavy in isolation, but it can be heavy for a specific task in a certain context. And through an assertion, a carpenter can point all of this out to someone on the job with her (Dreyfus 1991, 209). In this example, the assertion "The hammer is heavy" picks out an aspect of the work environment, "hammer," provides it with a predicate, "heavy," and in doing so is capable of indicating to others that this hammer is heavy for the task at hand. Assertions, in other words, take what is implicitly disclosed in our practical activity and make it explicit.

With that said, we are now in a position to see how unconcealment is a condition of possibility for propositional truth and our meaningful use of words more generally. Propositional truth presupposes the unconcealment achieved in our practical activities to the extent that assertions are about something in the world, and that which the assertion is about determines the assertion's truth-value. To continue with our talk of hammers, the assertion "The hammer is heavy" is true or false in virtue of being about a hammer. But for this assertion to be about a hammer, the hammer must be disclosed. As Heidegger puts it: "In order for something to be a possible about-which for an assertion," the about-which of the assertion "must *already* be somehow given for the assertion as *unveiled* and accessible" (*BP* 208). Assertions, however, are not only about something that has been disclosed, since they also make specific claims about that which is disclosed. "To make an assertion about a hammer," Mark Wrathall (1999, 82) says, "the assertion must focus on some particular involvement or characteristic of the hammer: 'The hammer is heavy.'" But in order for an assertion to focus on a definite aspect of a hammer, say, its heaviness, that aspect must itself be disclosed in the context of our activities. Finally, the ability of true or false assertions to communicate something meaningful depends on the communal context through which dimensions of the world are disclosed. In Wrathall's words:

> To say that we "communicate" with others, in Heidegger's "ontologically broad" sense, means that we share a background with them. . . . "Communication" is essential to meaningful assertion, for only on the basis of "communication" [as shared background] can what is asserted in the assertion be fixed. For instance, a sculptor and a carpenter might mean very different things in asserting "the hammer is heavy" as a result of the different practices, goals, equipmental contexts, etc., within which they each use a hammer. Likewise, whether the assertion "the hammer is heavy" is true will depend on the background which is "communicated" by the speaker and hearer. (Wrathall 1999, 81–82)

Wrathall's appeal to the distinct background significance of sculptors and carpenters highlights the fact that the meaning and truth of assertions are determined by the context in which they are used and the aspects of the world disclosed therein. And insofar as the meaning and truth of assertions presuppose the disclosure of aspects of our world in the context of our practical activities, Heidegger feels justified in calling the unconcealment achieved in the worldly nature of our pragmatic understanding "the *most primordial* phenomenon of truth" (*BT* 221/263).

2 HOW WORDS WORK

Although the unconcealment of dimensions of our world is necessary for assertions to correspond to them, the disclosure of these dimensions is not enough to explain how our words work. For propositions to point out specific entities and communicate insights about them, Heidegger is right to say that these entities "must *already* be somehow given for the assertion as *unveiled* and accessible" (*BP* 209). Yet the availability of an entity is not sufficient for showing how the content of an otherwise indeterminate sign is fixed by that entity. Take the assertion "The hammer is heavy." It can correspond to a given hammer only in a particular context through the unconcealment of that hammer in that context, but the availability of that hammer does not itself show how the sign "hammer," as opposed to the sign, "wrench," is taken to have its meaning fixed by the disclosed hammer. And in an effort to understand how this works, we will turn to Wittgenstein's writings on grammar, custom, and agreement as well as Heidegger's discussion of discourse and *das Man*.

While Wittgenstein never explicitly describes our practical activities disclosing aspects of our world, his claim in the *Blue Book* that "I know what a word means *in certain contexts*" (*BB* 9) and his remark in the *Philosophical Investigations* that "[e]very sign *by itself* seems dead. *What* gives it life?— In use it *lives*" (§432) resonate with Heidegger's depiction of assertions as tools that work in the context of a particular practical activity.[8] Heidegger's focus on words directing us toward entities in the context of a work-world should also remind us of what is often called the "Augustinian Picture" of language and the example Wittgenstein offers "for which the description [of language] given by Augustine is right" (*PI* §2).[9] According to this example,

> the language is meant to serve for communication between a builder A and an assistant B. A is building with building stones: there are blocks, pillars, slabs and beams. B has to pass the stones and to do so in the order in which A needs them. For this purpose they use a language consisting of the words "block," "pillar," "slab," "beam." A calls them out; B brings the stone which he has learnt to bring at such-and-such a call. (*PI* §2)

In this case, and like the hammer Heidegger appeals to in his account of worldhood, it is fair to say that the blocks, pillars, slabs, and beams are determined and disclosed as the entities that they are in the course of our practical activities. And like the meaning of the word "hammer," the meaning of the word "block" appears to be fixed by an object presented in a practical context. Of course, the disclosure of a block is not enough to explain how the meaning of the word "block" is fixed by said disclosure. And a good deal of the *Philosophical Investigations* is dedicated to a critique of the Augustinian Picture by showing how the meaning of a word is determined by a set of unique discursive norms that enable arbitrary signs to indicate aspects of the world.

Wittgenstein's word for the norms that enable signs to indicate dimensions of our world is "grammar." On Wittgenstein's account, "Grammar tells us what kind of object anything is" (*PI* §373). He also says that "[e]ssence is expressed in grammar" (*PI* §371). And in *Philosophical Grammar*, Wittgenstein asserts: "Grammar is not accountable to any reality. It is grammatical rules that determine meaning (constitute it) and so they themselves are not answerable to any meaning and to that extent are arbitrary" (*PG* 184). P. M. S. Hacker captures Wittgenstein's conception of grammar along with its arbitrary nature when he remarks:

> Grammar is not justified by the facts; indeed there is no such thing as justifying grammar by reference to reality on the model of verifying an empirical proposition by reference to what makes it true. Grammar consists of rules for the use of words and has no such justification. It determines what we count as possible descriptions of how things are in reality, fixing a logical space which the facts, so to speak, may then occupy or fail to occupy. Grammar is autonomous, not answerable to, but presupposed by, factual propositions. In this sense, unlike means/ends rules, it is arbitrary. (Hacker 1990, 60)

In sum, grammar consists in a set of rules that regulate our use of signs such that they are able to indicate dimensions of our world. Insofar as these rules underwrite our ability to indicate the entities and aspects in our world, grammar has a constitutive role to play in the way our world is presented. And striking a Heideggerian tone, we might say grammar alone brings what is, as something that is, into the open for the first time.

To clarify the content of our world-disclosing discursive norms and to illustrate how they enable signs to indicate aspects of our world, it is worth looking at Heidegger's kindred concept to Wittgenstein's grammar: "discourse." Discourse, for Heidegger, is the "Articulation of intelligibility" (*BT* 161/203–4) whereby "the intelligibility of Being-in-the-world . . . is articulated according to significations" (*BT* 162/206). In *Heidegger's Analytic*, Taylor Carman (2003, 205–6) says Heideggerian discourse "constitutes a kind of public space of expressive possibilities," and it refers to "the way in which our world is coherently articulated, not just pragmatically or teleologically in terms of ends and activities, but expressively and communicatively, that is, in terms of how it makes sense to express our understanding and convey it to others." The distinction Carman makes between the pragmatic and discursive articulations of our world rests on: (a) the conceptual relationship between discourse as "the articulation of intelligibility" and Heidegger's account of interpretation as "understanding made explicit"; and (b) the difference between our practical understanding and its articulation in interpretation. Specifically, discourse is a condition of explicit understanding insofar as the signs we use to interpret the world disclosed in our practical activities are subject to a set of norms that stand apart from the norms governing our practices. And to grasp the nature of these distinct discursive norms, we need to say more about the nature of our practical understanding and the relation between understanding, interpretation, and discourse.

Our practical understanding consists in *using* entities *as* the entities that they are in the course of our activities. This understanding is normative and aspectual, but also tacit and unthematic. The normativity involved in our practices is teleological: that is, success in any given activity is relative to a particular end, say, that of building a house, and subject to a certain set of rules that must be followed if the end is to be attained; in the case of building a house these rules are determined by the local environment, strength of materials, aesthetic considerations, and so on. Understanding is also aspectual insofar as it involves the competent use of entities *as* entities. Yet the aspects through which we deal with entities do not stand apart from the entities themselves but constitute those entities as the entities that they are. In his discussion of aspect seeing in *Philosophy of Psychology—a Fragment*, Wittgenstein suggests it would make little sense to look at a knife and fork and say: " 'Now I see this as a knife and fork.' This utterance would not be understood. Any more than: 'Now it is a fork for me' or 'It can be a fork too' " (*PPF* xi §122). And he goes on to write: "One doesn't '*take*' what one knows to be the cutlery at a meal *for* cutlery; any more than one ordinarily tries to move one's mouth as one eats" (*PPF* xi §123). Wittgenstein's claim is that a fork just *is* a fork in our daily activity, so it is pointless to insist that one *sees* it *as* a fork. And Carman (2003, 247) offers a felicitous gloss on this idea when he says that "we do not normally interpret things as the things they are, we just understand them by dealing with them appropriately." In short, the purposive structures of our practical activities disclose specific dimensions of the world as the dimensions that they are, but this disclosure is implicit and unexpressed.

The explicit expression of that which is disclosed in our practical understanding is achieved in interpretation. As Heidegger asserts:

> That which is disclosed in understanding—that which is understood—is already accessible in such a way that its "as which" can be made to stand out explicitly. The "as" makes up the structure of the explicitness of something that is understood. It constitutes the interpretation. (*BT* 149/189)

Whereas understanding discloses entities through a certain *use*, interpretation consists in abstracting from our practical engagement with the world and explicitly *seeing* what we understand *as* the entities that they are. This abstraction creates a gap between the signs we use to interpret the world and the world that we interpret, and this gap facilitates a distinction between the norms governing our practical activities and the rules regulating our use of signs. As Carman puts it:

> Interpretation involves practical norms at two distinct levels: first, in the practical intelligibility—the *how*—being made explicit itself; second, in the comportment effecting the explicitation. Interpretive activity, that is, makes manifest normative aspects of everyday intelligibility in a way that is itself sensitive to norms, in this case the norms governing *how* things are to be made properly manifest or explicit. (Carman 2003, 215)

The distinct discursive norms that regulate our expressive activities stand for the phenomenon Heidegger and Wittgenstein are trying to capture through their respective discussions of discourse and grammar. Like the rules regulating our practical activities, these discursive norms undergird our ability to present aspects of the world through concrete expressions. But unlike the teleological nature of purposive activity, the source of these distinct discursive norms is found in our ability to communicate with others.

Communication is a condition of expression insofar as the recognition and repetition of a given sign in specific contexts set the standards through which a sign is able to indicate dimensions of the world. Heidegger alludes to the recognition and repetition that enable our meaningful use of signs in his discussion of *das Man*. Wittgenstein describes the basis of our discursive norms through an appeal to agreement and custom. And to illustrate the extent to which recognition and repetition undergird expression, we will first turn to Wittgenstein's remarks on the incoherence of a private language that results from the public nature of following a rule.[10]

As in Wittgenstein's example, suppose that I write "S" in my diary every time I have a specific sensation. Wittgenstein claims, "I first want to observe that a definition of the sign cannot be formulated," and he goes on to ask: "What reason have we for calling 'S' the sign for a *sensation*?" (*PI* §258, §261). Briefly, a private definition regulating the correct use of "S" cannot be formulated because there is nothing independent of the language user to confirm whether she is *in fact* using the definition consistently or correctly. Wittgenstein asserts: "To *think* one is following a rule is not to follow a rule. And that's why it's not possible to follow a rule 'privately': otherwise, thinking one was following a rule would be the same thing as following it" (*PI* §202). Ultimately, the rule governing the proper use of a given expression, the meaning of the expression itself, and the expression's ability to refer to something in the world remains indeterminate in the absence of the consistency achieved through communal consensus. "A person goes by a sign-post," Wittgenstein says, "only insofar as there is an established usage, a custom" (*PI* §198). In *Zettel* he writes: "Our language-game only works when a certain agreement prevails" (*Z* §430). And Wittgenstein sums up his position in his *Remarks on the Foundations of Mathematics* when he says, "[T]he phenomenon of language is based on regularity, on agreement in action" (*RFM* VI §39).

Wittgenstein's invocation of agreement and custom as characteristics of the way our words work reflects the fact that our discursive norms are always bound by the normative authority of what Heidegger calls *das Man*. *Das Man* refers to an anonymous other who sets the standard for all of our intelligible interactions with the world, and it undergirds the efficient functioning of our work-world by ensuring that each individual interacts with signs in a similar fashion. *Das Man*, Heidegger says, "controls every way in which the world and Dasein get interpreted" (*BT* 127/165), and it is through *das Man* that "we have the *same thing* in view, because it is in *the same* averageness that we have a common understanding of what is said" (*BT* 168/212). The averageness that underwrites our common understanding of what is said refers to the communal consistency with which an expression is used to signify certain aspects of the world. And this consistency is achieved through the collective recognition of the way signs are used in a given context as well as the repetition of that use in corresponding contexts. The word "hammer," for example, is able to point out an object used to pound nails into a piece of wood because it has been consistently used in the context of a workshop to describe just such an object. Of course, the serviceability of a sign is extremely general, but the fact is that we find ourselves thrown into a world where a customary use of expressions determines the way the world shows up for us. And these customary uses amount to the specific discursive norms through which the intelligibility of our world is articulated or by which the essence of an entity is expressed.

Wittgenstein's and Heidegger's appeal to a distinct set of discursive norms that enable signs to indicate dimensions of our world disclosed in our practical activities addresses the fact that the disclosure of entities and aspects of our environment is alone not enough to explain how an arbitrary sign can correspond with an entity. And after examining some of the structural features of our existence that enable us to disclose the world and make that disclosure explicit through our use of signs—worldhood, understanding, discourse, and *das Man*, for Heidegger, and context, practical activity, grammar, custom, and agreement, for Wittgenstein—we are now able to offer an account of how our words work: certain practical contexts implicitly disclose entities as the entities that they are, and through the collective repetition and recognition of specific signs in a given context those signs are able to explicitly present the entities disclosed in said context.

3   HOW WORDS OPEN UP A WORLD

Although the discussion thus far has detailed the aspects of our existence that enable our words to work, focusing on assertions and propositional truth means we have more or less restricted ourselves to explicating just one way in which our signs are used: to indicate dimensions of our world. However, for both Wittgenstein and Heidegger words are capable of doing more than asserting or what the Augustinian Picture of "signs naming objects" suggests. Wittgenstein wonders, "How many kinds of sentences are there?" and then answers, "There are *countless* kinds: countless different kinds of use of all the things we call 'signs,' 'words,' 'sentences'" (*PI* §23). And Wittgenstein offers a host of examples, including: "making up a story; and reading one"; "singing rounds"; and "requesting, thanking, cursing, greeting, praying" (*PI* §23). In *Being and Time*, Heidegger says that a sign is not a thing that simply refers to another thing but rather is *"an item of equipment which explicitly raises a totality of equipment into our circumspection so that together with it the worldly totality of equipment announces itself"* (*BT* 80/110). And in a later essay called "Language," Heidegger asserts: "[O]nly speech enables man to be the living being he is as man" (*PLT* 187). Drawing on the work of both Wittgenstein and Heidegger, Charles Taylor (1985b, 259) writes, "[L]anguage creates what one might call a public space, or a common vantage point from which we survey the world together. . . . [I]t serves to found public space, that is, to place certain matters before *us*." As instruments that work in the context of our practical activities by enabling us to explicitly present the world disclosed in those activities, signs have a *constitutive* part to play in the opening up of our distinctly human world. And by bringing this distinct world into relief we will be able to address two outstanding and interrelated concerns: that characterizing the working of words as based on a world-disclosing, non-semantic practical significance raises doubts about the extent to which language alone brings what is, as it is, into the open for the first time; and conversely, if this practical significance is expressible, one may justifiably wonder if this "non-semantic" significance is just *implicitly* semantic.

In an essay on Heidegger's philosophy of language that deals with Heidegger's claim that "it is language that first brings man about" (*PLT* 190), Taylor (2005, 435) captures the distinction between practical significance and linguistic expression that opens the door to our uniquely human world when he remarks:

> Pre-linguistic beings can react to the things which surround them. But language enables them to grasp something *as* what it is. . . . [Here the] basic idea seems to be that while a pre-linguistic animal can learn to respond to some object appropriately in the light of its purpose, only the being with language can identify the object as of a certain kind, can, as we might put it, attribute such and such a property to it. An animal, in other terms, can learn to give the right response to an object—fleeing a predator, say, or going after food—where "rightness" means "appropriate to its (non-linguistic) purposes." But language use involves another kind of rightness. Using the right word involves identifying an object as having the properties that justify using that word. We can't give an account of

this rightness in terms of extra-linguistic purpose. Rightness is here irreducible to success in some extra-linguistic task. (Taylor 2005, 435)

For Taylor, the shift from animal understanding to linguistic expression amounts to a transition from purposive activity to what he calls the "semantic dimension." As beings that dwell in the semantic dimension, we are able to describe or identify aspects of the world *as* the aspects that they are. But Taylor (2005, 438) tells us that language does more than describe independent objects; it also "enables us to relate to things in new ways, e.g. as loci of features, and to have new emotions, goals, and relationships, as well as being responsive to issues of strong value." As an example of the new phenomena language makes possible, Taylor (2005, 437) says "gregarious apes may have (what we call) a 'dominant male,' but only language beings can distinguish between leader, king, president, and the like." Similarly, "[L]inguistic beings are capable of new feelings that affectively reflect their richer sense of the world: not just anger, but indignation; not just desire, but love and admiration" (Taylor 2005, 437). On Taylor's reading of Heidegger, linguistic expression partakes in both finding and making: that is, linguistic expressions *disclose* specific aspects of the world while *constituting* certain others. As he puts it: "In the case of natural science, one might define the end as more like depiction, the representation of an independent object, but in, for example, clarifying emotions, language also helps constitute or complete them" (Taylor 2005, 448). Lastly, linguistic communication creates the semantic dimension that constitutes the human world. Language, on Taylor's account, "opens access to meanings," and he goes on to say: "[L]anguage is the condition of the human world being disclosed"; "it occurs in the space between humans"; and indeed "it helps to define the space that humans share" (Taylor 2005, 442). In short, language constructs a communal space that cannot be reduced to practical activity, and in this space humans are able to explicitly articulate or create the various dimensions that make up their meaningful world.

Treating language as the site of our distinctively human world as well as the means through which we are able to explicitly articulate or create the dimensions of that world allows us to clarify Heidegger's claim that "language, by *naming* beings for the first time, first brings beings to word and appearance" (*PLT* 71), and explain a sign's relation to the practical significance that enables our words to work. Again, our practical activities implicitly disclose dimensions of our world as the dimensions that they are, but the grammar governing our use of individual words creates what Heidegger calls a "clearing" (*PLT* 53) in which aspects of our world are brought into the open for the first time. The explicit disclosure or concrete determination of a specific dimension of our world is achieved through a given word—hence, "naming nominates beings *to* their being *from out of* their being" (*PLT* 71)—and returning to the language of unconcealment used at the beginning of the chapter we can characterize the move from the implicit disclosure of an entity in practical activity to its explicit expression in a name as the move from the unconcealment that creates the context by which entities can be manifest to the unconcealment involved in making what is manifest explicitly understood. Of course, our language doesn't simply map onto a perfectly intelligible world of practical activity; rather, as an integrated aspect of our practical activities, language is a tool that generates and first makes possible our fully formed sense of that world.[11] "Words and language," as Heidegger puts it, "are not just shells into which things are packed for spoken and written intercourse. In the word, in language, things first come to be and are" (*IM* 11). The transition from the world-disclosure achieved in our practical activities to its explication in language should now be seen in terms of *increasing intelligibility* through which the human world is finally opened up. As a condition of our ability to use language that is expressible but functions without being expressed, the significance of our practical activities is neither semantic nor non-semantic but *proto*-semantic. And for Heidegger, "language alone brings what is, as something that is, into the Open for the first time" (*PLT* 71), because it is through language that dimensions of our world are *explicitly* or *fully* revealed *as* the dimensions that they are.

4   HOW WORDS WORK AS WORKS OF ART

After showing how truth happens, how words work, and how words open up a world, we are now in a position to see how words work as works of art. In "The Origin," Heidegger calls the disclosive power of words a "poetic projection" and he distinguishes this projection from our regular linguistic practices. Our ordinary experience with words can be understood in the terms we used earlier: certain holistic contexts disclose aspects of the world as the aspects that they are, and through the collective repetition and recognition of specific signs in a given context those signs are able to indicate the aspects that that context discloses as well as hold open our distinctly human world. This common engagement with words is a function of the familiarity that the collective repetition and recognition of a given sign in similar contexts make possible, and these ordinary words work in the context of our lives by pointing out specific characteristics of the situation we find ourselves in, providing predicates for subjects that are part of our environment, enabling expression to take place in the course of communal activity, and in doing so found our meaningful world. As Heidegger asserts: "Actual language at any given moment is the happening of this saying [i.e., the unconcealedness of what is] in which a people's world historically arises for it" (*PLT* 71), and ordinary language "stills" this world by "carrying out the bearing and enduring of world and things in their presence" (*PLT* 205). In contrast, the poetic projection of a word does not depend on a prior disclosure of our world or the adherence to common use in similar contexts. Rather, these projections disclose dimensions of the world and make that disclosure explicit by providing us with a new term or breaking away from our regular use of a familiar word. "Poetic projection," Heidegger writes, "never takes its gift from the ordinary and traditional" and "it always contains the abundance of the unfamiliar and extraordinary, which means that it also contains strife with the familiar and ordinary" (*PLT* 73, 74). Though Heidegger has relatively little to say about exactly how the introduction of a new word or the creative use of an old one is capable of revealing aspects of the world that were otherwise concealed, his neologisms, like *Befindlichkeit*, along with his own unusual use of terms, such as "truth," serve as a hint: by introducing new words or transgressing the norms with which ordinary terms are used, Heidegger points to something we didn't see with our current vocabulary (*Befindlichkeit* for the fact that we always find ourselves situated in and disposed to the world in a particular way) or frees common words from their typical associations and thereby opens them up to being used to direct us toward phenomena (truth to indicate unconcealment) that are otherwise overlooked in their ordinary use. In the end, the introduction of a new word or the innovative use of old ones alters the grammar that enables our current stock of signs to direct us toward the world in a specific way, and with such a shift dimensions of the world that were once dissembled are now disclosed. On Heidegger's account, this projective saying embodies all art, is essentially poetry, and is a "saying which, in preparing the sayable, simultaneously brings the unsayable as such into a world" (*PLT* 70–71).

If, for Heidegger, all art is poetry, all poetry is the happening of truth, and the happening of truth makes aspects of our world explicit or creates the context through which those aspects are initially disclosed, then words work as works of art by explicitly presenting aspects of reality or by creating the context through which those aspects are disclosed in the first place. Like the Van Gogh painting that presents peasant shoes *as* the peasant shoes that they are in relation to other parts of the peasant women's world, Heidegger writes: "Signs of the kind we have described let what is ready-to-hand be encountered; more precisely, they let some context of it become accessible in such a way that our concernful dealings take on an orientation and hold it secure" (*BT* 79/110). Seamus Heaney's meditations on his rural upbringing in *Death of a Naturalist* and David Foster Wallace's detailed description of rehab clinics in *Infinite Jest* stand out as two recent examples where words are used in creative ways to explicitly present aspects of our world that are often overlooked. But like the Greek temple that "opens up a *world* and keeps it abidingly in force" (*PLT* 43), words *also* work as works of art by altering current contexts or creating what Heidegger would call a new "clearing" and Wittgenstein would call a new "language-game"[12] whereby aspects of reality that were completely concealed are thereby revealed. Einstein's theory of special relativity and Locke's *Two Treatises of Government* (and its subsequent appropriation by the American Founders) serve as striking examples in which a system of meaningful signs creates the context through which dimensions of our world are initially disclosed. It is hardly a stretch to say of the developments in atomic physics and liberal democracy that they "fit together and at the same time gather around [themselves] the unity of those paths and relations in which birth and death, disaster and blessing, victory and disgrace, endurance and decline acquire the shape and destiny for human being" (*PLT* 41). And updating Heidegger, we could easily say that "the all-governing expanse of this open relational context [of nuclear technology and representative government, among other things] is the world of [*our*] historical people" (*PLT* 41).

Finally, Heidegger's reference to a concrete group of people points to the fact that the introduction of new words or the innovative use of old ones is not enough for words to work as works of art. For "just as a work cannot be without being created but is essentially in need of creators, so what is created cannot itself come into being without those who preserve it" (*PLT* 64). And this means "in the work, truth is thrown toward the coming preservers, that is, toward an historical group of men" (*PLT* 73). In alternative terms, words work as works of art by making the ordinary extraordinary or by breaking with the ordinary such that the extraordinary appears, but a certain amount of familiarity with and recognition of the extraordinary in a specific historical context is nevertheless required for truth to happen in the work of art. As Hölderlin puts it: "The poets found that which endures."[13]

NOTES

1. Such as the "richness of the soil" or the "ripening grain" (*PLT* 33).
2. "The work makes public something other than itself; it manifests something other; it is allegory. In the work of art something other is brought together with the thing that is made. To bring together is, in Greek, *sumballein*. The work is a symbol" (*PLT* 19).
3. In "The Origin of the Work of Art" Heidegger writes: "Poetry is thought of here in so broad a sense and at the same time in such an intimate unity of being with language and word, that we must leave open whether art, in all its modes from architecture to poesy, exhausts the nature of poetry" (*PLT* 72). Yet *Being and Time* provides an answer to this open question: for if art is identical with the happening of truth, and truth happens in, say, scientific research, then the traditional art forms do not exhaust the nature of art. See Heidegger's discussion of Newton's Laws (*BT* 226–27/269–70).
4. Translation in Wrathall (2011, 2).
5. For a detailed account of the relationship between concealment and uncealment, see Wrathall (2011, 1–2, 17–18, 57–71).
6. See Hunter (1968) for an account of the various interpretations of Wittgenstein's use of "*Lebensform*."
7. Heidegger's account of the worldhood is found in §18 of *Being and Time* and his discussion of understanding occurs in §31–32.
8. In *PI* §23 Wittgenstein speaks of language itself as made up of a set of tools: "It is interesting to compare the diversity of the tools in language and of the ways they are used, the diversity of the kinds of word and sentence, with what logicians have said about the structure of language."

9. This analogy does not mean Heidegger endorses the Augustinan Picture of language, for as we have seen, Heidegger's account of assertions takes us beyond "words as names for objects" such that we can predicate something about an object. And as we shall see, for both Wittgenstein and Heidegger words express our emotions and understanding, and are responsible for opening up our distinctly human world.

10. For a defense of reading Wittgenstein's argument against private language in light of his discussion of the public nature of following a rule, see Malcolm (1995). For an argument against this view, see Baker and Hacker (1985).

11. For a detailed discussion of this point see Guignon (1983, 115–32).

12. Here I take "language-game" to mean "the whole, consisting of language and the activities into which it is woven" (*PI* §7).

13. For Heidegger's discussion of this line from Hölderlin's poem "Remembrance" see "Hölderlin and the Essence of Poetry" in *HR* 117–29. The poem itself can be found in Hölderlin (1998, 252).

15 Wittgenstein and Heidegger as Romantic Modernists

Anthony Rudd

It has become quite common to class Wittgenstein and Heidegger together as the two most important—or at least, two of the most important—philosophers of the twentieth century. And it has become increasingly recognized that there are significant similarities between their ideas, despite the great differences in their styles of writing and philosophizing. In this chapter I want to consider not so much particular philosophical issues on which Wittgenstein and Heidegger agreed but the wider cultural background to their work. I shall argue that both of them were both romantics and modernists. That one can be both a romantic and a modernist may seem less than obvious; I will explain this in section 2. But I want to start by discussing what I mean by romanticism.[1]

1 ROMANTICISM

"Romanticism" and "modernism" are, of course, both extremely vague and ambiguous terms, and I'm not supposing that either of them designates a simple essence. The strand of romanticism I shall focus on here is its concern with the re-enchantment of the world, in opposition to the "disenchantment" produced by the utilitarianism and the mechanistic science that characterized the Enlightenment. Since at least Descartes, we have found it compelling to think of the physical world as brute matter, intrinsically purposeless, valueless, mindless, acting in accordance with mechanistic laws. At the same time we have found it equally compelling to think of the human mind as radically free, responsive to norms of reason and morality, and capable of recognizing or, more radically, projecting, norms of reasoning and right conduct. But if we think of reality as divided between mind and matter so conceived, how are we to find a way of unifying or connecting them? Ever since Descartes, philosophy has oscillated unhappily between forms of dualism, which simply restate the problem; of idealism or antirealism, in which the mind fails to connect with a reality genuinely external to it at all; and of materialism, which reduce the mind itself to disenchanted matter and, by so doing, threaten to make nonsense of the very science to which materialism itself appeals for its account of reality.[2]

Romanticism figures in this story as perhaps the most strenuous effort we have made to find a way of thinking of ourselves as parts of nature, without denying or reducing the distinctive powers and qualities of the mind. But this can be done only if we can think of nature itself as not alien to the mind but as continuous with it. The project of re-enchantment attempts to understand the physical world not simply as a dead mechanism but as expressive of the same essential Spirit that comes to a more articulate self-consciousness in our own mental and cultural life. Romanticism gave rise to an expressivist perspective that has been usefully characterized by Charles Taylor.[3] On his account, expressivism is initially a view about the human subject, which denies the Cartesian idea of the detached self. As such it involves three ideas: firstly, that individual subjects—but also collectives, such as nations—have an inner nature that demands expression in the outer world; secondly, that this inner nature is not something initially fixed and determinate but comes to be what it is only in and through the process of coming to expression; and thirdly, that the inner therefore essentially requires a medium in which it can express itself in order fully to be what it is. So language, the body, and cultural institutions are not just contingently related to a (Cartesian) mind but are the essential, expressive realizations of the human mind or spirit, which cannot exist prior to them. However, expressivism is a view not only about human subjects but also about their relation to the wider reality, for language, the body, and culture are themselves parts of a nature that, if it is to be understood as continuous with them, must itself be understood expressively. For the romantics, as Taylor says, I cannot be

> satisfied with an image of myself as a mind confronting internal and external nature, but must think of myself as life in which nature speaks through thought and will . . . if my life is to be fully reflected in my expressive activity . . . this feeling cannot stop at the boundary of my self; it has to be open to the great current of life that flows across it. . . . Thus our self-feeling must be continuous with this larger current of life which flows through us and of which we are a part. (Taylor 1975, 24–25)

My claim is that Wittgenstein and Heidegger both inherited the romantic ideal of re-enchantment, and that to understand that is crucial to a proper understanding of their philosophies, and the deep commonality between their superficially very different ways of thinking. This claim may seem strange. That Wittgenstein was in some sense an heir of the romantics is a thought that has occurred to various scholars,[4] but it may well seem peculiar to someone coming to his work after reading, say, Schelling or Coleridge. The *Tractatus* is a highly technical work on the philosophy of logic, which concludes with what seems to be a positivistic moral; we should "say nothing except what can be said, i.e. propositions of natural science" (*TLP* 6.53) and eschew "metaphysics" as meaningless. As for his later work, Wittgenstein takes pains to emphasize that he has no general doctrines at all. Philosophy is simply the piecemeal activity of disentangling conceptual confusions, as and when they arise. "The work of the philosopher consists in marshalling recollections for a particular purpose" (*PI* §127). This modest and essentially negative program seems to have little connection with grandiose, romantic visions of re-enchantment; indeed, its dry cutting-down-to-size may appear highly unromantic.

It is also hard to see much of a concern for romantic re-enchantment in Heidegger's early work. In *Being and Time*, things in the world around us are apprehended mostly as "ready-to-hand"—as "equipment"—tools to be manipulated and used. When we stand back from that pragmatic engagement, we experience them as "present-at-hand"—bits of stuff taking up space. It is this latter stance that gets refined into scientific understanding—which itself then takes us back to more complex techniques of manipulation. "The wood is a forest of timber, the mountain a quarry of rock; the river is water-power, the wind is wind 'in the sails'" (*BT* 70/100). Heidegger does go on to mention a different way of experiencing the things around us, but only briefly and by negation. When we see things either as ready-to-hand or present-at-hand, "the Nature which 'stirs and strives,' which assails us and enthralls us as landscape, remains hidden" (*BT* 70/100). But that is about as much as we get in *Being and Time* to suggest a Wordsworthian as distinct from a practical or scientific attitude to nature. The concern that we should think of Nature as a place in which to dwell, rather than as a collection of manipulable resources, *is* clearly manifest in Heidegger's later works. However, his connections with romanticism have continued to be underplayed—in part because the once widespread tendency to read Sartre back into Heidegger's early work has been replaced by a tendency to read Foucault and Derrida back into his later work.

We might also worry that it is simply anachronistic to identify Wittgenstein and Heidegger as romantics. And with respect to Wittgenstein in particular, the very austerity of his work—of the *Tractatus* and the *Investigations* in their different ways, as of the house he designed in starkly unornamented form in Vienna—seems to place him in the tradition of modernism rather than with the more exuberant style of romanticism. Now, I think it is true that Wittgenstein was a modernist (as, in a rather different way, was Heidegger). But modernism was—in important ways that were hidden by the antiromantic polemics of many leading modernists—a revival of rather than a denial of romanticism. To see this, and its significance, will require a little detour.

2   MODERNISM

We need to start by distinguishing between the scientifically oriented modernism of—to take a paradigm case—the logical positivists, and the radically different modernism of writers such as Yeats, Strindberg, Kafka, Rilke, Eliot, Pound, and Lawrence—and, though more ambiguously or skeptically, Joyce, Woolf, and Mann. These modernists were precisely reacting against the modernity of the nineteenth-century mainstream—industrialization, science, technology, secularism, positivism, liberalism, rationalism, etc. In so doing they were looking for the recovery of a metaphysical or mythological sensibility, a rediscovery of the depth beneath what they perceived to be the superficiality of the optimistic utilitarian culture in which they lived. And in this, as Taylor notes, they were the legitimate heirs of the great romantics. In Taylor's words:

> The modernists found themselves in opposition to their world for reasons which were continuous with those of the Romantics. The world seen just as mechanism, as a field for instrumental reason, seemed to the latter shallow and debased. By the twentieth century the encroachments of instrumental reason were incomparably greater, and we find the modernist writers and artists in protest against a world dominated by technology, standardization, the decay of community, mass society and vulgarization. (Taylor 1989, 456)[5]

This continuity of protest can be concealed by the distrust or repudiation of romanticism that was frequently expressed by the modernists. As Taylor goes on to note:

> For those who saw this whole [late-Victorian] world as spiritually hollow and flat, Romanticism could seem as integral to what they rejected as instrumentalism was. It merely offered trivialized, ersatz or inauthentic meanings to compensate for a meaningless world. . . . And so the modernists as heirs to the Romantics turned against what they saw as Romanticism. (Taylor 1989, 458)

So, even if they didn't see this clearly themselves, the modernists' argument really wasn't with romanticism as such but with its shallow inheritors. The modernists had to break the hold of certain expectations and conventions as to what a properly poetic manner was—hence the turn away from the hazy and indefinite to an art of precision, hardness, and clarity, and from the conventional prettiness of a cheaply enchanted nature to urban grittiness. As one important theorist of early modernism, T. E. Hulme, put it, poetry should bring us to see things as they are: "It always endeavours to arrest you, and to make you continuously see a physical thing, to prevent you gliding through an abstract process" (in Taylor 1989, 460). But this is really not so far from Shelley's statement that poetry "purges from our inward sight the film of familiarity which obscures the wonder of our being. It creates anew the Universe, after it has been annihilated in our minds by the recurrence of impressions blunted by reiteration" (in Abrams 1971, 384). Hulme's language is drier, more cautious. But the essential idea—that poetry is the attempt to make us really see things, to attend freshly and fully to what abstraction and familiarity have blinded us to—is the same.

However, despite this common concern with a visionary, epiphanic art that will make us see the world afresh, there are significant differences between the characteristic moods of romanticism and of modernism. Modernism tends toward

a) a skepticism about how or whether the metaphysical vision can be expressed; a loss of the romantic's faith in language to convey what needs to be conveyed. (Hofmannsthal's [1995] *The Lord Chandos Letter* is a classic statement of this theme.) Hence modernism tends toward a caution, a constantly self-questioning, even self-undermining, irony about its own moments of vision or epiphany; they are presented in a fragmentary, elusive way.

b) a skepticism about finding profound moral sources in what is metaphysically deepest. In a post-Schopenhauerian, post-Darwinian, post-Nietzschean world, it is still possible to see nature as the romantics had, as "a great reservoir of force, that we need to regain contact with" (Taylor 1989, 445). But there is a crucial difference, for

It is no longer seen as a domain of spirit, of goodness; quite the contrary. But to be cut off from it is to fall into desiccation, emptiness, dullness, a narrow and shriveled life. . . . But at the same time, we dare not plunge too deeply, too precipitously, too unguardedly into it, because it is wild, formless, unreason itself. (Taylor 1989, 445)

Important though these differences were, they can be overstated. The romantics were familiar with states of dejection, in which their visionary moments seemed delusive and nature blank or hostile (e.g., Coleridge, "Dejection: An Ode"). Irony was a pervasive theme of the early romantics at Jena in the 1790s (especially Friedrich Schlegel). And the idea of embracing the instinctive forces of nature against ethics was a commonplace of the Byronic strand of romanticism. On the other hand, there are epiphanies of being in modernism, invocations of a current of joy running through nature in which it is recognized not as mere amoral force but as something to which we can give a wholehearted and ethical response (for example, moments in Eliot's *Four Quartets*, or Pound's *Pisan Cantos*).

3 ROMANTIC MODERNISM IN WITTGENSTEIN AND HEIDEGGER

Wittgenstein and Heidegger can, I think, be best understood as providing the major philosophical articulations of this neo-romantic modernism. In so doing they set themselves against what one can call scientistic modernism. This latter form of modernism is simply the ideology of modernity—scientific rationalism, utilitarianism, secularism; in general the idea of a rationalized society, whether capitalist or socialist. Heidegger and Wittgenstein, as much as Rilke or Eliot, saw the dominance of that ideology as leaving the contemporary world spiritually bereft. In a draft preface for the *Philosophical Remarks* Wittgenstein notes the "disappearance of the arts," the "disappearance of a culture," and comments that "I have no sympathy for the current of European civilization, and do not understand its goals if it has any" (*CV* 6). These perceptions no doubt have much to do with Wittgenstein's doubts as to whether "in the darkness of this time" (*PI* p. 4) his work would have any effect, or would simply be assimilated into the *milieu* that he was writing against. There is mourning, but also a note of hope in a haunting remark from 1930: "The earlier culture will become a heap of rubble and finally a heap of ashes, but spirits will hover over the ashes" (*CV* 3). Similar views were frequently expressed by Heidegger:

> Devastation is more unearthly than destruction. Destruction only sweeps aside all that has grown up or been built up so far; but devastation blocks all future growth. The devastation of the earth can easily go hand in hand with a guaranteed supreme living standard for man and just as easily with the organized establishment of a uniform state of happiness for all men. Devastation is the high-velocity expulsion of Mnemosyne. (*WCT* 29–30)

Both philosophers connect this darkness and devastation with scientism and the mind-set characteristic of modern technology. Neither is calling for the abandonment of technology. But both are deeply troubled by the mentality that separates a detached, calculative subject from objects that are seen merely as "standing-reserve" (*QT* 20), stuff to be manipulated, whose only meaning or value is that which we have chosen to confer on it. This mind-set Heidegger calls "Enframing" (*Ge-stell*). It is primarily manifested in "Modern science's way of representing," which "pursues and entraps nature as a calculable coherence of forces" (*QT* 21). It is important to note that for Heidegger, this isn't simply a falsification of nature but also a kind of "revealing" of it. The scientifically calculable aspects of nature are perfectly real—the natural sciences do put us into contact with reality. But there are other aspects of reality that Enframing blinds us to, or has us redefine as "merely subjective"—in particular the aesthetic or religious perception of nature as expressive.

Wittgenstein's perspective was similar. For him, what is lost when scientific ways of thinking crowd out all others is *wonder*. In various places, Wittgenstein speaks of responding with wonder, both to particular phenomena (e.g., *PO* 129) and to the very existence of anything at all (*TLP* 6.44; *PO* 41).[6] And he explicitly contrasts this with what he sees as the scientific approach: "Man has to awaken to wonder. . . . Science is a way of sending him to sleep again" (*CV* 5). Obviously, Wittgenstein does not wish to abandon science, or even to oppose specific scientific statements,

234 of Anthony Rudd

but rather to set himself against the influence of a certain way of thinking that he saw as deriving from the sciences, and as pervading contemporary culture. In his *Lectures on Aesthetics,* Wittgenstein remarked, "I am in a sense making propaganda for one style of thinking as opposed to another. I am honestly disgusted with the other" (*LC* 28). Just before that remark, he had identified "the other" as "a kind of idol-worship, the idol being Science and the Scientist." This vehemence comes, I think, from the perception that the worship of science makes us distrust the expressive character of our normal experience. Scientism and the obsession with theory need to be combated, since they stand in the way of our experiencing phenomena as expressive.

4   HEIDEGGER: ROMANTICISM AND VOLUNTARISM

In both Heidegger and Wittgenstein romanticism had to struggle against certain countervailing tendencies. However, the often troubled and inhibited way in which they took up the insights of their romantic precursors is, as I noted earlier, very characteristic of the high modernist generation to which they belonged. In Heidegger's case the main inhibiting factor was what we can call a voluntaristic or "Promethean" tendency.[7] We have noted earlier that there seems to be very little by way of romantic re-enchantment in *Being and Time,* but critics—and admirers—did find in it a radical decisionism. That is, they saw its account of authenticity as affirming an individualism that disdains the anonymous "They" (*das Man*) and with proud resolution chooses its own values and way of being. More careful readers saw that *Being and Time* put great emphasis on community and history; the authentic Dasein chooses only to take on the possibilities of being as part of a historically grounded community that the current historical moment has made available.[8] So, far from excessive individualism, *Being and Time* could be accused of promoting a kind of collectivism that, in the retrospective light of Heidegger's Nazi involvements, could seem distinctly sinister. But this does not undermine the claims about Heidegger's voluntarism, for Promethean voluntarism can take a collectivist as well as an individualist form, and a distinctively voluntaristic mood or tone is certainly present in Heidegger's writings of the early to mid-1930s. During his Nazi period, the focus is on the great individual whose acts shape and carry forward the destiny of the community. Only after Heidegger's partial disillusionment with the Nazis in the mid-1930s does the concern with re-enchantment really come to the fore. And with this comes a lessening of the emphasis on will and, in its place, a concern with more passive states—openness, letting be (*Gelassenheit*).

This shift can be traced in an important transitional text, "The Origin of the Work of Art," published in 1936. (In my account of this I am largely following Julian Young's [2001, chap. 1] very helpful commentary.) There

Heidegger is concerned with works of art in a very broad sense—one might call them, following Hubert Dreyfus (1993, 298), "cultural paradigms." An artwork in this sense Heidegger defines as what "opens up a world" (*PLT* 44). One of his central examples is a Greek temple, which

> gathers around itself the unity of those paths and relations in which birth and death, disaster and blessing, victory and disgrace, endurance and decline acquire the shape of destiny for human being. The all-governing expanse of this open relational context is the world of this historical people. (*PLT* 41)

Heidegger is using "world" here much as he had used it in *Being and Time*—it is the network of meanings and significances in which we live our lives; the reality around us, apprehended in terms of its relevance to the projects that we (as members of a particular historical culture) pursue and the values that determine the success or failure of those projects. An artwork or cultural paradigm (such as the temple, or a medieval cathedral, but also a performance—for example, that of a Greek tragedy) serves to "open up" the world, to focus or articulate it. But Heidegger can be taken as saying something more—that the artwork "founds" or "creates" a world. This is what Young calls the "Promethean" idea of the will of the genius whose creation brings into being a world of meaning around itself. And this, as Young goes on to note, has serious political implications: "[I]t has led to 'The Origin' being read as a thinly disguised plea for the overcoming of European nihilism through the coming into being of a brave new world to be established by the Hitler-created artwork, by, in a word, (a refined version of) the Nuremburg rally" (Young 2001, 29).

So we have in "The Origin" the analysis of "world" from *Being and Time*, which is essentially "our" world, a humanized environment. And we have at least hints or overtones of the voluntaristic or Promethean view that the world, and the values and meanings it contains, is something that is created by the titanic will of a founder. So far, this seems to suggest precisely what the romantics were reacting against—the idea of reality as no more than raw material for a heroically detached will to impose its designs on. I do agree with Young, though, that "The Origin" also shows Heidegger starting, under (significantly) the influence of Hölderlin, to move away from Prometheanism toward an attitude of openness and receptivity.

This move is marked by his introduction, in addition to "world," of the concept of "earth." We come to know aspects of reality by taking them up into our networks of meaning. So we experience things as they show up for us in the world of science, or of business, or of pleasure seeking, or of revolutionary struggle. But this implies that there is a reality, some aspects of which show up to us in these ways, but which is not exhausted by them. To reveal some aspects of reality is precisely to conceal others, since we, as finite beings, cannot experience all aspects of reality at once. This dark, necessarily ungraspable background to all our articulations of world is what Heidegger means by "earth":

> [W]e know that belonging to our "truth," in the sense of "world," is an indefinitely large totality of other possible "truths," horizons of disclosure . . . that are equally disclosive of Being (reality) itself, yet blocked by our disclosure and, in fact, utterly unintelligible to us. It is this region of ineffability, this, as it were, epistemological "depth" to Being, which Heidegger calls "earth." (Young 2001, 40)

Young goes on to point out that "Heidegger's world-earth duality looks very like Nietzsche's duality between the Apollonian . . . and the Dionysian," and that this, given Heidegger's intense study of Nietzsche, was "no accident" (Young 2001, 40). Nietzsche's duality was itself derived from Schopenhauer's distinction between the world as Representation and as Will; and Schopenhauer's distinction was in turn derived from Kant's duality of phenomena and things in themselves. One shouldn't, of course, simply equate these distinctions with one another, but they all present the same basic structure—reality as we domesticate it, make sense of it to ourselves, and reality in itself. It should be noted that none of these dualities needs to be construed as an ontological dualism, a distinction between different kinds of stuff, or realms of being; but they should rather be seen as distinguishing between different ways of thinking about the same reality.[9]

But what makes Heidegger's position romantic and not just (in a broad sense) Kantian? Firstly, his claim that the "in-itself" is not just an intellectually inferred epistemological posit—rather, we can become *aware* of "earth"; not, of course, as something we can conceptualize and articulate, but precisely as the dark background to all of our conceptualizing and articulating. Secondly, this is not simply an operation of our minds; rather, we need to be receptive to earth's own manifestation to us. For Heidegger, as for the romantics, reality is expressive; earth expresses itself through world as the necessary background to it. But for us to experience it so doing, we need to turn off the busy theorizing activity of the scientific intellect. This does not mean that the process of apprehending earth is a merely passive one; on the contrary, Heidegger argues that a "cultural" paradigm like the Greek temple (in later works he mentions much humbler or more inconspicuous "paradigms," such as an earthenware jug, or a country bridge (see *PLT* 166ff. and 151ff.)) can make not only world but also the underlying earth properly manifest to us. "In setting up a world, the work sets forth the earth . . . the work moves the earth itself into the Open of a world and keeps it there. *The work lets the earth be an earth*" (*PLT* 46). But for the earth to be manifest to us is precisely for it to manifest itself as the excess, as what we cannot grasp. "The earth appears openly cleared as itself only when it is perceived and preserved as that which is by nature undisclosable, that which shrinks from every disclosure and constantly keeps itself closed up" (*PLT* 47).

But there is a third aspect of Heidegger's thought that needs to be recognized if we are to properly understand his romanticism. And this is the point that to experience earth through world is to be startled into amazement at the sheer existence of anything at all (see *BW* 110 and *IM* 1). To experience nature as *physis*—"emerging self-manifestation" (*IM* 109)—rather than dead mechanism, is to experience reality as calling for gratitude and awe; to experience it as a proper place, a context, for human dwelling. This is, I believe, what Heidegger ultimately meant by talking of "Being." (Although, confusingly, in some contexts *Sein* refers, roughly speaking, to "world"—or rather to the possibility of world as the transcendental horizon for any understanding—while elsewhere it refers to what Heidegger also calls "earth," *physis*, etc.—what is ultimately there beneath all our frameworks of understanding.[10]) That we can experience reality as exceeding all our conceptual frameworks is not simply one more fact to be dispassionately noted, for to experience things, not just as ready-to-hand, or present-at-hand, but as manifesting Being to us, is to experience them with awe and wonder—as in their moments of positive vision Hölderlin and Wordsworth did; and as, although more elusively and fleetingly, Eliot, Rilke, and Pound did also. It is, for Heidegger, the key to overcoming modern nihilism and thus the key to living well; to experience reality this way is to experience it as re-enchanted. To help prevent such a mode of experience falling into oblivion was, I believe, the ultimate aim of Heidegger's later writings—those he produced after, educated by Hölderlin, he had abandoned his flirtation with Promethean voluntarism.

5   WITTGENSTEIN'S ROMANTIC EXPRESSIVISM

While Heidegger's rejection of scientistic modernism seems to have been complete and wholehearted, Wittgenstein was in some ways more conflicted. (On the other hand, he seems to have had little if any attraction to the voluntarism that so tempted Heidegger.) His education was largely in science and engineering, and he had a real aptitude for and interest in mechanical problems, and also in the mathematical and logical questions that first drew him to philosophy. But there is also reason to think that he underwent the education he did largely to please his parents (see Monk 1990, 11, 14–15, 26, 27), and that his own inclinations were at least as much musical and artistic. Of course, one can be an engineer and a musician—but in Wittgenstein the distinction of these interests does seem to have symbolized a division in his intellectual sensibility, and indeed his personality as a whole.

This dividedness seems evident on the face of it in the *Tractatus*, which expresses that division in its very form; it is a collection of dense, technical remarks on the philosophy of logic, which ends with a few pages of enigmatic aphorisms about God, the mystical, death, and the sense of life. I think there is a coherence to the book, a continuity of theme between the "logical" and the "mystical" sections, but there is also a deep tension there, between the book's neo-romantic expressivism, and its essentially positivistic philosophy of language, according to which propositions are simply pictures of possible states of affairs. The most immediate source for the expressivism of the *Tractatus* is Schopenhauer, from whom Wittgenstein takes the distinction between the world as Will and as Representation. "I can also speak of a will that is common to the whole world. But this will is in a higher sense my will. As my representation is the world, in the same way my will is the world-will" (*NB* 85). However, for Wittgenstein, representation is an essentially linguistic matter; the world as representation becomes the world as we apprehend it in language.[11] Given his view of language as simply a medium for the representation of possible, contingent facts, this means that the world for us is the world experienced as a concatenation of discrete states of affairs. But the deeper noumenal reality may still express itself to us, make itself manifest, in and through the agglomeration of contingent facts that are all that literally meaningful language can describe.[12] As G. E. M. Anscombe says, "There is a strong impression made by the end of the *Tractatus*, as if Wittgenstein saw the world looking at him with a face . . . he speaks of the world 'waxing or waning as a whole,' i.e. in terms of my analogy, as having more or less expression, or a good or evil expression" (Anscombe 1959, 172).

The world is re-enchanted not by any of the facts that go to make it up being changed but by their all being seen together as forming a pattern through which their sense becomes manifest—though that sense is not something that can be separately stated:

> The facts all contribute only to setting the problem, not to its solution.
>   It is not *how* things are in the world that is mystical, but *that* it exists.
>   To view the world sub specie aeterni is to view it as a whole—a limited whole.
>   Feeling the world as a limited whole—it is this that is mystical. (*TLP* 6.4321–6.45)

But to see things in this way involves taking up a certain stance to them; it requires a kind of conversion, from simply seeing the things around one in terms of their usefulness to one's purposes, to seeing the world as a whole "sub specie aeterni."

> If the good or bad exercise of the will does alter the world, it can only alter the limits of the world, not the facts—not what can be expressed by means of language.
>   In short the effect must be that it becomes an altogether different world. It must, so to speak, wax and wane as a whole.
>   The world of the happy man is a different one from that of the unhappy man. (*TLP* 6.43)

But the *Tractatus'* philosophy of language—albeit self-destructively—rules out the use of language to state anything other than contingencies, tautologies, or contradictions, thus consigning the whole field of ethics, aesthetics, and religion (as well as logic, and, finally, itself) to the level of the inexpressible.[13] The spirit, it is hoped, will be manifest; but what it is to be manifested in is a severely positivistic world of mere facts. It is not entirely surprising then that the book was largely taken up at first as a sort of positivist manifesto, with a few irrelevant expressions of personal eccentricity tacked on to the end. The expressive vision in the *Tractatus* is almost stifled by the very medium of its expression. This has much to do with Wittgenstein's pessimism about the possibility of the spirit finding any genuine expression in contemporary culture, the general modernist tendency to ironize or retreat from the full-blown epiphanic art of romanticism, and Wittgenstein's own ascetic horror of making explicit what should be left implicit.[14] But it also probably derives in some part from the continuing influence of the positivistic/scientistic sensibility on Wittgenstein, his reluctance to depart too far from it.

There has been much discussion of the extent to which Wittgenstein's later work should be seen as continuous or as discontinuous with his earlier philosophy. There certainly are substantial differences—in particular, the picture theory is (happily) abandoned for a much richer and more flexible account of language and meaning. But Wittgenstein's concern with a kind of understanding that involves seeing connections between phenomena in such a way as to allow the underlying spirit expressed in those phenomena to become manifest remains constant. In his *Lectures on Aesthetics*, Wittgenstein emphasizes the importance of the search for this kind of understanding in our thinking about art. He dismisses with scorn the idea that there could be such a thing as a science of aesthetics—by which he seems to mean not a branch of philosophy but the first-order activity of art criticism: "You might think of Aesthetics as a science telling us what's beautiful—almost too ridiculous for words. I suppose it ought to include also what sort of coffee tastes well" (*LC* 11). What the good critic can do is try to get us to see a work of art in the right way, by pointing out connections and parallels, emphasizing some elements, showing how one figure in a painting balances another, how one theme is a variation on a melody heard earlier in the composition, and so on.

Wittgenstein mentions a couple of examples from his own experience. "I had an experience with the 18th century poet Klopstock. I found that the way to read him was to stress his metre abnormally. . . . I had read this kind of stuff [before] and had been moderately bored, but when I read it in this particular way, intensely, I smiled, said: 'This is grand,' etc." (*LC* 4). Later he mentions that "[y]ou can sometimes find the similarity between the style of a musician and the style of a poet who lived at the same time, or a painter. Take Brahms and Keller. I often found that certain themes of Brahms were extremely Kellerian" (*LC* 32n). This sort of suggestion may or may not be helpful to someone who knows the work of both Brahms and Keller; if accepted, it may deepen the understanding and appreciation of both. As a result of the comparison, one is brought to see a new dimension in already familiar works. This is, at any rate, one distinctive kind of understanding that the art critic or the cultural historian is aiming at. One can, I think, justly call it expressive; the aim is to point to a way of looking, reading, listening that enables one to appreciate the spirit of the work in question. Presumably Wittgenstein understood Klopstock's poetry in some sense before he hit on the right way to stress the meter, but it made no impression on him; he found it expressively dead. What he discovered was a way to read the poems that brought them to life. Similarly, not only may the Brahms-Keller comparison shed light on the artists concerned, but also a series of comparisons of that sort can bring out the spirit of a whole culture to which they belonged. As Wittgenstein noted, it would have had a quite different kind of interest if he had said that certain themes of Brahms seemed to him Shakespearean.

This expressive method is one that Wittgenstein follows in his own philosophical works, as he assembles reminders of how we use certain concepts, the different circumstances in which we do so, the similarities and the differences between the various cases. In the *Investigations*, he writes:

> A main source of our failure to understand is that we don't have *an overview* of the use of our words.—Our grammar is deficient in surveyability. A surveyable representation produces precisely that kind of understanding which consists in "seeing connections." . . .
>
> The concept of a surveyable representation is of fundamental significance for us. It characterizes the way we represent things, how we look at matters. (Is this a "Weltanschauung"?) (*PI* §122)

In this section, Wittgenstein outlines a form of understanding that is quite different from that which looks for (causal) explanations. One comes to an understanding of the phenomena in question by setting them out or surveying them in such a way as to "see the connections" between them. This is what he means when he speaks of gaining an "overview" (*Übersicht*) or a "surveyable representation" (*übersichtliche Darstellung*). This method is sometimes seen as implying a kind of anti-essentialism; instead of looking for the essence supposedly corresponding to a concept like "game," we should simply try to gain an overview of our usage of the word (see *PI* §65ff.). We need to be careful here, though. Wittgenstein explicitly rejects nominalism (*PI* §383), and when he says, "Essence is expressed by grammar" (*PI* §371), this is not intended in a reductive or dismissive sense. To understand the "grammar" of a word is to see a coherent pattern in its usage, not just, as in (a possibly straw man) nominalism, unrelated brute facts about the condition under which a noise is uttered. In discovering the crisscrossing pattern of similarities and differences in the use of terms, we may become aware, precisely, of what it is that connects them (their essence) but that would elude any attempt to state in a definition. This is why "Grammar [which expresses essence] tells us what kind of object anything is" (*PI* §373). Wittgenstein adds the example "theology as grammar" (*PI* §373). We are unlikely to be able to pin down the concept of God in a neat definition, but the assumption here is that the use of the word is not arbitrary or random. There is a coherent pattern to it, which can be found, and it is in finding it that we may come to understand what the word "God" means. To gain this sort of understanding, however, requires a sort of artistic tact, a sensitivity to which distinctions and which connections to emphasize.

The substantive issue in Wittgenstein's later work in which his romantic expressivism most clearly shows up is his account of, and attempt to dissolve, the traditional problems of mind and body and of our knowledge of other minds. These problems are a central legacy of the Cartesian attempt to ground science in a stance of pure objectivity. The human body, like any other part of the physical world, is to be understood in quantitative, mechanistic terms. Yet in order to do science at all, the scientist is committed to thinking of him- or herself as a free, detached, rational intelligence, able to transcend immediate surroundings and context. The problem of how my subjective sense of myself as a rational knower can be combined with my objective understanding of myself as a complex, physically determined, physiological mechanism also leads into the question of how, by observing someone else's body, I can infer that there is a mind, a subjective, self-conscious stream of experience, associated with that body. The traditional answer has been that this is achieved by a rational inference from the perceived behavior of that body to a hidden (mental) cause. Wittgenstein is sharply critical of this line of argument, and as a result, he has sometimes been suspected of an at least quasi-behaviorist stance.[15] If all the evidence I actually have for your state of mind is your observed bodily behavior, why suppose there is anything more going on than simply bodily behavior? Is the supposition even intelligible?

Wittgenstein's response to this is to argue that we are able to understand someone's state of mind by observing her bodily behavior, not by making an inference (consciously or otherwise) but simply because we naturally experience the behavior as expressive of inner states. We can see sadness, amusement, shock, curiosity, in the blink of someone's eyes, in the way she walks, her tone of voice. No inference goes on; we experience the human body not as a lump of matter, a complex machine, but as a medium of expression; as that in which the mental life of a person becomes manifest. There may indeed be problems encountered in everyday life about knowing what is going on in another person's mind. But we do not usually find ourselves wondering if anything at all is going on. We simply don't experience other human bodies in the same way that we experience inanimate things, and the difference is not adequately explained by a mere hypothesis that in the human case there is a hidden mental cause of the behavior:

But can't I imagine that people around me are automata, lack consciousness, even though they behave in the same way as usual? . . . But just try
to hang on to this idea in the midst of your ordinary intercourse with
others—in the street, say! Say to yourself, for example: "The children
over there are mere automata; all their liveliness is mere automatism."
And you will either find these words becoming quite empty; or you will
produce in yourself some kind of uncanny feeling, or something of the
sort. (*PI* §420)

Wittgenstein's criticisms of Cartesian appeals to hidden mental states can
easily seem to involve a denial of the "inner"—hence the tendency at one
time to assimilate his views to behaviorism, and the tendency even now for
some reductive materialist thinkers, such as Dennett, to suppose that they
are proceeding in the spirit of Wittgenstein (see Dennett 1993, 462–63). But
Wittgenstein's concern to reject the appeal to behind-the-scenes entities had
the radically different intention of bringing mind back into behavior, rather
than of banishing it in favor of behavior. His was the thoroughly romantic
aim of seeking the inner in the outer; of seeking to bring the mind back into
the world not by "physicalizing" the mind but by mentalizing the body. Or
more correctly, by reminding us just how mentalistic our understanding of
the body already is: "Consciousness in another's face. Look into someone
else's face, and see the consciousness in it, and a particular *shade* of consciousness. You see on it, in it, joy, indifference, interest, torpor and so on.
The light in other people's faces" (*Z* §220). So, like Heidegger, Wittgenstein
is concerned to deconstruct the assumptions of scientistically inspired philosophy in order to return us to the expressive quality of the world as we
do, or can, experience it.

6   CONCLUSION

There is, of course, much more that could be said to elucidate the claim that
Wittgenstein and Heidegger are romantic modernists. But I hope the foregoing sketch has at least shown in outline what the claim means and why it
might be thought plausible. Both philosophers show a deep hostility both
to scientism and to the Cartesian attempt to rescue at least something from
an otherwise scientistic worldview by isolating a pure immaterial self. Both
agree that human subjectivity cannot be accounted for in reductive terms,
but both also agree that the self cannot be separated from the wider world.
This is why they both look for a re-enchantment of the world as a whole. In
this they are romantics. What gives their romanticism its peculiarly modernist inflection is, in part, their refusal of metaphysics. Both repudiate the idea
that in order to re-enchant the world we need to provide a grand metaphysical picture of reality. (In this they differ strikingly from, for instance, Whitehead, who certainly shares their hostility to both reductive scientism and

dualism, but who attempts to replace them with an alternative metaphysical system of his own.[16]) The fragmentary, aphoristic nature of Wittgenstein's later work, its focus on particular problems, and the suggestive, exploratory character especially of Heidegger's later essays express the tentative, self-questioning character of the modernist sensibility, and so do their struggles with their own countervailing tendencies that I have reviewed in this chapter. But, for all that, the drive to re-enchantment, the radical critique of what are still some of our culture's most deeply entrenched assumptions, remains fundamental to the work of both Wittgenstein and Heidegger. And it is this shared sensibility, rather than agreement on particular philosophical doctrines or methods, that constitutes the connection between the two philosophers at its deepest level.

NOTES

1. I won't, in the space available, be able to give more than what I hope will be a suggestive and/or provocative overview of a huge field. So I will be simply asserting many exegetical claims that are, I am aware, highly controversial. It seemed better to do this boldly rather than attempt to support them in ways that would necessarily be inadequate because it simply isn't possible to go into the necessary detail here. Much of the detailed argument and exegesis in support of the views I develop here can be found in Rudd (2003).
2. On this last point see Putnam (1983; 1990, chap. 1–4) and Nagel (1997, chap. 5 and 7).
3. See Taylor (1975, 11–29).
4. The work of Stanley Cavell has been influential in suggesting such connections. See, for example, Cavell (1979, 1988). See also Lurie (1992) and Eldridge (1997).
5. For Taylor's extremely insightful account of Romanticism, Modernism, and the transition between them, see Taylor (1989, chap. 21–24).
6. Compare Heidegger on the question, "Why is there something at all, rather than nothing?" in *BW* 110 and *IM* 1.
7. I take this term from Julian Young; see Young (2001, 29–31).
8. See Vogel (1994, chap. 2 and 3) for good accounts of these two interpretations.
9. The locus classicus for the "two aspects" rather than the "two worlds" interpretation of Kant is Allison (2004).
10. On this distinction (which he marks by distinguishing "being" from "Being") see Young (2002, chap. 1).
11. For a more detailed presentation and defense of this Schopenhauerian reading of the *Tractatus* see Rudd (2004).
12. The distinction between what can be said and what can only be shown or "made manifest" is central to Wittgenstein's account of logic also. The truths of logic cannot be stated as if they were simply further facts: rather they make themselves manifest in the structure of the language that we use to state the facts.
13. In taking the *Tractatus* to claim that ethics, religion, logic, and the "picture theory" of language all express or point to truths that cannot be meaningfully stated, I am obviously rejecting the so-called "resolute" readings of the *Tractatus*, inspired by James Conant and Cora Diamond, which deny that it is trying to show something positive that cannot literally be said. See the essays

in part 2 of Crary and Read (2000) for some examples of such readings. For effective criticism, see Hacker (2000) and Hutto (2003, 90–98).

14. "[T]he spirit of a book has to be evident in the book itself and cannot be described. . . . It is a great temptation to try to make the spirit explicit" (*CV* 6, 7).

15. This reading is not as common as it once was, but for a recent instance see Forster (2004, 205–6, 219).

16. The opening chapters of Whitehead ([1925] 2011) offer his most forceful critique of scientistic disenchantment; the later chapters and, in greatest detail, Whitehead ([1929] 1978) set out his alternative metaphysical scheme.

16 Dwelling on Rough Ground
Heidegger, Wittgenstein, Architecture

David R. Cerbone

1 LE CORBUSIER: THE HOUSE-MACHINE

First published in 1923, Le Corbusier's *Toward a New Architecture* offers a breathtaking depiction of contemporary life. As Le Corbusier understands it, modern life has seen the largely beneficial spread of industrialization and with it a spread of rational planning and ordering. The modern age is marked by the triumph of *engineering*: the great structures and inventions of the day—large-scale factories, steamships, airplanes, motorcars, steel girders, and reinforced concrete—are the products of the new techno-scientific disciplines informed by calculation, rigor, and order. Along with these wondrous inventions, such feats of engineering provide new standards and conceptions of aesthetic beauty, an aesthetics of clean lines, orderly arrangements, and uncompromising efficiency. The new engineering aesthetic builds upon, and promotes further, an ideal of *standardization* that emerged with the rise of industrial, factory-based assemblage. The "industrial evolution" of building will see "the replacing of natural materials by artificial ones, of heterogeneous and doubtful materials by homogeneous and artificial ones (tried and proved in the laboratory) and by products of fixed composition" (Le Corbusier 1970, 214). The older, more "natural" materials are "doubtful" because they are "infinitely variable," admitting of unpredictable variety with unforeseeable consequences: for example, "in the old-world timber beam there may be lurking some treacherous knot" (Le Corbusier 1970, 214) that evades calculation and control. The new, artificial materials, because they have been fabricated from start to finish, are far more amenable to calculation, thereby allowing design and construction to be orderly and replicable from site to site, building to building.

Lighter, thinner, more readily manipulable, the new building materials and techniques are, by the time of *Toward a New Architecture*, firmly established in industrial design and construction: factories, bridges, storage silos, power plants, and the newly emerging means of transportation (automobiles and airplanes) proudly display their origins in this new spirit of engineering. Lagging behind, however, is the *house*, whose design and construction have yet to embrace the new technology and aesthetic. "All these objects of modern life create, in the long run, a modern state of mind," but this newly emerging "modern mind" recoils at the sight of its outmoded dwellings: "Bewilderment seizes us, then, if we bring our eyes to bear on the old and rotting buildings that form our snail-shell, our habitation, which crush us in our daily contact with them—putrid and useless and unproductive" (Le Corbusier 1970, 236–37). There is thus a disconnect—"no real link"—"between our daily activities at the factory, the office or the bank, which are healthy and useful and productive," and what the modern worker finds at home (Le Corbusier 1970, 256–57). Housing is "demoralizing" in that it lacks those admirable traits that the worker sees in the workplace, and reads and hears about in various media. Housing lags behind the surging industries of the day. A new kind of work, with its new scruples and new ideals, requires a new kind of *dwelling*, built in accord with the same scruples and ideals. Just "as so many cannons, airplanes, lorries and wagons had been made in factories, someone asked the question: 'Why not make houses?' There you have a state of mind really belonging to our epoch" (Le Corbusier 1970, 216). These homes will embody the same modern, clean aesthetic found in the modern machine and factory, power plant and bridge. It is imperative that industry "occupy itself with building and establish the elements of the house on a mass-production basis" (Le Corbusier 1970, 210). Doing so will "create the mass-production spirit. The spirit of constructing mass-production houses. The spirit of living in mass-production houses. The spirit of conceiving mass-production houses" (Le Corbusier 1970, 210). This new spirit will culminate in the realization of what Le Corbusier dubs the "House-Machine," the mass-produced antidote to the demoralization inherent in the "snail-shells" of old:

> If we eliminate from our hearts and minds all dead concepts in regard to the houses and look at the question from a critical and objective point of view, we shall arrive at the "House-Machine," the mass-production house, healthy (and morally so too) and beautiful in the same way that the working tools and instruments which accompany our existence are beautiful. (Le Corbusier 1970, 210)

2 AGAINST THE SPIRIT OF THE AGE: HEIDEGGER AND WITTGENSTEIN

Not everyone at the time shared Le Corbusier's enthusiasm for modernization. At the close of the same decade, in his 1929–30 lecture course, Fundamental Concepts of Metaphysics, in the midst of distinguishing between the notion of a *machine* and the broader category of *equipment*, Heidegger sees fit to make a not-so-veiled, and pointedly dismissive, reference to Le Corbusier:

> We talk about machine construction, but not everything which can and must be constructed is a machine. Thus it is only a further sign of the

prevailing groundlessness of thought and understanding today when we are asked to regard the house as a machine for living and the chair as a machine for sitting. There are people who even see this deluded approach as a great discovery ushering in a new culture. (*FCM* 215–16)

In stark contrast to Le Corbusier's image of the House-Machine—his celebration of the clean, modern, standardized residence—stands Heidegger's own celebration of rural life amid the peasants of the Black Forest. Starting in the 1920s, Heidegger would escape Freiburg as often as possible to his "hut" near the Black Forest village of Todtnauberg.[1] For Heidegger, the hut and its environs embodied a kind of vitality and authenticity lacking in city life, and so enabled the kind of genuine thinking he sought to articulate. In a 1934 essay, Heidegger connects his ability to do philosophy with the environs of his hut: "On a deep winter's night when a wild, pounding snowstorm rages around the cabin and veils and covers everything, that is the perfect time for philosophy" (*WP* 27–28). Heidegger sees his own work—his philosophizing—as entirely of a piece with the rural life that surrounds him at the hut: "And this philosophical work does not take its course like the aloof studies of some eccentric. It belongs right in the midst of the peasants' work. . . . It is intimately rooted in and related to the life of the peasants" (*WP* 28). The rustic vigor of peasant life that Heidegger cherishes and celebrates in this essay clashes with the ideal of the House-Machine, the sleek, standardized complement to the factory and the automobile.

Another, nearly contemporaneous, dissenting voice of sorts can be found in Wittgenstein's writings from the 1930s. Despite his own affinity for machines (Wittgenstein started out in aeronautics before turning to mathematical logic and philosophy) and despite his own foray into architecture in the 1920s resulting in a starkly modernist "house embodied logic"[2] that John Maynard Keynes would describe amusedly as "á la Corbusier" (cited in Monk 1990, 251), Wittgenstein's writings after his return to philosophy in the late 1920s express a marked antipathy for modernity. This is especially evident in the foreword he composed for the *Philosophical Remarks*: "This book is written for such men as are in sympathy with its spirit. This spirit is different from the one which informs the vast stream of European and American civilization in which all of us stand" (*PhR* 7). In an earlier version of this passage, Wittgenstein characterizes the spirit he finds "alien and uncongenial" as something that "makes itself manifest in the industry, architecture and music of our time, in its fascism and socialism" (*CV* 6). The first two items on this list—industry and architecture—are as we have seen the centerpiece of Le Corbusier's celebration of modernity: the "onwards movement" promoted by "the vast stream of European and American civilizations" is for Le Corbusier hardly something to be decried or lamented.

We have thus far one architectural manifesto celebrating the House-Machine and two philosophers seemingly united in opposition. But how are we to understand this opposition? This question actually contains several:

how closely aligned are Heidegger and Wittgenstein on these matters? Is it only a kind of incidental convergence? And what is the *source* of this opposition? Is it more reflective of personal temperament and preferences or is it connected to deeper and more pervasive aspects of their philosophical views?

3   THE GROUND OF DWELLING: HEIDEGGER

To begin to answer these questions, I want to first return to Heidegger's swipe at Le Corbusier in the *Fundamental Concepts of Metaphysics* and ask after the nature of Heidegger's complaint: in what way does talk of a house as "a machine for living" exemplify the "prevailing groundlessness of thought and understanding today"? When Heidegger says that calling a house a machine for living (and a chair a machine for sitting) is "groundless," the implication appears to be that there is no explanation or motivation for the use of that terminology. One way of teasing out this implication is to see the charge of groundlessness as meaning *empty*: calling a house or a chair a *machine* does not really mean anything, because the term "machine" is being applied so wantonly and indiscriminately. If a house can be called a machine, then just about *anything* can be called one as well: my coffee cup is a machine for holding coffee, my shoes are machines for walking, a bar of soap a machine for washing, and so on.[3]

This way of construing the charge of groundlessness strikes me as unpromising, as it simply ignores the motives at work in Le Corbusier's coinage. Far from applying the notion of a machine wantonly or indiscriminately, he is trying to articulate an *ideal*, something to which housing might aspire. Notice that Le Corbusier talks of the *creation* of the "mass-production spirit" for the house, a mind-set to be cultivated rather than already instantiated (except perhaps by Le Corbusier himself). In appealing to the House-Machine, Le Corbusier appeals to various features and virtues of machinery as things to be embodied in a new kind of housing: the modern house may not be literally a machine, but it will be *machine-like* in its design and functionality. Le Corbusier's use of "machine" is thus metaphorical rather than literal, and what Le Corbusier is trying to do throughout *Toward a New Architecture* and elsewhere is motivate the idea that the metaphor is an *apt* one. Remarking on the *basculant*, one of Le Corbusier's three innovative chairs (in addition to the *chaise-longue* and the *grand confort*), the architectural critic Charles Jencks notes that the chair, with its pivoting backrest, tightly strung armrests, and chrome tubes coupled with calf-hide convey the "overall feeling . . . of delicate fur being suspended within a frame of precise machinery" (Jencks 2000, 161). Jencks's point is that Le Corbusier's creations of this period *do* have the look and feel of machines, of "precise machinery," and thus he *shows* us what it might mean for a chair to *be* a "machine for sitting in." Whatever might be problematic about Le

Corbusier's choice of words—whatever Heidegger might mean in character-izing his talk as groundless—emptiness or a similar infelicity cannot be the source.

In light of these considerations, we should perhaps look for another way of understanding Heidegger's charge that talk of the house as a machine for living is symptomatic of "the prevailing groundlessness of thought and understanding today." Rather than read "groundlessness" here as indicat-ing some kind of semantic misfiring, the charge of groundlessness instead registers a kind of *existential* failure on the part of Le Corbusier and others. Likening—or even equating—a house to a machine displays a disregard or distortion of the phenomenon of *human dwelling*; that modern life seems poised in the 1920s to embrace Le Corbusier's language shows that it is not just his *take* on the phenomenon that is distorted but the very phenomenon itself. Although offered at the end of the 1920s, Heidegger's remark about Le Corbusier is best understood as pointing forward to his later work, most notably his essay of the 1950s, "Building Dwelling Thinking." Heidegger begins the essay by cautioning that the kind of thinking about building and dwelling he seeks to enact in the essay "does not presume to discover ar-chitectural ideas, let alone give rules for building" (*PLT* 145), but it has nonetheless served as a touchstone over the decades for architects and ar-chitectural theorists striving to break away from the modernist paradigm.[4] Insofar as we want to understand how the notion of the House-Machine might display a kind of "groundlessness of thought and understanding," this essay deserves careful attention.

Early in the essay, Heidegger asks, "Who gives us a standard at all by which we can take the measure of the nature of dwelling and building?" He answers:

> It is language that tells us about the nature of a thing, provided that we respect language's own nature. In the meantime, to be sure, there rages round the earth an unbridled yet clever talking, writing, and broadcast-ing of spoken words. Man acts as though *he* were the shaper and master of language, while in fact *language* remains master of man. Perhaps it is before all else man's subversion of *this* relation of dominance that drives his nature into alienation. (*PLT* 146)

Heidegger does not specify further the "unbridled yet clever talking" he has in mind here, and so it would be unwise simply to assume that he still has Le Corbusier in mind more than two decades after his earlier remark. None-theless, his remarks here about language might be understood as explicative of that earlier dismissal, and in the following way. Talk of a house as "a machine for living in" is groundless in the sense that it violates, and so is not grounded in, the deep senses of words such as *Bauen* and *Wohnen*; by wrest-ing words away from their deep senses—by disrespecting "language's own

nature"—Le Corbusier's coinage thereby displays an impoverished understanding of the very notion of dwelling.[5] *Groundless* thus means something
like *uprooted*, torn from the ground that gives sense to the notions in question, *house, home, building*, and *dwelling*. Groundless indicates a lack of
sense, not in the manner of emptiness but more as emptied out, denatured.

   Talk of a House-Machine is groundless in that it is forgetful or dismissive
of the deep resonances and affinities laid up in the origins and history—and
so the meaning of—words. Attention to these origins shows that *building* and *dwelling* are not two separate notions but are instead intertwined
with one another: *Bauen*, Heidegger notes, comes from the Old English
and High German *buan*, which means to dwell, which Heidegger connects
with the notions of *remaining* and *staying in a place* (*PLT* 146). Traces of
the connectedness of building and dwelling remain in *Nachbar* (*neighbor*,
"he who dwells nearby"), but also in "*ich bin*" (*I am*) and "*du bist*" (*you
are*) and so intimates something fundamental about the nature of human
existence: "The way in which you are and I am, the manner in which we
humans *are* on earth, is *Buan*, dwelling. To be a human being means to be
on the earth as a mortal. It means to dwell" (*PLT* 147). Further attention
to *Bauen* reveals more about the character of human dwelling, as "this
word *bauen* however *also* means at the same time to cherish and protect, to
preserve and care for, specifically to till the soil, to cultivate the vine. Such
building only takes care—it tends the growth that ripens into its fruit of
its own accord" (*PLT* 147). Heidegger further develops "the primal nature
of these meanings" by tracing *Wohnen* to the Old Saxon *wuon* and the
Gothic *wunian*, where the latter further articulates the character of dwelling as staying in a place: "*Wunian* means: to be at peace, to be brought to
peace, to remain in peace," while peace, *Friede*, in turn, "means the free,
das Frye, and *fry* means: preserved from harm and danger, preserved from
something, safeguarded. To free really means to spare" (*PLT* 149). Thus,
Heidegger declares that "to dwell, to be set at peace, means to remain at
peace within the free, the preserve, the free sphere that safeguards each
thing in its nature. *The fundamental character of dwelling is this sparing
and preserving*" (*PLT* 149).

   With even just this much in place, we might begin to appreciate the
distance between Heidegger's conception of full or genuine dwelling and
Le Corbusier's engineering aesthetic, and so his celebration of the House-
Machine. Recall Le Corbusier's disdain for "natural" materials, which he
considers "doubtful" owing to their unforeseeable variations; instead, he
prefers synthetic materials, the products of laboratories and factories, made
according to rigid standards with maximally predictable results. There is little that is "sparing and preserving" about Le Corbusier's approach to building, no sense of safeguarding "each thing in its nature." On the contrary, the
engineering aesthetic exemplifies the understanding of being Heidegger finds
at work in modern technology, what he calls in "The Question Concerning
Technology" *challenging* (see *QT*, especially 14–16). The goal is always and

everywhere to challenge what there is, to rearrange, reconstitute, reconfigure raw materials to maximize efficiency, durability, pliability, and so on. Le Corbusier's ideal engineer does not seek to reach an accommodation with things, but treats what there is as *resources* (*Bestand*, sometimes translated as standing-reserve) to be manipulated and exploited. From an engineering standpoint, to do otherwise would be at best rather quaint and benighted, and at worst downright irrational.

That things are disclosed in terms of challenging is not just a matter of raw materials for building—concrete versus stonework, for example—but the *products* made from such materials are also revealed in such terms: that a house should aspire to the ideal of the House-Machine means that one's dwelling place is likewise to be challenged, to be refined and adjusted to maximize its provision of comfort, satisfaction, and security. A machine is to be evaluated solely in terms of how well it does what it does, how well it provides something for its "end user." If a better machine is available, then *ceteris paribus* there is no reason whatsoever not to replace the current one with a better one. There is nothing *intrinsic* to a machine to recommend its retention in the face of superior competitors.

A machine *always* allows for the possibility of substitution or replacement, and so, from Heidegger's perspective, cannot gather in the manner of a genuine dwelling place. To occupy a House-Machine, to take up and maintain a purely instrumental relation to where and how one lives, is not really to dwell at all but to be, after all, *groundless*. As a site of dwelling, the house is not merely *instrumental*—a means to an end—but *constitutive* of a particular way of life. Heidegger's depiction of the Black Forest farmhouse in "Building Dwelling Thinking" is offered as illustrative of the way that kind of building is interwoven with the lives of the farmers who built it and live there: the orientation and placement of the house, as well as everything from its roofing to its rooms, reflect and express both *where* the farmers live with its distinctive climate and terrain, *how* they live in terms of daily patterns of activities and rituals, family roles and lineage, and *what matters* to them, their understanding of the significance of birth and death, the hope or promise of something better beyond their daily toil (see *PLT* 160). The farmhouse is both literally and figuratively grounded and grounding for the farmers, and so is not merely a machine that they make use of or employ toward a particular, independently specifiable end.

Although Heidegger's opposition to Le Corbusier's ideal of the House-Machine ends, as we have seen, with an account of the way that ideal is hostile to the very possibility of dwelling, that opposition begins by reflecting on the *language* denoting that possibility: the resonances and affinities laid up in the histories of the relevant vocabulary are revelatory of the true nature of human dwelling. Language, properly understood, tells us what human dwelling, properly understood, is all about, and a respect for such dwelling begins and is concomitant with a respect for language. Equating a house with a machine, even if metaphorically, might be understood as an act of *disrespect*, a willful severing of the connections between the words' origins and deep senses so as to serve an entirely contemporary agenda. Le Corbusier's coinage in some way violates the grammar, we might say, of the constellation of terms at work in the articulation of human existence. That the term "House-Machine" might be understood as a kind of grammatical mistake suggests a point of entry for thinking about Le Corbusier in relation to Wittgenstein, for whom grammar, of course, stands as the central preoccupation of the later philosophy.

4 MACHINES AND GRAMMAR: WITTGENSTEIN

While suggestive in many ways, the path laid down by Heidegger's investigations does not indicate in a clear way how to proceed into Wittgenstein's thinking. The difficulties here are multiple. First, consider Wittgenstein's foray into architecture in the late 1920s, when he designed and oversaw the construction of the Palais Stonborough for his sister Margaret. I noted previously that Keynes referred to Wittgenstein as building something "à la Corbusier." No doubt Keynes was led to this bit of wit by the austere modernist design Wittgenstein developed, starting from initial plans by his friend Paul Engelmann. Although the lack of ornamentation suggests the influence more of the Viennese architect Adolf Loos, author of "Ornament and Crime," mentor of Engelmann, and personal acquaintance of Wittgenstein, Keynes may be forgiven the misreading: to the casual observer, the house certainly *looks* like the kind of modernist house one would expect of Le Corbusier or any of the other up-and-coming modernist architects in that decade. Severe, austere, geometrically rigid: the house appears to be nothing else but high modernism. Moreover, many of the details in the design and construction of the house might be read as enacting Le Corbusier's ideal of the House-Machine (although there is no evidence that Wittgenstein had any awareness of that notion). Wittgenstein insisted on metal shutters for all the windows, rather than any kind of drapery; the shutters could be raised and lowered mechanically, with the machinery for doing so lodged out of sight in the basement. The shutters were thus literally machines for blocking and letting in sunlight (and for securing privacy). All of the hardware for the house—door and window latches and handles, locks and other fittings—was also designed by Wittgenstein himself and machined to exacting specifications. The tall, metal doors separating interior rooms are so carefully hung and balanced that they can be pushed closed with a single finger, despite their great weight.[6]

But there are aspects of the house that interrupt the assimilation to Le Corbusier, and so reveal the casual nature of Keynes's remark. The interior of the house is not designed on the model of the "open plan" characteristic of modernism. The interior is carefully divided into public and private spaces, with an overall layout that reflects by then fairly traditional Viennese salon culture. In general, the proportions of the rooms are far more classical than modernist. Moreover, the house displays an exceedingly high level of craftsmanship, even, or especially, with those parts involving machinery and machine-work; Wittgenstein even insisted upon changing the elevation of a ceiling by three centimeters when the house was near completion (Wittgenstein 1981, 9). Wittgenstein's sister, Hermine, recounts that in the design and construction of the house, "[N]othing was unimportant except time and money" (Wittgenstein 1981, 7), which indicates that there is little about the house that displays any of the "mass-production spirit" Le Corbusier envisions in *Toward a New Architecture*. That the design of the house was intensely *personal* further underscores this point; its layout and ordering were entirely governed by the sensibilities and desires of its eventual occupant, Wittgenstein's sister.[7] The house is thus tailor-made for one particular occupant and for her manner of dwelling, which is again antithetical to the ideal of factory-made, one-size-fits-all housing.[8] Although these considerations perhaps drive a wedge between Wittgenstein and Le Corbusier, they do not bring him all that much closer to Heidegger.

If we turn our attention to more centrally philosophical matters, Wittgenstein's concern with language does not map neatly onto Heidegger's. Although a hallmark of Wittgenstein's practice is its endeavoring to ferret out and dissolve the perversities of speech to which philosophy is prone, that endeavor is coupled with a recognition of, and insistence upon, the *open* character of human language. Whatever perversities of speech arise on the way to, and in the course of, philosophizing are not to be accounted for in terms of their violation of the rules of "ordinary" language—that is, their failure to adhere to the standards laid down in everyday speech. Language is not "everywhere bounded by rules" (*PI* §84), and so all speaking involves projecting words into new contexts, new situations, where their sense is not always guaranteed in advance and where the speaker assumes the ultimate responsibility for ensuring whatever sense they have (that speakers of a language generally understand one another reflects the "agreement in judgments" (*PI* §242) constitutive of a shared form of life). Wittgenstein's suspicion of philosophical language is that such a burden has not been borne by the philosopher, that the philosopher speaks "outside language-games" not in the sense of violating the rules of speech but in the sense of refusing or resisting the demand to account for his uses of words in ways that render them genuinely intelligible. If philosophy issues in nonsense, it is not because of what the words involved really mean, but because no real meaning has yet been determined in the way the philosopher wishes—or thinks he wishes—to project them.[9]

If the term "House-Machine" and the attending idea that a house is "a machine for living in" are indeed perversions of speech, establishing this from the perspective of the *Investigations* is thus a delicate matter. Nothing about the "rules" for using the words "house" and "machine" forbid or prevent their being combined in the manner Le Corbusier uses them. The combination is certainly striking, perhaps even jarring, but part of his intent is to shake up our sensibilities a bit, to get us thinking about just what a house *is* and what it *could be*. Le Corbusier certainly projects "house" and "machine" in a novel way, so that the meaning is not *obvious* in the way it might be when I say, for example, "Do you want to go play at Sara's house?" or "His new car is one sleek machine." But just the fact that the sense is not obvious does not mean it is altogether lacking; rather, it means that it is incumbent upon Le Corbusier to make that sense clear, so that we might follow along (or forego doing so).

As I suggested earlier, when first considering Le Corbusier's coinage, likening a house to a machine might be illuminating or insightful: think of the virtues of a machine, such as functionality, efficiency, smooth operation and handling, and so on. In what ways might it be desirable for a house to embody those sorts of virtues? In asking this, I do not just mean the various machines that a house contains (laundry machines, central heating, and so on), although it is clear that we generally want those (literal) machines to have such virtues, but the house *as a whole*. Is it desirable to have a house that is itself functional and efficient, where the space in the house is ordered so as to permit easy movement and promote a general sense of comfort and well-being? Does the house—like a good machine—cater to the inhabitant's needs and desires? Is it well designed—that is, is the design *rational*? Does the look and feel of the house clash with or complement the rest of one's modern life? Insofar as these questions are in order, or at least make some purchase on our comprehension, then the notion of the House-Machine cannot readily or obviously be dismissed as a kind of nonsense. Insofar as Le Corbusier projects these words in this new way, a motivation for so projecting them can be made out, and indeed quite clearly so. Le Corbusier, we might say, shows us the "form of life" in which the phrase "House-Machine" has a place—namely, an ultra-modern way of living ordered around the ideals of rationality and efficiency. Such a way of life is certainly both intelligible and possible.

Endorsing the intelligibility of Le Corbusier's projection is not the same as endorsing it full stop in the sense of finding its image of the house as a machine to be as virtuous or welcome as he makes it out to be. Do we necessarily want to live in machines? Do we want our houses to embody, or even aspire to, the virtues we associate with machines? Heidegger's thoughts about dwelling might serve to give us pause here, but what of Wittgenstein? Consider the following remark from *Culture and Value*:

> It is very *remarkable* that we should be inclined to think of civilization—houses, trees, cars, etc.—as separating man from his origins, from what is lofty and eternal, etc. Our civilized environment, along with its trees and plants, strikes us then as though it were cheaply wrapped in cellophane and isolated from everything great, from God, as it were. That is a remarkable picture that intrudes on us. (CV 50)[10]

It is not entirely clear how to understand the sense of *intrusion* Wittgenstein registers here with respect to his "picture," in the sense of how we are to measure the force and significance of its doing so.[11] That civilization might "strike us" in this way, "as though it were cheaply wrapped in cellophane," is noted by Wittgenstein as being only "remarkable," but that does not mean our being so struck intimates some deep fact about how civilization really stands in relation to something else, "what is lofty or eternal." But Wittgenstein's imagery of cheap cellophane wrapping suggests a feeling of impoverishment and sterility, something distinctively *inorganic* about how human beings live and the places they have created for themselves. Such an inclination is perhaps at work in a critical remark Wittgenstein made about the house he had built:

> [T]he house I built for Gretl is the product of a decidedly sensitive ear and *good* manners, and expression of great *understanding* (of a culture, etc.). But *primordial* life, wild life striving to erupt into the open—that is lacking. And so you could say it isn't *healthy* (Kierkegaard). (Hothouse plant). (*CV* 38)

Although Wittgenstein does not single out modern civilization as especially occasioning the intrusion of this picture of civilization as "isolated from everything great," ideals such as Le Corbusier's House-Machine might be thought of as epitomizing such sterility: just as being "cheaply wrapped in cellophane" runs counter to an idea of "primordial life," so too does the House-Machine, a decidedly *inorganic* image.

In earlier describing Wittgenstein's conception of language as open-ended, as "not everywhere bounded by rules," in order to distance that vision from Heidegger's reverence for etymology, I omitted other dimensions of that conception that might be seen as closing the gap considerably. While Wittgenstein's "grammatical investigations" do not take the form of attending to the etymologies of various words, there is nonetheless an emphasis throughout his later philosophy on the *organic* and *living* character of language. Very early in the *Investigations*, Wittgenstein likens language to a slowly evolving "ancient city" consisting of "a maze of little streets and squares, of old and new houses, of houses with extensions from various periods, and all this surrounded by a multitude of new suburbs with straight and regular streets and uniform houses" (*PI* §18). Although Wittgenstein here does not accord to the older parts of this "ancient city" any special value or reverence (as Heidegger might), a certain reverence for historically anchored speech can be seen in his contempt for Esperanto, a form of language whose development and promotion were of interest to Carnap and other logical positivists. At the Vienna Circle's first meeting with Wittgenstein, Carnap reports that:

> Schlick unfortunately mentioned that I [Carnap] was interested in the problem of an international language like Esperanto. As I had expected, Wittgenstein was definitely opposed to the idea. But I was surprised by the vehemence of his emotions. A language which had not "grown organically" seemed to him not only useless but despicable. (Carnap 1963, 26)

That this was more than a passing feeling on Wittgenstein's part is illustrated by the following remark, written nearly twenty years after the encounter Carnap reports:

> Esperanto. The feeling of disgust we get if we utter an *invented* word with invented derivative syllables. The word is cold, lacking in associations, and yet it plays at being "language." A system of purely written signs would not disgust us so much. (*CV* 52)

Lacking in Esperanto is any of the kind of rich history that informs non-invented language. Notice the emphasis here on *associations*, as these are precisely what Heidegger emphasizes in his etymological remarks such as those between *dwelling*, *preserving*, *freeing*, and *remaining at peace*. The poverty of Esperanto, its frigidity, is owing to its lack of such connections and associations. Wittgenstein's disdain for Esperanto could be interpreted as motivating an equal disdain for Le Corbusier's ideal of the House-Machine, insofar as it is a radical departure from more traditional styles and methods of building. The House-Machine, built with synthetic materials and modern construction techniques, is like a word in Esperanto, "cold, lacking in associations," and is motivated by the same wholesale repudiation of tradition (what Le Corbusier dismisses contemptuously as "snail-shell" dwellings).

On those occasions in Wittgenstein's philosophical writings where the machine makes an appearance, it typically stands in stark opposition to the kind of "primordial life" Wittgenstein finds lacking in his own house. Consider the following passage from the first volume of *Remarks on the Philosophy of Psychology*:

> First of all it is clear that the tendency to regard the word as something intimate, full of soul, is not always there, or always in the same measure. But the opposite of being full of soul is being mechanical. If you want to act like a robot—how does your behaviour deviate from our ordinary behaviour? By the fact that our ordinary movements cannot even approximately be described by means of geometrical concepts. (*RPPI* §324)

Something that is "full of soul" displays a kind of variability, flexibility, and indeterminacy radically unlike the workings of a machine, whose movements may be more precise but also more rigidly parameterized. Elsewhere, Wittgenstein explicitly connects this idea of being full of soul with the notions of unforseeability and indeterminacy: "But with a human being, the assumption is that *it is impossible* to gain an insight into the mechanism. Thus indeterminacy is postulated" (*RPPII* §666). No such "assumption" is involved in the idea of a machine or a mechanism: "Looking at it one might think: if I knew what it looked like inside, what was going on right now, I would know what to expect" (*RPPII* §665). While the laws of its operation may be very complicated, such that predicting its movements might elude the casual observer, there is certainly no "postulated" indeterminacy at work. But this lack of indeterminacy is precisely what underwrites the opposition between being mechanical and being full of soul: mechanized, rigid motions are marked by an absence of the kind of expressiveness and meaning conveyed in the fluid and variable actions of living beings. In the *Investigations*, Wittgenstein asks, almost despairingly, "How could one so much as get the idea of ascribing a *sensation* to a *thing*?" What dispels the sense of despair is the image of an organic, animalistic kind of movement, albeit of a very primitive kind: "And now look at a wriggling fly, and at once these difficulties vanish, and pain seems to get a *foothold* here, where before everything was, so to speak, too *smooth* for it" (*PI* §284). *Wriggling* is "full of soul" in the sense that it expresses and conveys the organism's *suffering*, its plight as something trapped, perhaps even doomed. And wriggling is not a sharply bounded kind of movement: if the fly only flipped one way and another in a perfectly rigid way, without any variation, its movements would likely remain "too smooth" for the ascription of any kind pain.

Among the remarks collected in *Culture and Value* are two concerning architecture that connect it to *gesture* and *expression*. The earlier of the two is from the early 1930s: "Remember the impression one gets from good architecture, that it expresses a thought. It makes one want to respond with a gesture" (*CV* 22). Wittgenstein does not elaborate on the kind or range of gestures good architecture might elicit, which suggests that what matters is the *fact* of eliciting such a response. That a building evokes such a response is a mark of its appearing to express a thought, to engage us as something meaningful and expressive, rather than something inert and unthinking. Good architecture has a kind of vitality that allows the notions of thought and expression to gain a foothold, much as the fly's wriggling motion anchors the ascription of sensation. Lifeless, mechanical architecture, by contrast, leaves us likewise feeling lifeless, feeling unprompted to respond in any particular way, if at all. The second remark, from roughly a decade later, locates the gesture not in our response to architecture but in architecture itself: "Architecture is a *gesture*. Not every purposive movement of the human body is a gesture. And no more is every building designed for a purpose architecture" (*CV* 42). The possibility of gesturing, of making movements that express a meaning, depends upon their fluidity and variability: rigid, uniform movements, even if "purposeful," are lacking in gestural expressiveness. The more the body approximates the workings of a machine, the more its possibilities of meaningful expression diminish. The House-Machine, as rigid, uniform, standardized, might thus be understood as a diminished or impoverished gesture, as a kind of architecture seeking to limit and even undermine its own gestural possibilities.

5   CODA: TOWARD THE POSTMODERN

That something might both present itself as an *ideal* and yet work contrary to the aims the ideal is meant to serve is one of Wittgenstein's central lessons in his explorations of logic and language in the *Investigations*. Motivated by a desire to secure transparent linguistic communication—a form of communication where misunderstandings are no longer possible—the ideal of a logically perfect language disregards—even effaces—just those things that make communication and understanding possible in the first place, the kind of shared and imparted sensibility—what Stanley Cavell calls the "whirl of organism" (Cavell 1976a, 52)—that constitutes our form of life. Pursuit of such an ideal puts us "on to slippery ice where there is no friction." Lacking friction, "the conditions are ideal, but also, just because of that, we are unable to walk. We want to walk: so we need *friction*. Back to the rough ground!" (*PI* §107).

In his architectural manifesto, *Complexity and Contradiction in Architecture*, Robert Venturi declares: "I am for messy vitality over obvious unity" (Venturi 2002, 16). Venturi's declaration is a measure of the distance between his conception of architecture and that of what he refers to as "orthodox Modern architecture." Employing an approach and style governed by what Charles Jencks refers to as "univalence"—"an architecture created around one (or a few) simplified values" (Jencks 1977, 15)—modern architects, according to Venturi:

> Have tended to recognize complexity insufficiently or inconsistently. In their attempt to break with tradition and start all over again, they idealized the primitive and elementary at the expense of the diverse and the sophisticated. As participants in a revolutionary movement, they acclaimed the newness of modern functions, ignoring their complications. In their role as reformers, they puritanically advocated the separation and exclusion of elements, rather than the inclusion of various requirements and their juxtapositions. . . . Modern architects with few exceptions eschewed ambiguity. (Venturi 2002, 16)

In the view of architects and theorists like Jencks and Venturi, modernism's puritanism has failed both aesthetically and socially by producing drab, uniform, monotonous structures people tend to dislike looking at and cold, hostile, impractical environments that people dislike inhabiting even more.[12] Captivated by an ideal of simplicity and uniformity—an ideal codified in Le Corbusier's vision of the house as a machine for living in—modern architecture ignored the "rough ground" of human dwelling and its need for "friction," what Venturi here calls "messy vitality."

That modernism's failure lies partly in its desire "to break with tradition and start all over again" is an idea shared by both Heidegger and Wittgenstein, in their shared sense of language being a historical phenomenon, something shaped by ongoing patterns of use and enmeshed in likewise ongoing human practices. Their shared suspicion of radical novelty, radical innovation, and wholesale rejection of the past in favor of something entirely (and excitingly) new typically invites charges of a problematic nostalgia, conservatism, and in Heidegger's case, far worse (Heidegger's political biography does little to deflect such accusations). Heidegger's appeals to Black Forest farmhouses and his own claims to identification with his hardscrabble farming neighbors make it seem that the solution to modernity's problems lies in finding our way back to some past way of life. But Heidegger is careful to point out at the close of "Building Dwelling Thinking" that his "reference to the Black Forest farm in no way means that we should or could go back to building such houses; rather, it illustrates by a dwelling that *has been* how *it was* able to build" (*PLT* 160). Instead, Heidegger insists that we "*must ever learn to dwell*" (*PLT* 161), which suggests that the question of what it is to dwell as a human is inevitably an open question. The ideal that gives life to the House-Machine tries to settle that question, like a perfect mechanism whose movements are rigidly determined.

Ultimately, the allure of synthetic materials, prefabrication, and standardization lies in their contribution to more predictable, uniform houses: the House-Machine is a structure where the steps of how to live in it have already been taken, solved beforehand by the engineer's calculations. The House-Machine is itself a kind of fantasy of friction-free living, where the manner of building and the manner of dwelling are perfectly controlled, perfectly predicted in advance. Perhaps Le Corbusier himself came to see the fantastical nature of his ideal. In the mid-1920s, Le Corbusier designed a worker housing complex at Pessac, using a small handful of elements— a cube or cell, concrete beam, and ribbon window—that could be combined in a variety of ways to avoid monotony while maintaining a kind of "visual consistency" (Jencks 1973, 74). Over the years, residents disrupted this "visual consistency," altering and adjusting the layout and appearance of the complex in various ways: living spaces were divided, windows were walled up, and so on. Remarking on the undoing of his original standardized and visually consistent design, Le Corbusier remarked: "You know, it's life that's always right and the architect who's wrong" (cited in Jencks 1973, 74).[13]

NOTES

1. See Sharr (2006) for an account of both the history and design of Heidegger's hut.
2. The phrase is Hermine Wittgenstein's, cited in Monk (1990, 237). See also Wittgenstein (1981) for more of her recollections regarding the house and its construction.
3. Understanding the charge of groundlessness in this way connects Heidegger's remark to his discussion of *idle talk* in *Being and Time*. There, Heidegger describes the processes involved in idle talk (such as "gossiping" and "passing the word along") as one where the talk's "initial lack of grounds to stand on becomes aggravated to complete *groundlessness*" (*BT* 168/212; my emphasis). Despite the proximity of these lectures to *Being and Time*, I do not think Heidegger's charge of groundlessness is best cashed out with reference to that earlier work. As I suggest, we gain more by looking ahead to his later work.

4. See, for example, Norberg-Schulz (1971); Frampton (1996); and Sharr (2007).

5. Heidegger's ideas about dwelling are understood as applicable in this way to Le Corbusier by James C. Edwards, who appeals to Le Corbusier as an example of the kind of thinking about dwelling that Heidegger is opposing. See Edwards (1990, 98), where Heidegger's description of a Black Forest farmhouse is read as a corrective to Le Corbusier's talk of a house as a machine for living in. Likewise, Miguel de Beistegui sees Le Corbusier as exemplifying the kind of impoverishment of the possibility of dwelling in the technological age Heidegger is seeking to diagnose and perhaps remedy. He asks: "Has the home been *reduced* to a mere 'machine for living in,' as Le Corbusier so famously declared?" (de Beistegui 2003, 158; my emphasis). See also Borgmann (1984, 64–65).

6. I am indebted to Wijdeveld (1999) and Leitner (2000) for these details about the Palais Stonborough, as well as for a more general orientation with respect to the house's history and structure.

7. See Wittgenstein (1981, especially 6–9) and Leitner (2000, 30–31). The house was also intensely personal in terms of Wittgenstein himself, as the following remark from *Culture and Value* suggests: "Working in philosophy—like work in architecture in many respects—is really a working on oneself. On one's own interpretation. On one's way of seeing things. (And what one expects of them)" (*CV* 16).

8. Although the Wittgenstein house is often viewed as reflecting the philosophical sensibilities of the *Tractatus*, Nana Last (2008) argues that the design and construction of the house constitute a kind of pivot from the early to later philosophy, a rejection of the "verticality" of the *Tractatus* in favor of a ground-level, internal view of the *Investigations*.

9. The *locus classicus* for this way of reading the later Wittgenstein is the work of Stanley Cavell. See, for example, Cavell (1976a; 1979), especially chapter 7 ("Excursus on Wittgenstein's Vision of Language").

10. Although written in 1946, well after the composition of *Philosophical Remarks*, there is an echo here of what he says there regarding its "spirit" as "different from the one which informs the vast stream of European and American civilizations in which all of us stand." Those words are followed by Wittgenstein reporting that he "would like to say 'This book is written to the glory of God'" (*PhR* 7). Both passages register a kind of spiritual destitution in the modern age, which is reflected in its architecture.

11. *Picture* is also, of course, a term of art (and criticism) throughout the *Investigations*. There, pictures hold us "captive" (*PI* §115) and Wittgenstein's efforts can in larger part be directed toward *freeing* us from them. I am, however, not inclined to read this remark from outside of the *Investigations* as employing "picture" in this way. While remarkable, Wittgenstein does not here suggest that it is distorting or debilitating.

12. Consider, for example, Jencks's "obituary" for modern architecture, which begins by recounting the destruction of the Pruitt-Igoe housing project in St. Louis, Missouri. See Jencks (1977, 9–10), and part 1 more generally.

13. Many of the ideas leading to this chapter were first presented in a very different form at the Regional Wittgenstein Workshop, held at Washington and Lee University in March 2012. I would like to thank Charles Lowney for organizing the conference and all the participants (especially Christopher Hoyt and Simon Levy) for their challenging (and helpful) comments and questions. I would also like to thank Randall Havas, Christopher Hoyt, Edward Minar, Duncan Richter, Iain Thomson, and the editors of this volume for their comments, criticisms, and helpful discussion of previous drafts of this chapter.

Bibliography

1 WORKS BY WITTGENSTEIN

AWL: Wittgenstein's Lectures: Cambridge, 1932–1935: From the Notes of Alice Ambrose and Margaret Macdonald. Edited by Alice Ambrose. Amherst, NY: Prometheus Books, 2001.

BB: The Blue and Brown Books: Preliminary Studies for the "Philosophical Investigations." 2nd ed. Oxford: Blackwell, 1969.

BTS: The Big Typscript. Edited and translated by C.G. Luckhardt and M.E. Aue. Oxford: Wiley-Blackwell, 2005.

Conv: Wittgenstein: Conversations 1949–1951. By O.K. Bouwsma. Edited by J.L. Craft and Ronald E. Hustwit. Indianapolis: Hackett, 1986.

CV: Culture and Value. 2nd ed. Edited by G.H. von Wright, Hekki Nyman, and Alois Pichler. Translated by Peter Winch. Oxford: Blackwell, 1998.

LC: Lectures and Conversations on Aesthetics, Psychology and Religious Belief. Edited by Cyril Barrett. Oxford: Blackwell, 1966.

LFM: Lectures on the Foundations of Mathematics: Cambridge, 1939. Edited by Cora Diamond. Chicago, IL: University of Chicago Press, 1976.

LPP: Wittgenstein's Lectures on Philosophical Psychology: 1946–47. Edited by P.T. Geach. Chicago, IL: University of Chicago Press, 1988.

LWL: Wittgenstein's Lectures: Cambridge, 1930–32. Edited by Desmond Lee. Chicago, IL: University of Chicago Press, 1980.

LWPPI: Last Writings on the Philosophy of Psychology. Edited by G.H. von Wright and Heikki Nyman. Translated by C.G. Luckhardt and Maximilian A.E. Aue. Vol. 1. Oxford: Blackwell, 1982.

LWPPII: Last Writings on the Philosophy of Psychology. Edited by G.H. von Wright and Heikki Nyman. Translated by C.G. Luckhardt and Maximilian A.E. Aue. Vol. 2. Oxford: Blackwell, 1992.

LWVC: Ludwig Wittgenstein and the Vienna Circle: Conversations Recorded by Friedrich Waismann. Edited by Brian McGuinness. Oxford: Blackwell, 1979.

NB: Notebooks, 1914–1916. 2nd ed. Edited by G.H. von Wright and G.E.M. Anscombe. Translated by G.E.M. Anscombe. Oxford: Blackwell, 1979.

OC: On Certainty. Edited by G.E.M. Anscombe and G.H. von Wright. Translated by G.E.M. Anscombe, G.H. von Wright, and Denis Paul. Oxford: Blackwell, 1975.

PG: Philosophical Grammar. Edited by Rush Rhees. Translated by Anthony Kenny. Oxford: Blackwell, 1980.

PhR: Philosophical Remarks. Edited by Rush Rhees. Translated by Raymond Hargreaves and Roger White. Oxford: Blackwell, 1975.

PI: Philosophical Investigations. 4th ed. Edited by P.M.S. Hacker and Joachim Schulte. Translated by G.E.M. Anscombe, P. M. S. Hacker, and Joachim Schulte. Oxford: Wiley-Blackwell, 2009.

PO: Philosophical Occasions: 1912–1951. Edited by James Klagge and Alfred Nordmann. Indianapolis: Hackett, 1993.

PPF: Philosophy of Psychology—a Fragment. In *PI*, 182–243.

RC: Remarks on Colour. Edited by G.E.M. Anscombe. Translated by Linda L. McAlister and Margarete Schättle. Oxford: Blackwell, 1977.

RFM: Remarks on the Foundations of Mathematics. 3rd ed. Edited by G.H. von Wright, Rush Rhees, and G.E.M. Anscombe. Translated by G.E.M. Anscombe. Oxford: Blackwell, 1978.

RPPI: Remarks on the Philosophy of Psychology. Edited by G.E.M. Anscombe and G.H. von Wright. Translated by G.E.M. Anscombe. Vol. 1. Oxford: Blackwell, 1980.

RPPII: Remarks on the Philosophy of Psychology. Edited by G.H. von Wright and Heikki Nyman. Translated by C.G. Luckhardt and M.A.E. Aue. Vol. 2. Oxford: Blackwell, 1980.

SP: Wittgenstein: Sources and Perspectives. Edited by C.G. Luckhardt. Ithaca, NY: Cornell University Press, 1979.

TLP: Tractatus Logico-Philosophicus. Translated by D.F. Pears and B.F. Mc Guinness. London: Routledge, 1974.

Z: Zettel. Edited by G. E. M. Anscombe and G.H. von Wright. Translated by G.E.M. Anscombe. Oxford: Blackwell, 1967.

2 WORKS BY HEIDEGGER

AM: Aristotle's Metaphysics Θ 1–3: On the Essence and Actuality of Force. Translated by Walter Brogan and Peter Warnek. Bloomington: Indiana University Press, 1995.

Basic: Basic Concepts. Translated by Gary E. Aylesworth. Bloomington: Indiana University Press, 1993.

BaT: Being and Truth. Translated by Gregory Fried and Richard Polt. Bloomington: Indiana University Press, 2010.

BCAP: Basic Concepts of Aristotelian Philosophy. Translated by Robert D. Metcalf and Mark B. Tanzer. Bloomington: Indiana University Press, 2009.

BH: Becoming Heidegger: On the Trail of His Early Occasional Writings, 1910–1927. Edited by Theodore Kisiel and Thomas Sheehan. Evanston, IL: Northwestern University Press, 2007.

BP: The Basic Problems of Phenomenology. Rev. ed. Edited by Albert Hofstadter. Bloomington: Indiana University Press, 1988.

BQ: Basic Questions of Philosophy: Selected "Problems" of "Logic." Translated by Richard Rojcewicz and André Schuwer. Bloomington: Indiana University Press, 1994.

BT: Being and Time. Translated by John Macquarrie and Edward Robinson. New York: Harper & Row, 1962. Page references give the page numbers from the original German edition followed by the page numbers from the Macquarrie and Robinson translation.

BW: Basic Writings. Edited by David Farrell Krell. New York: HarperCollins, 1993.

CP: Contributions to Philosophy (From Enknowing). Translated by Parvis Emad and Kenneth Maly. Bloomington: Indiana University Press, 1999.

CPC: Country Path Conversations. Translated by Bret W. Davis. Bloomington: Indiana University Press, 2010.

DT: Discourse on Thinking. Translated by John M. Anderson and E. Hans Freund. New York: Harper & Row, 1966.

EGT: Early Greek Thinking: The Dawn of Western Philosophy. Translated by David Farrell Krell and Frank A. Capuzzi. New York: Harper & Row, 1975.

EP: Einleitung in die Philosophie (GA 27). Frankfurt am Main: Vittorio Klostermann, 1996.

ET: The Essence of Truth: On Plato's Parable of the Cave Allegory and Theaetetus. Translated by Ted Sadler. London: Continuum, 2002.

FCM: The Fundamental Concepts of Metaphysics: World, Finitude, Solitude. Translated by William McNeill and Nicholas Walker. Bloomington: Indiana University Press, 1995.

FS: Four Seminars. Translated by Andrew Mitchell and François Raffoul. Bloomington: Indiana University Press, 2003.

GA: Gesamtausgabe. 102 vols. Frankfurt am Main: Vittorio Klostermann, 1975–present.

HCT: History of the Concept of Time: Prolegomena. Translated by Theodore Kisiel. Bloomington: Indiana University Press, 1985.

HH: Hölderlin's Hymn "The Ister." Translated by William McNeill and Julia Davis. Bloomington: Indiana University Press, 1996.

HR: The Heidegger Reader. Edited by Günter Figal. Translated by Jerome Veith. Bloomington: Indiana University Press, 2009.

ID: Identity and Difference. Translated by Joan Stambaugh. New York: Harper & Row, 1969.

IM: An Introduction to Metaphysics. Translated by Gregory Fried and Richard Polt. New Haven, CT: Yale University Press, 2000.

IPR: An Introduction to Phenomenological Research. Translated by Daniel O. Dahlstrom. Bloomington: Indiana University Press, 2005.

ITP: Introduction to Philosophy—Thinking and Poetizing. Translated by Phillip Jacques Braunstein. Bloomington: Indiana University Press, 2011.

KPM: Kant and the Problem of Metaphysics. 5th ed. Translated by Richard Taft. Bloomington: Indiana University Press, 1990.

LQT: Logic: The Question of Truth. Translated by Thomas Sheehan. Bloomington: Indiana University Press, 2010.

M: Mindfulness. Translated by Parvis Emad and Thomas Kalary. London: Continuum, 2006.

MFL: The Metaphysical Foundations of Logic. Translated by Michael Heim. Bloomington: Indiana University Press, 1992.

N: Nietzsche. Translated by David Farrell Krell. 4 vols. New York: Harper & Row, 1979–87.

OBT: Off the Beaten Track. Edited and translated by Julian Young and Kenneth Haynes. Cambridge: Cambridge University Press, 2002.

OHF: Ontology—the Hermeneutics of Facticity. Translated by John van Buren. Bloomington: Indiana University Press, 2008.

OWL: On the Way to Language. Translated by Peter D. Hertz. New York: Harper & Row, 1971.

P: Parmenides. Translated by André Schuwer and Richard Rojcewicz. Bloomington: Indiana University Press, 1992.

PIA: Phenomenological Interpretations of Aristotle: Initiation into Phenomenological Research. Translated by Richard Rojcewicz. Bloomington: Indiana University Press, 2001.

PIE: Phenomenology of Intuition and Expression. Translated by Tracy Colony. London: Continuum, 2010.

PIK: Phenomenological Interpretation of Kant's Critique of Pure Reason. Translated by Parvis Emad and Kenneth Maly. Bloomington: Indiana University Press, 1997.

PLT: Poetry, Language, Thought. Translated by Albert Hofstadter. New York: Harper & Row, 1971.

PM: Pathmarks. Translated by William McNeill. Cambridge: Cambridge University Press, 1998.

PR: The Principle of Reason. Translated by Reginald Lilly. Bloomington: Indiana University Press, 1991.

PRL: The Phenomenology of Religious Life. Translated by Matthias Frisch and Jennifer Anna Gosetti-Ferencei. Bloomington: Indiana University Press, 2004.

PS: Plato's Sophist. Translated by Richard Rojcewicz and André Schuwer. Bloomington: Indiana University Press, 1997.

PT: The Piety of Thinking. Translated by James C. Hart and John C. Maraldo. Bloomington: Indiana University Press, 1976.

QT: The Question Concerning Technology and Other Essays. Translated by William Lovitt. New York: Harper & Row, 1977.

SA: The Self-Assertion of the German University. In *The Heidegger Controversy: A Critical Reader,* edited by Richard Wolin, 29–40. Cambridge, MA: MIT, 1993.

STF: Schelling's Treatise on the Essence of Human Freedom. Translated by Joan Stambaugh. Athens: Ohio University Press, 1985.

Supp: Supplements: From the Earliest Essays to Being and Time *and Beyond.* Edited by John van Buren. Albany: State University of New York Press, 2002.

TB: On Time and Being. Translated by Joan Stambaugh. New York: Harper & Row, 1972.

TDP: Towards the Definition of Philosophy. London: Continuum, 2000.

WCT: What Is Called Thinking? Translated by J. Glenn Gray. New York: Harper & Row, 1968.

WIP: What Is Philosophy? Translated by Jean T. Wilde and William Kluback. New Haven, CT: College & University Press, 1956.

WP: Why Do I Stay in the Provinces? In *Heidegger: The Man and the Thinker,* edited by Thomas Sheehan, 27–30. New Brunswick, NJ: Transaction.

WT: What Is a Thing? Translated by W.B. Barton Jr. and Vera Deutsch. Chicago, IL: Henry Regnery, 1967.

Zo: Zollikon Seminars: Protocols—Conversations—Letters. Edited by Medard Boss. Translated by Franz Mayr and Richard Askay. Evanston, IL: Northwestern University Press, 2001.

3   OTHER WORKS CITED WITH ABBREVIATIONS

AT: Descartes, René. *Oeuvres Complètes de René Descartes.* Edited by Charles Adam and Paul Tannery. 13 vols. Paris: Léopold Cerf, 1897–1913.

CPR: Kant, Immanuel. *Critique of Pure Reason.* 1781. Translated by Paul Guyer and Allen W. Wood. Cambridge: Cambridge University Press, 1998. Page references give the page numbers in the German first (A) and second (B) editions.

4   OTHER WORKS CITED

Abrams, M.H. 1971. *Natural Supernaturalism: Tradition and Revolution in Romantic Literature.* London: W.W. Norton.

Allison, Henry. 2004. *Kant's Transcendental Idealism: An Interpretation and Defense.* Rev. ed. New Haven, CT: Yale University Press.

Anscombe, G.E.M. 1959. *An Introduction to Wittgenstein's "Tractatus."* London: Hutchinson.

Apel, Karl-Otto. 1980. *Towards a Transformation of Philosophy*. Translated by Gwyn Adey and David Frisby. London: Routledge & Kegan Paul.

———. 1998. *From a Transcendental-Semiotic Point of View*. Edited by Marianna Papastephanou. Manchester: Manchester University Press.

———. 1998a. Wittgenstein and Heidegger: Language Games and Life Forms. In Apel 1998, 122–59.

Arendt, Hannah. 1958. *The Human Condition*. Chicago, IL: University of Chicago Press.

Ayer, A. J. 1936. *Language, Truth, and Logic*. London: Victor Gollancz.

———, ed. 1959. *Logical Positivism*. New York: Free Press.

Baker, G. P., ed. 2003. *The Voices of Wittgenstein: The Vienna Circle*. London: Routledge.

———. 2004. *Wittgenstein's Method: Neglected Aspects*. Edited by Katherine Morris. Oxford: Blackwell.

———. 2004a. "Our" Method of Thinking about "Thinking." In Baker 2004, 144–78.

———. 2004b. Wittgenstein: Concepts of Conceptions? In Baker 2004, 260–78.

Baker, G. P., and P. M. S. Hacker. 1985. *Rules, Grammar, and Necessity*. Vol. 2 of *Wittgenstein*. Oxford: Blackwell.

———. 2005. *Understanding and Meaning, Part I: Essays*. Vol. 1 of *Wittgenstein*. 2nd ed. Oxford: Blackwell.

Bambrough, Renford. 1979. *Moral Scepticism and Moral Knowledge*. London: Routledge.

Bennett, M. R., and P. M. S. Hacker. 2003. *Philosophical Foundations of Neuroscience*. Oxford: Blackwell.

Black, Max. 1964. *A Companion to Wittgenstein's* Tractatus. Ithaca, NY: Cornell University Press.

Blattner, William D. 2007. Ontology, the A Priori, and the Primacy of Practice. In Crowell and Malpas 2007, 10–27.

Bloor, David. 1996. The Question of Linguistic Idealism Revisited. In Sluga and Stern 1996, 354–82.

Borgmann, Albert. 1984. *Technology and the Character of Contemporary Life: A Philosophical Inquiry*. Chicago, IL: University of Chicago Press.

Bourdieu, Pierre. 1990. Fieldword in Philosophy. In *In Other Words: Essays towards a Reflexive Sociology*, 3–33. Stanford, CA: Stanford University Press.

Bouveresse, Jacques. 1987. *Le Mythe de l'intériorité: Experience, signification et langage privé chez Wittgenstein*. Paris: Éditions de Minuit.

———. 1995. *Wittgenstein Reads Freud: The Myth of the Unconscious*. Translated by Carol Cosman. Princeton, NJ: Princeton University Press.

———. 2003. *Essais III: Wittgenstein et les sortileges du langage*. Agone: 2003.

———. 2008. Wittgenstein's Critique of Frazer. In *Wittgenstein and Reason*, edited by John Preston, 1–20. Oxford: Blackwell.

Braithwaite, R. B. 1978. An Empiricist's View of the Nature of Religious Belief. In *The Philosophy of Religion*, edited by Basil Mitchell, 72–91. Oxford: Oxford University Press.

Brandom, Robert. 1994. *Making It Explicit: Reasoning, Representing, and Discursive Commitment*. Cambridge, MA: Harvard University Press.

———. 2002. *Tales of the Mighty Dead: Historical Essays in the Metaphysics of Intentionality*. Cambridge, MA: Harvard University Press.

Braver, Lee. 2007. *A Thing of This World: A History of Continental Anti-realism*. Evanston, IL: Northwestern University Press.

———. 2012. *Groundless Grounds: A Study of Wittgenstein and Heidegger*. Cambridge, MA: MIT.

———. Forthcoming. Never Mind: Thinking of Subjectivity in the Dreyfus-McDowell Debate. In *Mind, Reason and Being-in-the-World: The McDowell-Dreyfus Debate*, edited by Joseph K. Schear. London: Routledge.

Burge, Tyler. 1979. Individualism and the Mental. *Midwest Studies in Philosophy* 4: 73–121.

Burtt, E. A. 1954. *The Metaphysical Foundations of Modern Science*. Garden City, NY: Doubleday.

Camerlingo, Francesco. 2011. *La questione del senso: Con Heidegger e Wittgenstein sull'enigma dell'esistenza*. Genoa: Il Melangolo.

Carman, Taylor. 2003. *Heidegger's Analytic: Interpretation, Discourse, and Authenticity in* Being and Time. Cambridge: Cambridge University Press.

Carnap, Rudolf. 1932. Überwindung der Metaphysik durch logische Analyse der Sprache. *Erkenntnis* 2: 219–241.

———. 1956. *Meaning and Necessity*. 2nd ed. Chicago, IL: University of Chicago Press.

———. 1963. Carnap's Intellectual Autobiography. In *The Philosophy of Rudolf Carnap*, edited by Paul Arthur Schilpp, 3–84. La Salle, IL: Open Court.

———. 1967. *The Logical Structure of the World & Pseudoproblems in Philosophy*. Translated by Rolf A. George. Berkeley: University of California Press.

Cavell, Stanley. 1976. *Must We Mean What We Say?: A Book of Essays*. Cambridge: Cambridge University Press.

———. 1976a. The Availability of Wittgenstein's Later Philosophy. In Cavell 1976, 44–71.

———. 1979. *The Claim of Reason: Wittgenstein, Skepticism, Morality, and Tragedy*. Oxford: Oxford University Press.

———. 1988. *In Quest of the Ordinary: Lines of Skepticism and Romanticism*. Chicago, IL: University of Chicago Press.

———. 1988a. The Uncanniness of the Ordinary. In Cavell 1988, 153–80.

———. 1989. Declining Decline. In *This New Yet Unapproachable America: Lectures after Emerson after Wittgenstein*, 29–76. Albuquerque, NM: Living Batch Press.

———. 1991. The Argument of the Ordinary: Scenes of Instruction in Wittgenstein and in Kripke. In *Conditions Handsome and Unhandsome: The Constitution of Emersonian Perfectionism*, 64–100. Chicago, IL: University of Chicago Press.

Conant, James. 2002. The Method of the *Tractatus*. In *From Frege to Wittgenstein: Perspectives on Early Analytic Philosophy*, edited by Erich H. Reck, 374–462. Oxford: Oxford University Press.

Conant, James, and Ed Dain. 2011. Throwing the Baby Out: A Reply to Roger White. In Read and Lavery 2011, 66–83.

Conant, James, and Cora Diamond. 2004. On Reading the *Tractatus* Resolutely: Reply to Meredith Williams and Peter Sullivan. In *The Lasting Significance of Wittgenstein's Philosophy*, edited by Max Kölbel and Bernhard Weiss, 46–99. London: Routledge.

Cooper, David E. 2002. *The Measure of Things: Humanism, Humility, and Mystery*. Oxford: Oxford University Press.

Crary, Alice, and Rupert Read, eds. 2000. *The New Wittgenstein*. London: Routledge.

Crowe, Benjamin D. 2006. *Heidegger's Religious Origins: Destruction and Authenticity*. Bloomington: Indiana University Press.

Crowell, Steven. 2001. *Husserl, Heidegger, and the Space of Meaning: Paths toward Transcendental Phenomenology*. Evanston, IL: Northwestern University Press.

Crowell, Steven, and Jeff Malpas, eds. 2007. *Transcendental Heidegger*. Stanford, CA: Stanford University Press.

Dahlstrom, Daniel O. 1994. Heidegger's Method: Philosophical Concepts as Formal Indications. *Review of Metaphysics* 47: 775–95.

———. 2001. *Heidegger's Concept of Truth*. Cambridge: Cambridge University Press.

Danto, Arthur. 1965. Basic Actions. *American Philosophical Quarterly* 2: 141–48.

De Beistegui, Miguel. 2003. *Thinking with Heidegger: Displacements*. Bloomington: Indiana University Press.

Dennett, Daniel. 1993. *Consciousness Explained*. London: Penguin.

DeRose, Keith. 1995. Solving the Skeptical Problem. *Philosophical Review* 104: 1–52.

Diamond, Cora. 1990. Rules: Looking in the Right Place. In *Wittgenstein: Attention to Particulars*, edited by D. Z. Phillips and Peter Winch, 12–34. New York: St. Martin's.

———. 1991. *The Realistic Spirit: Wittgenstein, Philosophy, and the Mind*. Cambridge, MA: MIT.

———. 1991a. Frege and Nonsense. In Diamond 1991, 73–94.

———. 1991b. The Importance of Being Human. In *Human Beings*, edited by David Cockburn, 35–62. Cambridge: Cambridge University Press.

———. 1991c. Throwing Away the Ladder: How to Read the *Tractatus*. In Diamond 1991, 179–204.

———. 2005. Wittgenstein on Religious Belief: The Gulfs Between Us. In *Religion and Wittgenstein's Legacy*, edited by D. Z. Phillips and Mario von der Ruhr, 99–138. Aldershot: Ashgate.

Dretske, Fred. 1970. Epistemic Operators. *Journal of Philosophy* 67: 1007–23.

Dreyfus, Hubert L. 1991. *Being-in-the-World: A Commentary on Heidegger's* Being and Time, *Division I*. Cambridge, MA: MIT.

———. 1992. *What Computers Still Can't Do: A Critique of Artificial Reason*. Cambridge, MA: MIT.

———. 1993. On the Connection between Nihilism, Art, Technology, and Politics. In Guignon 1993, 345–72. Cambridge: Cambridge University Press.

Dreyfus, Hubert L., and Mark A. Wrathall, eds. 2005. *A Companion to Heidegger*. Oxford: Wiley-Blackwell.

Drury, Maurice O'Connor. 1984a. Conversations with Wittgenstein. In Rhees 1984, 97–171.

———. 1984b. Some Notes on Conversations with Wittgenstein. In Rhees 1984, 76–96.

Dummett, Michael. 1978. *Truth and Other Enigmas*. Cambridge, MA: Harvard University Press.

———. 1996. *Origins of Analytical Philosophy*. Cambridge, MA: Harvard University Press.

Edwards, James C. 1990. *The Authority of Language: Heidegger, Wittgenstein, and the Threat of Philosophical Nihilism*. Tampa: University of Southern Florida Press.

Edwards, Paul. 1979. *Heidegger and Death*. La Salle, IL: Hegeler Institute.

———. 1989. Heidegger's Quest for Being. *Philosophy* 64: 437–70.

Egan, David. 2011. Pictures in Wittgenstein's Later Philosophy. *Philosophical Investigations* 34 (1): 55–76.

———. 2012. *Das Man* and Distantiality in *Being and Time*. *Inquiry* 55 (3): 289–306.

Eldridge, Richard. 1997. *Leading a Human Life: Wittgenstein, Intentionality, and Romanticism*. Chicago, IL: University of Chicago Press.

Finch, Henry LeRoy. 1977. *Wittgenstein—the Later Philosophy: An Exposition of the "Philosophical Investigations."* Atlantic Highlands, NJ: Humanities Press.

Finkelstein, David H. 2003. *Expression and the Inner*. Cambridge, MA: Harvard University Press.

Flatscher, Matthias. 2011. *Logos und Lethe: Zur phänomonologischen Sprachauffassung im Spätwerk von Heidegger und Wittgenstein*. Freiburg: Karl Alber.

Fogelin, Robert J. 1995. *Wittgenstein*. 2nd ed. London: Routledge.

Forster, Michael. 2004. *Wittgenstein on the Arbitrariness of Grammar*. Princeton, NJ: Princeton University Press.

Foucault, Michel. 1972. *The Archaeology of Knowledge*. Translated by A. M. Sheridan Smith. New York: Harper Colophon.

———. 1988. The Return of Morality. In *Politics, Philosophy, Culture: Interviews and Other Writings, 1977–1984*, edited by Lawrence D. Kritzman, 242–54. London: Routledge.

Frampton, Kenneth. 1996. On Reading Heidegger. In *Theorizing a New Agenda for Architecture: An Anthology of Architectural Theory 1965–1995*, edited by Kate Nesbitt, 442–46. New York: Princeton Architectural.

Frege, Gottlob. (1884) 1980a. *The Foundations of Arithmetic*. Translated by J. L. Austin. Evanston, IL: Northwestern University Press.

———. (1892) 1980b. On Concept and Object. In Frege 1980c, 42–55.

———. 1980c. *Translations from the Philosophical Writings of Gottlob Frege*. Edited by Peter Geach and Max Black. Oxford: Basil Blackwell.

Friedlander, Eli. 2001. *Signs of Sense: Reading Wittgenstein's* Tractatus. Cambridge, MA: Harvard University Press.

Gadamer, Hans-Georg. 1976. The Phenomenological Movement. In *Philosophical Hermeneutics*, Edited and translated by David E. Linge, 130–81. Berkeley: University of California Press.

———. 1997. Reflections on My Philosophical Journey. In *The Philosophy of Hans-Georg Gadamer: The Library of Living Philosophers*, edited by Lewis E. Hahn, 3–63. La Salle, IL: Open Court.

Galilei, Galileo. 1842. *Opere Complete di Galileo Galilei*. Edited by Eugenio Alberi. Vol. 4. Florence: Società Editrice Fiorentina.

Gallagher, Shaun, and Dan Zahavi. 2008. *The Phenomenological Mind*. 2nd ed. London: Routledge.

Gaukroger, Stephen. 1995. *Descartes: An Intellectual Biography*. Oxford: Oxford University Press.

Genova, Judith. 1995. *Wittgenstein: A Way of Seeing*. London: Routledge.

Gier, Nicholas F. 1981. *Wittgenstein and Phenomenology: A Comparative Study of the Later Wittgenstein, Husserl, Heidegger, and Merleau-Ponty*. Albany: State University of New York Press.

Glendinning, Simon. 1998. *On Being with Others: Heidegger—Wittgenstein—Derrida*. London: Routledge.

———. 2011. Europe, for Example. *Moving Worlds: A Journal of Transcultural Writings* 11 (2): 35–47.

Glock, Hans-Johann. 1992. *Philosophical Investigations* Section 128: "Theses in Philosophy" and Undogmatic Procedure. In *Wittgenstein's* Philosophical Investigations: *Text and Context*, edited by Robert L. Arrington and Hans-Johann Glock, 69–99. London: Routledge.

———. 2007. Perspectives on Wittgenstein: An Intermittently Opinionated Survey. In Kahane, Kanterian, and Kuusela 2007, 37–65.

———. 2008. *What Is Analytic Philosophy?* Cambridge: Cambridge University Press.

Goldfarb, Warren. 1997a. Metaphysics and Nonsense: On Cora Diamond's *The Realistic Spirit. Journal of Philosophical Research* 22: 57–73.

———. 1997b. Wittgenstein on Fixity of Meaning. In *Early Analytic Philosophy: Essays in Honor of Leonard Linsky*, edited by William W. Tait, 75–89. Chicago, IL: Open Court.

———. 2011. *Das Überwinden*: Anti-metaphysical Readings of the *Tractatus*. In Read and Lavery 2011, 6–21.

Gram, Moltke S. 1981. Intellectual Intuition: The Continuity Thesis. *Journal of the History of Ideas* 42 (2): 287–304.

Grondin, Jean. 1994. The Ethical and Young Hegelian Motives in Heidegger's Hermeneutics of Facticity. In Kisiel and van Buren 1994, 345–57.

Guignon, Charles. 1983. *Heidegger and the Problem of Knowledge*. Indianapolis: Hackett.

———. 1990a. Philosophy after Wittgenstein and Heidegger. *Philosophy and Phenomenological Research* 50 (4): 649–72.

———. 1990b. Truth as Disclosure: Art, Language, History. In *Heidegger and Praxis*, edited by Thomas J. Nenon, supplement, *Southern Journal of Philosophy* 28: 105–20.

———. 1991. Heidegger: Language as the House of Being. In *The Philosophy of Discourse*, edited by Chip Sills and George H. Jensen, 163–87. Portsmouth, NH: Boynton/Cook.

———, ed. 1993. *The Cambridge Companion to Heidegger*. Cambridge: Cambridge University Press.

Habermas, Jürgen. 1988. *On the Logic of the Social Sciences*. Translated by Shierry Weber Nicholsen and Jerry A. Stark. Cambridge, MA: MIT.

———. 1992. Work and *Weltanschauung*: The Heidegger Controversy from a German Perspective. In *Heidegger: A Critical Reader*, edited by Hubert L. Dreyfus and Harrison Hall, 186–208. Oxford: Blackwell.

———. 1998. *On the Pragmatics of Communication*. Edited by Maeve Cook. Cambridge, MA: MIT.

Hacker, P. M. S. 1986. *Insight and Illusion*. Rev. ed. Oxford: Oxford University Press.

———. 1987. *Appearance and Reality: A Philosophical Investigation into Perception and Perceptual Qualities*. Oxford: Blackwell.

———. 1990. *Part I: Essays. Wittgenstein: Meaning and Mind: Volume 3 of an Analytical Commentary on the Philosophical Investigations*. Oxford: Blackwell.

———. 1993. *Part II: Exegesis §§243–427. Wittgenstein: Meaning and Mind: Volume 3 of an Analytical Commentary on the Philosophical Investigations*. Oxford: Blackwell.

———. 1996. *Wittgenstein's Place in Twentieth-Century Analytic Philosophy*. Oxford: Wiley-Blackwell.

———. 2000. Was He Trying to Whistle It? In Crary and Read 2000, 353–88.

———. 2003. Wittgenstein, Carnap and the New American Wittgensteinians. *Philosophical Quarterly* 53 (210): 1–23.

———. 2007. Gordon Baker's Late Interpretation of Wittgenstein. In Kahane, Kanterian, and Kuusela 2007, 88–122.

Hanfling, Oswald. 1981. *Logical Positivism*. Oxford: Blackwell.

Heaney, Seamus. 2006. *Death of a Naturalist*. London: Faber and Faber.

Haugeland, John. 1982. Heidegger on Being a Person. *Noûs* 16 (1): 15–26.

———. 1998. *Having Thought: Essays in the Metaphysics of Mind*. Cambridge, MA: Harvard University Press.

———. 2013. *Dasein Disclosed: John Haugeland's Heidegger*. Cambridge, MA: Harvard University Press.

Hegel, G. W. F. (1816) 2010. *The Science of Logic*. Translated by George di Giovanni. Cambridge: Cambridge University Press.

Hintikka, Merrill B., and Jaakko Hintikka. 1989. *Investigating Wittgenstein*. Oxford: Blackwell.

Hofmannsthal, Hugo von. (1902) 1995. *The Lord Chandos Letter*. Translated by Michael Hofmann. London: Penguin.

Hölderlin, Friedrich. 1998. *Selected Poems and Fragments*. Translated by Michael Hamburger. London: Penguin

Hoy, David. 2009. *The Time of Our Lives: A Critical History of Temporality*. Cambridge, MA: MIT.

Hume, David. (1748) 1975. *An Enquiry Concerning Human Understanding*. In *Enquiries Concerning Human Understanding and Concerning the Principles of Morals*, edited by P. H. Nidditch. 5–165. Oxford: Clarendon.

————. (1739/40) 1978. *A Treatise of Human Nature*. Edited by L.A. Selby-Bigge and P.H. Nidditch. Oxford: Clarendon.

Hunter, J.F.M. 1968. Forms of Life in Wittgenstein's *Philosophical Investigations. American Philosophical Quarterly* 5 (4): 233–43.

Husserl, Edmund. (1929) 1969. *Formal and Transcendental Logic*. Translated by Dorion Cairns. The Hague: Martinus Nijhoff.

————. (1913) 1976. *Ideen zu einer reinen Phänomenologie und phänomenologischen Philosophie, Erstes Buch: Allgemeine Einführung in die reine Phänomenologie*. Edited by Karl Schumann. The Hague: Martinus Nijhoff.

Hutto, Daniel D. 2003. *Wittgenstein and the End of Philosophy: Neither Theory nor Therapy*. New York: Palgrave.

Hyman, John. 1999. Wittgensteinianism. In *The Blackwell Companion to the Philosophy of Religion*, edited by Philip Quinn and Charles Taliaferro, 150–58. Oxford: Blackwell.

Janik, Allan, and Stephen Toulmin. 1973. *Wittgenstein's Vienna*. New York: Simon & Schuster.

Jencks, Charles. 1973. *Le Corbusier and the Tragic View of Architecture*. Cambridge, MA: Harvard University Press.

————. 1977. *The Language of Post-Modern Architecture*. Rev. ed. New York: Rizzoli International.

————. 2000. *Le Corbusier and the Continual Revolution in Architecture*. New York: Monacelli.

Johnston, Paul. 1993. *Wittgenstein: Rethinking the Inner*. London: Routledge.

Kahane, Guy, Edward Kanterian, and Oskari Kuusela, eds. 2007. *Wittgenstein and His Interpreters: Essays in Memory of Gordon Baker*. Oxford: Blackwell.

————. 2007a. Introduction. In Kahane, Kanterian, and Kuusela 2007, 1–36.

Kant, Immanuel. (1783) 1950. *Prolegomena to Any Future Metaphysics*. Translated by Lewis White Beck. New York: Library of Liberal Arts.

————. (1790) 2001. *Critique of the Power of Judgment*. Translated by Paul Guyer and Eric Matthews. Cambridge: Cambridge University Press.

Käufer, Stephan. 2001. On Heidegger on Logic. *Continental Philosophy Review* 34: 455–76.

Kenny, Anthony. 2006. *Wittgenstein*. 2nd ed. Oxford: Blackwell.

Kierkegaard, Søren. (1846) 1992. *Concluding Unscientific Postscript to* Philosophical Fragments. Edited and translated by Howard and Edna Hong. Princeton: Princeton University Press.

Kisiel, Theodore. 1993. *The Genesis of Heidegger's* Being and Time. Berkeley, CA: University of California Press.

————. 1994. Heidegger (1920–21) on Becoming a Christian: A Conceptual Picture Show. In Kisiel and van Buren 1994, 175–92.

Kisiel, Theodore, and John van Buren, eds. 1994. *Reading Heidegger from the Start*. Albany: State University of New York Press.

Kleinberg, Ethan. 2005. *Generation Existential: Heidegger's Philosophy in France, 1927–1961*. Ithaca, NY: Cornell University Press.

Kober, Michael. 1996. Certainties of a World-Picture: The Epistemological Investigations of *On Certainty*. In Sluga and Stern 1996, 411–41.

Krell, David Farrell. 1992. *Diamon Life: Heidegger and Life-Philosophy*. Bloomington: Indiana University Press.

Kripke, Saul. 1982. *Wittgenstein on Rules and Private Language*. Cambridge, MA: Harvard University Press.

Kuhn, Thomas. 1962. *The Structure of Scientific Revolutions*. Chicago, IL: University of Chicago Press.

Lafont, Cristina. 2002. Replies. *Inquiry* 45: 229–48.

Last, Nana. 2008. *Wittgenstein's House: Language, Space, and Architecture*. New York: Fordham University Press.

Lear, Jonathan. 1998. *Open Minded: Working out the Logic of the Soul*. Cambridge, MA: Harvard University Press.

Le Corbusier. 1970. *Toward a New Architecture*. Translated by Frederick Etchells. New York: Praeger.

Leitner, Bernhard. 2000. *The Wittgenstein House*. New York: Princeton Architectural.

Levinas, Emmanuel. 1969. *Totality and Infinity*. Pittsburgh, PA: Duquesne University Press.

Lewis, David. 1996. Elusive Knowledge. *Australasian Journal of Philosophy* 74: 549–67.

Locke, John. 1960. *Two Treatises of Government*. Cambridge: Cambridge University Press.

Lurie, Yuval. 1992. Culture as a Form of Life: A Romantic Reading of Wittgenstein. *International Philosophical Quarterly* 32 (2): 193–204.

Lyotard, Jean-François. 1984. *The Post-Modern Condition: A Report on Knowledge*. Translated by Geoff Bennington and Brian Massumi. Minneapolis: University of Minnesota Press.

Malcolm, Norman. 1982. Wittgenstein and Idealism. *Royal Institute of Philosophy Lecture Series* 13: 249–67.

———. 1994. *Wittgenstein: A Religious Point of View?* Ithaca, NY: Cornell University Press.

———. 1995. Wittgenstein on Language and Rules. In *Wittgensteinian Themes: Essays 1978–1989*, 145–71. Ithaca, NY: Cornell University Press.

Malpas, Jeff. 2007. *Heidegger's Topology: Being, Place, World*. Cambridge, MA: MIT.

Marion, Mathieu. 1998. *Wittgenstein, Finitism, and the Foundations of Mathematics*. Oxford: Oxford University Press.

McDowell, John. 2000. Non-cognitivism and Rule-Following. In Crary and Read 2000, 38–52.

———. 2009. Are Meaning, Understanding, Etc. Definite States? In *The Engaged Intellect: Philosophical Essays*, 79–95. Cambridge, MA: Harvard University Press.

McGrath, Alister. 1990. *Luther's Theology of the Cross: Martin Luther's Theological Breakthrough*. Oxford: Blackwell.

———. 2005. *Iustitia Dei: A History of the Christian Doctrine of Justification*. Cambridge: Cambridge University Press.

———. 2009. *Reformation Thought: An Introduction*. Oxford: Blackwell.

McGrath, S. J. 2006. *The Early Heidegger and Medieval Philosophy: Phenomenology for the Godforsaken*. Washington, DC: Catholic University of America Press.

McManus, Denis. 2006. *The Enchantment of Words: Wittgenstein's* Tractatus Logico-Philosophicus. Oxford: Oxford University Press.

———. 2007. Heidegger, Measurement and the "Intelligibility" of Science. *European Journal of Philosophy* 15: 82–105.

———. 2008. Rules, Regression and the "Background": Dreyfus, Heidegger and McDowell. *European Journal of Philosophy* 16: 432–58.

———. Forthcoming a. Austerity, Psychology, and the Intelligibility of Nonsense. *Philosophical Topics*.

———. Forthcoming b. *Heidegger and the Measure of Truth*. Oxford: Oxford University Press.

———. Forthcoming c. Heidegger and the Supposition of a Single, Objective World. *European Journal of Philosophy*.

———. Forthcoming d. Heidegger, Wittgenstein and St Paul on the Last Judgment: On the Roots and Significance of the "Theoretical Attitude." *British Journal for the History of Philosophy*.

———. Unpublished. Ontological Pluralism and the *Being and Time* Project.

Medina, José. 2002. *The Unity of Wittgenstein's Philosophy: Necessity, Intelligibility, and Normativity*. Albany: State University of New York Press.

Minar, Edward H. 1994. Paradox and Privacy: On §§201–202 of Wittgenstein's *Philosophical Investigations*. *Philosophy and Phenomenological Research* 54 (1): 45–77.

———. 2001. Heidegger's Response to Skepticism in *Being and Time*. In *Future Pasts: The Analytic Tradition in Twentieth-Century Philosophy*, edited by Juliet Floyd and Sanford Shieh, 193–214. Oxford: Oxford University Press.

———. 2011. The Life of the Sign: Rule-Following, Practice and Agreement. In *The Oxford Handbook of Wittgenstein*, edited by Oskari Kuusela and Marie McGinn, 276–93. Oxford: Oxford University Press.

Monk, Ray. 1990. *Wittgenstein: The Duty of Genius*. New York: Free Press.

Moore, A.W. 2007. Wittgenstein and Transcendental Idealism. In Kahane, Kanterian, and Kuusela 2007, 174–99.

———. 2012. *The Evolution of Modern Metaphysics: Making Sense of Things*. Cambridge: Cambridge University Press.

Moore, G. E. 1922. Some Judgments of Perception. In *Philosophical Studies*, 220–52. London: Kegan Paul, Trench, Trubner.

———. 1959. *Philosophical Papers*. New York: Collier Books.

———. 1959a. A Defence of Common Sense. In Moore 1959, 32–59.

———. 1959b. Proof of an External World. In Moore 1959, 126–48.

Mulhall, Stephen. 1990. *On Being in the World: Wittgenstein and Heidegger on Seeing Aspects*. London: Routlege.

———. 1994. Wittgenstein and Heidegger: Orientations to the Ordinary. *European Journal of Philosophy* 2 (2): 143–164.

———. 1996. *Heidegger and* Being and Time. London: Routledge.

———. 2001a. *Inheritance and Originality: Wittgenstein, Heidegger, Kierkegaard*. Oxford: Oxford University Press.

———. 2001b. Wittgenstein and the Philosophy of Religion. In *Philosophy of Religion in the 21st Century*, edited by D. Z. Phillips and Timothy Tessin, 95–118. London: Palgrave Macmillan.

———. 2008. "Hopelessly Strange": Bernard Williams' Portrait of Wittgenstein as a Transcendental Idealist. *European Journal of Philosophy* 17 (3): 386–404.

Murray, Michael, ed. 1978. *Heidegger and Modern Philosophy*. New Haven, CT: Yale University Press.

Nagel, Thomas. 1997. *The Last Word*. Oxford: Oxford University Press.

Norberg-Schulz, Christian. 1971. *Existence, Space, and Architecture*. New York: Praeger.

Nozick, Robert. 1981. *Philosophical Explanations*. Oxford: Oxford University Press.

Nussbaum, Martha C. 1986. *The Fragility of Goodness: Luck and Ethics in Greek Tragedy and Philosophy*. Cambridge: Cambridge University Press.

Okrent, Mark. 1988. *Heidegger's Pragmatism*. Ithaca, NY: Cornell University Press.

O'Neill, Martin. 2001. Explaining "The Hardness of the Logical Must": Wittgenstein on Grammar, Arbitrariness and Logical Necessity. *Philosophical Investigations* 24 (1): 1–29.

Park, Byong-Chul. 1997. *Phenomenological Aspects of Wittgenstein's Philosophy*. Dordrecht: Kluwer Academic.

Pears, David. 1987. *The False Prison: A Study of the Development of Wittgenstein's Philosophy*. Vol. 1. Oxford: Oxford University Press.

———. 1988. *The False Prison: A Study of the Development of Wittgenstein's Philosophy*. Vol. 2. Oxford: Oxford University Press.

Petzet, H.W. 1993. *Encounters and Dialogues with Martin Heidegger 1929–1976*. Translated by Parvis Emad and Kenneth Maly. Chicago, IL: University of Chicago Press.

Philipse, Herman. 1992. Heidegger's Question of Being and the "Augustinian Picture" of Language. *Philosophy and Phenomenological Research* 52 (2): 251–87.
———. 1995. Transcendental Idealism. In *The Cambridge Companion to Husserl*, edited by Barry Smith and David W. Smith, 239–322. Cambridge: Cambridge University Press.
———. 1998. *Heidegger's Philosophy of Being: A Critical Interpretation*. Princeton, NJ: Princeton University Press.
———. 2007a. Heidegger's "Scandal of Philosophy": The Problem of the "Ding an sich" in *Being and Time*. In Crowell and Malpas, 2007, 169–98.
———. 2007b. Overcoming Epistemology. In *The Oxford Handbook of Continental Philosophy*, edited by Brian Leiter and Michael Rosen, 334–78. Oxford: Oxford University Press.
Phillips, D. Z. 1999. *Philosophy's Cool Place*. Ithaca, NY: Cornell University Press.
Pippin, Robert. 2008. *Hegel's Practical Philosophy: Rational Agency as Ethical Life*. Cambridge: Cambridge University Press.
Pitcher, George. 1965. Wittgenstein, Nonsense, and Lewis Carroll. *Massachusetts Review* 6 (3): 591–611.
Pöggeler, Otto. 1991. *Martin Heidegger's Path of Thinking*. Translated by Daniel Magurshak and Sigmund Barber. Atlantic Highlands, NJ: Humanities Press.
Polanyi, Michael. 1967. *The Tacit Dimension*. Garden City, NY: Doubleday.
Priest, Graham. 2002. *Beyond the Limits of Thought*. 2nd ed. Oxford: Oxford University Press.
Pritchard, Duncan. 2002. Recent Work on Radical Skepticism. *American Philosophical Quarterly* 39: 215–57.
———. 2005. The Structure of Skeptical Arguments. *Philosophical Quarterly* 55: 37–52.
———. Forthcoming. Wittgenstein and the Groundlessness of Our Believing. *Synthese*.
Proops, Ian. 2001. The New Wittgenstein: A Critique. *European Journal of Philosophy* 3: 375–404.
Putnam, Hilary. 1981. *Reason, Truth and History*. Cambridge: Cambridge University Press.
———. 1983. Why Reason Cannot Be Naturalized. In *Realism and Reason*, 229–247. Vol. 3 of *Philosophical Papers*. Cambridge: Cambridge University Press.
———. 1990. *Renewing Philosophy*. Cambridge, MA: Harvard University Press.
———. 2001. Was Wittgenstein *Really* an Anti-realist about Mathematics? In *Wittgenstein in America*, edited by Timothy G. McCarthy and Sean C. Stidd, 140–94. Oxford: Oxford University Press.
Quine, W. V. O. 1951. Two Dogmas of Empiricism. *Philosophical Review* 60: 20–43.
Read, Rupert, and Matthew A. Lavery, eds. 2011. *Beyond the* Tractatus *Wars*. London: Routledge.
Rentsch, Thomas. 2003. *Heidegger und Wittgenstein: Existential- und Sprachanalysen zu den Grundlagen philosophischer Anthropologie*. Stuttgart: Klett-Cotta.
Rhees, Rush. 1970. "The Philosophy of Wittgenstein". In *Discussions of Wittgenstein*, 37–54. London: Routledge & Kegan Paul.
———, ed. 1984. *Recollections of Wittgenstein*. Oxford: Oxford University Press.
———. 1984a. Postscript. In Rhees 1984, 172–209.
———. 1998. *Wittgenstein and the Possibility of Discourse*. Edited by D. Z. Phillips. Cambridge: Cambridge University Press.
Richardson, William J. 1993. *Heidegger: Through Phenomenology to Thought*. 4th ed. Bronx, NY: Fordham University Press.
Ricketts, Thomas. 1996. Pictures, Logic, and the Limits of Sense in Wittgenstein's *Tractatus*. In Sluga and Stern 1996, 59–99.

Rorty, Richard. 1979. *Philosophy and the Mirror of Nature*. Princeton, NJ: Princeton University Press.

———. 1991. *Essays on Heidegger and Others*. Vol. 2 of *Philosophical Papers*. Cambridge: Cambridge University Press.

———. 1993. Wittgenstein, Heidegger, and the Reification of Language. In Guignon 1993, 337–57.

Rouse, Joseph. 1987. *Knowledge and Power: Toward a Political Philosophy of Science*. Ithaca, NY: Cornell University Press.

Rudd, Anthony. 2003. *Expressing the World: Skepticism, Wittgenstein, and Heidegger*. Chicago, IL: Open Court.

———. 2004. Logic and Ethics as Limits of the World. In *Post-Analytic Tractatus*, edited by Barry Stocker, 47–58. London: Ashgate.

Rundle, Bede. 2001. Meaning and Understanding. In *Wittgenstein: A Critical Reader*, edited by Hans-Johann Glock, 94–118. Oxford: Blackwell.

Russell, Bertrand. 1951. Obituary: Ludwig Wittgenstein. *Mind* 60 (239): 297–98.

———. 1959. *My Philosophical Development*. New York: Simon and Schuster.

Ryle, Gilbert. (1928) 2009. Review of Heidegger's *Sein und Zeit*. In *Critical Essays*, 205–22. London: Routledge.

Sallis, John. 1986. *Delimitations: Phenomenology and the End of Metaphysics*. Bloomington: Indiana University Press.

Schatzki, Theodore R. 1996. *Social Practices: A Wittgensteinian Approach to Human Activity and Social Life*. Cambridge: Cambridge University Press.

———. 2005. Early Heidegger on Sociality. In Dreyfus and Wrathall 2005, 233–47.

———. 2010. *The Timespace of Human Activity: On Performance, Society, and History as Indeterminate Teleological Events*. Lanham, MD: Lexington Books.

Schear, Joseph. 2007. Judgment and Ontology in Heidegger's Phenomenology. *New Yearbook for Phenomenology and Phenomenological Research* 7: 127–58.

———. Forthcoming. Historical Finitude. In *The Cambridge Companion to Heidegger's Being and Time*, edited by Mark Wrathall. Cambridge: Cambridge University Press.

Schönbaumsfeld, Genia. 2010. *A Confusion of the Spheres: Kierkegaard and Wittgenstein on Philosophy and Religion*. Oxford: Oxford University Press.

Schürmann, Reiner. 1990. *Heidegger on Being and Acting: From Principles to Anarchy*. Bloomington: Indiana University Press.

Sefler, George F. 1974. *Language and the World: A Methodological Synthesis within the Writings of Martin Heidegger and Ludwig Wittgenstein*. New York: Humanities Press.

Sellars, Wilfrid. 1963. Philosophy and the Scientific Image of Man. In *Science, Perception, and Reality*, 1–40. London: Routledge & Kegan Paul.

Sharr, Adam. 2006. *Heidegger's Hut*. Cambridge, MA: MIT.

———. 2007. *Heidegger for Architects*. London: Routledge.

Sluga, Hans. 2011. *Wittgenstein*. Oxford: Wiley-Blackwell.

Sluga, Hans, and David G. Stern, eds. 1996. *The Cambridge Companion to Wittgenstein*. Cambridge: Cambridge University Press.

Standish, Paul. 1992. *Beyond the Self: Wittgenstein, Heidegger, and the Limits of Language*. Aldershot: Avebury.

Staten, Henry. 1986. *Wittgenstein and Derrida*. Lincoln: University of Nebraska Press.

Stern, David G. 1995. *Wittgenstein on Mind and Language*. Oxford: Oxford University Press.

Strawson, P. F. 1985. *Skepticism and Naturalism: Some Varieties*. London: Methuen.

Streeter, Ryan. 1997. Heidegger's Formal Indication: A Question of Method in *Being and Time*. *Man and World* 30: 413–30.

Stroll, Avrum. 2002. *Wittgenstein*. Oxford: Oneworld.

Stroud, Barry. 1984. *The Significance of Philosophical Skepticism*. Oxford: Oxford University Press.

———. 2000. *Meaning, Understanding, and Practice*. Oxford: Oxford University Press.

———. 2011. *Engagement and Metaphysical Dissatisfaction: Modality and Value*. Oxford: Oxford University Press.

Taylor, Charles. 1975. *Hegel*. Cambridge: Cambridge University Press.

———. 1985. *Human Agency and Language*. Vol. 1 of *Philosophical Papers*. Cambridge: Cambridge University Press.

———. 1985a. Language and Human Nature. In Taylor 1985, 215–47.

———. 1985b. Theories of Meaning. In Taylor 1985, 248–92.

———. 1989. *Sources of the Self: The Making of the Modern Identity*. Cambridge: Cambridge University Press.

———. 1995. *Philosophical Arguments*. Cambridge, MA: Harvard University Press.

———. 1995a. Heidegger, Language, and Ecology. In Taylor 1995, 100–126.

———. 1995b. The Importance of Herder. In Taylor 1995, 79–99.

———. 2005. Heidegger on Language. In Dreyfus and Wrathall 2005, 433–55.

Thomson, Iain. 2005. *Heidegger on Ontotheology: Technology and the Politics of Education*. Cambridge: Cambridge University Press.

———. 2011. Heidegger's Aesthetics. *Stanford Encyclopedia of Philosophy*. http://plato.stanford.edu/entries/heidegger-aesthetics/.

Travis, Charles. 2000. Philosophy in the Twentieth Century: A Revolutionary Path. *Disputatio* 8: 3–16.

Trigg, Roger. 1991. Wittgenstein and Social Science. In *Wittgenstein: Centenary Essays*, edited by Allen Phillips Griffiths, *Royal Institute of Philosophy Supplement* 28: 209–22.

Tugendhat, Ernst. 1986. *Self-Consciousness and Self-Determination*. Translated by Paul Stern. Cambridge, MA: MIT.

Van Buren, John. 1994a. Martin Heidegger, Martin Luther. In Kisiel and van Buren 1994, 159–75.

———. 1994b. *The Young Heidegger: Rumor of the Hidden King*. Indianapolis: Indiana University Press.

Venturi, Robert. 2002. *Complexity and Contradiction in Architecture*. New York: Museum of Modern Art.

Vogel, Lawrence. 1994. *The Fragile "We": Ethical Implications of Heidegger's "Being and Time"*. Evanston, IL: Northwestern University Press.

Von Hartmann, Eduard. 1907. *System der Philosophie im Grundriß 1: Grundriß der Erkenntnislehre*. Bad Sachsa im Harz: Hermann Haacke.

Waismann, Friedrich. 1997. *The Principles of Linguistic Philosophy*. London: Palgrave Macmillan.

Wallace, David Foster. 1997. *Infinite Jest*. London: Abucus

Warburton, Nigel. 2011. *A Little History of Philosophy*. New Haven, CT: Yale University Press.

Whitehead, Alfred North. (1929) 1978. *Process and Reality*. New York: Free Press.

———. (1925) 2011. *Science and the Modern World*. Cambridge: Cambridge University Press.

Wijdeveld, Paul. 1999. *Ludwig Wittgenstein, Architect*. Amsterdam: Pepin Press.

Williams, Bernard. 1976. Wittgenstein and Idealism. In *Understanding Wittgenstein*, edited by George Vesey, 76–95. Ithaca, NY: Cornell University Press.

Williams, Meredith. 1999. *Wittgenstein, Mind and Meaning: Towards a Social Conception of Mind*. London: Routledge.

Williams, Michael. 1996. *Unnatural Doubts: Epistemological Realism and the Basis of Scepticism*. Princeton, NJ: Princeton University Press.

Witherspoon, Edward. 2002. Logic and the Inexpressible in Frege and Heidegger. *Journal of the History of Philosophy* 40: 89–113.

Wittgenstein, Hermine. 1981. My Brother Ludwig. In *Ludwig Wittgenstein: Personal Recollections*, edited by Rush Rhees, 1–13. Totowa, NJ: Rowman and Littlefield.

Woessner, Martin. 2011. *Heidegger in America*. Cambridge: Cambridge University Press.

Wolfe, Judith. Forthcoming. *Heidegger's Eschatology: Theological Horizons in Heidegger's Early Work*. Oxford: Oxford University Press.

Wolin, Richard. 2001. *Heidegger's Children: Hannah Arendt, Karl Löwith, Hans Jonas, and Herbert Marcuse*. Princeton, NJ: Princeton University Press.

Wrathall, Mark A. 1999. Heidegger and Truth as Correspondence. *International Journal of Philosophical Studies* 7: 79–88.

———. 2005. *How to Read Heidegger*. London: Granta.

———. 2011. *Heidegger and Unconcealment*. Cambridge: Cambridge University Press.

Wright, Crispin. 1980. *Wittgenstein on the Foundations of Mathematics*. Cambridge, MA: Harvard University Press.

———. 2004. Wittgensteinian Certainties. In *Wittgenstein and Scepticism*, edited by Denis McManus, 22–55. London: Routledge.

Young, Julian. 2001. *Heidegger's Philosophy of Art*. Cambridge: Cambridge University Press.

———. 2002. *Heidegger's Later Philosophy*. Cambridge: Cambridge University Press.

Zimmerman, Michael E. 1986. *Eclipse of the Self: Development of Heidegger's Concept of Authenticity*. Athens: Ohio University Press.

Index